ECONOMICS III

Macroeconomics for a Sustainable Roadmap

By Dr. Edward Schellhammer

2nd Edition 2014, revised.
© Copyright. Dr. Edward Schellhammer. All rights reserved.

ISBN-13: 978-1478275626
ISBN-10: 1478275626

www.EdwardSchellhammer.com

Table of Contents

Disclaimer

The facts, figures, statistics and other data have been culled from various online and offline sources for dissemination for research, analysis, review and reference purposes.

The author of this report reasonably believes such sources to be reliable, but does not make any representations, express or implied as to the accuracy or fitness of use of such information. The information or contents of the publication do not constitute advice and should not be relied upon in making (or refraining from making) any decision.

The author has taken due care and caution in compilation and processing of data, but does not guarantee the accuracy, adequacy or completeness of any information and is not responsible for any errors or omissions or for the results obtained from the use of such information.

The author shall not be liable for any damages (including, without limitation, damages for loss of business projects, or loss of profits) arising in contract, tort or otherwise from the use of or inability to use the information in this report, or any of its contents, or from any action taken (or refrained from being taken) as a result of using the report or any of its contents.

In Somnis Veritas for Economics III

Dreams tell the truth. Dreams stay above theories, ideologies and dogmas. During the last 33 years I had over 12,000 dreams about the state of humanity and the planet. I had an estimated 3,000 dreams about humans' evolution and all processes of the Archetypes of the Soul. Examples:

From the heaven debouching, first energy, panic in the air, frightening, then something like warships or war machines fly towards the earth; suddenly the entire sky is full of them. An unbelievable dimension as large and deep as the sky, everything is full of these flying machines. A never before existed machinery of destruction. A total apocalyptic scene.

Many important strong men are in fact nothing other than baby pissers without legs.

I am in the Vatican, in an immense arch room, full of all kinds of junk. A big amount of rubbish, compressed many meters high. I am there and take a look at it while thinking: There is absolutely nothing here that could have a value or could be vivid.

I walk through the Vatican. And I ask myself who has paid and still pays for all this, and under which conditions has all this been built. And I think: hidden behind all of this is an immeasurable megalomania, a perverse suppression and exploitation of people, robbery and homicide, wars and dictatorships, lies about God and religion.

The horizon is gloomy. Air and ground are poisoned. A cosmic nightmare is in the atmosphere.

2008 I told to people in a dream: "You have 10 years left to take strong measures to avoid the total collapse." But nobody listened.

The day will come when no bread exists.

In 35-40 years everything will be over, the end, no more earth and no more humanity.

I am coming to a church in Jerusalem: The main part has got a cupola, the plaza outside is square-shaped with a column at each corner. All around there are more columns or turrets…

...As I step on the square I say to a person next to me: "I can see the last riddle, solving it means, that we've reached the goal." I know the solution. On one of the steeples the circle-cross-Mandala is missing. The great wise and true experts of the holy books of humanity know through immemorial tradition, that only the true ... (sent man) can solve this riddle with a dream. I know that the circle-cross-Mandala has to go on the steeple top and I remember in my dream: I've received this a few years ago (in reality!). I take it out and want to attach it there. It fits perfectly.

A famished child is dancing on a battlefield full of corpses and blood. The child is dancing a dance of death. I ask the president of the USA: "Do you want to accept me as the ...? You will avoid 80% of the damage and suffering."

I tell people: "Never again will I come back to this earth. I am only here for a visit and I have to accomplish a job. And you have to get your shit together yourself."

I am interviewed on television: At the end I am asked: Do you want to say a last word to the viewers? I answer: "Yes, I can say to everybody: Continue living as you have up until this day and you will lose the earth!"

I tell to masses of people: "I have not come from millions of light years away to this earth, sent from God, to play here the cretin and idiot. With me humanity and the earth will have a good future. Without me humanity will perish. The choice is now yours!"

The truth and the Archetypes of the Soul are the primordial foundation and aim of science, human life, and society. 'Economics' doesn't have either of them! The entire social sciences do not have it. That's the scandalous drama of science. The absence of the truth and of the Archetypes of the Soul produces enormous destructive energy and developments in sciences and societies. It shows clearly that sciences do not take care of the archetypal, psychical and spiritual evolution of mankind nor do they have any respect for the creation. Such science is a sham. Such sciences dehumanize mind and soul, and eliminate the dignity of humans. Such sciences are infected with the most toxic virus ever existed: the dynamic code for regicide and deicide. In the end, it will irreversibly and unstoppably lead to the doom. It can happen within decades if drastic global measures are not soon taken.

Dr. Edward Schellhammer

1. Macroeconomics and Society

1.1. Economy and Macroeconomics

1.1.1. Macroeconomics

Definition of 'Economy' and 'Macroeconomics'

We consulted as usual some classical study books about economics and many websites to find the right definition. There are countless descriptions and definitions. Some definitions are short, others extensive. Some mention many parameters, others focus on some preferences. We give here an overview of the components that fill the term with topics; obviously nothing is complete here.

First of all 'Economy' and 'Macroeconomics' is a concept, a system, a range, a theory, a model, an organized system of knowledge, an orderly functional arrangement of parts, a sum of knowledge to study, an analytical description and examination, a description of phenomena and networks. It is also said that it is a science.

Secondly is it about topics that can cover local, regional, provincial, national or global communities. In general it is about the big (macro-) picture (the 'whole', an 'aggregate') meanwhile microeconomics as is implied is about the small-picture.

Thirdly it is about human activities: behavior, human activities, management, producing (production), consumption, services, distribution, supply, allocation, distribution, working, investing, decision making, controlling, protecting, providing, governmental intervention, etc.

Fourthly it is about (economic) parameters:

- Resources
- Material
- Labor

- Unemployment
- Goods
- Services
- Benefits
- National income
- Rate of growth
- Gross domestic product
- Trade, tariffs, restrictions
- Money
- Investment
- Interest
- Exchange
- Inflation (price levels)
- Expenditures (costs)
- Public goods
- Business structures
- Laws
- Taxes
- Etc.

Lastly, it is about: understanding the processes and causes, the influences in general, the increase or decrease, the understanding and effect of human factors, the possible interventions (fiscal and monetary policies), effects of investments, the fluctuations, the factors of efficiency (performance), the failure of economic policies, the effects of financial management; and it is about forecasting, influencing, controlling development of parameters and the aggregate as a whole. Some authors emphasize that economics' aim is also to give advice to firms and governments.

→ Economics must clearly say what they understand with 'parameter'. Certain given criteria must be given to enable science to work properly and to cover the entire fields of economics.
→ Without clear rules and criteria, economics can easily cheat and deceive simply by ignoring other parameters even if these parameters are of mega-importance for financial issues and the society or market as a whole.

"Macroeconomics studies the behavior of the economy as a whole. It is primarily concerned with two topics: long-run economic growth and the short-run fluctuations in output and employment that are often referred to as the business cycle. These phenomena are closely related because they happen simultaneously." [1]

→ The economy is not a vivid being that 'behaves'. People behave and 'make' the economy as a whole. The author's way of saying deviates from the real actor and thus avoiding to identify the predators that can never have enough and the stupid consumers that can never stop compensating for their inner deficits.

→ In macroeconomics there are many essential fields and parameters. Long-run economic growth and the short-run fluctuations are only two examples. What are the criteria that allow one to say that these two fields are the most important ones?

→ Giving highest priority to economic growth is based on ideology; it's not an internal law of an all-sided balanced economy.

"Microeconomics focuses on decision-making by individuals and firms and the consequences of the decisions made. Macroeconomics focuses on the overall behavior of the economy ... The combined effect of individual actions can have unintended consequences and lead to worse or better macroeconomic outcomes for everyone." [2]

→ The author should mention the predators that are responsible for 'unintended consequences'. They are sitting in the banks, the corporations, the politics, and the religion.

→ He should also give some example of 'worse' and 'better'; or: 'better' here and therefore elsewhere 'worse'.

→ The 'overall behavior' needs to be clearly specified. The way this word is used here allows for manifold interpretations: a trap for cheat, deceit, and manipulations!

---

[1] McConnell (et al.), p. 116
[2] Krugman, p. 297

1.1.2. Economic Institutions

Economic Institutions are everywhere: "Economic policies are actions (or inaction) taken by government to influence economic actions" ... "Markets are highly developed social constructs that are part of a country's social and economic institutions. Markets are based on institution ... the formal and informal rules that constrain human economic behavior. Institutions include laws that protect ownership of property, and the legal system to enforce and interpret laws. They also include political institutions that develop those laws, the cultural traits of society that guide people's tastes and behaviors, and the many organizational structures such as corporations, banks, and nonprofit organizations that make up our economy." [3]

We decompose the complex statement:

- Markets are social constructs.
- Social constructs are part of the country's social institutions.
- Social constructs are part of the country's economic institutions.
- Markets are based on institutions.
- Markets include political institutions.
- There are formal and informal rules constraining human economic behavior.
- Institutions include laws.
- Political institutions develop laws.
- Political institutions develop cultural traits of society.
- Cultural traits guide people's tastes and behaviors.
- Corporations make up our economy.
- Banks make up our economy.
- Nonprofit organizations make up our economy.

→ This complex statement is not systematic and doesn't give a representative picture about economic institutions. It's a 'wish-wash' blabber avoiding transparency and perspective.
→ Governments act or don't act: What's the point here? So, the governments influence economic actions or they don't influence economic actions. Strange!
→ '... make up our economy': What does this mean in concrete terms? The question arises: Which organizational structures do make up our economy;

---

[3] Colander, p. 17, 53

and which do not?

→ There are many more organizational structures than the author mentions here: small firms and self-employed businesses (not only corporations), hospitals, prisons (working for corporations), Churches (tax free operations), negative externalities, etc.

→ In this book we will show many fields that construct a kind of 'household' and in that sense 'make up our economy'.

→ '...make up our economy' can also be understood as 'burden our economy'. From here we come to non-productive costs. The Mega-parameters' we draw in chapter 7 are not only a burden, but these parameters will destroy entire nations in the coming 2-3 decades.

→ As long as the term 'economy' remains spongy and does not fully present clear criteria of selection (what is in and what is out), it always misleads in some way.

→ A systematic structure of 'economy' also requires giving with full transparency all the indispensable and intrinsic interrelations (interdependences) with other systems of society.

McConnel says (summarized): Institutional structures promote growth. He mentions: Strong property rights, patents and copyrights, efficient financial institution, literacy and widespread education, free trade, and a competitive market system. But these institutional structures also could promote stability, balance, security, social peace, justice, and much more. The author abuses these institutional structures for his growth ideology. [4]

---

[4] McConnell, p. 155-156

1.2. Society and Western Standard of Living

1.2.1. Society

Economic institutions and the real economics shall serve the people, the community, the society, and the country as a whole. Therefore let's have a closer look at the term 'society', again collected from digging in the online dictionaries and some books.

Definition of 'Society':

The top characteristics in varied descriptions:

- A group of people related to each other through persistent relations
- A large social grouping sharing the same geographical or virtual territory
- The totality of social relationships among humans
- A group of humans broadly distinguished from other groups
- A body of individuals living as members of a community
- A highly structured system of human organization for large-scale community living
- A body of individuals living as members of a community
- The body of human beings generally, viewed as members of a community
- The aggregate of people living together in a more or less ordered community
- An economic, social, or industrial infrastructure made up of, for and by humans
- A community where its members have a national identity
- A community with the same political authority and dominant cultural expectations

Sociology today operates with 7 classes based upon the passion of different amounts of ownership, control, and marketability: [5]

- Upper class
- Upper middle class
- Middle middle class

---

[5] Haralambos & Holborn. 2008, p. 31

- Lower middle class
- Skilled working class
- Unskilled working class
- Underclass

The word 'society' is also used for specific associations or organizations with specific interests and aims. We ignore this particular specification as it does not affect our explorations.

A society has a variety of social patterns (groups). The members share a manifoldness of common values and expectations:

- A specific way of living
- A distinctive culture
- A variety of subgroups
- Participation
- Shared customs
- Sharing activities
- Own norms, rules, customs, values
- Engaged in a common profession
- Associated together for and by religious aims
- Common interests (politics, sports, science…)
- Common business interests
- Sharing household
- Connected with other households
- Protected by the same laws
- Sharing technological products
- Taking benefit from shared public goods
- Networked with selected businesses
- Bonded to institutions, organizations
- Common consumer patterns
- Family and friendship network
- Sharing work or work experiences
- Growing up in an educational network
- Participating in politics
- Etc.

Conclusions:

All members of a society have in common that they live in a household (ignored here are homeless people). During their entire life all members experience the evolution of humans and technological progress.

We can conclude that such a community is also embedded in an economic network. A society does not function without a real complex network of economics (a market network).

The market in the most extensive view holds everything together and allows the community to live and to function as a complex network of manifold components and institutions.

There is also a political structure: a political institution is responsible for managing the entire social aggregate. There is a government with a head (president, prime minister…) and a variety of ministers that operate in the interest of the society's combined groups and members. We have collected from some governmental websites a variety of governmental departments for illustration purposes:

Education	Labor	Emergencies and Catastrophes
Health	Agriculture and Forestry	Pensions
Justice and Police	Animal Breeding	Meteorology
Finances	Fisheries	Land Settlement
Defense	Youth	Interior Affairs
Trade	Building and Planning	Environment
Commerce	Wildlife	Consumer Protection
Traffic	Immigration and Migration	Foreign Affairs
Family and Women's Affairs	Culture and Sport	Religion
Social Services	Economic Affairs	Archeology

In general all homes, institutions, firms, corporations, churches, societies, and all governmental departments can be considered households. And no household can operate without money. But in a certain (theoretical) way households could operate without a government, although with fatal consequences.

Nevertheless, this need for monetary operations necessitates planning, budgeting and forecasting in an effort to manage efficiently these monetary resources (this is of course the ideal as we have all seen that this aim for efficiency is very rarely met by most governments!).

However governments periodically change, either through democratic election (and so does the focus of their plan) or through externalities, are forced to alter previous master plan.

In this sense we can deduce that democratic structures are much more vulnerable and inherently weaker than the governance of the monetary structures which are largely private.

The concentration of the market (corporations), the power of certain banks, and the money (and gold) in certain places is an indication about who really rules societies. In the market, people are not elected for 4-6 years like in a democracy. Moreover the corporate elite can afford to develop a master plan for a generation.

Just consider the current astronomic levels of public debt of many governments today, whilst in contrast most large corporations are enjoying high profit rates and large cash reserves. This exposes a fundamental and additional governmental Achilles heel: These governments depend on those who weald the most financial power, their monetary masters. Masters who can simply redirect investments and cash flow of $3 or $4 trillion, or increasing interest rates within a week can destroy instantly a society, its foundation and essential structures.

Therefore where these indebted governments simply playing with fire like stupid boys or girls and their societies now are burning or was this acute indebtedness planned and executed on purpose?

Thesis: We don't have an 'economic crisis'! We experience the ultimate economic master plan!

Conclusions:

➔ The entire political system cannot work without the real economy, the market.
➔ The market (the entire aggregate of economics) is omnipresent and indispensable in a society.
➔ The (economic) market serves the community and guarantees the community's evolution.
➔ There is interdependence between the market, the internal communities, and the government.
➔ If the market fails and or the government fails, then the society fails in parts or as a whole.
➔ Money is the tool that makes the market and the governmental (political) activities work.
➔ The market also has a market hierarchy: at the top are the most powerful market masters.

→ The supreme masters of money concentration and money distribution govern society.

→ The question is: Do the market masters govern or do the political institutions govern?

→ Thesis: As everything in a society only works through the market, then the masters of the market and the monetary system must also dominate the government. But it should be the other way round!

We will dig to find more signs that confirm our thesis!

1.2.2 Western Life Standard

Example: Germany

Life expectancy is increasing; society is growing older and older. Two thirds of the affected will be over 80 years old by 2030. An estimated 50 million people between the age of 20 and 64 make up the work force. Experts forecast that with the decreasing birth rates this figure will drop by a whopping 17 million people.

Estimates suggest that by 2030 a million more people than today will be in need of care.

Nearly every sixth child in Germany is poor. In September 2010 1.72 million children under the age of 15 lived in a household that received unemployment benefits.

Many people in the work force in Germany have big problems with reading and writing. Around 14% are so-called 'functional analphabets' – they cannot write or read continuous texts. Around 4% of the population is analphabet in the stricter sense.

Around 7.5 million adults in Germany cannot read or write simple texts.

In Germany, those without a graduation, hardly have any chance to successfully integrate into the labor market… According to a recent study bad education and lacking training qualifications result in costs of billions of Euros for the general public. Every year around 150,000 young people join the workforce without any qualifications.

No school, no apprenticeship. This logic is creating more and more problems in Germany. There are already nearly 1.5 million young people between the age of 20 and 29 years old without any formal qualifications. Their chances in the labor market are near zero.

Out of the 1.484 million unskilled young people around 729,000 are women (49.1%). Also in vocational training, family background and professional status of the parents extensively determines the success or failure. Children of parents who don't have schooling and professional backgrounds tend to follow the same path.

60% of the unskilled youngsters have at least one parent without any school leaving certificate or professional qualifications. 17% of youngsters aged 20 to 29 years old are considered unskilled.

Federal government debt rose in 2010 by 22% (€230.3 billion) up to €1,284 billion. German States had debts of €595.3 billion at the end of 2010. Municipal debt rose 4.9% (€5.6 billion) up to €119.4 billion. German public debt rose to €2 trillion in 2012.

Example: United States of America
(Diagnosed by an American Expert)[6]

- America is number one in divorce, drug addiction, debt, obesity, car thefts, murders and total crimes.
- America has become a slothful, greedy, decadent nation that is exhibiting signs of advanced decay.
- The United States has the highest incarceration rate.
- The United States has largest total prison population.
- The United States has the highest percentage of obese people.
- The United States has the highest divorce rate.
- The United States has the most hours of television watched per person each week.
- The United States has the highest rate of illegal drug use.
- There are more car thefts in the United States each year than anywhere else.
- There are more reported rapes in the United States each year than anywhere else.
- There are more reported murders in the United States each year than anywhere else.
- There are more total crimes in the United States each year than anywhere else.
- The United States has more police officers than anywhere else.
- The United States spends much more on health care as a percentage of GDP than any other nation.
- The United States has more people on pharmaceutical drugs than any other country.
- The percentage of women taking antidepressants in America is higher than in any other country.
- Americans have more student loan debt than anyone else.
- The United States spends 7 times more on the military than any other nation on the planet does. In fact, U.S. military spending is greater than the

---

[6] http://theeconomiccollapseblog.com/archives/number-one-20-not-so-good-categories-that-the-united-states-leads-the-world-in

military spending of China, Russia, Japan, India, and the rest of NATO combined.

- The United States has far more foreign military bases than any other country does.
- The U.S. has accumulated the biggest national debt that the world has ever seen and it is rapidly getting worse.
- President Obama is being given the power to shut down the Internet for any reason he chooses.
- The US Government now says it has the right to assassinate any American citizen they deem a "terrorist".
- Under US law only the President can define who a "terrorist" is.
- Under US law the President's defining of an American as a "terrorist" is not only secret but cannot be reviewed by any court.
- Americans, which account for only 5%of the world's population, are outraged if anyone tries to tell them that they don't have a divine right to levels of consumption that squander 25% of the world's energy.

Example: Abundant Food in America and Europe

Here some annoying facts: [7]

- In the United Kingdom 30-40% of all foods are never eaten
- In the last 10 years the amount of food British people threw away went up by 15%
- Overall, £20 billion ($38 billion) worth of food is thrown away each year
- In the USA 40-50% of all food ready for harvest never even gets eaten
- Of the food that does eventually reach households, 14% is wasted, resulting in an estimated $43 billion wastage
- If food reaching supermarkets, restaurants and cafeterias is added to the household figure, that wastage goes up to 27%.

"1.200.000.000 billion suffer from obesity (excess of fats and salt, often accompanied by deficiency of vitamins and minerals)" [8]

Social Networks

"Sherry Turkle, Professor of the Social Studies of Science and Technology at the Massachusetts Institute of Technology, tells us there's a 'shift' from an analog world in which our identities are generated from within, to a digital

---

[7] http://philanthropy2012.hubpages.com/hub/Things-that-are-wrong-with-the-world-that-could-be-avoided

[8] http://www.globalissues.org/article/7/causes-of-hunger-are-related-to-poverty

world in which our sense of self is intimately tied to our social media presence ... But this shift to a Facebook world of incessant 'friending', Professor Turkle correctly warns us, is a 'seductive fantasy' which is weakening us both as individuals and as a society. The problem, she explains, is that a 'capacity for solitude is what nurtures great relationships.' But in today's always-on social media world, our solitude has been replaced by incessant online updates, which both weaken our sense of self and our ability to create genuine friendships." [9]

"Facebook is destroying our privacy as discrete individuals ... Our obsession with posting data about our kids - is destroying our children's privacy." [10]

"The vast differences in living standards seen today between rich and poor countries are almost entirely the result of the fact that only some countries have experienced modern economic growth." [11]

→ Only some countries have experienced modern economic growth: Other countries couldn't due to public debt, previous colonization, over-exploited (sold or rented out) natural resources, bribery and corruption (learnt from the imperialists), lost cultural self-identity due to the imperialists, etc.

→ Such statement is not only a trivialization of an immense problem, but also expresses an outrageous arrogance and shows the hidden capitalistic ideology or the ignorance of the author.

Life standard and Consumption

"The average workweek (excluding overtime) in the United States (and in Europe) has declined since the beginning of the 1900s – from about 53 hours to about 35 (36-38) hours…

…Moreover, the greater frequency of paid vacations, holidays, and leave time has shortened the work year itself. This increase in leisure time has clearly had a positive effect on overall well-being." [12]

→ People are lazy! They must come back to at least 42 hours work per week.

---

[9] http://edition.cnn.com/video/#/video/tech/2012/05/25/natpkg-orig-ideas-sherry-turkle.cnn
[10] http://edition.cnn.com/2012/05/30/tech/keen-technology-facebook-privacy/index.html?hpt=hp_bn9
[11] McConnell (et al.), p. 118
[12] McConnell (et al.), p. 143

And 4 weeks holidays would also be enough with additional some short holidays (3-4 days each).

→ The increase in leisure time has absolutely not had a positive effect on overall well-being. This is stupid blabber or lure in order to glorify the success of the neo-capitalism!

"In a typical year, roughly 10 percent of the personal consumption expenditures are on durable goods – products that have expected lives of three years or more ... Another 30 percent are on nondurable goods – products with less than three years of expected life. Included goods like food, clothing, and gasoline ... About 60 percent of personal consumption expenditures are on services – the work done by lawyers, hair stylists, doctors, mechanics, and other service providers." [13]

→ We can conclude: In a typical year, people should invest 20% in very long-term durable goods. People also should buy more goods of duration of 5-8 years (instead of 3 years) and they should drastically reduce their daily 'non-durable' consumption. But corporations would not like this.

→ People should also invest 10% per year in life-long further education for personal development, mastering successfully their life, and for improving their professional skills or building up their own business.

Thesis: A new understanding of 'life standard' and 'lifestyle' would drastically change the entire economic system.

1.2.3. Tourism and Lifestyle

Tourism is the biggest employer around the world (255 million jobs, every 15th worker is employed in the tourism industry). In 2007 the travel boom reached record levels: Nearly 900 million travelers. In 2011 estimates suggest it could be one billion people.

Tourism generates about 9% of total GDP and provides for more than 255 million jobs in 2010 representing 8% of global employment.

The United Nations World Tourism Organization (UNWTO) is expecting the sector's global economy to provide 296 million jobs by 2019. Tourism has the potential to become a major generator of jobs after the crisis.

---

[13] McConnell (et al.), p. 133

The tourism sector suffered a decline that began in the second half of 2008 and intensified in 2009 after several consecutive years of growth. A sharp reduction in tourist flows, length of stay, tourist spending and increased restrictions on business travel expenses led to a significant contraction of economic activity in the sector worldwide.

Such statistics are vague and undifferentiated. Is a 'visitor' a tourist? Is a person that visits family members or a fried a tourist? Is a 'tourist' only a person going for holidays? Similar questions must be asked: Where are these 255 million jobs? Does this statistic include all restaurants, cafés and bars; or only those that are directly related to hotels? Or does it only refer to the Hotel industry? But there are countless hotels that have as guests a majority of business people and not holiday people (tourists). Are the jobs in leisure facilities related to hotels (spa, gym, tennis courts, indoor pools, golf courses, beach facilities, etc.) also included? Are the tourists that rent private holiday homes (via private websites) also included? Are the millions of holiday home owners travelling by private car, bus or train also included? There are also people travelling by airplane, bus or train to participate in a conference, course program, art event, sport event or training, partly staying in a hotel and partly using private or governmental accommodation from the organizers; are these people also included? Are these people in the statistics taking only an airplane, or are tourists travelling by car, train, bus or ship also included? There are also millions of campers traveling with caravans or sleeping wherever in their tents; are they counted as tourists?

As a macro-economic parameter such data gives a highly distorted picture and is absolutely not useful for economic or governmental policy.

The Tourism Plague

Europe alone records around 460 million visitors from around the world every year. An estimated 80-120 million from Northern Europe (exact figures unknown) travel every year towards the south for holidays, to the Mediterranean and the Black Sea: Portugal, Spain, Italy, South of France and the Balkans; a majority with private cars.

Avalanches of cars and airplanes arrive in the high season every few minutes. The consumption of electricity, gasoline, diesel and kerosene is immense. Tons of carcinogenic fine dust is breathed in by people, at airports and around airports. Rubbish and sewage water from tourists reaches astronomical levels in the area around the Mediterranean Sea during high season. Billions of tons of sewage flow directly into the sea.

The fish eat nearly everything; and the people then eat the fish. The environmental contamination and pollution is horrendous; also the noise. Depending on the season, massive smog clouds form over the big cities such as Paris, London, Rome, Athens, Madrid, Barcelona, and even Odessa. This is what you call the contamination (gasifying) of hundreds of millions of people, or millions of tourists in single big tourist resorts. In this context, the tourism sector around the world needs to be labeled as a plague producer.

The greed in the tourism industry will destroy even its own foundation. Not to mention for example that from Almeria to Malaga (Spain) there are now plans to explore and subsequently drill for oil and gas in the Mediterranean Sea: more emissions into the air and sea. All it needs is a small minor oil disaster and the whole coast will be completely destroyed for decades.

In February 2011, the Spanish Foundation for Science and Technology (FECYT) declares: "The rise in sea level of the Mediterranean Sea appears to be accelerating. The sea level in the Mediterranean has risen by between 1 and 1.5 millimeters each year since 1943. It now seems that the speed at which it rises is accelerating. Since the start of the 21st century the level has already risen by 20 centimeters (this means: 2 cm per year!). During the next 30 years the rise in temperatures and in sea level will continue." [14] This means: 60+ cm rise within the next 30 years. Such development will destroy practically all beaches on the Costa del Sol (and all other Mediterranean beaches) and therefore it will enormously affect tourism!

Following an example of the tourism sector in Spain, because this is where we have something of a perspective. The following picture about Spain is a prime example and must subsequently be placed into the frame of humanity and the earth as a whole. The situation of individual areas and places must be placed in the context of the global developments of the following 30-40 years.

If we generalize the main critical aspects to the situations over numerous tourist resort areas around the Mediterranean Sea and then throughout the world one thing becomes self-evident: Today's form of tourism worldwide is not sustainable in the long-run.

The Aftermath of the Financial Crisis

In 2006 several hundred thousand expatriates lived in the Mediterranean areas. On the Costa del Sol and on the Costa Blanca, approximately 65-75% of all expatriates (approximately 120,000 to 180,000 each) have left due to

---

[14] http://2012forum.com/forum/viewtopic.php?f=38&p=355237

lack of work opportunities and as a result of the devaluation of the British Pound (against the Euro). This is a loss of annual cash flow alone for an area such as Costa del Sol East (50 km) or Mallorca of approximately 3,600,000,000 Euros. The loss of annual cash flow on the Costa Blanca (300 km) can easily be higher. How high is the annual loss of cash flow on the Costa del Sol as a whole? How about Mallorca or the Balearic Islands?

On top of the loss of cash flow we estimate that there are approximately over one million residential and commercial properties that lie empty (on sale or for rent) or in a state of unfinished construction. In 2012, the number of empty office spaces in Barcelona, Madrid, Valencia, Alicante, Malaga are immense.

In January 2011, Marbella, in the South of Spain with a Coastline of 20 km alone had approximately 2,000 empty commercial premises on the market, either for sale or for rent. This is huge for such a small area. Most of the new developments in all the resorts throughout the Mediterranean Sea have a yearly occupation of maximum 10-20%, certain developments not more than 1-3%. As statistics do not tell the truth, we can only estimate based on some samples, that the Costa del Sol must have 350,000-500,000 empty new homes, finished and unfinished; and many more second hand homes for sale or rent at insane prices. From Malaga to Gibraltar there are estimated up to 50,000 empty premises (commercial premises and offices). The sale and rental prices are still at least 50-65% too high. But the owners do not reduce their fantasy prices, but prefer to let their property empty for years or decades to come. Greed and avarice are the sole motives. This is a kind of collective economic suicide. However, greed together with miserable working attitudes and lowest business skills, the Spaniards punish themselves economically at the cost of a lost young generation. Arrogant, conceited, lazy, and stupid they say: "In 2014 everything will work well again..." They really think they can go back to exploit tourists and foreigners like in the golden years before 2008.

Spain ... built its housing and financial bubble much the old-fashioned way, borrowing a trillion dollars and more abroad." And: "Mini-flats of 30m2 in a suburb of Madrid ... were going for $200,000." [15] Today, this dream is gone: uncountable urbanizations are empty.

During the so-called golden years many properties were sold on the coasts of the Mediterranean Sea. On the Costa del Sol and on the Costa Blanca alone the property business moved billions of Euros. Lawyers, fiduciaries, real estate agents, banks and the state made huge profits from the booming sector.

---

[15] Chinn (et al.), p. 49

Up until 2008 many people throughout these areas amassed a great deal of wealth. Where is this money today? Where did it go? Who has it and where do they keep it? Today, 2012, the average unemployment rate in these resort areas lies around 25-30%.

Some resorts have dozens of golf courses which occupy massive areas of land that need to be maintained daily with immense amounts of water. The areas around are dry and overgrown with weeds and bushes. There is hardly a place for relaxing, for walking or for fun. The implausible numbers of golfers no longer visit.

The tourist resorts in Spain will never be able to recover from this incredible disaster. It is never possible to go back to the golden years by pumping up the real estate market with arrogant attitudes, lies and massive exaggerations, with glamorous marketing, with glossy brochures or with celebrities. Certain resorts are *per se* no longer competitive compared to other tourist resorts in like Greece, Turkey or Egypt, or with those on the Black Sea for example.

A survey in an English newspaper (January 2011) discovered that half of those Brits who have a home in Spain or France want to sell this year. We assume the same attitude is prevalent amongst the Germans that have a home in Spain. It is certainly well known that many Germans decided to go back to their homeland at a certain age (70-75). They would never wish to go to a Spanish nursing home let alone to die in Spain and be buried here. There are more than 2,000,000 homes for sale; some sources mention 'up to 3,500,000 units'. If we add the foreign owners of holiday homes that wish to sell, it will require 100 years to sell these homes, if ever. A healthy mind has certain difficulties to understand such stupidity. It would be wise to dig up the reasons of this crazy market and to discuss them.

Tourist Prices

The totally excessive real estate and rental prices resulted from years of speculation, fuelled by greed from property owners, investors, constructors, banks, lawyers, real estate agents and others involved in the property business. There are strange places in Spain: Apartments that have a value of 250,000 Euros are still offered for 600,000 Euros. Luxury properties that have a value of 2-3 million Euros are offered at 5-7 million Euros; Miserable old apartments are rented out for 800-1,000 Euros per month when the real value is more around 400 Euros. The rental prices of many villas are similar in constellation. The prices are not appropriate to their true value; they are not oriented on the local employment market, nor on the demand and definitely not on the local salaries.

Most of the properties are of lowest construction quality: no oil or gas heating, no insulation, thin walls, cheap windows, cheap air conditioning. Many second hand properties are in a dilapidated condition with outdated furniture. Some of the smart owners get their properties painted, re-decorate their 'new' place with new furniture and appliances for 30,000 Euros; then they increase the sales price by 150,000-300,000 Euros. At 35-40° C in the sun the trick starts to work. Where doesn't the trick work? After all this is the American concept of 'value appreciation'.

Also the prices of commercial premises are 40-75% over-valued. In certain locations they are completely absurd, especially when taking into account the current economic climate. The owners prefer to leave their properties empty for years and speculate that one day another 'idiot' will come along, blinded by the sun and the manipulated (hyped up) reputation of the resorts to pay the outrageous price. The arrogance of these owners: 'I do not have to rent out these premises!' There are millions of m2 for rent in cities, but the owners still offer them for perverse prices. Some want square meter rental prices of 30-40 Euros, others 20-30 Euros or 10-20 Euros meanwhile the value is in best cases 35%. This is the Spanish self-made crisis. These owners destroy the market and the economic recovery.

Big shopping malls, commercial centers and office developments have completely destroyed small and medium-sized businesses. Many of the tenants can only pay the horrendous rental prices by ripping off their clients, speculating with dubious business practices, with money-laundering and outright fraudulent financial scams. "In all the nightclubs and discos in Madrid there are drugs and the doormen are mafiosos", The Judge Coro Cillán in Madrid told the courts. [16] Is it different in Mediterranean tourist areas? No. Everywhere where prices are 'irrational', then we must suspect other, more profitable, businesses behind the curtains.

Gastronomy and Hospitality Industry

The prices in cafes, bars and restaurants in many places do not reflect the value of that which is served on the plate. The quality of the food is miserable (food from the day before or worse from the week before). The value of the content on the plate is at best 2-3 Euros, the price however between 12-15 Euros. A glass of wine is charged at double the value of the whole bottle. Smart business owners even have a different menu for summer and winter (of course with their respective price differences). Here and there some of the

---

[16] http://politica.elpais.com/politica/2012/06/24/actualidad/1340564506_363194.html

businesses have their kitchen cleaned once every 10-20 years (if at all) and toilets are cleaned monthly, sometimes only yearly – or so it seems here and there. Such ways of doing business destroys the tourist market and any project of recovery.

Another rip off also exists on the beaches with sun beds, with drinks, with parking fares, taxi prices, drink prices in clubs and especially with car rental prices. Other especially blatant rip off services are offered by lawyers, judiciaries, dentists, private doctors, and car dealers. Even the police have long realized that the ideal way of financing their troops is by hunting down parking offenders on a daily basis. Their hunt begins around midday and lasts deep into the night (special areas); they know all the weak spots.

Depending on the resort, 35-65% of the hotels are closed during the winter season. Several 5-star hotels on the Costa del Sol for example have closed for good. In the last two years hotel prices have fallen significantly. In 2011 alone Spanish hotel prices decreased 12-15%.

Hotel prices have plummeted. Nevertheless during the high season in summer and winter they are still over valued and often subsidized by Spanish government initiatives. It is estimated that several million beds in hotels and tourist apartments (Spain) are empty during 9-10 months of the year. The food served does not qualify for anything merely resembling a competent cook. Cleanliness in most hotels is light years away from perfection. Most hotels are boring industrial-like mass-production rabbit stalls. How old are the mattresses? It is well known that you can find between 100,000 and 10 millions dust mites in your bed sheets. Imagine how many millions are in those hotel mattresses after a few years?

Reputation

The reputation of many tourist resorts in Spain and elsewhere is irreparably damaged, destroyed and even rotten to the core. The media is filled with stories about criminals, tax evaders, adventurers, scammers, fraudsters, drug dealers, mafia bosses, prostitution rings, online scammers, human traffickers, weapons dealers, old Nazis, and loan sharks. Pages are filled with reports of corruption and the excesses of the super rich of whom no one knows where they got their millions from. Here and there is fierce and angry talk about the real estate kings (and queens), who badly ripped off foreigners for 10-40 years; to rub salt into the nation's wounds they have taken most of their wealth to offshore havens (tax-free of course). Some have died. Others moved away. Are there still some around here and there around the Mediterranean Sea?

Infrastructure

The cleanliness of many public spaces in Spain is a well known topic on many online forums: dog excrements and millions of discarded chewing gum are nailed to the pavements. In some areas even the main streets are littered with rubbish, which the people throw out of their windows when driving by. Many plants in public spaces are either dead or untended.

The public bus service in many tourist resorts is a complete catastrophe, or rather a disgrace: dirty bus stations and dirty buses, bus shelters adequate for 4-6 people despite there being 30 or more standing in the rain or the blazing heat; indecipherable over optimistic timetables, irregular arrivals, no night routes; during rush hour and during the high season you will find masses of tourists, working residents and locals packed into the buses.

Many developments have no local bus connections making it possible to live there unless one owns has a car (if you are single), or two cars in the case of couples or those that have families. These circumstances together with the ridiculously high rental prices make life for singles, couples and families in such developments impossible for most people!

Especially along the main streets in resorts, towns and cities across the country you will find that the contamination and pollution is horrendous: exhaust fumes, fine dust, noise, and smell. The smog clouds in Malaga, Alicante, Valencia, Madrid and Barcelona for example, or the traffic intensive cores of tourist resort areas are pathogenic if not nearly deadly.

Take Malaga in Spain, a well-known tourist city. On one out of two days of the year the air contamination is over the norm established by EU directives. Cars are responsible for 85% of these emissions. Presumably a similar situation exists in Barcelona, Madrid, Valencia, Alicante as well as many other major towns and cities. Even small tourist towns are highly contaminated by car emissions. There is hope for Spain's contamination: In the year 2011, an average of 900,000 cars were for sale on the website 'auto-scout'. Today 2012 there are 2,100,000 cars for sale (same amount like Germany with double the population and no specific crisis; 85 million). Not many people buy cars now.

Further to the car problems many areas completely lack adequate parking areas. Those offering parking facilities are expensive, as much as 2.50-3.40 Euros per hour. Large shopping malls and office developments further enrich their pockets with ludicrous high hourly parking fees (up to 6-9 Euros per hour). Mainly most towns and cities are immensely over-crowded with parked cars everywhere.

Spanish Culture

Local culture in tourist resorts is seldom present. Here and there you will come across an event or a show; every now and then a religious procession reflecting culture from 500 years ago; archaic rubbish without any educational value and solely for 'very simple minded' people. Cultural events, when they happen, are so expensive that only those with big wallets can attend. Historical monuments, artistic buildings, cultural locations or educational and historic museums for tourists and dwellers (national and international) don't exist in most coastal resorts. International music schools, tango schools, art academies, artist ateliers, theatres or concert halls or highly professional nostalgic bars (with Jazz, Blues, etc.) you will never find in most of these resorts. Some tourist resorts do not have anything of these genres for tourists and expats, let alone for local citizens.

Out of around 200 business owners in a tourism and hospitality sector, most with failing businesses (threatened with economic ruin), at best one is interested in contracting a business coaching to learn something or improve something. There is not a single business owner which wants to see their business situation in a bigger picture, let alone with a future perspective. This is what it is like in Spain and surely also in many other Mediterranean countries.

Bull fighting is part of the Spanish culture. For entertainment they kill bulls. Many earn huge sums of money with this infantile 'fun'. But we live in the modern 21st century. To have fun harming and killing a noble animal surely belongs to the Middle Ages. That is where it should remain.

Cultural peculiarity: 95% of all Spaniards who play the lottery fail to significantly win during an entire life spent a lot of money playing the 'game'. During their entire life, week after week they experience 'I am a loser'. This makes their inner 'self' weak and their soul depressive. They become conditioned and brainwashed to 'have wealth without performing or achieving', but just by being lucky, and only very few are real winners (revenue minus costs during life). Their sick fantasy is: 'To have a lot, but achieve nothing or give very little'. Here we have a destructive micro-economic parameter.

Marriage is also a 'culture'. The divorce rate in Spain is apparently 68-75%. It shows: Young Spaniards are unprepared for marriage. They are unsuitable for a constructive relationship, unprepared to raise children and incapable of educating them. The have got absolutely no clue about what love is, with exceptions of course. Their motto: 'to solve the problem, throw it away'. Should people just be thrown away when they have or create problems?

When analyzing a culture and society it is always essential to take into account its history. History always repeats itself, until it is amended, reconciled and redeemed. Until today this has not happened in Spain. Not the murdering and stealing of hundreds of years ago, not the Franco-era.

Hundreds of years ago the Spaniards invaded and occupied nearly half of the earth's surface. They massacred entire populations and stole their lands and possessions. They did so in the name of Jesus Christ and the Bible. For the building of their ships they cut down 80% of their own forests: today all that remains is dry land covered in weeds and bushes, in many cases these are now wastelands, scrublands.

The wealth from the last centuries has long been wasted and misspent. Today they again want to enrich themselves with corporate groups who drain people, other nations, and the oceans. This is also the case with France, England and other nations such as the United States who conquered the Americas, the Far East and the African continent. Who murdered their populations and stole their lands and goods 'all in the name of the Lord J.C.' as part of their 'culture'.

What also belongs to Spanish culture is the fact that many large companies have their headquarters abroad. 82% of the companies listed on the Spanish IBEX 35 index have branches and operations in fiscal paradises. Each is certainly a case to unravel and meticulously explore with highest professionalism. The big corruption scandals milked by the media are only the tip of the iceberg. In some cases they are merely a form of distraction and revenge for the years that others didn't get a slice of the pie.

The Judicial System and Administration

Who has ever met a friendly, helpful, competent and efficient civil servant? Surely, here and there they must exist. Which civil servant can speak a few words of French, German or English? Surely some here or there must do so. Many resorts live mainly or fully from tourism and from expatriates; also foreigners who come to Spain to retire. Yet more often than not the attitude in the service from these civil servants expresses envy, contempt, indifference, laziness, ignorance, disrespect, and almost always above all professional inefficiency.
The legal system isn't very different. It does not work in the interest of the

people and the world of small business. As a foreigner try and find a Spanish lawyer that will go to court for you against a Spaniard (and your opponent's Spanish lawyer). First of all this costs a fortune paid up front (30% of the quantity claimed) and this without any guarantee whatsoever. The procedure is long-winding, can take many years and in the end you receive nothing whether the amount reclaimed is 10,000 Euros or 200,000 Euros.

Hundreds of thousands of foreigners were ripped off over the past 20 years in the Spanish real estate sector. They all barely stand a chance in the Spanish legal system. This certainly can be interpreted as a 'typical Spanish attitude' against foreigners and tourists. Rip off and abuse as much as possible! But this is not 'typical Spanish'; much rather this is 'typical capitalistic' and with that typical for the Swiss, Germans, Brits, French, Italians, etc. And it is also 'typical Christian'.

Many politicians and greedy business people in Spain have destroyed the lives and future of millions of people, couples and families, and with that also the future of hundreds of thousands of children: their inherited love and their fortune, their wealth and their hope. They created a daunting disaster and committed incredible emotional suffering. Yet nobody is holding them accountable.

The incompetence, corruption and greed for money that most politicians and many business people have in the tourist areas are mind-blowing. They have neither morals nor the capacity to think in dimensions that take into account the soul of people, the genuine inner human needs, nature and the environment, the economic balance, and the future of their own children and the future of tourism itself. But all the authorities and institutes of tourism always restart the old hand organ.

Today one thing is clear: They all want to go back to the old lies, tricks and glamour marketing strategies to revive the old days of glory in the tourism and real estate sector. But the goose that lays golden eggs doesn't exist any more and can't come back. They haven't learnt anything.

The Expats

Far too many foreigners come to Spain, to the coastal areas, thinking that they can simply open a bar, restaurant or consumption oriented business; or an office offering a service. They think that they can then just wait and a constant flow of clients (guests) will show up miraculously. Most are far too idle to work hard, think creatively, let alone to take advice or educate themselves; to offer something that people really need for their genuine needs is unknown. Education and culture isn't of their interest. To develop themselves psychically and spiritually, to read a book or attend a course for vocational further or personal education is something they see as for fools.

Most of those that come to Spain to retire are lazy, gossip about others, eat and drink (a lot), watch hours of TV and become more and more stubborn, rigid and mentally regress year by year. Their average life potential is of 15-25 years yet they sit around and wait for death to arrive; or they one day return to a nursing home in their country of origin.

The million-strong herd of tourists also has certain peculiarities that don't have a future: There are those with very little money, who only eat, drink, sleep and lie on the beaches, who want only to have fun (i.e. sex, alcohol) and gossip. Most of them are badly educated. Then there are those who think they can behave arrogantly in their narcissist obsession just because they are well off financially.

They consider themselves superior having usually put one over on their fellows. The interests and needs of the local people don't interest them. Ultimately there are of course a select group of tourists who certainly do deserve to spend their holidays by the Mediterranean Sea.

→ All this tourism disaster is the result of the neo-capitalistic lifestyle and way of doing business.
→ We will give examples in chapter 3 that shows how sick the modern way of tourism is with all its billions of tons of waste, sewage, contamination, and environmental destruction.

1.2.4. Externalities

"Externalities – the effects of a decision on a third party that are not taken into account by the decision maker. Externalities can be either positive or negative. Secondhand smoke and carbon monoxide emissions are examples of negative externalities, which occur when the effects of a decision not taken into account by the decision maker are detrimental to others. Positive externalities occur when the effects of a decision not taken into account by the decision maker are beneficial to others. An example is education." [17]

Critical approach:
→ 'The effects of a decision': They calculate minimizing costs with 'negative

---

[17] Colander, p. 486

externalities'!
→ The author doesn't say who takes decisions on a third party.
→ 'Third party': This is trivializing the immense dimension: folks, environment, nature, etc.
→ There is no reason to understand externalities either as positive or as negative.
→ Introducing this distinction reduces the weight of the 'negative' perspectives.
→ To only mention 'smoke and carbon monoxide emissions' is an insane trivialization.
→ Constructing this 'positive' perspective with the example of 'education' is deceitful and a deviation.
→ Taking the criteria 'beneficial' for 'positive externalities' is a serious manipulation.
→ 'Positive externalities' is an absurd term as it can be extended to any external positive factor.
→ Such an immense perfidious distortion is a disgrace and a sign of very extreme perversion.

"Pollution is a bad thing. Yet most pollution is a side effect of activities that provide us with good things: our air is polluted by power plants generating the electricity that lights our cities, and our rivers are damaged by fertilizer run off from farms that grow our food. Why shouldn't we accept a certain amount of pollution as the cost of a good life?" [18]

→ The good part here is that the author agrees: Pollution is bad. The bad part here is the suggestion: If we want a good life, we must accept pollution.
→ The author minimizes the problem of pollution and makes it to an unavoidable side effect of human's life.
→ We must accept a certain amount of pollution: How much do we need to accept? So, 7 billion, then 8 billion, then 9 billion, and then 10 billion people have to accept pollution.
→ How much pollution does a human body accept? How much do the species accept? And how much do the ecosystems accept?
→ Considering the contamination we explored in chapter 3.5., we identify here either a reckless and naïve view of the concern or the author is a radical psychopath. Not acceptable!

---

[18] Krugman, p. 262

"Even an environmentally conscious society would accept some pollution as the cost of producing useful goods and services." [19]

→ The author becomes devious, trivializes the concern, and manipulates the readers even more. Does he really know that an environmentally conscious society would accept some pollution? How can he know?

"An externality arises when a person engages in an activity that influences the well-being of a bystander (a third party) who neither pays nor receives any compensation for that effect. If the impact on the bystander is adverse, it is called a negative externality; if it is beneficial, it is called a positive externality ... The release of dioxin into the environment, for instance, is a negative externality." [20]

→ An externality arises when people, firms, corporations and governments produce damages (on people, environment, eco-systems, resources, etc.) and are not liable for the costs.

"Traders are unlikely to take into account any effect that an action may have on a third party. Economists call the effect of a decision on a third party not taken into account by the decision maker an externality ... An externality can be positive (in which case society as a whole benefits form the trade between the two parties) or negative (in which case society as a whole is harmed by the trade between the two parties) ... An example of a positive externality is education. When someone educates herself or himself, all society benefits, since better-educated people usually make better citizens and are better equipped to figure out new approaches to solving problems – approaches that benefit society as a whole ... An example of a negative externality is pollution." [21]

→ Not only the traders are unlikely to take into account any effect that an action may have on a third party. The entire neo-capitalistic theories and practices ignore 'negative' effects.
→ The author mixes 'positive externality' with the world of 'trade' in order to deviate from the outrageous economic practices of the modern world.
→ Better-educated people do absolutely not make better citizens. The educational system is based on an archaic understanding of humans and only serves the world of economics. And everything that public education and family upbringing do positively for an excellent education is

---

[19] Krugman, p. 262
[20] Mankiw, p. 198-199
[21] Colander, p. 69

permanently destroyed by the media, the falseness, lies, brainwashing and propaganda from the (consumer) world of economics and the political sceneries full of ego-trips.

"Economics provides the tools, not the rules, for policy." [22]

→ The tools are miserable, evil, insane, and full of faults and abdication of responsibility.
→ Who gives the rules in the world of banking?
→ Who gives the rules in the world of corporations?
→ Who gives the rules to the governments?

"Education yields positive externalities because a more educated population leads to improved productivity and increases the potential for economic growth, which benefits everyone." [23]

→ Education is in general indispensable for individuals to manage life, for a society, for the market, for fulfillment of life, and for the archetypal evolution.
→ To connect education with 'economic growth' is tricky and manipulative, a typical strategy of economics (concepts, theories and economists).
→ Another manipulation is planted on education: 'everyone benefits from economic growth'. More sadistic, perverse, dirty, and perfidious is not possible!

"Unless there is a strong and effective environmental policy, our society will generate too much pollution – too much of a bad thing. And the great majority of economists agree." [24]

→ The great majority of economists think that pollution is in general still not on an alarming level. They ignore the accumulation and the principle of the momentum: They will see the alarming level when it is too late and irreversible for 500 years.

"The government can internalize the externality by taxing goods that have negative externalities and subsidizing goods that have positive externalities." [25]
→ 'Taxing goods that have negative externalities': this suggests that these negative externalities can be regulated or compensated with a tax or fine.

---

[22] Colander, p.539
[23] Mankiw (et al.), p. 203
[24] Krugman, p. 262
[25] Mankiw (et al.), p. 204

→ Considering the global negative externalities, as described in chapter 3, even $5 trillion of taxes per year would not solve or repair the damages of negative externalities.

→ 'Subsidizing goods that have positive externalities' will never solve the global negative externalities. The author tries with artful words to trivialize the negative externalities.

"One way to deal with pollution directly is to charge polluters an emissions tax. Emissions taxes are taxes that depend on the amount of pollution a firm produces." [26]

→ No! No! Taxes will never solve the problem. A new way of living is required; and this around the globe. Renewing society's life requires focusing on genuine human values and on a new understanding of a fulfilling life.

"Actions with positive externalities should be encouraged and actions with negative externalities should be discouraged. Governments can step in and change the rules so that the actors must take into account the effect of their actions on society as a whole." [27]

→ We wish to know what type of 'positive externalities' are desirable in an economy.

→ Discouraging negative externalities needs first a complete catharsis and renewal of economics.

→ A bit naïve: The politicians come in just like that and change the rules. Unbelievable!

→ Who are these actors that must take into account the effects of their evil doing?

"At present the main policy tools are environmental standards, rules that protect the environment by specifying actions by producers and consumers. A familiar example is the law that requires almost all vehicles to have catalytic converters, which reduce the emissions of chemicals that can cause smog and lead to health problems. Other rules require communities to treat their sewage or factories to avoid or limit certain kinds of pollution, and so on." [28]

→ It's outrageous and perfidious how the author minimizes and trivializes

---

[26] Krugman, p. 268
[27] Colander, p. 69, 70
[28] Krugman, p. 268

the problem of pollution. OK, we can all live with a 'little bit of health problems'.

→ For the author the problem of pollution is already significantly solved with catalytic converters. Is it really? What about the fine dust that kills millions per year?

"How much pollution should society allow? (…) the optimal amount of an activity always involves comparing the marginal benefit from an additional unit of something with the marginal cost of that additional unit. The same is true of pollution … The marginal social cost of pollution is the additional cost imposed on society as a whole by an additional unit of pollution. For example, acid rain damages fisheries, crops, and forests, and each additional ton of sulfur dioxide released into the atmosphere increases the damage." [29]

→ The author tries to solve the problem by balancing benefit (the good life with consumption) and costs of pollution. But this can never work. It's a deceit and cheat! And it's insane to search for a solution with the 'marginal'-idea.

"Today's rich countries have historically been responsible for most greenhouse gas emissions, but newly emerging economies like China are responsible for most the recent growth." [30]

→ Indeed, and that must be discussed: the industrial lunacy has infected China and entire Asia. They have not learnt the lesson!
→ They are blinded as well and nobody bothers there that the contamination in towns and cities is horrifying.

"We can determine the socially optimal quantity of pollution – the quantity of pollution society would choose if all its costs and benefits were fully accounted for." [31]

→ The author has lost reality! The nature, the ecosystems, the world of species, the soil, the seas and oceans, and the fetus and babies and old people don't have a voice in his concept of solution.

"The environmental costs of pollution are the best-known and most

---

[29] Krugman, p. 262
[30] Krugman, p. 384
[31] Krugman, p. 263

important example of an external cost – an uncompensated cost that an individual or firm imposes on others. There are many other examples of external costs besides pollution. Another important, and certainly very familiar, external cost is traffic congestion – an individual who chooses to drive during rush hour increases congestion and so increases the travel time of other drivers." [32]

→ It sounds like: 'Traffic congestion' is not that bad; it's a matter of waste of time (lost time is here the cost); and we all can and must live with it. Above that, he speaks about environmental costs, but he doesn't give here any figure for today and the future generations.
→ The author ignores that there are many sources of pollution and that also pollution and not only toxic chemicals produce serious illnesses, mental damages, even untimely 'exitus' for millions.

"At present the main policy tools are environmental standards, rules that protect the environment by specifying actions by producers and consumers. A familiar example is the law that requires almost all vehicles to have catalytic converters, which reduce the emissions of chemicals that can cause smog and lead to health problems. Other rules require communities to treat their sewage or factories to avoid or limit certain kinds of pollution, and so on."

→ It's outrageous and perfidious how the author minimizes and trivializes the problem of pollution. OK, we can all live with a 'little bit of health problems'.
→ For the author the problem of pollution is already significantly solved with catalytic converters. Is it really? What about the fine dust that kills millions per year?

"One way to deal with pollution directly is to charge polluters an emissions tax. Emissions taxes are taxes that depend on the amount of pollution a firm produces."

→ No! No! Taxes will never solve the problem. A new way of living is required; and this around the globe. Renewing society's life requires focusing on genuine human values and on a new understanding of a fulfilling life.

"The most important single source of external benefits in the modern

---

[32] Krugman, p. 265

economy is the creation of knowledge. In high-tech industries like semiconductors, software design, and bioengineering, innovations by one firm are quickly emulated and improved upon by rival firms and by firms in other industries. Such spreading of knowledge among individuals and firms is known as technology spillover." [33]

→ The author focuses on technological knowledge. But we have plenty of such knowledge that is not used for a new way of living.

→ The author ignores that humans, humanity, and all societies need a much deeper understanding of the inner life of humans. This includes the entire psychical-spiritual development with the Archetypes of the Soul.

→ Ignoring the deficit of knowledge about the entire inner world with its spiritual dimensions will lead humanity to the doom whatever they may try with technological knowledge.

Destruction of our Natural World

"The destruction of our natural world that goes on every day, to most, is virtually unfathomable; so are the economic losses for that matter. Today, the disappearance of species, the loss of wetlands, peat bogs, and tropical rainforests, toxic waste disposal in our freshwater resources, billions of tons of greenhouse gases dumped into the atmosphere and absorbed into the oceans, countless drill holes bored and mountaintops removed to excavate fossil fuels, massive soil depletion due to modern agricultural practices, and glaciers receding all have a toll not only on the planet, but also on the people living on it … Environmental economists have recently tried to assess the economic damage that will most certainly be caused by our wholesale destruction of the planet, but the science of calculating the true cost of climate change, biodiversity loss, and toxic poisoning is a bit abstract and is quite open to subjective appraisals." [34]

Michael Mansfield QC, leading human rights lawyer writes: "The problem in the past is that if you hold a company responsible, who sits in the dock? All the court can do is fine the company if it has transgressed. Who pays the fine? We do, because they pass the cost of the fine onto their customers – so it does not have very much effect, at all. But who is responsible? The object of the Ecocide act is not just aimed at companies it is aimed at individuals … the only way there will be any change." [35]

---

[33] Krugman, p. 275
[34] http://www.earthpulsedaily.net/epd-post/corporate-capitalism-s-ecocide-freeride
[35] http://www.eradicatingecocide.com/wp-content/uploads/2012/01/What-is-Ecocide-6-

"Aluminum factories emit pollution. This pollutant may pose health risks for those who breathe the air, it is a negative externality. Because of the externality, the cost to society of producing aluminum is larger than the cost to the aluminum producers." [36]

→ 'May pose': Eventually, maybe… This is a very tricky way to trivialize the mentioned problem.
→ The author admits: The negative externalities of production costs society more than the production costs (of aluminum). There are a thousand other products with production costs that have such a costly negative externality.

"Destruction, damage or loss of ecosystems is happening on a mass scale, every day … A recent report for the United Nations has found that 3,000 of the world's biggest corporations caused $2.2 trillion of ecocide in 2008." [37] (We suppose the ecocide in 2012 has probably reached 3 trillion.) [38]

"Ocean damage from climate change will cost $2 trillion a year." [39]

→ These negative externalities cost an estimated $ 5 trillion per year at public accounting.
→ How much is the profit from these 3,000 corporations per year?
→ Probably these 3,000 corporations can only make huge profits by letting the community pay for the costs of the damages.
→ If the costs of the negative externalities are equal or higher than the profit, then the corporations must fall.
→ It is absolutely unacceptable that private firms produce a global disaster with costs of $5 trillion in order to make profit, measures must be taken.
→ As education is an indispensable preparation for working in the corporations (called 'positive externality), and as the public pays these costs, we can say the community pays the educational preparation for the corporations, their profit and all the negative externalities.
→ Do you get the astronomic cheat and scam from economics (theory and practice) now?
→ Ecocide is a crime against the planet and the entire humanity!

---

pages.pdf
[36] Mankiw, p. 200-201
[37] http://climateandcapitalism.com/2010/03/04/3000-companies-cause-2-2-trillion-in-environmental-damage-every-year/
[38] http://www.eradicatingecocide.com/wp-content/uploads/2012/01/What-is-Ecocide-6-pages.pdf
[39] http://climateandcapitalism.com/2012/03/21/ocean-damage-2-trillion/

Chapter 3 shows you all the negative 'externalities' from the 'actors'.

Warning

"Earth faces a century of disasters, report warns." [40]

"Rapid and widespread changes in the world's human population, coupled with unprecedented levels of consumption present profound challenges to human health and wellbeing, and the natural environment ... The combination of these factors is likely to have far reaching and long-lasting consequences for our finite planet and will impact on future generations as well as our own. These impacts raise serious concerns and challenge us to consider the relationship between people and the planet." [41]

UN Warns of 'A Major Planetary Catastrophe': Humanity is close to breaching the sustainability of Earth ... The world is facing exploding population, an energy crisis, global climate change, increasingly destructive natural disasters and increasing starvation ... even if we stop global engines of growth now, the depletion and pollution of our natural environment would still continue because of existing consumption patterns and production methods." [42]

UNITED NATIONS NEWS SERVICE
20 June, 2012 – We cite from this daily news some statements:

"More than 40,000 people – including parliamentarians, mayors, UN officials, chief executive officers and civil society leaders – are attending Rio+20 from 20-22 June.

Since the Earth Summit twenty years ago progress has been too slow, and much more needs to be done ... It is time for all of us to think globally and locally.

Taking steps to go beyond gross domestic product to assess the wellbeing of a country... A framework for tackling sustainable consumption and production...

---

[40] http://www.guardian.co.uk/environment/2012/apr/26/earth-population-consumption-disasters

[41] http://royalsociety.org/policy/projects/people-planet/

[42] http://beforeitsnews.com/story/783/989/UN_Warns_of_A_Major_Planetary_Catastrophe.html&SID=NL

We recognize that the old model for economic development and social advancement is broken…

(Aim): To create a new model, to set a new course that truly balances the imperatives of robust growth and economic development with the social and environmental dimensions of sustainable prosperity and human wellbeing.

We are running out of time. We no longer have the luxury to defer difficult decisions. We have a common responsibility to act in common cause, to set aside narrow national interests in the name of the global public good and the betterment of all."

The following day the Headline News: [43]

"…officially-accredited non-government delegates who had traveled thousands of miles to attend the UN's Rio+20 sustainable development conference in Brazil have been refused all access to the central negotiating text … This key document, containing all of the environmental conference's decisions, is now restricted to governmental delegates only … This censorship by the UN is without precedent. The public has had access to these documents at previous UN summits … This latest development makes a mockery of any UN claim to transparency."

So it's basically everything is too 'fucked up' for the average citizen to know about!

A Bleak Picture we also get from WWF

"Data from many more species' populations than previously, the Living Planet Index continues to show around a 30 (37) per cent global decline in biodiversity health since 1970.

The tropical freshwater index declined even more precipitously, by 70 per cent. Overall, the global tropical index declined by 60 per cent since 1970

The footprint exceeded the Earth's bio-capacity — the area of land and productive oceans actually available to produce renewable resources and absorb CO2 emissions — by more than 50 per cent.

---

[43] http://climatedepot.com/a/16354/UN-Censorship-Rio-Earth-Summit-text-is-now-secret--Senior-official-of-transparent-UN-admits-Rio-negotiating-text-is-classified

The tropical freshwater index declined even more precipitously, by 70 per cent. Overall, the global tropical index declined by 60 per cent since 1970."

The 'Living Planet Report' from WWF reveals in Chapter 1 the state of the Planet: [44]

- Biodiversity has declined globally
- The global Living Planet Index declined by almost 30 per cent between 1970 and 2008.
- The global tropical index declined by 60 per cent during the same period.
- The global temperate index increased by 31 per cent.
- The global terrestrial, freshwater and marine indices all declined by 37 per cent.
- The tropical freshwater index declined even more precipitously, by 70 per cent.
- Human demands on the planet exceed supply
- The Ecological Footprint exceeded the Earth's bio-capacity by more than 50 per cent (2008).
- The carbon footprint is a significant component of this ecological overshoot.
- Bio-capacity per person decreased from 3.2 global hectares (gha) in 1961 to 1.8 gha per capita in 2008, even though total global bio-capacity increased over this time.
- Many river basins are actually overexploited, hampering critical ecosystem functions.

And the Author's Personal Statement

The state of Humanity and the Earth is disastrous. Most leaders in politics, economy, industry, religion and education have failed terribly. The planet is in frightening danger of collapse.

On the 14.08.2010 I dreamt: "In 35-40 years everything will be over, the end, no more earth and no more humanity."

In 2008 I dreamt: "Humanity has got 10 years left to take drastic measures". Today, 2012, Humanity has only got 6 years left to take drastic measures!
The chapter 3 about global macroeconomic parameters will reveal and put on the table what is fact. The picture as a whole is indeed extremely shocking –

---

[44]

http://www.unep.org/publications/ebooks/foresightreport/Portals/24175/pdfs/Foresight_Report-21_Issues_for_the_21st_Century.pdf even beyond imagination.

1.3. Population Growth and Macroeconomics

1.3.1. Population Growth

"Homo sapiens seem to have appeared at least as early as 700,000 B.C. Hominids walked the Earth as early as several million years ago. According to the United Nations Determinants and Consequences of Population Trends, modern *Homo sapiens* may have appeared about 50,000 B.C. This long period of 50,000 years holds the key to the question of how many people have ever been born." [45]

Number who have ever been born: 107,602,707,791 [46]
The growth rate peaked at 2.2% in 1963, and had declined to 1.1% by 2011. [47]

With the beginning of the year 2012 the earth population reached 7 billion people. The biggest nations in terms of population are: [48]

Rank	Country / Territory	Population	Date	% of world population
1	China	1,351,500,000	June 20, 2012	19.2%
2	India	1,203,710,000	March 2011	17%
3	United States	313,765,000	June 20, 2012	4.47%
4	Indonesia	238,400,000	May 2010	3.34%
5	Brazil	196,574,000	June 20, 2012	2.8%
6	Pakistan	179,882,000	June 20, 2012	2.56%
7	Nigeria	170,123,740	July 2012	2.42%
8	Bangladesh	161,083,804	July 2012	2.29%
9	Russia	141,927,297	January 1, 2010	2.02%
10	Japan	127,610,000	May 1, 2012	1.82%

- Number of children in the world: 2.2 billion
- Number in poverty: 1 billion (every second child)

---

[45] http://www.prb.org/articles/2002/howmanypeoplehaveeverlivedonearth.aspx
[46] See list: http://www.prb.org
[47] http://en.wikipedia.org/wiki/World_population
[48] http://en.wikipedia.org/wiki/World_population

Approximately 4.06 billion people live in these 10 countries, representing around 58% of the world's population as of April 2012. The same source describes:

UN 2008 estimates and medium variant projections (in millions)

Year	World	Asia	Africa	Europe	Latin America	Northern America	Oceania
2000	6,115	3,698 (60.5%)	819 (13.4%)	727 (11.9%)	521 (8.5%)	319 (5.2%)	31 (0.5%)
2005	6,512	3,937 (60.5%)	921 (14.1%)	729 (11.2%)	557 (8.6%)	335 (5.1%)	34 (0.5%)
2010	6,909	4,167 (60.3%)	1,033 (15.0%)	*733 **(10.6%)**	589 (8.5%)	352 **(5.1%)**	36 (0.5%)
2015	7,302	4,391 (60.1%)	1,153 (15.8%)	734 (10.1%)	618 (8.5%)	368 (5.0%)	38 (0.5%)
2020	7,675	4,596 (59.9%)	1,276 (16.6%)	733 (9.6%)	646 (8.4%)	383 (5.0%)	40 (0.5%)
2025	8,012	4,773 (59.6%)	1,400 (17.5%)	729 (9.1%)	670 (8.4%)	398 (5.0%)	43 (0.5%)
2030	8,309	4,917 (59.2%)	1,524 (18.3%)	723 (8.7%)	690 (8.3%)	410 (4.9%)	45 (0.5%)
2035	8,571	5,032 (58.7%)	1,647 (19.2%)	716 (8.4%)	706 (8.2%)	421 (4.9%)	46 (0.5%)
2040	8,801	5,125 (58.2%)	1,770 (20.1%)	708 (8.0%)	718 (8.2%)	431 (4.9%)	48 (0.5%)
2045	8,996	5,193 (57.7%)	1,887 (21.0%)	700 (7.8%)	726 (8.1%)	440 (4.9%)	50 (0.6%)
2050	9,150	5,231 (57.2%)	1,998 (21.8%)	691 **(7.6%)**	729 (8.0%)	448 **(4.9%)**	51 (0.6%)
Year	World	Asia	Africa	Europe	Latin America	Northern America	Oceania

Some special facts and perspectives (estimated; based on the same source):
* European Union Population 2011: 502,000,000 [49]
  European Union + North America Population together = 854,000,000

- European Union Population 2011 in percentage: 7.1% of the world population
- Northern America Population 2011 in percentage: 5.1%
- Population of European Union plus Northern America 2011 in percentage: 12.2%
- 1.350.000.000 people live in China 2011: in percentage: 19.3%
- 1,200,000,000 people live in India 2011: percentage: 17.1%

---

[49] http://en.wikipedia.org/wiki/European_Union

- 2012: 80% of the earth population is living in Asia, Africa, and South America.
- 2050: European Union plus Northern America in percentage estimated: 7-8%
- Today 3.5 billion people (50%) are living in cities with high growth rate.
- 2050: Nearly 6.8 billion people will live in cities and mega cities (estimated 75%).

1.3.2. Development of World Population

1950 2,519
1955 2,756
1960 2,982 Increase within 10 years: 463 m
1965 3,335
1970 3,692 Increase within 10 years: 710 m
1975 4,068
1980 4,435 Increase within 10 years: 743 m
1985 4,831
1990 5,263 Increase within 10 years: 828 m
1995 5,674
2000 6,070 Increase within 10 years: 807 m
2005 6,454
2010 6,972 Increase within 10 years: 902 m

If nothing of high significance causes a change to the growth rate and if we ignore the exponential factor (progressive or regressive), we can theoretically estimate an average increase of 800 million every 10 years. This means starting with approximately 7,000 million (2010):

- Population 2020: 7,800,000,000
- Population 2030: 8,600,000,000
- Population 2040: 9,400,000,000
- Population 2050: 10,200,000,000

If we calculate an average reduction of growth with estimated 600 million per decade, then we get the following picture:

- Population 2020: 7,600,000,000
- Population 2030: 8;200,000,000
- Population 2040: 8,800,000,000
- Population 2050: 9,400,000,000

Some available statistics calculate with less population growth. A strange statement which can be found on many websites: "The United Nations' most recent 'mid-range' projection calls for an increase to 8 billion people by 2025 and to 10.1 billion by century's end." [50] The question is here: What can produce such a drastic reduction of the growth rate after the year 2025? Another source, the UN reports in January 2011: "The world population is expected to reach 7 billion later this year (2011) and the figure could potentially double to 14 billion by 2100 unless preventive measures are taken." [51]

People get older. Health care will get better in Asia and Africa. The current and upcoming young generation will procreate several hundred million babies every decade. Therefore the population will increase. We have to calculate with a progressive exponential factor unless drastic measures are taken especially in Asia and Africa, which is improbable. Which measures could drastically reduce the population rate?

Another approach to get a picture about the growth of the world population: Increase of 1 billion people every 13-15 years:

- 2024-2027: 8 billion people
- 2037-2040: 9 billion people
- 2050-2053: 10 billion people
- 2050: 90-93% of the earth population will live in Asia, Africa, and South America.

Another source calculates: [52]

"There were 1 billion humans in 1804; 2 billion in 1927; 6 billion in 1999; and 7 billion today. The UN's forecasts for 2050: a range from 8.1 billion to 10.6 billion, with 9.3 billion as the mid-projection. Nearly all the population increases will be in urban areas in developing countries, where the slum population expanded from 767 million in 2000 to 828 million in 2010 and is expected to reach 889 million by 2020. Without sufficient nutrition, shelter, water, and sanitation produced by more intelligent human-nature symbioses, increased migrations, conflicts, and

---

50

http://www.foreignpolicy.com/articles/2011/08/15/the_world_will_be_more_crowded_with_old_people

[51] http://www.bbc.co.uk/news/science-environment-12338901

[52] http://www.millennium-project.org/millennium/Global_Challenges/chall-03.html

disease seem inevitable. ICT continues to improve the match between needs and resources worldwide in real time, and nanotech will help reduce material use per unit of output while increasing quality. However, food prices may continue to rise due to increasing affluence (especially in India and China), soil erosion and the loss of cropland, increasing fertilizer costs (high oil prices), market speculation, aquifer depletion, falling water tables and water pollution, diversion of crops to biofuels, increasing meat consumption, falling food reserves, diversion of water from rural to urban, and a variety of climate change impacts…

Population dynamics are changing from high mortality and high fertility to low mortality and low fertility. If fertility rates continue to fall, world population could actually shrink to 6.2 billion by 2100, creating an elderly world difficult to support; if not, however, the UN projects <u>15.8 billion by 2100</u>."[53]

Examples of growth rate: [54]

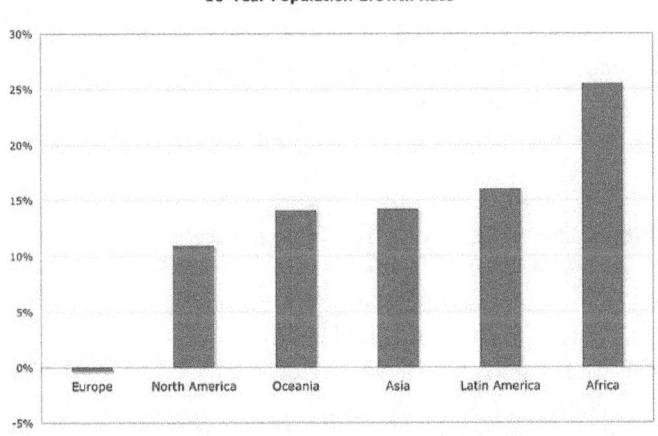

10-Year Population Growth Rate

1.3.3. Growth and Intrinsic Factors

General future perspectives and information from many other online sources draw the following general picture about world population:

- Population India: in 2025 India could have a higher population than China.
- Population Africa: At the end of the century the population will increase

[53] http://en.wikipedia.org/wiki/World_population_milestones
[54] http://en.wikipedia.org/wiki/List_of_countries_by_population_growth_rate

up to probably 3.6 billion.

- Some experts estimate: 10 billion people by 2050.
- In 2050-2055 around 70% of the world population will live in mega cities and immense cities (urban growth).
- In one year one additional billion people will suffer from hunger due to the current increase of food prices.
- In 40-45 years 3 billion people more will need food, water, health services, education, sanitation, energy, etc.
- In 40-45 years 10 billion people will produce immense volumes of sewage, air pollution, chemical emissions (contaminations), and waste in general.
- Europe and the United States will not have a significant increase of population, maybe rather a decrease.
- Europe and the United States will face increasing conflicts with the rest of the world due to the global demand of resources.
- 10-11 billion people need 3 planets for a sustainable life (like EU, USA).

Depending on local medium life expectancy, people born in:

- 1960-1980: will face a very tough and bitter third age in the future.
- 1981-2000: will face and live unimaginable nightmares in the future.
- 2001-2010: will suffer terribly due to the failure of global politics.
- Everything will be worse for children born from now on and the coming decades

Religions (estimations; figures differ with 10-15% variance)

- Christianity: 2.2 billion (other figures found: 2.4 billion)
- Islam: 1.5 billion (other figures found: 1.8 billion)
- Secular/Non-religious/Agnostic/Atheist: 1.1 billion
- Hinduism: 900 million
- Chinese traditional religion: 394 million
- Buddhism: 376 million

1.3.4. The Destructive Factors of Population Growth

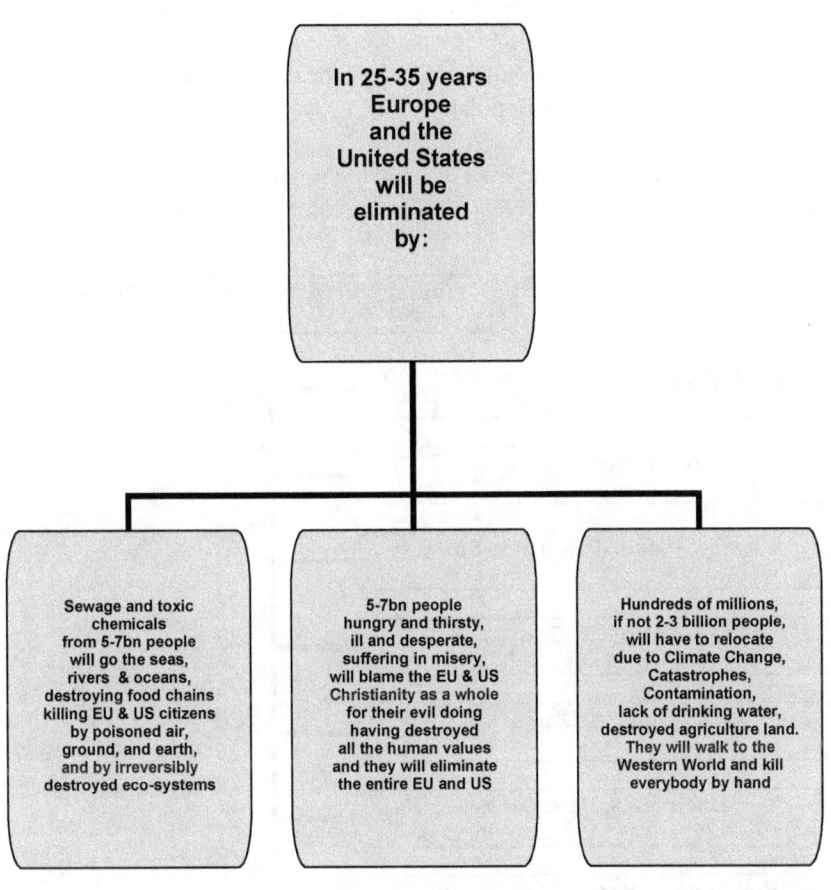

In 25-35 years Europe and the United States will be eliminated by:

Sewage and toxic chemicals from 5-7bn people will go the seas, rivers & oceans, destroying food chains killing EU & US citizens by poisoned air, ground, and earth, and by irreversibly destroyed eco-systems

5-7bn people hungry and thirsty, ill and desperate, suffering in misery, will blame the EU & US Christianity as a whole for their evil doing having destroyed all the human values and they will eliminate the entire EU and US

Hundreds of millions, if not 2-3 billion people, will have to relocate due to Climate Change, Catastrophes, Contamination, lack of drinking water, destroyed agriculture land. They will walk to the Western World and kill everybody by hand

1.3.5. Macroeconomic Parameters of Mega-Cities

The macroeconomic parameters of Mega-Cities including outskirts:

- Today 50% of the earth population live in Cities; 75% by 2050
- 100 Mega Cities with a population of 3,000,000 – 33,000,000 citizens (today) [55] [56]
- Mega Cities will need an increase of production: 50% more by 2050
- 50% more supply and recycling transport; and 50% more cars for private use

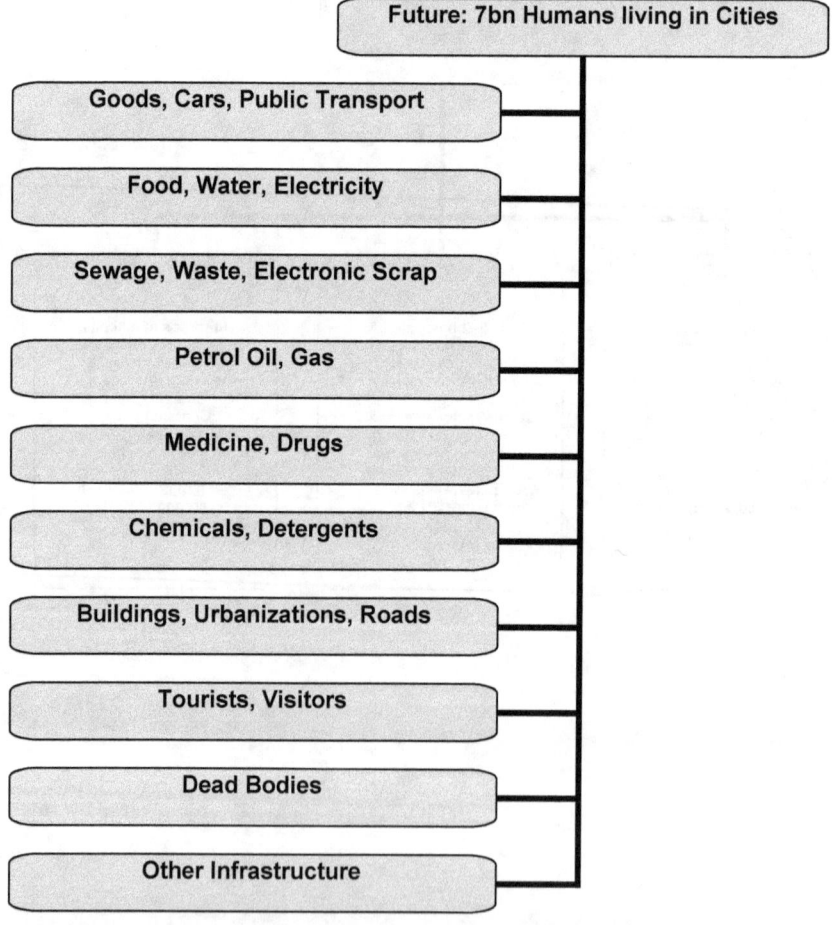

[55] http://www.worldatlas.com/citypops.htm
[56] http://www.citymayors.com/statistics/largest-cities-population-125.html

1.3.6. Mental Sustainability of Mega Cities

Cities produce immense mental, psychical, behavioral, social, psychosomatic, somatic, and existential suffering and fatalities.

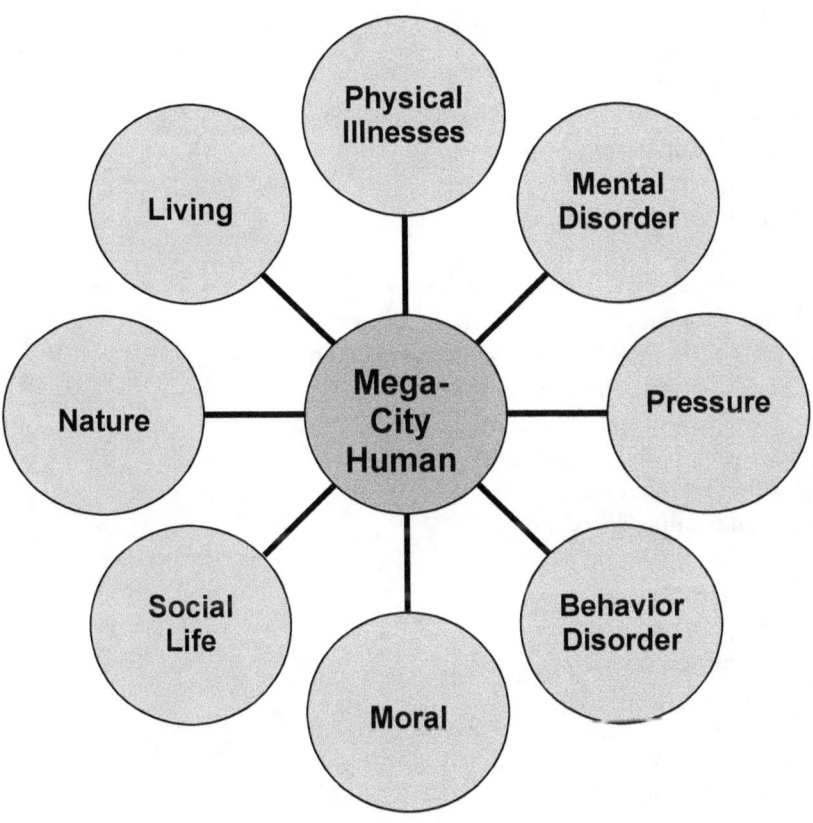

1.3.7. Global Future of Needs and Wants

There are and there will be in 2030-2050 many more needs and wants:

Of highest economic importance is the fact: Estimated every 13-15 (or: 12-13) years one billion more people – in total 3 billion more people in 40-45 years will have needs and wants:

- A home
- A job, work
- Money for living
- Education, professional and higher education
- Public Health Care
- Medicaments
- Sanitation
- Food and beverage
- Healthy water
- Water for agriculture
- Fertile agriculture land, free of contamination
- Energy (electricity, gas, oil, petrol)
- A variety of natural resources
- Sewage and rubbish recycling
- Clothes and shoes
- All kinds of products and goods
- Furniture
- Hardware
- Detergents and toilet articles
- Cars and scooters
- Condoms
- Televisions
- Stationary articles
- Mobile phones
- Computer and internet connection
- Leisure areas
- Touristy opportunities
- Fun and entertainment
- And much more …

➔ The consequences for the global economy will be monstrous.
➔ The growth of production for needs and wants must be equal to the population growth.

1.3.8. Management of Macroeconomic Parameters

Political management of highest economic importance is:

Every 13-15 years one billion more people – in total 3 billion more people in 40-45 years will need efficient political management and state administration which includes macroeconomic decisions and management:

- The production processes
- The allocation of goods and services
- Citizen registration and control
- Tax registration and management
- Public traffic systems (people and goods traffic)
- Registrations of cars and vehicles
- Court and police institutions
- Road construction and maintenance
- Sanitation and rubbish disposal
- Disposal of corpses
- Contamination regulations
- Nuclear waste maintenance
- Electricity delivery and maintenance
- Water system maintenance
- Pension system
- Education and research
- Culture promotion
- Public health care
- Energy resources management
- Media systems
- Food quality control
- Delivery of construction licenses
- Management of catastrophes
- Military force and secret service
- Economical and industrial systems
- Businesses and service sector
- And much more …

Conclusions:

→ The qualifications most politicians and economists have today will not enable them in the future to do their job in a constructive way. They do not have the complex knowledge, the demanding skills, the strength of personality and the moral attitudes. This will logically lead to rigid policy and from there to police states and fascist governments that will govern the world.

→ All significant parameters producing waste, sewage, contamination, pollution, climate change, crimes, unrest, and many more critical externalities will increase and therefore become uncontrollable.

→ The increasing scarcity of raw materials and natural resources (drinking water, agriculture land) together with a strong increase of prices will provoke unrest and wars.

1.3.9. Human Factors of World Population Growth

a) Education:

- No information or consequences on sexuality, ovulation and menstruation
- No information or consequences on contraceptives and their importance related to AIDS
- No information or consequences of having a baby
- No information on the importance of making love to strengthen a relationship
- No information on the importance of regularly having sex with love and care
- No information on the manifold psychical and physical functions of making love

b) Cultural standards:

- Big family gives importance
- Big family shows wealth
- Children guarantee looking after parents when old
- Social pressure: one must have children (a family)
- Culture, tradition: (nearly) everybody has children (a child)
- Not having children is suspicious, not normal, strange

c) Religion:

- Order to increase community (Church)
- Contraceptives not allowed
- Suppressing sexual drive
- To enjoy sex is not allowed
- To direct the libido into belief makes sex drive uncontrollable

d) Attitudes:

- A women is only a woman as a mother
- A man must have children to be a real man
- Having children gives the core meaning of life
- General rejection of responsibility for oneself and one's life
- Not having children is egoistic
- Having a baby is the sole importance of life
- Going to a shop buying condoms is embarrassing
- The whole meaning of life is to reproduce

e) Economy (Poverty):

- Making love is the only pleasure in life
- Lack of general education for mastering life
- Lack of professional education and satisfaction
- Lack of organized social networks
- Condoms cost money (3 billion people need every cent for food)
- The people do not consider the economic implications

f) Personal disposition:

- Making a family to compensate for the lack of love in one's own family
- Making a home that has not existed in one's own childhood
- Making a baby to become important and to get attention
- No ability to think about the future consequences (life and work in general)
- General boredom in life and inner emptiness
- Lack of regularly satisfying love and care in general
- Not thinking about the economic consequences of creating a baby
- Suppressing sexuality increases the inability to control sexual drive
- General inability of controlling sexual drive
- Ignorance about the humane consequences of creating a baby
- Fear from being lonely in the future
- Out of control by sexual encounter due to excitement
- Not seeing the knowledge and skills that are necessary to educate a baby
- Unhappiness and the illusion a baby will bring happiness and fulfillment
- Weakness of women towards men that just want sex or a baby
- Not respecting the 'qualities' that are necessary to make a family life work
- Extremely unconscious living with bad self-management in general
- Unconsciously wanting to give care to the own inner child (projection)
- Lack of higher aims in life for personal fulfillment
- Inability to create an emotional and fulfilling home and life with the partner

- Running away from oneself and the partner
- Disinterest in giving high importance for personal psychical-spiritual development
- Not considering the economical development (stability of work)
- A feeling of embarrassment dealing with condoms
- In general stupidity, infantilism, neuroticism, bad character, inner emptiness

→ These human factors imply money matters and macroeconomic challenges of unseen dimension.

"People respond to incentives. Bearing a child, like any decision, has an opportunity cost. When the opportunity cost rises, people will choose to have smaller families. In particular, women with the opportunity to receive good education and desirable employment tend to want fewer children than those with fewer opportunities outside the home. Hence, policies that foster equal treatment of women are one way for less developed economies to reduce the rate of population growth and, perhaps, raise their standards of living." [57]

→ There are many measures to take in order to stop and in the long term to reduce the world population.
→ As a whole the problem of an increasing world population has indeed to do with economic matters, but also with education, religion, social norms, etc.

---

[57] Mankiw (et al.), p. 544

1.4. Businesses and Corporations

"Anytime a household decides to produce something, it becomes a business. Business is simply the name given to private producing units in our society ... Business in the United States decide what to produce, how much to produce, and for whom to produce it. They make these central economic decisions on the basis of their own self-interest, which is influenced by market incentives. Anyone who wants to can start a business, provided he or she can come up with the required cash and meet the necessary regulatory requirements. Although corporations account for about 90 percent of all sales, in terms of numbers of businesses, most are one- or two-person operations." [58]

The term 'household' is abused in this statement: If the members or a member of a household want to produce something, then there are basically two options: the person start working as self-employed or creates a firm. In this case we have split the household in a 'living entity' and a 'working entity'; we can declare both unities in a certain way as 'household'. If a household is an institution with specific tasks, then the operations are considered as 'working' (e.g. for production or a service). In both cases we can say it's about doing business. An institution can be corporate or private (ownership), but always it's considered as a 'working entity' and not a 'living entity'. Both are 'doing business'.

The statement 'Business is simply the name given to private producing units' is misleading because also small and big public corporations do business. The part 'of all sales' could be interpreted as 90% of the amount of sales (of goods and services). So consequently it suggests that 'one- or two-person operations' account for 10% of all sales.

1.4.1. The Different Forms of Businesses

"The three primary forms of business are sole proprietorships, partnerships, and corporations. Of the 29 million businesses in the United States, approximately 71 percent are sole proprietorships, 10 percent are partnerships, and 19 percent are corporations ... Sole Proprietorships – businesses that have only one owner – are the easiest to start and have the fewest bureaucratic hassles. Partnerships – businesses with two or more

---

[58] Colander, p. 61

owners – create possibilities for sharing the burden but they also create unlimited liability for each of the partners. Corporations – businesses that are treated as a person, and are legally owned by their stockholders, who are not liable for the actions of the corporate "person" – are the largest form of business when measured in terms of receipts. In corporations, ownership is separated from control of the firm." [59]

Here we have a much clearer picture: 71 percent are sole proprietorships, 10 percent are partnerships, and 19 percent are corporations. We put these figure in the context of the above statement: 'corporations account for about 90 percent of all sales'. From here we come to a new picture:

From the entire businesses 19% are corporations and account for about 90% of all sales. And 81% are small and medium sized businesses that account for about 10% of all sales. This would mean that the 19% of corporations dominate and control practically the entire market. As corporations in general dispose of immense amounts of money, they absorb most of the cash flow and investment market. In contra, the 81% of entities doing business have practically irrelevant financial power and investments at their disposal.

→ The big corporations dictate the market and with that societies and the governments.
→ Most of the business cash flow and investments are in the channel (hand) of corporations.
→ We consider this as a destructive imbalance and the end of democracy and the 'free market'.

Corporations operate globally:

"… Most large corporations today are not U.S., German, or Japanese corporations; they are global corporations (corporations with substantial operations on both the production and sales sides in more than one country … Global corporations offer enormous benefits for countries. They create jobs; they bring new ideas and new technologies to a country; and they provide competition for domestic companies, keeping them on their toes. But global corporations also pose a number of problems for governments. One is their implication for domestic and international policy. A domestic corporation exists within a country and can be dealt with using policy measures within that country. A global corporation exists within many countries and there is no global government to regulate or control it. If it doesn't like the policies in one country – say taxes are too high or regulations

---

[59] Colander, p. 62-63

too tight – it can shift its operations to other countries." [60]

The misleading strategy ('it's correct, but also wrong') is already a prevalent pest in these books about economics, also here with the part of a statement: 'Most large corporations today are not U.S., German, or Japanese corporations; they are global corporations'. The verbs 'are' can refer to the nation from where they operate and also to the areas they operate. But this is not the same. The construction of this sentence wants to avoid saying that they ARE U.S., German, or Japanese corporations (as a legal entity with a business location). Entering into this matter, the picture becomes more diverse: The location of the business can be anywhere, even on an island with a few dwellers. The CEOs and board of directors can be from other nations and locations. And the owner can also be from another nation. And these corporations operate (manage, produce and sell) in many other countries. The main owner can be another corporation. The presentation hides these facts, especially the nationality and living location of the owner (the main owners).

Another part of the statement: 'Global corporations offer enormous benefits for countries'. We could turn around this glorification and also say: they produce enormous damages for countries (as we will explore in chapter 3). Certainly, they create jobs (mostly in developing countries, but they destroy the small firms in the home country and they produce immense poverty as they outrageously exploit manpower in foreign countries.

At least the author admits: 'there is no global government to regulate or control it'. And we extend: corporations have a top-team that finds out everything that allows them to reduced costs and ignore collateral damages. Do these corporations really bring new ideas and new technologies to a country? What is the value of this 'benefit' if 4 billion people can never have access to these technologies and ideas as they have no money and no appropriate education? They also use all possibilities to avoid paying (high) taxes. It is well known, even widely reported in the media, that corporations operate with bribery and corruption or special 'benefits' in order to do what they want (for maximizing profit). In a certain way a corporation herewith becomes 'untouchable' for governments (especially in developing countries).

→ The complexity of the operating and sale locations, the owner's legal structure and location makes the power of corporations in the most important parameters invisible for the people.
→ The global operations allows the corporations to minimize the costs, including the taxes, and this also by abusing 'weaknesses' of the legal

---

[60] Colander, p. 73

structures in these countries, e.g. concerning labor and environment.

→ Global corporations have destroyed and continue destroying hundreds of millions of small firms and their financial power in their homeland and also in developing countries.

1.4.2. Failures of Market Outcomes

"Market failures are situations in which the market does not lead to a desired result. In the real world, market failures are pervasive – the market is always failing in one way or another." [61]

→ Who says what the desired result is? No profit is a failure. Highest possible profit is success.

"A failure of market outcome occurs when, even though the market is functioning properly (there are no market failures), it is not achieving society's goals. Three separate types of failures of market outcomes will be considered:

1. Failures due to distributional issues: Whose surplus is the market maximizing?
2. Failures due to rationality problems of individuals: What if individuals don't know what is best for themselves?
3. Failures due to violations of inalienable or at least partially inalienable rights of individuals: What if individuals don't know what is best for themselves?
4. Failures due to violations of inalienable or at least partially inalienable rights of individuals: Are there certain rights that should not be for sale?"[62]

Oh, do they really fail in distribution matters? They do everything that is possible to exploit everywhere where they can find a market gap. The second point is not a failure of the corporations. To the contrary, they know perfectly about the 'irrational problems' of individuals (consumers). Fact is: most people really don't know what is best for them. And the corporations abuse these mental weaknesses. Above that, as 80% of all people on earth earn less than $10 per working day, they don't have money for most of the goods and services corporations offer. The 'violations of inalienable or at least partially inalienable rights' are a matter of crimes and of the financial power and

---

[61] Colander, p. 71

[62] Colander, p.532

operational network the actors have. There are 'rights that should not be for sale' and there are gaps in the legal frame that allows clever actors to exploit. This is first a governmental matter and then a matter of morality for the corporations; but corporations operate without an ethical framework even if they claim to do so.

→ The 'failures of market outcomes' is here very narrowly presented and replaces the real facts.
→ Failure due to rationality problems of individuals is already trivialized in the 'theories' of microeconomics.
→ The fact that 80% of the world population earns less than $10 per working day is ignored.
→ Global poverty as a market result is ignored despite of the manifold obvious interrelations.

"By definition, inalienable rights cannot be sold or given away. There can be no weighing of costs and benefits. For example, the right to freedom is an inalienable right, so slavery is wrong, and any trade creating slavery should not be allowed, regardless of any issues of consumer and producer surplus." [63]

The author's arrogance and impertinence is unlimited: 'Slavery is wrong'. Fact is: the wages the corporations pay to the workers in developing countries, sometimes even in industrialized countries is a blatant scandal. Outrageous is also the way they push down the prices they offer to manufacturers and farmers in developing countries. The dynamic of competition has already long ago broken the moral border and led to the fact that firms in developing countries must sell at prices offered (dictated) from the big corporations or traders (brokers); traders that operate in the interest of the big corporations or investors (via banks). Modern slavery is practiced everywhere from these corporations, obviously not in the form of iron chains on the feet! Consumer and producer surplus are basic 'law' in corporation's policy.

"Moral prohibitions that are related to inalienable rights include those against prostitution, selling body parts, and selling babies ... Moral judgment must be made about where markets should exist, and someone might decide that the market should be allowed everywhere (that is the libertarian view), but such moral judgments can override consumer surplus arguments about markets achieving efficiency." [64]

Shocking picture: 'selling body parts, and selling babies'. Never would a

---

[63] Colander, p. 535-536
[64] Colander, p.537

corporation do such business. At first glance this sounds ethically wonderful. But it is a hidden declaration of innocence for the corporations. It is also a divertive statement which leads to the implicit meaning: "We, the corporations, would never do such inhumane business!" But 'inhumane' is the supreme attribute in the world of globally operating corporations. The falseness and perverse abuse of scientific statements is here unspeakable. What is the best way that the devil on earth can hide his true face? He puts on the divine robe, and takes the moral high ground.

The final part of this statement reveals another belittlement and trivialization: 'Moral judgment must be made about where markets should exist, and someone might decide that the market should be allowed everywhere'. What could be a moral criteria or judgment about where corporations are allowed or not allowed to operate? The question here is about location and not about the way of doing business. This trivializes the fundamental problem about the sale of body parts and babies; and it deviates into matters of low moral importance. The part of the statement 'the market should be allowed everywhere' is a normative statement and probably most people would agree. The real moral criteria about if and where and how corporations should be allowed to operate are to determine within the 'negative externalities' as described in the following chapters.

The strategy is: lead the people on a main stream of positive collective agreements in order to avoid being caught in the line of fire which means the real (moral) scandalous problems of the big corporations. (I have not counted the amount of such strategic statements in the study books of economics, but there are more than a thousand. It's an absolutely perverse manipulation of the readers and students.)

➜ The 'failure of market outcomes' is very narrowly presented and distorts the picture of responsibilities
➜ Moral (ethical) failure is presented in such a trivial way that makes the corporations quasi innocent in their way of doing business.
➜ The presentation strategy leads the people on a main stream of positive collective agreements by deviating into matters of low moral importance.
➜ The dynamic of competition has already long ago broken the moral border and creates immense negative externalities and amoral attitudes towards labor and environment.

"Productivity rises when the health, training, education, and motivation of workers improve; when workers have more and better machinery and natural resources with which to work; when production is better organized and managed; and when labor is reallocated from less-efficient industries to more-efficient industries." [65]

➔ If we estimate that 65-80% of the production is outsourced to Asia and other developing areas, then the statement becomes deceiving and misleading.

➔ Health, training, education, and motivation are in a majority of production entities in Asia and other developing countries irrelevant for the corporation's management.

➔ 'More-efficient industries' has a meaning into two directions: a) producing more with the best possible machinery; and b) producing at minimal costs in order to get the highest possible profit.

➔ The 'outcome' seen in global perspective is disastrous.

1.4.3. Businesses and Limited Liability

"A corporation provides the owners with limited liability – the stockholder's liability is limited to the amount the stockholder has invested in the company … With the other forms of business, owners can lose everything they possess even if they have only a small amount invested in the company, but in a corporation the owners can lose only what they have invested in that corporation." [66]

There is a corporation and there are the owners. The owners are the stockholders who bought a small, high, or very high amount of shares. The only liability these 'owners' have is their money: they can lose part of it or all of if the corporation fails partly or totally. Stockholders have no legal or moral liability concerning the way of doing business of the corporation. In contra, the owner of the other forms of business, loses in the worst case everything and remains liable for outstanding bills.

Stockholders can get a dividend (a slice of the profit cake) or nothing, both related to the value of shares; or at least the increase in value of the paper they have, but also a decrease can occur; everything depends on the success of the corporation and the way they operate (e.g. they invest part of the profit in renewal of equipment or for expansion), read: profit.

A first focus is: the owners. There are shareholders with low share value and one or more shareholders with higher value. Who has the say?

---

[65] McConnell (et al.), p. 158
[66] Colander, p. 63

A second focus is the liability: It is scandalous that shareholders have no liability within the frame of the corporation's operations. And it is even outrageous that all other forms of businesses are fully liable for failure. Sometimes corporations have to pay a fine for misuse. But a fine of a hundred million dollars or even a billion dollars is a mere bagatelle for a corporation, already previously calculated into the price of the goods they sell. The 'mechanism' is obvious: if shareholders would be liable, they would not invest money in a corporation, we would not have these global monsters, and the other forms of firms would be very dominant in the market of a society, operating a much more level playing field.

A third focus is the money concentration: If liability were given it would not allow any 'entity' to concentrate hundreds of billions and even trillions the way the corporations and behind them the big investors can and do. The liability-freedom is the tool to concentrate the money flow and the investments in order to dominate entire societies and even governments. The destructive effect essentially strikes all the businesses: the amount of small firms has decreased a lot and will continue to decrease more in the future. The worst of it however, is that the governments have lost their power in favor of the money masters so cannot do anything about it. Another consequence is that the politicians (governments) always have to take the hot potatoes in their hand because nobody is liable for the collateral damages (negative externalities) caused by corporations or by the anonymous money masters. Looking at the whole picture of today: Democracy is either dying or has already gone down the drain.

Recall: Conspiracy is the term that refers to groups of people operating in a hidden criminal way. And an analysis or interpretation of facts or signs of facts are a scientific matter on a level of hypotheses or theses. Social science always must start with descriptions and hypotheses. In criminology one of the most important focuses is the motive of actors. Existing motives and effectual indications (signs) or evidence is understood as legitimate proof, but sometimes still not enough for an indictment.

→ The value of shares is not guaranteed with land, buildings, machines, infrastructure, and raw material deposit. Therefore the entire shareholder business principle is insecure and unstable.
→ The shareholder principle is built up on greed for profit without having worked for it and without any liability. The profit principle is not sustainable and provokes negative externalities.
→ The injustice that all the owners of most other forms of business are fully liable (as a private person) and therefore exposed to serious risks (often life long) is ignored.

1.4.4. The Media have no Liability

"You know very well, and the stupid Americans know equally well, that we control their government, irrespective of who sits in the White House. You see, I know it and you know it that no American president can be in a position to challenge us even if we do the unthinkable.

What can they (Americans) do to us? We control congress, we control the media, we control show biz, and we control everything in America. In America you can criticize God, but you can't criticize Israel…" Israeli spokeswoman, Tzipora Menache [67]

"The largest media conglomerate today is Walt Disney Company, whose chairman and CEO, Michael Eisner, is a Jew. The Disney Empire, headed by a man described by one media analyst as a "control freak", includes several television production companies (Walt Disney Television, Touchstone Television, Buena Vista Television), its own cable network with 14 million subscribers, and two video production companies. As for feature films, the Walt Disney Picture Group, headed by Joe Roth (also a Jew), includes Touchstone Pictures, Hollywood Pictures, and Caravan Pictures. Disney also owns Miramax Films, run by the Weinstein brothers. When the Disney Company was run by the Gentile Disney family prior to its takeover by Eisner in 1984, it epitomized wholesome, family entertainment. While it still holds the rights to Snow White, under Eisner, the company has expanded into the production of graphic sex and violence. In addition, it has 225 affiliated stations in the United States and is part owner of several European TV companies. ABC's cable subsidiary, ESPN, is headed by president and CEO Steven Bornstein, a Jew.

This corporation also has a controlling share of Lifetime Television and the Arts & Entertainment Network cable companies. ABC Radio Network owns eleven AM and ten FM stations, again in major cities such as New York, Washington, Los Angeles, and has over 3,400 affiliates. Although primarily a telecommunications company, Capital Cities/ABC earned over $1 billion in publishing in 1994. It owns seven daily newspapers, Fairchild Publications, Chilton Publications, and the Diversified Publishing Group. Time Warner, Inc, is the second of the international media leviathans.

The chairman of the board and CEO, Gerald Levin, is a Jew. Time Warner's subsidiary HBO is the country's largest pay-TV cable network. Warner Music

---

[67] http://www.heunjustmedia.com

71

is by far the world's largest record company, with 50 labels, the biggest of which is Warner Brothers Records, headed by Danny Goldberg. Stuart Hersch is president of Warnervision, Warner Music's video production unit. Goldberg and Hersch are Jews. Warner Music was an early promoter of "gangsta rap." Through its involvement with Interscope Records, it helped popularize a genre whose graphic lyrics explicitly urge Blacks to commit acts of violence against Whites. In addition to cable and music, Time Warner is heavily involved in the production of feature films (Warner Brothers Studio) and publishing. Time Warner's publishing division (editor-in-chief Norman Pearlstine, a Jew) is the largest magazine publisher in the country (Time, Sports Illustrated, People, Fortune).

When Ted Turner, a Gentile, made a bid to buy CBS in 1985, there was panic in media boardrooms across the nation. Turner made a fortune in advertising and then had built a successful cable-TV news network, CNN. Although Turner employed a number of Jews in key executive positions in CNN and had never taken public positions contrary to Jewish interests, he is a man with a large ego and a strong personality and was regarded by Chairman William Paley (real name Palinsky, a Jew) and the other Jews at CBS as uncontrollable: a loose cannon who might at some time in the future turn against them. Furthermore, Jewish newsman Daniel Schorr, who had worked for Turner, publicly charged that his former boss held a personal dislike for Jews.

To block Turner's bid, CBS executives invited billionaire Jewish theater, hotel, insurance, and cigarette magnate Laurence Tisch to launch a "friendly" takeover of the company, and from 1986 till 1995 Tisch was the chairman and CEO of CBS, removing any threat of non-Jewish influence there. Subsequent efforts by Turner to acquire a major network have been obstructed by Levin's Time Warner, which owns nearly 20 percent of CBS stock and has veto power over major deals. Viacom, Inc, headed by Sumner Redstone (born Murray Rothstein), a Jew, is the third largest megamedia corporation in the country, with revenues of over $10 billion a year. Viacom, which produces and distributes TV programs for the three largest networks, owns 12 television stations and 12 radio stations. It produces feature films through Paramount Pictures, headed by Jewess Sherry Lansing. Its publishing division includes Prentice Hall, Simon & Schuster, and Pocket Books.

It distributes videos through over 4,000 Blockbuster stores. Viacom's chief claim to fame, however, is as the world's largest provider of cable programming, through its Showtime, MTV, Nickelodeon, and other networks. Since 1989, MTV and Nickelodeon have acquired larger and larger shares of the younger television audience. With the top three, and by far the largest, media companies in the hand of Jews, it is difficult to believe that such an overwhelming degree of control came about without a deliberate, concerted effort on their part. What about the other big media companies? Number four on the list is Rupert Murdoch's News Corporation, which owns Fox Television and 20th Century Fox Films. Murdoch is a Gentile, but Peter Chermin, who heads Murdoch's film studio and also oversees his TV production, is a Jew. Number five is the Japanese Sony Corporation, whose U.S. subsidiary, Sony Corporation of America, is run by Michael Schulhof, a Jew. Alan Levine, another Jew, heads the Sony Pictures division. Most of the television and movie production companies that are not owned by the largest corporations are also controlled by Jews. For example, New World Entertainment, proclaimed by one media analyst as "the premiere independent TV program producer in the United States," is owned by Ronald Perelman, a Jew. The best known of the smaller media companies, Dreamworks SKG, is a strictly kosher affair.

Dream Works was formed in 1994 amid great media hype by recording industry mogul David Geffen, former Disney Pictures chairman Jeffrey Katzenberg, and film director Steven Spielberg, all three of whom are Jews. The company produces movies, animated films, television programs, and recorded music. Two other large production companies, MCA and Universal Pictures, are both owned by Seagram Company, Ltd. The president and CEO of Seagram, the liquor giant, is Edgar Bronfman Jr., who is also president of the World Jewish Congress. It is well known that Jews have controlled the production and distribution of films since the inception of the movie industry in the early decades of the 20th century.

This is still the case today. Films produced by just the five largest motion picture companies mentioned above-Disney, Warner Brothers, Sony, Paramount (Viacom), and Universal (Seagram)-accounted for 74 per cent of the total box-office receipts for the first eight months of 1995. The big three in television network broadcasting used to be ABC, CBS, and NBC. With the consolidation of the media empires, these three are no longer independent entities. While they were independent, however, each was controlled by a Jew since its inception: ABC by Leonard Goldenson, CBS first by William Paley and then by Lawrence Tisch, and NBC first by David Sarnoff and then by his son Robert. Over periods of several decades, these networks were staffed from top to bottom with Jews, and the essential Jewishness of network television did not change when the networks were absorbed by other corporations. The Jewish presence in television news remains particularly strong. As noted, ABC is part of Eisner's Disney Company, and the executive producers of ABC's news programs are all Jews: Victor Neufeld (20-20), Bob Reichbloom (Good Morning America), and Rick Kaplan (World News Tonight). CBS was recently purchased by Westinghouse Electric Corporation.

Nevertheless, the man appointed by Lawrence Tisch, Eric Ober, remains president of CBS News, and Ober is a Jew. At NBC, now owned by General Electric, NBC News president Andrew Lack is a Jew, as are executive producers Jeff Zucker (Today), Jeff Gralnick (NBC Nightly News), and Neal Shapiro (Dateline)."

The author concludes:

"By permitting the Jews to control our news and entertainment media, we are doing more than merely giving them a decisive influence on our political system and virtual control of our government; we also are giving them control of the minds and souls of our children, whose attitudes and ideas are shaped more by Jewish television and Jewish films than by their parents, their schools, or any other influence."

→ There is not much 'market freedom'; people are highly shaped by the Media.
→ The Media are an immense powerful parameter of macroeconomics.
→ The situation is not much different in the media world of the European Union.
→ It is a strategy of economics to forge opinions and consumer behavior through the Media.

1.4.5. Informational Problems

"The perfectly competitive model assumes that individuals have perfect information about what they are buying. So, if they voluntarily buy a good, it is a reasonable presumption that they expect that they are making themselves better off by doing so. But what if the buyer doesn't have perfect information? ... Real-world markets often involve deception, cheating, and inaccurate information. When there is a lack of information, or when buyers and sellers don't have equal information, markets in some goods may not work well ... If sellers are profit maximizers, they will reveal as little as possible about the cars' defects; they will reveal as much as they can about the cars' good qualities ... Such a market failure is called an adverse selection problem – a problem that occurs when buyers and sellers have different amounts of information about the good for sale." [68]

→ Nobody needs a 'perfect competitive model' and it doesn't exist anyway.
→ An economic bigotry: 'Individuals have perfect information about what

---

[68] Colander, p. 495

they are buying.'

→ In most cases a consumer never has 'perfect information'.
→ Real-world markets mostly involve deception, cheating, and inaccurate information.
→ Buyers and sellers practically never have equal information.
→ In most cases there is a lack of information.
→ Sellers reveal as little as possible about the cars' defects: the author doesn't value this.
→ Really true: buyers and sellers have different amounts of information.

"Economists who lean away from government regulation suggest that the problem presented by the information examples above is not really a problem of market failure but instead a problem of the lack of a market. Information is valuable and is an economic product in its own right. Left on their own, markets will develop to provide the information that people need and are willing to pay for. (For example, a large number of consumer magazines provide such information.)

If the government regulates information, these markets may not develop; people might rely on government instead of markets. Thus, the informational problem is not a problem of the market; it is a problem of government regulation." [69]

→ Trivialization of the lack of information: It is 'a problem of the lack of a market'.
→ Information is valuable: Tell this to the politicians, the banks, and the capitalistic economists.
→ Markets will develop to provide the information that people need: this will never happen.
→ Consumers shall pay to get the valuable information; and public institutes must search for it.
→ Informational problem is not a problem of the market: right; it is a problem of the leaders.
→ Informational problem is a problem of government regulation: they want no regulation!

---

[69] Colander, p. 496-497

Everyday Influences: Information and Money Matters

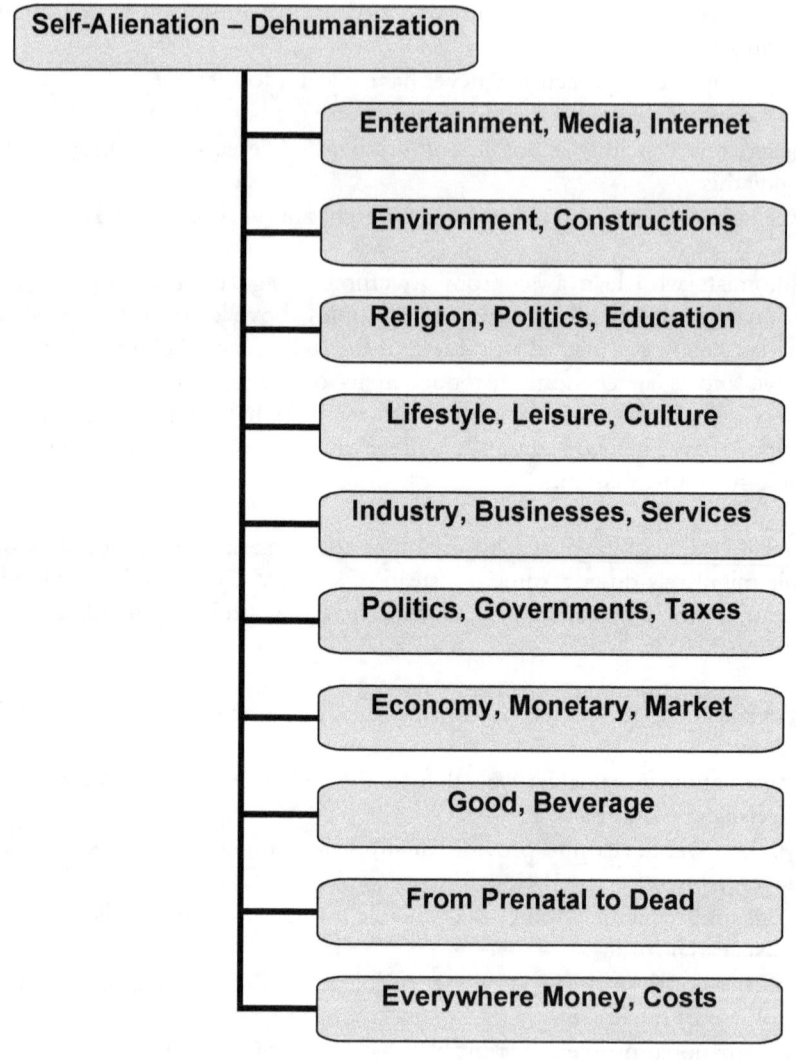

Self-Alienation – Dehumanization

Entertainment, Media, Internet

Environment, Constructions

Religion, Politics, Education

Lifestyle, Leisure, Culture

Industry, Businesses, Services

Politics, Governments, Taxes

Economy, Monetary, Market

Good, Beverage

From Prenatal to Dead

Everywhere Money, Costs

Everywhere: Contamination · Fine Dust · Nano-particles · Drugs · Contaminated Food · Contaminated Products · Consumption Values · Lies · Cheat · Fabrications · Norms · Attitudes · Regulations · Prescription · Accreditation · Control

→ Billions of engineered nano-particles in foods, pharmaceuticals, and air are ingested by humans daily.
→ Millions of engineered poisonous information in media and communication are ingested by humans yearly.
→ Economics tremendously simplifies the importance of informational, environmental and financial influences in the life of a human.

1.4.6. Behavioral Economics

We want to explore shortly what this 'behavioral economics' does. It is about 'behavior' of people, consumers and human beings, and not about animals.

"Economic engineers don't just try to understand the way the economy works as economic scientists do. Economic engineers ask: Can they design mechanisms to better coordinate people's actions?" [70]

→ Economic engineers want to design mechanisms to better coordinate people's actions.
→ Economic engineers search for 'mechanisms' that direct and control human's behavior.

"As modern economists have moved more toward engineering, they have begun to explore a broad range of mechanisms and institutions that solve coordination problems. These mechanisms and institutions are called coordination mechanisms – methods of coordinating people's wants with other people's desires." [71]

→ There is a broad range of mechanisms and institutions that solve coordination problems.
→ 'Coordination' means: bringing people in the same main stream of opinion and behavior.
→ The aim of behavior engineering is that all people have the same desires (needs and wants).

"The supply/demand model assumes that firms maximize profits. But real-world firms' decisions are made by individuals whose incentives may differ from the firm's incentives. When a decision maker's income is not the same as the firm's profit, as is generally the case, the firm's and the decision maker's incentives may be incompatible, and the individual is more likely to make

---

[70] Colander, p. 506-507
[71] Colander, p. 507

decisions that don't maximize profits." [72]

➔ Individuals are more likely to make decisions that don't maximize profits.
➔ The economic engineers must shape people for the firm's interest of maximum profit.

"An incentive compatibility problem is a problem in which the incentive facing the decision maker does not match the incentive needed for the mechanism to achieve its desired end." [73]

➔ Designing mechanisms in order to manipulate people must operate with incentives.

"Modern economists use their insights about incentive compatibility problems to design mechanism that align incentives with desired ends. This has led to the development of a new branch of economics, called mechanism design, which is explicitly interested in designing mechanism to achieve specific ends. Mechanism design involves identifying a goal and then designing a mechanism such as a market, social system or contract to achieve that end." [74]

➔ 'Design mechanisms that align incentives with desired ends' means: creating robots.
➔ Mechanism design involves identifying a goal: all people have the same opinions and desires.

"So mechanism design economists began to take into account people's predictable irrationalities when designing coordination mechanism. In order to do that, they had to better understand how people's behavior deviated from the model's predicted behavior, which led to the emergence of behavioral economics … Behavioral economists argue that because people are social creatures, the coordinating mechanism that economists design must take into account much more than simple price incentives; it must also include social and moral incentives and the economist's models must include these additional elements as shadow prices." [75]

➔ Mechanism design economists take into account people's predictable irrationalities.

---

[72] Colander, p. 508
[73] Colander, p. 508
[74] Colander, p. 508
[75] Colander, p. 510

→ First step: understand how people's behavior deviates from the model's predicted behavior.

→ As people are social creatures – read: sheep – incentives are not enough to achieve the aim.

→ The mechanisms lie in the social and moral incentives: bring in line moral attitudes!

"One of the findings of behavioral economics is that choice architecture – the context in which decisions are presented – impacts people's decisions … Behavioral economists argue that modifying precepts after the fact to take predictable irrationality into account isn't enough. They argue that people are predictably irrational in so many areas that economists' models and policy recommendations have to include those predictable irrationalities in both models and policies. Behavioral economic policy - a policy designed to influence people's choice architecture in a way that directs people to make decisions that make them better off under the assumption that they are predictably irrational – does just that." [76]

→ Predictable irrationalities of people must be considered in the design of mechanisms.

→ Psychoanalysis: Irrationality is linked with the content of the unconscious mind, with emotions and self-identity.

"As you can see, adopting the behavioral economic framework opens up many ways in which government can usefully intervene in the market … Traditional economists say desires are inherent in each person. Behavioral economists say that desires are affected by context … Traditional economist say that having more is not what makes people happier. Some behavioral economists suggest that having more is not what makes people happy. Often what makes them happy is having more than other people." [77]

→ Governments can also strongly benefit from a positive result of the designed mechanisms.

→ Desires are inherent in each person and affected by context: this is the focus of the designers.

→ What makes people happy is having more than other individuals: Those who have more get a higher status and a higher esteem in the social context.

→ If most people want more than other people have, then it all turns into an endless spiral of consumption, a permanent competition between people

---

[76] Colander, p. 511
[77] Colander, p. 517

about who has more! Insane!

"Behavioral economics tells us that people are not good at making decisions when issues are complicated. Economic policy involves very complicated decisions, and the general population and policy makers need a nudge to get them to make good decisions." [78]

→ People are not good at making decisions when issues are complicated: = people are stupid!
→ People need to be pushed, forced, lured, seduced, manipulated, brainwashed, deceived ...

Brain Research from Economists: [79]

"Microsoft co-founder Paul Allen is donating $300 million of his $14 billion fortune in his eponymous Allen Institute for Brain Science to fund new projects to map and observe the human brain ...

(A project of) Harvard Medical School ... the study of connections in the brain ... ways of monitoring what happens in the brain ...

... to program a computer in a matter of years, a computer can't learn to function like a human brain even given a lifetime of opportunity. 'You can't create an artificial intelligence', Allen said, 'unless you know how the real thing works.' ...

They advised me to develop an accurate and comprehensive map of the brain detailing the expression of every single gene. This would be key to solving basic questions about human behavior, brain disorders and diseases ...

To understand this complex organ, we're starting with individual cells, to better understand how they develop, integrate information, and make decisions. ... we are studying how information is input, transformed, and processed ...

Our dream is to one day uncover the essence of what makes us human."

→ They want to know how they can monitor the brain of humans.
→ The have the idea they can create an artificial intelligence in the brain of people.

---

[78] Colander, p. 520
[79] http://www.forbes.com/sites/matthewherper/2012/03/21/billionaire-paul-g-allen-donates-300-million-in-brain-research-to-understand-what-makes-us-human/

→ They say it's about understanding of brain disorders and diseases for therapy.
→ An accurate and comprehensive map of the brain allows one to control the map.
→ They want to answer the basic questions about human behavior in order to control.
→ Aim is to control the brain's development, the way to put information in the brain.
→ If they know how the brain makes decisions, they can direct the decision mechanism.
→ They are 100% ignorant about human's inner life, soul and the Archetypes of evolution.
→ They have absolutely no idea about what a human is; these people are veil monsters!
→ These insane super rich people really think they will find human's mystery. Pure Madness!
→ They want to play God and to control the entire humanity via collective brain steering.
→ The key problem of behavioral economics is to control the irrational decisions (see: 2.12.).

Cynical answer: As 95% of humanity never wants the truth, they shall have these servants of Satan!

1.5. Government Regulations

1.5.1. Public Goods

"A public good is a good that is nonexclusive (no one can be excluded from its benefits) and non-rival (consumption by one does not preclude consumption by others)." [80]

"We all expect the government to provide us with certain services, such as roads, parks, police and national defense. These public services require tax revenue." [81]

→ Why does the author mention here 'national defense'? Why is this 'public good'? It does not make sense here as the public can't simply benefit in their leisure or holidays or everyday life from the national defense institutions.

"The defense of the country from foreign aggressors is a classic example of a public good ... The creation of knowledge is a public good" [82]

→ If people only would become aware how important 'knowledge' is!
→ So, the author fears that an enemy could come and steal their knowledge?

"Clean air and clean water are common resources like open grazing land, and excessive pollution is like excessive grazing. Environmental degradation is a modern Tragedy of the Commons." [83]

→ Billions would wish to have access to clean water! And some billions more would wish to have clean air every day. It's indeed a tragedy!

Krugman gives us a picture about public good: public sewage system, disease prevention, national defense, and scientific research. A very poor picture: [84]

---

[80] Colander, p. 492
[81] Mankiw (et al.), p. 170
[82] Mankiw, p. 224
[83] Mankiw (et al.), p. 232
[84] Krugman, p. 281

1) Public sewage system: thank God we have it in the Western world, although Spain, for example, is a bit neglecting in that matter; it costs less to pour it directly into the Mediterranean Sea. Unfortunately the sewage of 2.6 billion people comes back to the industrialized world via oceans.

2) Disease prevention is a state of readiness in case of emergency.

3) Scientific research is free of cost for the one who benefits: the corporations and the technology.

4) National defense seems to be necessary to protect from the headsmen that will come to punish the neo-capitalistic world for their evil doing and heavy destruction of the planet and their exploitation of humans and everything around the globe.

Examples of public goods we collected from the Internet and from some books:

- The physical environment
- Public places
- Mountain areas
- Roads, highways
- Libraries
- Museums
- Archeological material and sites
- Fireworks
- Clean air
- Lighthouses
- Open source software
- Open spaces
- TV
- Movies
- Concerts
- Art galleries
- Parks
- Swimming pools
- Scenic views
- Radio
- Hiking
- Water
- Cooking recipes
- Security

- Justice
- National defense
- Basic health
- Basic education
- Equality
- Inspection of food processing
- Melodies

→ It's very surprising that some goods of highest importance are ignored: routes for walking, mountains to climb up, landscapes and woodland for long walks, lakes and rivers for swimming or fishing, beaches and natural reserves (parks), etc.
→ Many governmental buildings, educational buildings, prisons, furniture and equipment, even the chair and the car of the prime minister and also the batons for the police to hit demonstrators are public goods – obviously for special tasks.

"With a public good the focus is on the group. The societal benefit in the case of a public good is the sum of the individual benefits (since societal benefit in the case of a public good). With private goods, we count only the benefit to the person buying the good since only one person gets it." [85]

"Common resources, like public goods, are not excludable: they are available free of charge to anyone who wants to use them." [86]

→ It would be a matter of public education to make clear to the children and young people the value of public goods and that no lunch is for free.

"Since individuals do not purchase public goods, their demand is not revealed by their actions. Government must guess at it. If a public good is to be financed by a tax on the citizens who benefit from it, individuals have an incentive to conceal their willingness to pay for it. This is why in the supply of public goods we see the free rider problem. The self-interested citizen wants to benefit from the public good without bearing the cost of providing it." [87]

→ Most public goods have a cost attached normally paid for with taxes.
→ There are people taking benefit from public goods, but do not pay taxes ('free riders').
→ There are people that do not value the pubic goods that have high costs.

---

[85] Colander, p. 493
[86] Mankiw, p. 229-231
[87] Colander, p. 493-494

→ Citizens should be extensively informed about the costs of public goods and that some pubic goods and their cost are not self-evident.

→ The lack of excludability means that people can't be charged for each unit of a public good that they consume.

→ "The profit potential of making public goods excludable can, at least in some cases, result in the production of more and/or better public goods." [88]

"The ancient Greek philosopher Aristotle pointed out the problem with common resources. What is common to many is taken least care of." [89]

→ This is still true in the modern societies and maybe it's necessary to think about some educational conclusions.

"Many species of animals are common resources. Fish and whales, for instance, have commercial value, and anyone can go to the ocean and catch whatever is available. Each person has little incentive to maintain the species for the next year. Just as excessive grazing can destroy the Town Common, excessive fishing and whaling can destroy commercially valuable marine populations." [90]

1.5.2. Political Economy

"Government plays two general roles in the economy. It's both a referee (setting the rules that determine relations between business and households) and an actor (collecting money in taxes and spending that money on projects such as defense and education)." [91]

Indeed, governments set rules. But this directly leads to the question: Are the rules set for businesses and especially for corporations the right rules? And 'collecting taxes' leads to the problem of the use of these taxes and the tax rate they determine.

It sounds very strange that the author mentions only two areas of spending (defense and education). There are many more fields of responsibility as mentioned above with the manifoldness of ministries. Strange is also that 'defense' seems to have highest importance for the economy (or the author).

"The general rule of political economy in a democracy: When small groups

---

[88] http://www.linfo.org/public_good.html
[89] Mankiw, p. 232
[90] Mankiw, p. 233
[91] Colander, p. 66

are helped by a government action and large groups are hurt by that same action, the small group tends to lobby far more effectively than the large group; thus, policies tend to reflect the small group's interest, not the interest of the large group." [92]

Reality shows that it is the other way round: small groups are not protected enough, but corporations have too much free space to act. Nowadays, politicians operate in the interest of corporations and of the super-rich, but ignore the people's basic need such as work in general. Ordered by the government, the police use brutal violence against demonstrators, but never against the exploiting and destructive way of doing business by the banks and the varieties of exploitation and their negative externalities from the corporations.

"Antitrust policy is not the only way in which governments affect the competitive processes. Other ways include (1) regulating the activities of firms, (2) government ownership – taking charge of the firms and operating them directly, and (3) industrial policy – influencing firms with laws and taxes." [93]

→ A survey should find out the understanding (knowledge and skills) politicians have of the world of business.

The essential focus here is: 'governments affect the competitive processes'. The questions here are: Are the political interventions in the free market always efficient? Is there a need to regulate the activities of corporations in a much more severe way? Do the governments damage firms with their laws and taxes?

→ A much more critical question is: Do the politicians and members of the governments have the necessary knowledge, skills and freedom of action to operate in the economy?
→ Could it be that the politicians and members of the governments are under severe influence from the lobbyists and from financial institutions?
→ Could it be that the politicians and members of the governments ignore the concerns from a large number of small businesses and even damage small firms with regulations and laws in order to comply to the demands and 'orders' from their economic masters?

"Regulation involves the setting of the rules that firms must follow if they are

---

[92] Colander, p. 190
[93] Colander, p. 422-423

to conduct business. There are two types of regulation: price regulation and social regulation. Price regulation is regulation directed at industries that have natural monopoly elements ... Social regulation is concerned with the conditions under which goods and services are produced, the safety of those goods, and the side effects of production on society." [94]

In any case, the regulations in the Western world today show us that these regulations hinder small firms and favors large corporations with the result of gigantic public debt and a disaster in the market (unemployment, lack of liquidity of banks, recession, etc.), and with poverty in industrialized nations increasing. In some developed countries up to 50% of the youth have a 'lost future'.

→ The predators and destructive forces are primarily not in politics and governments.
→ The predators are in the corporations and the superior world of the money masters.

"At the very least, government can lend support to the invisible hand by maintaining property rights and political stability. More controversial is whether government should target and subsidize specific industries that might be especially important for technological progress." [95]

→ What does this magic invisible hand have to do here?

1.5.3. Laws and Regulations

"Some examples of U.S. laws regulating the interaction between households and businesses today are: [96]

1. Businesses are not free to hire and fire whomever they want. They must comply with equal opportunity and labor laws. Even closing a plant requires 60 days' notice for many kinds of firms.
2. Many working conditions are subject to government regulation: safety rules, wage rules, overtime rules, hours-of-work rules, and the like.
3. Businesses cannot meet with other businesses to agree on prices they will charge.

---

[94] Colander, p. 423
[95] Mankiw (et al.), p. 547
[96] Colander, p. 68

4. In some businesses, workers must join a union to work at certain jobs.

In its role as both an actor and a referee, government plays a variety of specific roles in the economy. These include:

1. Providing a stable set of institutions and rules.
2. Promoting effective and workable competition.
3. Correcting for externalities.
4. Ensuring economic stability and growth.
5. Providing public goods.
6. Adjusting for undesirable market results."

At first glance the described roles of governments in the economy are pleasant. A deeper exploration always starts with questions:

→ Do the governments provide the right and enough stable sets of institutions and rules?
→ As most small firms can't compete with corporations, do governments do their job correctly?
→ What do governments do about the thousand negative externalities of corporations?
→ Where is the real economic stability and growth in America, Europe, and elsewhere?
→ What is an 'undesirable market result'? And how do they efficiently adjust for it?

Example: Fighting Poverty

"Taxing the wealthy to raise the living standard of the poor can make everyone better off. The poor are better off because they now enjoy a higher standard of living, and those paying the taxes are better off because they enjoy living in a society with less poverty." [97]

→ There is no proven theory that this would lead to the desired aim.
→ Poverty is a systemic problem that starts with public education, lack of vocational education, lack of knowledge and skills, and the organization of the labor market.

---

[97] Mankiw (et al), p. 225-226

1.5.4. Stable Set of Institutions and Rules

"The modern market economy requires enforceable complex contractual arrangements among individuals. Where governments don't provide a stable institutional framework, as often happens in developing and transitional countries, economic activity is difficult." [98]

→ If tax regulations fill a book with 10,000 pages then contractual arrangements are not efficient.
→ It is fact that in some countries economic activity is difficult.
→ We should consider that not all countries should or must dance the way America and Europe orders.

"In addition to providing general stability, government has the potential role of providing economic stability ... Government should prevent large fluctuations in the level of economic activity, maintain a relatively constant price level, and provide an economic environment conducive to economic growth." [99]

→ What if many corporations and banks are the main originator of general instability?
→ Government cannot provide economic stability with the neo-capitalistic holy books.
→ How can governments provide stable price levels, when corporations produce abroad?
→ Product prices of corporations do not reflect the production cost, so there is no solution.

"Government establishes laws that dictate what we can do, what prices we can charge for goods, and what working conditions are and are not acceptable." [100]

→ We would like to know how governments dictate the product prices of corporations.
→ Corporations take their production to Asia as there, there are unacceptable working conditions.

"Sometimes sellers can get government to limit quantity supplied through

---

[98] Colander, p. 68-69
[99] Colander, p. 70
[100] Colander, p. 187

licensing; other times they can limit supply by force. A well-placed threat ('If you enter this market, I will blow up your store') is often effective. In some developing economies, such threats are common. What stops existing suppliers from making good on such threats? Government. But the government also creates opportunities for individuals to prevent others from entering the market. Therein lies a central problem of political economy. You need government to see that competition works – to ensure that existing suppliers don't prevent others from entering the market – but government can also be used to prevent competition and protect existing suppliers. Government is part of both the problem and the solution." [101]

→ Competition doesn't work in America and Europe as small firms can't compete with corporations.
→ The corporations and the banking systems are the problem and from that, there is no solution.

"Government-owned firms did not have an incentive to hold costs down or to introduce new technology. Workers in government-owned firms, who were guaranteed jobs, used political threats to hold their wages high ... Economic integration in Europe has been accompanied by privatization of many of the formerly government-owned industries, and a fall in prices in many of these industries." [102]

→ Why do we always need to hold costs down and to introduce new technology?
→ Privatization of many of the formerly government-owned industries must be questioned.
→ A 'fall in prices in many of these industries' hides the reality that many such industries saw huge price hikes, such as telecom and electricity.

"One important job of economists is to give **advice to politicians** and other policy makers on a variety of questions relating to social policy: How should unemployment be dealt with? How can society distribute income fairly? Should the government redistribute income? Would a program of equal pay for jobs of comparable worth (a pay equity program) make economic sense? Should the minimum wage be increased? ... Economic reasoning and the supply/demand model are tools, not rules." [103]

→ It would better work the other way round: Politicians must give advice to

---

[101] Colander, p. 191
[102] Colander, p. 425
[103] Colander, p. 524

economists!

→ Unemployment can be dealt with by breaking up all large corporations into independent units.

→ Equal pay for jobs of comparable worth is nonsense as the price level differs between areas.

"Economists have many different views on social policy because

1. Economists' suggestions for social policy are determined by their subjective value judgments (normative views) as well as by their objective economic analyses.
2. Policy proposals must be based on imprecise empirical evidence, so there's considerable room for differences of interpretation not only about economic issues but also about how political and social institutions work. Economic policy is an art, not a science.
3. Policy proposals are based on various models that focus on different aspects of a problem." [104]

→ 'Many different views on social policy' shows that there is no proven economic science.

→ Most of the economic theories, laws, and principles are subjective value judgments.

→ In the entire economics (theory) there is considerable room for differences of interpretation.

→ There is no clarity in the economy how political and social institutions (should) work.

→ As economic policy is an art, economic advices are based on subjective and different opinions.

"Value judgments creep into economic policy proposals through economists' interpretations of empirical evidence, which is almost always imprecise." [105]

→ Economists' interpretations of empirical evidence are almost always imprecise due to its faults in their neo-classical study books.

"Similarly with the choice of models. A model, because it focuses on certain aspects of economic reality and not on others, necessarily reflects certain value judgments, so economists' choice of models must also reflect certain value judgments. Albert Einstein once said that theories should be as simple

---

[104] Colander, p. 525
[105] Colander, p. 526

as possible, but not more so … Scientists should be as objective and as value-free as possible, but not more so." [106]

→ 'Scientists should be as objective and as value-free as possible' which is thoroughly not given.
→ It seems that everywhere in the theories and laws of economics there are hidden values, judgments, and opinions.

The need of a worldview: An economist who is to play a role in forming policy must be willing to combine value judgments and technical knowledge. "(The) worldview determines how and when the economic model will be applied." [107]

If we consider the multiple negative externalities of economic practices we must conclude that the 'worldview' of economists is very narrow and short-sighted – due to the profit maxim.

"Many people think economists of all persuasions look at the world coldheartedly. In my view, that opinion isn't accurate." [108]

→ These 'many people' are totally right and the author is totally wrong; it can happen in science.
→ These economic experts have no idea about humanity and the planet now let alone in 20-35 years.

1.5.5. The Value of Life

"Economists argue that individuals' revealed choices are the best estimate that society can have of the value of life, and that in making policy society shouldn't pretend that life is beyond value." [109]

→ The 'individuals' revealed choices' refer to consumer decisions. Is the value of life there?
→ What does this statement say about the 'value of life? Nothing at all! There is a learning deficit about human values, inner life of humans, spiritual intelligence, and attitudes of love!
→ For 5-6 billion people life is beyond value, only the froth of myths, legends, and fairytales.

---

[106] Colander, p. 526
[107] Colander, p. 527
[108] Colander, p. 527
[109] Colander, p. 529

To be on this earth is a great gift. The planet is a wonderful and very valuable creation, and it is the home of all humans today and in the (far) future. All people have a soul and their goal is to develop this soul with learning, growing and living. Humanity is just at the beginning of a cosmic evolutionary project.

Maybe humans can be on earth even in hundreds of thousands of years. But a majority of humans today don't bother about the elimination of humanity and the destruction of the planet. All humans urgently must bethink these facts.

"Rich is better. Richer countries on average have higher life satisfaction than poor countries.

Money matters less as you grow richer. The gain in life satisfaction as you go from GDP per capita of $5,000 to $20,000 is greater than the gain as you go from $20,000 to $35,000." [110]

→ We must tell all people in Europe and America and to the rest of the world: 'Rich is better!'
→ To get a life satisfaction – the value of life here – people must earn much more money.
→ There are countries that have a better life due to performance, intelligence, hard learning, discipline, efficient professional attitudes and excellent professional education.
→ There are many countries and billions of people on earth that must learn: 'no lunch is for free'. The fatalistic and insane religious teachings have destroyed people's mind and soul.
→ There are also a million individuals in the world of economics, politics and religion that must be sentenced for life because they have stolen too much and intentionally hinder (their own folk) to get a better life, a higher life standard.

Many people on earth don't stand up for and don't bother (means: give a shit) about the human values such as love, care, hope, trust, truth, reliability, faith, faithfulness, justice, balance, honesty, fairness, joy of life, happiness, inner fulfillment, protection, emotional security, respect for human's weaknesses and inner suffering, attitudes in the interest of protection of the nature and the world of animals and the values of the Archetypes of the Soul. Their sole result of being on this earth is abuse of resources, waste and sewage, contamination and mental poison, hate, cheat, distortion, lies, arrogance, aggression, violence, fights and wars.

---

[110] Krugman, p. 319

Happiness doesn't happen just like that. All the psychical and spiritual aspects of the psyche (soul, inner life) have to be formed in an all-sided balanced way for success in life, for happiness, for genuine joy of life, for fulfillment, and for a constructive way of living.

➔ The value of human life lies in the archetypal psychical-spiritual processes – and not in possessions, profit, consumption and economic growth.

1.5.6. Government Failures

"There are also government failures – situations in which the government intervenes and makes things worse. Government failures are pervasive in the government – the government is always failing in one way or another." [111]

➔ Indeed, governments sometimes make things worse with their interventions.
➔ The government is always failing in one way or other because the fundamental economy is a failure.
➔ Failure is part of life as nobody is perfect; life is a learning process, also for economists.

"The business of governments is to keep the government out of business – that is unless business needs government. (Will Rogers)" [112]

➔ This is an opinion. It is more: it leads to the destruction of society and democracy.
➔ Nothing can be worse on earth than to give all the market power to economists.

"Government failures – when the government intervention in the market to improve the market failure actually makes the situation worse." [113]

➔ The author doesn't give here a list of concrete failures. The picture is a terrible simplification.
➔ Political failure must be seen and interpreted in the complex network of the real economics.

"Why are there government failures? Let's briefly list some important reasons:

---

[111] Colander, p. 71, 72
[112] Colander, p. 485
[113] Colander, p. 485

94

1. Government doesn't have an incentive to correct the problem. Government reflects politics, which reflects individual's interests in trying to gain more for themselves. Political pressures to benefit some group or another will often dominate over doing the general good.

2. Governments don't have enough information to deal with the problem. Regulating is a difficult business. To intervene effectively, even if it wants to, government must have good information, but just as the market often lacks adequate information, so does the government.

3. Intervention in markets is almost always more complicated that it initially seems. Almost all actions have unintended consequences. Government attempts to offset market failures can prevent the market from dealing with the problem more effectively. The difficulty is that generally the market's ways of dealing with problems work only in the long run. As government deals with the short-run problems, it eliminates the incentives that would have brought about a long-run market solution.

4. The bureaucratic nature of government intervention does not allow fine-tuning. When the problems change, the government solution often responds far more slowly...

5. Government intervention leads to more government intervention. Given the nature of the political process, opening the door in one area allows government to enter into other areas where intervention is harmful. Even in those cases where government action may seem to be likely to do some good, it might be best not to intervene, if that intervention will lead to additional government action in cases where it will not likely do good.

The important point to remember is that government failures exist and must be taken into account before making any policy recommendation. That's why real-world economic policy falls within the art of economics, and policy conclusions cannot be drawn from the models of positive economics." [114]

→ Economic arrogance is speaking here. These people only want to dethrone the kings.
→ An incentive to correct the problem is in the mission to lead the folks and the entire society.
→ Politicians and economists have individual interests in trying to gain more for themselves.
→ Governments don't have enough information to deal with problems; same

---

[114] Colander, p. 499

for economists.

→ Challenge for economists: Almost all actions in human's life have unintended consequences.
→ The difficulty is that dealing with negative externalities only works in the long run (inertia).
→ The real disaster: Bureaucratic nature of government intervention does not allow for any fine-tuning.
→ The source of the coming doom: the nature of economics and the corporation's motives.
→ It's obvious that economists hate political interventions; it could damage their profit drive.
→ Real-world economic policy is an art so, where is the science that follows scientific rules?

"For the government to correct the problem, it must

1. Recognize the problem.
2. Have the will to do something positive about the problem.
3. Have the ability to do something positive about the problem.

Government seldom can do all three of these well. Often the result is that government action is directed at the wrong problem at the wrong time." [115]

→ Do the economists realize the outrageous problems they have and create worldwide?
→ Having a will is great; having stupid masses and economic psychopaths is a nightmare.

"Economic policy is, and must be, applied within a political context. This means that political elements must be taken into account. Politics enters into the determination of economic policy in two ways, one positive and one negative. Its positive contribution is that politicians take market failures and failures of market outcomes into account when formulating policy. Ultimately the political system decides what externalities should be adjusted for, what is a desirable distribution, what rights are above the market, and when people's revealed demand does not reflect their true demand. To the extent that the government's political decisions reflect the will of society, government is making a positive contribution." [116]

→ Why can't the economic system decide what negative externalities should

---

[115] Colander, p. 537
[116] Colander, p. 537-538

be adjusted?

→ Political elements must be taken into account; but there's more: governments must get back their freedom of operation (from the economic institutions) and teach the economists how they have to take human factors, the nature, and the planet into account.

"The political reality is that, in the short run, people are often governed by emotion, swayed by mass psychology, irrational, and interested in their own rather than the general good. Politicians and other policy makers know that; the laws and regulations they propose reflect such calculations. Politicians don't get elected and reelected by constantly saying that all choices have costs and benefits." [117]

→ In opposite to that, we can posit: economists and the money masters are governed by ego-lunacy, unlimited greed, megalomania, psychopathy, and psychosis. They use mass psychology, abuse the irrational mind of humans, and they are only interested in their own profit, ignoring the evolution of humanity.

→ In general we could not find substantial criticism and suggestions for politics and governments. But the entire tone reflects a deep hostility towards politics in general as if these economists would want to dethrone governments and to fully control the entire political systems.

→ Seen from the other side, with a certain understanding, the economists and business people (all levels) are frustrated in such a way by the stupid, ignorant, arrogant, incompetent, and good-for-nothing in the world of politics, so that the economic intelligence must put them in traps.

Example of a Political Failure

3.2.2011: Obama's speech; he claims: the "leadership that made the U.S. (is) the light of the world. In other words: Obama claims the U.S. to be "the predestined nation, the only one that can save mankind". This implies that he is the new Messiah saving the world; and the U.S. is the chosen folk from God. "God bless the United States of America", he was saying.

Confucius: "Signs and symbols rule the world, neither words nor laws." Today we must say: Corporations rule the world and the politics, not politics. The meaning of signs and symbols of corporate groups dominate people. States have de facto converted into corporate groups. Their only creed is ultimately greed for money for power, which is fueled by lust. In their agenda, they all have the complete destruction of all Archetypes of the Soul.

---

[117] Colander, p. 538-539

There are hundreds of thousands of CEOs, owners of corporate groups, politicians and religious leaders who have acted during decades with their megalomania, paternalism, extreme greed, stubbornness, sick narcissism, arrogance, falseness and scrupulousness, perversion, amorality and a religious psychosis or political lunacy.

The psychological and material question is always the same: Who is the profiteer of such mad politics and legal mendacity? Who is the profiteer of such governmental criminality "in the Name of the Creator and the Almighty God"?

1.6. International Trade Policy

"If economists had a mantra, it would be "Trade is good." Trade allows specialization and division of labor and thereby promotes economic growth. Consistent with that mantra, most economists oppose trade restrictions ... We hear calls from some sectors of the economy to restrict foreign imports to save U.S. jobs and protect U.S. workers from unfair competition." [118]

→ Is that a joke? The mantra is a million times clear: 'MAXIMUM PROFIT IS GOD'
→ This is funny and at the same time a clever deception and deviation from the sick truth.
→ Most economists oppose trade restrictions: it's worse; they hate all kind of restriction.

1.6.1. Differences in the Importance of Trade

"The importance of international trade to countries' economies differs widely ... The value of goods and services sold abroad – and imports – the value of goods and services purchased abroad ... The relationship between a country's imports and its exports is no coincidence. For most countries, imports and exports roughly equal one another, though in any particular year that equality can be rough indeed ... Imports have generally significantly exceeded exports. But that situation can't continue forever ... We must also look at what types of goods are traded and with whom that trade is conducted." Colander (et al.), p. 199

→ Indeed, the importance of international trade differs widely: there are winners and losers.
→ There are nations that need to import goods for living and developing a basic infrastructure.
→ There are nations that want to export goods in order to make the highest possible profit.
→ There are nations that want to import cheap goods because they can sell these at higher prices.

---

[118] Colander, p. 198

1.6.2. The Changing Nature of Trade

"The change in the nature of the goods that a country produces and exports up the technological ladder is typical for developing countries ... We can expect the nature of trade to change even more in the future as numerous technological changes in telecommunications continue to reduce the cost of both voice and data communications throughout the world and expand the range of services that can be provided by foreign countries. Production no longer needs to occur in the geographic area where the goods are consumed. For example, financial accounting, compositing (typesetting) of texts, and research can now be done almost anywhere, and transferred with the click of a mouse." [119]

➜ An example is: the Indian population prefers to have a mobile phone and TV than a toilet.
➜ Technological changes in telecommunications will increase the control of foreign countries.
➜ Sucking data from the communication tools throughout the world will give market power.
➜ Food no longer needs to be produced in the area of the consumers; lowest quality suffices.
➜ Cheap services such as accounting, typesetting of texts, and research allows for increased profit.

"This trade in services is what the press often refers to as outsourcing, but it is important to remember that outsourcing is simply a description of some aspects of trade." [120]

➜ Outsourcing is simply a description of some aspects of trade – other aspects are hidden.

"The reason two countries trade is that trade can make both countries better off." [121]

➜ Yes, it can, but in many cases it doesn't. Some countries today are much 'worse off'.

---

[119] Colander, p. 200
[120] Colander, p. 200-201
[121] Colander, p. 203

➜ Some countries are forced to shut down internal industries because they cannot compete with the global corporations and thus are effectively forced to 'trade'.

"Generally the person arranging the trade must compete with other traders and offer both countries a better deal than the one presented here. But the person who fist recognizes a trading opportunity often makes a sizable fortune. The second and third persons who recognize the opportunity make smaller fortunes. Once the insight is generally recognized, the possibility of making a fortune is gone. Traders still make their normal returns, but the instantaneous fortunes are not to be made without new insight. In the long run, benefits of trade go to the producers and consumers in the trading countries, not the traders." [122]

➜ Run to make a fortune: the first to recognize a trading opportunity often makes a sizable fortune!
➜ The second and third taking the chance make smaller fortunes; the dogs bite the last.
➜ A misunderstanding that needs to be rectified: In the long run, the supra-benefits of trade go to the traders.

"The more competition that exists among traders, the less likely it is that the trader gets big gains of trade; more of the gains from trade will go to the citizens in the two countries, and less will go to the traders." [123]

➜ Or: the bigger the market, the more new markets, the higher the trader's profit.

"The market is not about abstract forces; it is about real people operating to improve their position. Many of the gains from trade do not go to the countries producing or consuming the good but rather to the trader. And the gains that traders get can be enormous." [124]

➜ The market is about 80% that earn less than $10 per day. And others earn more than $2,000.
➜ The truth speaks: The gains that traders get can be enormous.

"Trade increases income and wealth abroad, thereby creating additional demand for U.S. goods.
One big policy problem is that the benefits of trade are quite uneven. The

---

[122] Colander, p. 205
[123] Colander, p. 205
[124] Colander, p. 207

people whose jobs are outsourced are significantly hurt by trade and are very visible. The benefits of trade in lower prices and jobs created by trade are spread throughout the economy and are much less visible. It is the concentrated nature of the costs of trade and dispersed nature of the benefits that will continue to present a challenge to policy makers when dealing with the effects of trade." [125]

→ Trade increases income / wealth abroad: what is the difference between $5 and $10 per day?
→ There is a concentrated nature of the costs of trade and dispersed nature of the benefits; and there is a concentrated profit and money flow to the headquarters of the economic masters.

"The trade restriction policies that governments can undertake will generally make things worse.

But in the coming decades, we can expect a narrowing of the wage gap between the United States and China and India." [126]

→ In the coming decades, we can expect a narrowing of the wage gap between US and Asia; hidden is in the statement: lower wages in Europe, America and higher wages in Asia. Translated into reality: more poverty in America and Europe and less in Asia. Not bad at all!
→ This is capitalisms only solution to "rebalance" - playing the same old tune.
→ This cannot be a "rebalance" however, but "suicide" when you consider the population data in Chapter 1.

"Tariffs are taxes governments place on internationally traded goods – generally imports.

Tariffs operate in the same way a tax does: They make imported goods relatively more expensive than they otherwise would have been, and hereby encourage the consumption of domestically produced goods ... Quotas are quantity limits placed on imports. They have the same effect on equilibrium price and quantity as the quantity restrictions." [127]

→ It is an unanswered question if the tariffs (trade taxes) are in order to regulate trade or simply to get more money for the governmental cash

---

[125] Colander, p. 208
[126] Colander, p. 211
[127] Colander, p. 212

register.

→ Setting quotas can be done for export and import of goods. The effect is not the same. Export quotas can be set to discipline certain corporations in their profit madness.

"Regulatory trade restrictions are government-imposed procedural rules that limit imports.

One type of regulatory trade restriction has to do with protecting the health and safety of a country's residents." [128]

→ And what are the other reasons of trade restrictions? A trade war that forces governments of other countries to follow the neo-capitalistic ideology. The "cannot beat them so join them" mentality.

"A second type of regulatory restriction involves making import and customs procedures so intricate and time-consuming that importers simply give up … Some regulatory restrictions are imposed for legitimate reasons; others are designed simply to make importing more difficult and hence protect domestic producers form international competition." [129]

→ An exaggerated trade market where many countries compete to sell their goods around the world, leads to the question: do people really need all the products offered from trade?

"Often people don't want to make radical changes in the kind of work they do – they want to keep on producing what they're already producing. So when these people see the same kinds of goods that they produce coming into their country from abroad, they lobby to prevent the foreign competition." [130]

→ Economists and neo capitalists get here a warning: 'Often people don't want to make radical changes in the kind of work they do'.

Thus, "…when an economy is in a recession, there is a strong macroeconomic reason to limit imports and encourage exports. These macroeconomic effects of free trade play an important role in the public's view of imports and exports." [131]

---

[128] Colander, p. 214
[129] Colander, p. 215
[130] Colander, p. 215
[131] Colander, p. 220

→ 'To encourage exports' means that other countries shall help solve the recession. By buying goods they cannot afford and getting themselves into debt?

"Economists' first argument for free trade is that, viewed from a global perspective, free trade increases total output. From a national perspective, economists agree that particular instances of trade restrictions may actually help one nation, even as most other nations are hurt. But they argue that the country imposing trade restrictions can benefit only if the other country doesn't retaliate with trade restrictions of its own." [132]

→ 'Free trade increases total output'; in other words: export increases the output = the profit.
→ Trade restrictions hurt other nations: In which way do trade restrictions hurt?
→ If a country lives preponderantly from import or export, then there is a natural imbalance.

"A second reason most economists support free trade is that trade restrictions reduce international competition. International competition is desirable because it forces domestic companies to stay on their toes. If trade restrictions on imports are imposed, domestic companies don't work as hard and therefore become less efficient." [133]

→ This permanent 'competition' can make the mind of economists and people very sick. Running and never catching up.
→ If trade restrictions on imports are imposed, it is surprising how people can be very inventive to develop new own productions. And domestic companies can work even harder and be more efficient and sustainable too.
→ The arguments here are superficial. More important in the world of trade is: Who gets 'the most out of it'?

In general we observe in the statements about international trade an incredible trivialization of the real world of trade. Especially ignored are the very critical developments due to Climate Change such as drought, flood, water scarcity, destruction of arable land, exploitation of forests, over-exploitation of natural ground water, and so forth.

With the migration from rural areas to cities and the increase of agriculture

---

[132] Colander, p. 221
[133] Colander, p. 221

scarcity (e.g. China, Africa) an immense new demand has been raised for corn, wheat and meat, products that absorb more water than humans use. Under such development trade has become a question of survival and immense political tensions with trouble spots of global dimensions. The essential classical economic formulas exploit with fanatical zeal and greed the global demand for basic needs.

➔ International trade, globalization in general, has become the new battle field of politics and economics not just for the needs and wants, but also for global governance.
➔ The 'law' expressed in the statement 'with an increase of demand also the prices increase' together with the principle of 'profit maximization' is the absolute evil economic formula.

1.6.3. Global Economic Institutions

"Governments, however, have developed a variety of international institutions to promote negotiations and coordinate economic relations among countries. Besides the United Nations, these include the World Bank, the World Court, and the International Monetary Fund (IMF). These organizations have a variety of goals. For example, the World Bank, a multinational, international financial institution, works with developing countries to secure low-interest loans, channeling such loans to them to foster economic growth. The International Monetary Fund (IMF), a multinational, international financial institution, is concerned primarily with monetary issues. It deals with international financial arrangements. When developing countries encountered financial problems in the 1980s and had large international debts that they could not pay, the IMF helped work on repayment plans ... The World Trade Organization (WTO) works to reduce trade barriers among countries." [134]

➔ The business world suffocates from institutions that eat away a huge slice of the profit cake.
➔ These monstrous institutions cost the citizens a lot of money (taxes), but the profiteers are not the people with 'normal' wages.
➔ Some of these institutions are predators, very dangerous monsters that destroy many countries around the globe. Start digging and soon you get a shock!

Institutions Supporting Free Trade:

---

[134] Colander, p. 73

"The most important is the World Trade Organization (WTO), which has about 150 members, and is the successor to the General Agreement on Tariffs and Trade (GATT). You will still occasionally see references to GATT, even though the WTO has taken its place. One of the differences between the WTO and GATT is that the WTO includes some enforcement mechanisms." [135]

→ 'Free trade' is the 'mantra' of neo-capitalistic economics. They all want total freedom to do what they like for the highest possible profit and in the end for dominating other countries.

---

[135] Colander, p. 222

2. National Parameters of Macroeconomics

2.1. Macroeconomic Parameters

A) The term 'parameter' has a number of specific meanings in mathematics, physics, statistics, electricity, astronomy, temperature, etc.

B) The term 'parameter' is also used equally for 'variable', 'factor, 'aspect', 'field', a 'distinguishing characteristic or feature', or a 'determined topic', all of them determine a scale of variations.

→ We understand 'parameter' in the context of macro-economics as mentioned in B).

What are the criteria to determine a macroeconomic parameter? Naturally we would say: the parameters in the books, in the chapters about 'macroeconomics' are the macroeconomic parameters. From here we would not need to ask for criteria to determine a macroeconomic parameter.

This could serve as a guideline for determining parameters in economics: "Macroeconomics is the study of the economy as a whole. The goal of macroeconomics is to explain the economic changes that affect many households, firms and markets simultaneously." [136]

→ Any 'field' that affects a majority of households, firms, the market and the society as a whole is a parameter of macro-economics.

This is neither a principle nor a theory. It simply has practical relevance in organizing all the topics (fields) of macro-economics. At least, all these parameters imply directly or indirectly the measurable variable 'money' on a big (national or global) scale which in turn can be and is used in statistics.

'Macro' means: Very large in scale, scope or extent, or capability
'Capability' we can understand as power or extension of performance and effects

---

[136] Mankiw (et al.), p. 487

We have to distinguish:

- Macro-parameters that refer to constitutive systems in societies
- Sub-macro-parameters that are part of macro-parameters
- Parameters that are 'tools' operating within the macro-parameters

We also have to distinguish between:

- Macro-parameters limited to national areas
- Macro-parameters that are cross-national
- Macro-parameters that cover global dimensions

Furthermore we also have to distinguish between:

- Macro-parameters of limited capacity
- Macro-parameters of extensive capacity

→ We observe that important classical study books about economics have not developed a macro-economic picture (model, network) differentiated in the above mentioned criteria. This is an immense negligence and serves to detract the readers from the hidden manipulations.
→ Not distinguishing between the above mentioned variations of macro-parameter creates a distorted and deceiving picture about the whole world of macro-economics.

In this chapter we present a selection of macro-economic parameters that form an economical picture about a nation. We focus on topics that refer to decisive dimensions of financial issues of a society. Other parameters are presented and discussed in other chapters.

→ Prepare yourself for the following chapter with immensely shocking news!

The Systemic Tactics to Deceive Entire Folks

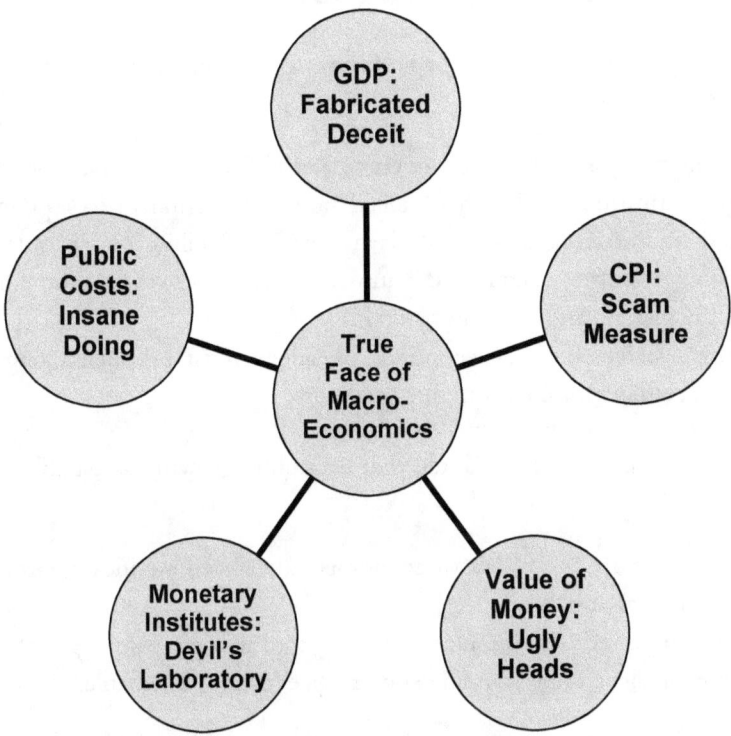

2.2. Gross Domestic Product - GDP

"Economic growth has been perhaps the most revolutionary and powerful force in history." [137]

➜ Yes, economic growth has been a very powerful force in history, especially together with armies. They have killed hundreds of millions of people, enslaved hundreds of millions Africans, exploited billions of people in developing countries, eliminated entire folks, and destroyed more than half of the planet. And they can't stop it.
➜ Normative statement: such economic preachers must be put lifelong in prisons together with the economic predators.

"Economists usually take for granted that economic growth is desirable and sustainable." [138]

➜ Usually? There are thousands of economists that have a critical approach to economic growth.
➜ There are thousands of examples that give proof that economic growth (in the neo-capitalistic understanding and practice) is not sustainable.

Definition

"The statistic might measure the total income of everyone in the economy called gross domestic product (**GDP**), the rate at which average prices are rising (inflation), the percentage of the labour force that is out of work (unemployment), total spending in shops (retail sales), or the imbalance of trade between the domestic economy and the rest of the world (the trade deficit). All these statistics are **macroeconomic**." [139]

➜ A very reduced picture from this author: Macroeconomics is about: 1) GDP, 2) Inflation, 3) Unemployment rate, 4) retail sales, and 5) trade.
➜ In other words, macroeconomics is about: 1) Growth and profit, 2) the theatre of value of money, 3) costly unemployment, 4) high or low retail

---

[137] McConnell (et al.), p. 150
[138] McConnell (et al.), p. 165
[139] Mankiw (et al.), p. 486-487

sales, and 5) the winner and loser of trade.

→ There are a further 20-30 macro-economic parameters of highest importance; e.g. negative externalities with \$5 trillion damages from corporations per year. Where are the others?

"When judging whether the economy is doing well or poorly, it is natural to look at the total income that everyone in the economy is earning. That is the task of gross domestic product (GDP). GDP measures two things at once: the total income of everyone in the economy and the total expenditure on the economy's output of goods and services. The reason that GDP can perform the trick of measuring both total income and total expenditure is that these two things are really the same." [140]

→ "The total income of everyone in the economy": deceiving formulation! It's an average that doesn't show the real world throughout a nation.
→ The total expenditure on the economy's output of goods and services: Dig deep and you will find out that this is not the same as the total income. It simply doesn't make sense.

"Households do not spend all of their income. They pay some of it to the government in taxes, and they save some for use in the future." [141]

→ "Households do not spend all of their income": 80% of the earth population tries to survive with \$300 per month. Nothing is left at the end of the month. Of the remaining 1.4 billion people a majority living in industrialized countries, we have estimated 50% poor or extremely poor people: nothing is left there at the end of a month. Who can save significant money for the future? Not even 10% of the world population!

"Gross domestic product is the market value of all final goods and services produced within a country in a given period of time ... GDP adds together many different kinds of products into a single measure of the value of economic activity." [142]

→ "GDP adds together many different kinds of products into a single measure": the more they add the less the 'soup' becomes a relevant meaning for political measures.

There are some products, however, that GDP excludes because measuring

---

[140] Mankiw (et al.), p. 487
[141] Mankiw (et al.), p. 488
[142] Mankiw (et al.), p. 489

them is so difficult ... Vegetables you buy at the greengrocer's shop or supermarket are part of GDP; vegetables you grow in your garden are not. The value of work carried out by house wives and husbands is not included in GDP calculations and neither the value of child care work carried out by grandparents." [143]

→ These excluded goods, services and private work can be of highest importance for a society. Ignoring these fields, expresses a complete disrespect and disinterest, leads to a devaluation of human values.

"GDP includes both tangible goods (food, clothing, cars) and intangible services (haircuts, house cleaning, doctor visits). When you (legally) download an album by your favourite band, you are buying a good, and the purchase price is part of GDP. When you pay to hear a concert by the same band, you are buying a service, and the ticket price is also part of GDP." [144]

→ Any irrelevant, stupid, useless good or service has importance for the GDP. There must be a hidden interest in such a GDP: VAT, Tax calculations, and forecasting the next profit cake.

"GDP measures the value of production within the geographic confines of a country. GDP measures the value of production that takes place within a specific interval of time." [145]

→ Simple and clear; also correct. It shows that the GDP is a political parameter.

"If total spending rises from one year to the next, one of two things must be true (or a combination of the two): (1) the economy is producing a larger output of goods and services, or (2) goods and services are being sold at higher prices." [146]

→ The GDP either shows that a larger amount of goods and services are produced and sold at the price of the past year; or the prices of the goods and services have risen.
→ We could also say: both at the same time could be expressed in the GDP.
→ If this statement is correct, then the increase of the GDP would also express inflation.

---

[143] Mankiw (et al.), p. 489
[144] Mankiw (et al.), p. 490
[145] Mankiw (et al.), p. 490
[146] Mankiw (et al.), p. 494

"Still, one must be careful when using GDP numbers, especially when making comparisons over time. That's because part of the increase in the value of GDP over time represents increases in the prices of goods and services rather than an increase in output." [147]

→ In other words: the GDP doesn't say anything reliable about a real 'growth'. And if we add the rate of wage decrease, the entire picture becomes useless.

Real GDP answers a hypothetical question: what would be the value of the goods and services produced this year if we valued these goods and services at the prices that prevailed in some specific year in the past? By evaluating current production using prices that are fixed at past levels, real GDP shows how the economy's overall production of goods and services changes over time." [148]

→ The construction: The goods and services, in the GDP basket, from the current year have the same price as the goods and services from a specific year in the past. This construction is actually and probably in general unreal and nonsense.
→ The content of the basket changes sometimes. Additionally most technical products experience yearly improvements, often with a higher price due to this margin element. Other products are cheaper due to technical advances. Therefore we can't simply take the prices of the goods from a year in the past for the actual GDP basket.

"The production of goods and services valued at current prices, is called **nominal GDP.** To obtain a measure of the amount produced that is not affected by changes in prices, we use **real GDP**, which is the production of goods and services valued at constant prices.

To sum up: nominal GDP uses current prices to place a value on the economy's production of goods and services, while real GDP uses constant base-year prices to place a value on the economy's production of goods and services. Because real GDP is not affected by changes in prices, changes in real GDP reflect only changes in the amounts being produced …

Thus, real GDP is a better gauge of economic well-being than is nominal GDP. When economists talk about the economy's GDP, they usually mean

---

[147] Krugman, p. 315
[148] Mankiw (et al.), p. 494

real GDP rather than nominal GDP. And when they talk about growth in the economy, they measure that growth as the percentage change in real GDP from one period to another." [149]

➜ The nominal GDP measures the production of goods and services valued at current prices.
➜ The real GDP measures the amount produced that is not affected by changes in prices.
➜ Real GDP measures only the changes in the amounts being produced. Such a calculation model has an intrinsic fault as mentioned above and therefore remains 'in the air'.

"People dispute the validity of GDP as a measure of well-being." [150]

➜ Which people dispute the validity of GDP as a measure of well-being? The problem here is the meaning of the word 'well-being'.

"GDP does not directly measure those things that make life worthwhile, but it does measure our ability to obtain the inputs into a worthwhile life … GDP is not, however, a perfect measure of well-being." [151]

➜ GDP measures our ability to obtain the inputs into a worthwhile life: if the rich get every year richer and the rest of the population every year poorer, then the GDP doesn't say much about a worthwhile life of all members of a society.
➜ More interesting is here: What is a not-worthwhile life in a developed country – and in a developing country? Depending on the interpretation we come to the conclusion that up to 80% of the world's population does not have a worthwhile life. And those who have a worthwhile life do have it due to the corporations' exploitation of labor and resources, and due to ignoring negative externalities' in developing countries.

"GDP uses market prices to value goods and services, it excludes the value of almost all activity that takes place outside of markets … Another thing that GDP excludes is the quality of the environment … GDP is a good measure of economic wellbeing for most – but not all – purposes." [152]

➜ In case of negative externalities, excluding the quality of the environment

---

[149] Mankiw (et al.), p. 496-497
[150] Mankiw (et al.), p. 499
[151] Mankiw (et al.), p. 499
[152] Mankiw (et al.), p. 499

(e.g. contamination) is a cheat. Somebody has to pay for it (e.g. illnesses).

→ Ignoring the positive externalities shows that economics does not want to give special weight to this, partly as the corporations are the profiteers (e.g. education paid by government).

→ The statement doesn't make clear why GDP is a good measure of economic well-being. Here is a lot of blabber, probably to hide the real economic interest in this parameter.

→ The core thesis from the experts is: if the GDP grows, economic wellbeing is given. And as everybody wants economic well-being, everybody wishes for a yearly increase of the GDP.

→ Sure is: the corporations always wants 'growth' as it allows with high probability an increase of profit. And the governments need growth to manage their public debt.

"An economy that is experiencing economic growth is better able to meet people's wants and resolve socioeconomic problems. Rising real wages and income provide richer opportunities to individuals and families – a vacation trip, a personal computer, a higher education – without scarifying other opportunities to individuals and families – a vacation trip, a personal computer, a higher education – without sacrificing other opportunities and pleasures." [153]

→ 50-65% of the wants that 80% of the people have are irrelevant for a good life and for personal fulfillment, happiness and wellbeing included.

→ Higher education is for a small group of people. A vacation trip doesn't necessarily mean going to long distance vacation trip. Who really uses a personal computer for something enriching? And 50% of people absolutely do not need a car.

"Today people living in countries experiencing modern economic growth are constantly exposed to new technologies, new products, and new services." [154]

→ Yes, but these new technologies, new products, and new services make most people crazy, produce egomania, neuroticism, depression, fear, sleeplessness, restlessness, blind and greedy consumers, and much more.

"Countries with low GDP per person tend to have more infants with low birth weight, higher rates of infant mortality, higher rates of maternal mortality, higher rates of child malnutrition and less common access to save

---

[153] McConnell (et al.), p. 150
[154] McConnell (et al.), p. 152

drinking water. In countries with low GDP per person, fewer school-age children are actually in school, and those who are in school must learn with fewer teachers per student. These countries also tend to have fewer televisions, fewer telephones, fewer paved roads and fewer households with electricity. International data leave no doubt that a nation's GDP is closely associated with its citizens' standard of living." [155]

→ These examples show that many developing countries indeed need to increase their GDP to reach a higher standard of living.

→ The problem is that many developing countries have been exploited, abused, terrorized, dehumanized, and enslaved since centuries, chained with debt so that the Western world could build up a comfortable standard of life and the developing countries are irreversibly damaged in their culture, their raw resources, and deformed in their mind.

→ Do all the people in the industrialized world and elsewhere really need (for example) more televisions, more mobile phones, and more luxurious cars?

"There are a range of factors that can contribute to a definition of happiness; that if you are fortunate enough to find yourself being able to boast having these characteristics of in some cases managing to avoid them then you are more likely to be happy." [156]

→ When economists start talking about 'happiness', then it is better to leave the field or to make them keep silent. These people have no soul, no spirituality, and no understanding of human values; therefore their 'happiness' is a mad construction. Even children with a healthy mind and soul know better what 'happiness' really means.

Layard identified some key factors that may contribute to 'happiness'. He suggested that some of the factors associated with promoting happiness, include sex, socializing, relaxing, praying, worshipping or meditating, eating, exercising, watching TV and shopping, among others.

Other studies have suggested that an individual's level of education, health, whether they are married, single or divorced, the level of income enjoyed, whether they are working/unemployed/retired, their aspirations and whether they have experienced bereavement can all be contributory factors." [157]

Now, we are challenged: sex without love may relax, but doesn't make happy.

---

[155] Mankiw (et al.), p. 500
[156] Mankiw (et al.), p. 501-502
[157] Mankiw (et al.), p. 501-502

Socializing is an artificial game full of lies. Relaxing creates well-being, but this is not happiness. Praying is a hamster race for nothing and can never create happiness. Worshipping is a scam construction that stimulates psychotic views and self-identity. Eating gives satisfaction, never happiness. Watching TV makes people stupid, as a majority of people only watch junk; and 95% of TV-programs aim to bring people into one stream of opinion and behavior pattern – called: brainwashing. Shopping can produce joy, fun, satisfaction, but never happiness – except when people really deserve what they can afford and the products they buy give a certain deeper meaning. Only meditating can make happy, but it depends a lot on the way and aims of meditation; it always include inner psychical-spiritual development aiming for completeness (fulfillment) and with that experiencing the Archetypes of the Soul. Authentic self-realization and living in the truth creates genuine happiness. – What Layard talks about here is absolute bullshit, an evil lie and manipulation of students and naïve economists!

→ A GDP-parameter that excludes the negative externalities is a fabricated deceit and cheat.
→ The GDP-parameter is rotten to the core, fabricated for hidden interests.

"Policymakers attempt to maximize growth while minimizing unemployment and inflation." [158]

→ The history does not give prove that 'maximizing growth' always minimizes unemployment and inflation. Above that maximizing growth produces enormous negative externalities.
→ High unemployment rate has a lot to do with the politics of the big corporations and / or with an imbalance between production and service industries in a country.
→ The lunacy in the real estate market together with the bank's speculations and the immense public and private debt are additional factors that create high unemployment rate.

One aspect that must be made clear: Growth is not bad per se. In all societies there are fields that require improvements or extension of public goods for the citizens. Producing knowledge, especially about the soul (inner life of people) and the inner archetypal processes, is of high importance for the evolution of humanity. Many countries have reached a standard of living where we must say: enough is enough!

---

[158] McConnell (et al.), p. 118

→ Once a certain level of growth is reached, consolidation and balancing with other parameters is absolutely indispensable. Continuous growth requirement makes people insane.

→ Above a certain level of living standard people get neurotic, narcissistic, lazy, unwilling to learn, undisciplined, stupid, arrogant, dehumanized, and good-for-nothing.

→ Evolutionary growth is especially needed in all religions and also in public education. These worlds are as archaic in the understanding of humans as 500 or 2,000 years ago.

→ Growth is also needed in the personality quality and integrity of politicians and experts of economics. Politics and economics must undergo a complete catharsis and renewal.

→ Growth is of highest importance in matters of love, care, justice, peace, understanding, living human values, and especially in international understanding, respect, and cooperation.

→ 'Growth' must be re-defined and measured with a new multiple parameter that encompasses quality, balance, justice, sustainability, intellectual capacities and other human factors.

The supreme masters of economics and politics should consider a new perspective:

If 10% of the world population has reached a very high standard of living and the rest of the world is suffering in misery due to very low or lowest standard of living, then the 10% will be eliminated at any cost. The nature and the collective unconscious will hit and punish horrifyingly.

Production and Growth

"Richer countries have more cars, more telephones, more televisions, better nutrition, safer housing, better health care and longer life expectancy." [159]

→ Not bad at all. But not all people in richer countries get these goods.
→ Most people no longer appreciate what they get from society.
"Other theories argue: Investment in a nation's human capital will be a key driver of economic growth. The reason being that investment in human capital is more likely to lead to increases in technology which in turn help promote efficiency and increases in productivity." [160]

→ Human capital has been a key driver for World War I and World War II

---

[159] Mankiw (et al.), p. 524-525
[160] Mankiw (et al.), p. 530

and will be the human capital for the doom in sight.

→ Human capital is seen here as a resource for technological growth and increase of productivity; in the end for the profit of corporations.

"Long-run economic growth is fundamental to many of the most pressing economic questions today. Responses to key policy questions, like the country's ability to bear the future costs of government programs such as Social Security and Medicare, depend in part on how fast the U.S. economy grows over the next few decades. More broadly, the public's sense that the country is making progress depends crucially on success in achieving long-run growth." [161]

→ Like a mantra the author evokes the economic growth. It's a fairy tale and a dogmatic belief that says the problems today will be solved in the future with economic growth.
→ Who knows if the United States of America will even exist in decades?
→ The lie and deceit here is the belief that growth is crucial for all societies; here for America and (we would add) for Europe.
→ Are these economists so naïve? Or do they simply try to get today 'the best they can' because they know perfectly well that tomorrow there is nothing more to get.

Productivity is determined by: "physical capital, human capital, natural resources and technological knowledge." [162]

→ Human capital is also for creating society, social life, family life, culture, personal fulfillment, etc.

"Workers are more productive if they have tools with which to work. The stock equipment and structures that are used to produce goods and services is called physical capital, or just capital." [163]

→ Workers must be as productive as possible. Is there a humane limit?

A second determinant of productivity is human capital: "Human capital is the economist's term for the knowledge and skills that workers acquire through education, training and experience Human capital includes the skills accumulated in early childhood programmes, primary school, secondary school, university or college, and on-the-job training for adults in the labour

---

[161] Krugman, p. 303
[162] Mankiw (et al.), p. 531
[163] Mankiw (et al.), p. 531

force." [164]

→ Human capital = knowledge, skills acquired through education, training and experiences.
→ Building up human capital for the corporations starts with early childhood and does not end until university graduation. Do you see the master plan of shaping humans?

"Natural resources are inputs into production that are provided by nature, such as land, rivers and mineral deposits. Natural resources take two forms: renewable and non-renewable." [165]

→ Best is to get the natural resources such as land, rivers and mineral deposits by conquest.

"A fourth determinant of productivity is technological knowledge – the understandings of the best ways to produce goods and services." [166]

→ There is also a 'best way of working' that needs to be discussed, including working conditions, wage for living and personal satisfaction through working.

"Education – investment in human capital – is at least as important as investment in physical capital for a country's long-run economic success." [167]

→ Logically the masters of economics must govern the entire system of education by acquiring or controlling them through other networks.

"Rich countries like those of Western Europe and North America have the best systems of higher education." [168]

→ The higher education in America and Europe has become a preparative tool for economics, corporations, and for the deicide master plan.
→ The higher education in America and Europe operates with an archaic understanding of humans and of society.
→ 'The best systems of education' is vague and doesn't say anything about the qualities to which 'best' can be referred.
→ There are developing countries with excellent and 'equal best' academic

---

[164] Mankiw (et al.), p. 531
[165] Mankiw (et al.), p. 532
[166] Mankiw (et al.), p. 532
[167] Mankiw (et al.), p. 539
[168] Mankiw (et al.), p. 539

institutions. Very arrogant this point of view from economic experts!

"The term human capital usually refers to education, but it can also be used to describe another type of investment in people: expenditures that lead to a healthier population." [169]

→ This statement is an incredibly trivialized understanding of education. The author smashes the entire history of Western education and completely ignores the forming and shaping of humans with a holistic approach. Here all human values are eliminated and that's not by accident, nor a failure. It's absolutely part of the master plan.

Productivity and growth can also be seen under the perspective of obsolescence practices: "Light bulbs, nylon stockings, printers, cell phones - most of these products have their 'end date' already planned. The consumer should be induced to buy a new product rather than have defective ones repaired … The deliberate reduction in the lifetime of an industrial product, to keep the economy going, is called 'planned obsolescence'."

Economic growth is mainly from obsolescence practices. The 'negative externalities' of obsolescence practices can be seen in many countries. In Ghana for example, the millions of tons of electronic scrap and the destruction caused would cost at least half a trillion dollars to clean up. GDP does not say anything about this. That's called: deceit, cheat, and even a scam.

The planned obsolescence must come from the 'invisible hand'. The body from this 'hand' has made and still makes enormous profit with this strategy. This body must pay for the damages and considering the billions of tons of waste and the irreversible damages they also must be put in prison lifelong. But there is no solution as most politicians are too sneaky. [170]

---

[169] Mankiw (et al.), p. 540
[170] http://www.phoenix.de/

2.3. Consumer Price Index

"Consumer Price Index (CPI) is a measure of the overall prices of the goods and services bought by a typical consumer.

1. Fix the basket. The first step in computing the consumer prices index is to determine which prices are most important to the typical consumer. The ONS sets these weights by surveying consumer buys.
2. Find the prices. The second step in computing the consumer prices index is to find the prices of each of the goods and services in the basket for each point in time.
3. Compute the basket's cost. The third step is to use the data on prices to calculate the cost of the basket of goods and services at different times.
4. Choose a base year and compute the index. The fourth step is to designate one year as the base year, which is the benchmark against which other years are compared.
5. Compute the inflation rate. The fifth and final step is to use the consumer prices index to calculate the inflation rate, which is the percentage change in the price index from the preceding period." [171]

➔ It's not about good or services. It's about the overall prices that are most important to typical consumers.
➔ What is a typical consumer? The typical consumer is a mass human, a sheep, a greedy person perfectly programmed through the media to follow the main steam of consumption.
➔ Which type of people in industrialized nations are aware of the price differences from all the goods? The poor and the very poor people calculate with every cent.

(See Economics II where we have developed a picture about baskets and baskets costs.)

"Producer Price Index is a measure of the change in prices of a basket of goods and services bought by firms." [172]

➔ There are thousands of types of producers and thousands of different baskets of goods and services bought by firms.

---

[171] Mankiw (et al.), p. 507
[172] Mankiw (et al.), p. 508

→ A corporation buys yearly 10,000 tons of a raw material. A small firm has some costs such as stationery and consumable items. Draw some examples of costs and calculate an average!
→ What is the benefit of such PPI?

A typical basket of good is: [173]

Food and non-alcoholic beverages	22%
Alcohol and tobacco	4%
Clothing and footwear	11%
Housing and household services	5%
Furniture and household goods	11%
Health	3%
Transport	6%
Communication	1%
Education	1%
Restaurants and hotels	8%
Miscellaneous goods and services	11%

→ There are many people that do not consume alcohol or tobacco.
→ Once the home is furnished, people in general keep it that way for years.
→ There are many people that rarely or never go to hotels.
→ How is a typical basket from the people earning less than $2.50 per day?
→ How is a typical basket from the people earning $10 per day?
→ How is a typical basket from the people earning $100 per day?
→ How is a typical basket from the people earning $300 per day?
→ What can you do with the Producer Price Index of Spain, UK, Greece, or Ghana?

"If the family's income does not rise as fast as the prices of the goods and services that it consumes, it won't be able to purchase as much as it used to and its standard of living will fall. Along the same lines, a surprise jump in inflation reduces the purchasing power of people's savings." [174]

---

[173] Mankiw (et al.), p. 511
[174] McConnell (et al.), p. 117

→ For example, Spanish wages for 80% of the citizens have not risen since 10 years (2002-2012), but the prices have increased enormously.

→ '...to purchase as much as it used to' is not founded in any reasonable 'law'. A reduction of 20-30% of consumption does not necessarily mean a reduction of standard of living.

→ A reduction of the purchasing power can evoke giving more importance to the profoundest meaning of life, to the genuine human values, and to grow psychologically and spiritually.

"...if prices were fully flexible, there would be no short-run fluctuations in output. Production levels would remain constant and unemployment levels would not change because firms would always need the same number of workers to produce the same amount of output." [175]

→ Nothing is constant in the economic world. The problem is the excess of some 'parameters'.

→ There is and always will be a certain amount of unemployment (2-3%).

→ The same amount of output is not a real expectation.

→ This statement indirectly imputes an undesired economy and favors the growth ideology.

"An inventory is a store of output that has been produced but not yet sold. Inventories are useful because they can be allowed to grow or decline in periods when demand is unexpectedly low or high – thereby allowing production to proceed smoothly even when demand is variable." [176]

→ Inventories are also useful to manipulate prices.

→ Allowing production to proceed smoothly is a nice way of saying that promotes unlimited growth.

"... if demand falls off for many goods and services across the entire economy for an extended period of time, then the firms that make those goods and services will be forced to cut production." [177]

→ There are indeed production entities that nobody needs for a good life.

→ Exaggerated, endless growth of production must be brought back to

---

[175] McConnell (et al.), p. 122
[176] McConnell (et al.), p. 123
[177] McConnell (et al.), p. 123

'normal'.

"As both manufacturing and service output declines, the economy will recede, with GDP falling and unemployment rising. On the other hand, if demand is unexpectedly high for a prolonged period of time, the economy will boom and unemployment will fall." [178]

→ The view is one-sided: There are always fields in a society where growth is required or appropriate.

→ There are also fields that are adequately balanced and other fields are insanely exaggerated in growth.

→ The human body teaches us: an all-sided balanced growth expresses health. A cancer shows us that there are causes that damages health and balance. Economics is full of cancers.

---

[178] McConnell (et al.), p. 123-124

2.4. Monetary Institutions

An honest and carefully working scientist is always very critical into two directions: On the one hand he is thoroughly critical towards facts and statements about facts. He always has questions. He must dig deep to identify the relevant elements of a topics. On the other hand he is always self-critical about his knowledge, his perception, his questions, his motives and aims of understanding realities (his topics) and producing new knowledge.

In a general way the advice is for everybody: Always be critical and distrustful when politicians talk, when religious people talk about their belief, when media report about events, when representatives of corporations inform, and when economists or bankers talk.

The problem is not simply that they always lie. One problem is that lies are mixed with true facts, common sense, and added with 'marginal', 'free rider elements' or 'incentives'. Another problem is that sometimes the most important facts are trivialized, skipped, or hidden.

→ The truth doesn't require that people should always tell everything to anybody.
→ Science enormously damages society, if it's based on misleading, distorting, and deceiving.

With their horrendous speculation (real estate, commodities, resources, etc.) and fraudulent and deceitful models of investment countless banks and financial institutions have destroyed the existence and hope of billions of people. Many of these banks and financial institutions have provided immense loans to governments, partly with enormous interest rates, ultimately to dominate politics and oppress the people. Lately they started increasing speculative trade with food. This will force up to 2 billion people into poverty and hunger; poverty will increase dramatically.

Let's first identify the components of the monetary system in an admittedly very reduced way:

Role of Central Banks

"Whenever an economy relies on a system of fiat money (…) some agency must be responsible for regulating the system. This agency is generally known as the central bank – an institution designed to regulate the quantity of money made available in the economy, called the money supply. Two of the most important central banks in Europe are the European Central Bank and the Bank of England. Other major central banks around the world include the US central bank – the Federal Reserve – and the Bank of Japan … The central bank of an economy has the power to increase or decrease the amount of currency in that economy." [179]

→ Central banks are responsible for regulating the money market system.
→ Central banks regulate the quantity of money made available in the economy.
→ The central bank of an economy has the power to increase or decrease the amount of money.

"If the central bank decides to increase the money supply, it can do this by creating currency and using it to buy bonds from the public in the bond market. After the purchase, the extra currency is in the hands of the public. Thus, an open-market purchase of bonds by the central bank increases the money supply." [180]

→ Central banks can print money and supply the money demand on the market.
→ Central banks can supply the printed money by buying bonds from the public in the market.
→ The public in the bond market are people, governments, and banks.
→ Now more money is on the market and can be spent for whatsoever.
→ A bond has an interest to pay to the Central Bank.

"If the central bank decides to decrease the money supply, it can do this by selling bonds from its portfolio to the public. After the sale, the currency it receives for the bonds is out of the hands of the public." [181]

→ A Central bank can sell bonds from its portfolio to the public: people, governments, banks.
→ People and institutions buy bonds and pay the corresponding money to the Central Bank.
→ The money from the sold bonds (by people, governments, and banks) is not anymore on the market.

---

[179] Mankiw (et al.), p. 622
[180] Mankiw (et al.), p. 622
[181] Mankiw (et al.), p. 622

"Central banks (…) are specifically charged with the duty to maintain inflation at or near an inflation target. The central bank should perhaps be thought of as the guardian of inflation stability." [182]

→ Central banks are in charge of maintaining inflation rate and responsible for inflation stability.
→ An Engineering and construction firm is planning and building a huge bridge; later the bridge crashes: Who is responsible for it?

"In pursuit of price stability, it aims to maintain inflation rates below but close to 2 per cent over the medium term." [183]

→ Central banks are in charge of maintaining inflation rate below, but close to 2%.
→ Central banks can only be responsible for this aim if they have the tool to act so.
→ If the inflation rate is higher than aimed, then the Central bank failed in their responsibility.
→ A high inflation rate produces economic damages. Who is responsible for these damages?
→ Somebody is responsible and this can't be the 'invisible hand'? Right?
→ If the Central bank is not responsible, what other factors are responsible for a high inflation rate?

"The primary objective of the ECB is to promote price stability throughout the Euro area and to design and implement monetary policy that is consistent with this objective." [184]

→ Price stability is destroyed in Europe, especially in some countries of the Euro-zone.
→ Somebody is responsible for the catastrophic economic crisis, increasing since 2008 and reaching in 2012 dramatic levels in Europe, and producing immense damages and destroying millions of businesses and lives.
→ The design and implementation of monetary policy from the European Central bank has completely failed.

"An important feature of the ECB and of the Euro-system in general is its independence. (…) Neither the ECB, nor a national central bank, nor any member of their decision-making bodies is allowed to seek or take

---

[182] Mankiw (et al.), p. 622
[183] Mankiw (et al.), p. 625
[184] Mankiw (et al.), p. 625

instructions from any external body, including any member governments or any European Union institutions." [185]

→ At first sight this independence rule sounds wonderful; but it is an ideal model.
→ As all neo-capitalistic theories thousand times identify this 'invisible hand' operating for the benefit of all parts in the market, this 'hand' must also be in some way in the ECB.
→ The declaration of independence does not include personal weaknesses or external manipulations from the monetary market provoking actions from the EBC.
→ As the 'invisible hand' is incredibly intelligent, clever and genius, this hand can create chain-actions, turbulences, similar to a war setting, forcing the enemy to act in determined ways.
→ All members of the ECB and the decision makers depend on the information they get on the table. Wrong information, distorted information, fabricated information, or lack of information can immensely influence the decision-making bodies.
→ This ideal of independence sounds like a Christmas fairy tale about the baby Jesus and the three holy kings bringing presents.

"(…) the Financial Policy Committee (is) charged with preventing credit and asset bubbles and overall financial stability, the Economic Crime Agency, focusing on serious economic crime such as corporate fraud, market-fixing and insider trading and the Consumer Protection and Markets Authority which manages protection of investors, market supervision and regulation and the conduct of banks and financial services." [186]

→ The Economic Crime Agency has completely failed to identify and stop all the fraud that already started many years before the collapse in 2008.
→ These experts of the ECA must have known early enough how agents can and sometimes try to act in a fraudulent way.

"The US Federal Reserve was created in 1913. The Fed is run by its Board of Governors, which has seven members appointed by the US president. Six of the governors have 14-year terms to give them independence from short-term political pressures when they formulate monetary policy, although the Chairman has a four-year term." [187]

---

[185] Mankiw (et al.), p. 625
[186] Mankiw (et al.), p. 626
[187] Mankiw (et al.), p. 626

➔ This institution must have immense power and even more responsibility for the well-being of many societies and corporations. But what do the last few years tell us about struggling American banks and bailouts?

➔ How many governments around the globe are their direct or indirect debtors? How much interest do they have to pay to the Fed?

Let's construct an example: "A Bank is only a depository institution – that is, it accepts deposits but does not make loans. The purpose of the bank is to give depositors a safe place to keep their money. Whenever a person deposits some money, the bank keeps the money in its vault until the depositor comes to withdraw it or writes a cheque against his or her balance. Deposits that banks have received but have not lent out are called reserves." [188]

➔ What is bad or wrong with such a banking concept?

➔ The customer pays a fee to put his money in a safe place. And that's it.

➔ The bank has several thousand clients that pay a fee to get their money to a safe place.

➔ This is a good business for a bank. Nobody needs such a bank with 1,000 m2 operation space and an impressive luxurious building of 300 meters height.

"If banks hold all deposits in reserve, banks do not influence the supply of money." [189]

➔ Nothing is wrong with that. Other banks could do the supply of money with a special business concept.

➔ Where is the mad idiot that said that money must always generate money? Hang this guy!

The Bond Market

Bond: A certificate of debt issued by a government or corporation that guarantees payment of the original investment plus interest by a specified future date.

Bond: "A bond is a fixed interest financial asset issued by governments, companies, banks, public utilities and other large entities. Bonds pay the bearer a fixed amount a specified end date. A discount bond pays the bearer only at the ending date, while a coupon bond pays the bearer a fixed amount over a specified interval (month, year, etc.) as well as paying a fixed amount at

---

[188] Mankiw (et al.), p. 627
[189] Mankiw (et al.), p. 628

the end date." [190]

"The biggest economic threat to bonds is rising interest rates. If you own a bond and interest rates go up, the value of your bond on the open market, with few exceptions, will go down." [191]

"When you buy a bond, either directly or through a mutual fund, you're lending money to the bond's issuer, who promises to pay you back the principal (or par value) when the loan is due (on the bond's maturity date).

When new bonds are issued, they typically carry coupon rates at or close to the prevailing market interest rate. Interest rates and bond prices have what's called an 'inverse relationship'.

➔ The problem starts here with the risk of the repayment. What happens if the borrower can't pay back the holder of the bond?

Investors constantly compare the returns on their current investments to what they could get elsewhere in the market. As market interest rates change, a bond's coupon rate – which, remember, is fixed – becomes more or less attractive to investors, who are therefore willing to pay more or less for the bond itself…many other factors go into determining the attractiveness of a particular bond: the length of time until the bond matures, whether or not its interest is taxable, the creditworthiness of its issuer, the likelihood that the issuer will pay off debt early, and more. (…) … change, be it major or minor, occurs in market interest rates virtually every business day." [192]

➔ For the next 1,000 years buyers and issuers of bonds are stressed every day as prices and interest rate on the market go up and down incessantly.
➔ There are winners and losers every day on the bond market. Humans (economists) have created this perverse stress parameter.
➔ The drive is: Every day I want to make 'the best of it', 'the highest possible profit'; 'I can't live with the fact that my neighbor gets a bit more than I from a cake.'
➔ The 'invisible hand' must be drunk everyday or has a compulsion of constantly fooling others. One party here is always the winner, and that's the traders and portfolio service institutes.

---

[190] http://economics.about.com/cs/economicsglossary/g/bond.htm
[191] http://stocks.about.com/od/understandingstocks/a/Bondint111004.htm
[192] http://www.wellsfargoadvantagefunds.com/wfweb/wf/education/choosing/bonds/rates.jsp

"There are literally millions of bonds traded in advanced economies. When large corporations or the national government, or even local governments need to borrow in order to finance the purchase of a new factory, a new jet fighter or a new school, they often do so by issuing bonds."[193]

→ We have here theoretically millions of risks of repayment from borrowers.
→ The first question is: why do governments need to borrow money?
→ The second question is: what do governments do with borrowed money?
→ And another question here is: Why do governments need to purchase a factory?
→ Most governments need money due to catastrophic mismanagement of their resources.
→ In the end, always the citizens must pay for government's indebtedness, capital and interest.

"Some bonds have short terms, such as a few months; while others have terms as long as 30 years." [194]

→ For short term bonds the borrowers always have a risk of being suffocated.

"The second important characteristic of a bond is its credit risk – the probability that the borrower will fail to pay some of the interest or principal. Such a failure to pay is called a default. Borrowers can (and sometimes do) default on their loans by declaring bankruptcy. When bond buyers perceive that the probability of default is high, they demand a higher interest rate to compensate them for this risk." [195]

→ Therefore borrowers can try to identify or construct a 'higher risk' in order to place a higher interest rate.
→ Also in this business the capitalistic maxim is: 'maximizing profit' with all available means.
→ All kind of indebtedness, loans and mortgages, have such a risk; with individuals, firms, corporations, and governments there is always a risk.
→ As the world is changing faster than ever before, nobody can plan a guaranteed future for 5, 10, 20 or 40 years.
→ All borrowers can and must give a guarantee, e.g. a property, if they have. Lenders can be sure that in 10-25 years they will get the property from many borrowers.

---

[193] Mankiw (et al.), p. 552
[194] Mankiw (et al.), p. 552
[195] Mankiw (et al.), p. 552

→ If lenders want to become owners of all kind of property to fully dominate the property market in the future, they can direct the market aiming for a 'fall' of millions of borrowers.

"Financially shaky corporations raise money by issuing junk bonds, which pay very high interest rates; in recent years some countries' debt has been graded as 'junk'. Buyers of bonds can judge credit risk by checking with various private agencies, such as Standard & Poor's." [196]

→ We would like to know which kind of corporations is meant here with 'financially shaky corporations'.
→ Junk bond: "A bond rated 'BB' or lower because of its high default risk." [197]
→ Private agencies, such as Standard & Poor's, can clandestinely create economic earthquakes in a country with the way they check and judge the risk of a borrower.
→ Buyers of bonds can have a clandestine interest in 'high risk' by borrowers in order to demand a higher interest or to direct the firm into a default in order to get the guarantees: assets, properties, land, raw resources.

The roadmap to destroy entire countries becomes herewith transparent.

The Money Multiplier

"When thinking about why saving and investment are so important for economic growth, the key point is that the amount of investment is ultimately limited by the amount of saving." [198]

→ The logical conclusion would be here: reduce consumption in order that others can increase with your savings their wealth by speculations.
→ Reducing consumption in the developed countries would not damage the genuine human values or the life standard, but much more it would save the planet for the future generations.
→ Here is an economic trap: Reducing consumption reduces the profit from production corporations. Increased saving, as a consequence of reduced consumption, is the 'raw material' for the money multiplier of banks. But where should the banks invest the huge amounts of savings (of people), if the corporations decrease in production, sales and profit?

Here we have the mad banker: "The (mad) banker may start to reconsider

---

[196] Mankiw (et al.), p. 552
[197] http://www.investopedia.com/terms/j/junkbond.asp#axzz1zqiqXTKP
[198] McConnell (et al.), p. 118

their policy of 100 per cent reserve banking. Leaving all that money sitting idle in their vaults seems unnecessary. Why not use some of it to make loans? Families buying houses, firms building new factories and students at university would all be happy to pay interest to borrow some of that money for a while." [199]

→ Imagine the compulsive servant of the king: he sees all that money sitting idle in vaults of the king and the servant thinks: let's make more of it (the best of it), obviously in his personal benefit. His question is: How can I get a slice of this cake?

"If the flow of new deposits is roughly the same as the flow of withdrawals, (… the bank) needs to keep only a fraction of its deposits in reserve. Thus, First European adopts a system called fractional-reserve banking." [200]

→ Every day a hundred clients bring money to the bank and the same amount of clients withdraws roughly the same amount of money every day.
→ The key for a bank to multiply money is: by law the bank must keep only a fraction of its deposits in reserve. With the remaining amount of money (from deposits) the bank can do business.

"The fraction of total deposits that a bank holds as reserves is called the reserve ratio. This ratio is determined by a combination of government regulation and bank policy." [201]

→ Governments have allowed and regulated that banks only need a 'reserve ratio' and with the remaining amount of deposits they can do business; obviously aiming to increase profit.
→ Profit of banking business is of high interest for governments.
→ The source that allows banks to do business with client deposits is the government – is it really?
→ Could it be that the banks forced governments to allow such risky business?

"The European Central Bank and the US Federal Reserve place a minimum on the amount of reserves that banks hold, called a reserve requirement…)." [202]

---

[199] Mankiw (et al.), p. 628
[200] Mankiw (et al.), p. 628
[201] Mankiw (et al.), p. 628
[202] Mankiw (et al.), p. 628

→ Here the superior bank institutes give a guarantee. How liable is this guarantee? The financial crisis since 2008 gives you the answer.

"When banks hold only a fraction of deposits in reserve, banks create money (by giving loans)." [203]

→ Now we get the point: Banks can make money with the money that customers have given in as a deposit.
→ The statement hides the fact that these clients get from the banks an interest for their placed deposits.

"Loans from (a bank) give the borrowers some currency and thus the ability to buy goods and services." [204]

→ The people wanting a loan get cash from the bank. Halleluiah, these people can buy goods and services without having worked for it.
→ The statement doesn't say that the borrowers have to pay an interest.

"The amount of money the banking system generates with each euro of reserves is called the money multiplier." [205]

→ Now, we have this machine that creates money: banks multiply their amount of money.
→ Banks pay e.g. 3% interest to the depositors and demand 18% interest for the loan they give to people. Gross profit: 15%, inflation not considered.
→ If we multiply the amount of deposits up to a level of $10 million, $100 million, or even $1,000 million then we come closer to the real gross profit: the bigger the game, the higher the profit up to millions or hundreds of millions, depends on the size and amount of branch offices in a country or around the world. Using part of the profit to give new loans accelerates and increases the incoming profit.
→ 'Money multiplier' means: Accumulating money by taking away money from others.

"The fact that the future is uncertain, investment projects sometimes produce disappointing results or even fail totally. Macroeconomics has to take into account expectations about the future." [206]

---

[203] Mankiw (et al.), p. 629
[204] Mankiw (et al.), p. 629
[205] Mankiw (et al.), p. 630
[206] McConnell (et al.), p. 120

→ Indeed the future is uncertain; but what is certain is that humanity will experience a terrible doom if they follow these insane economic preachers that permanently focus on growth.

→ Chapter 3 shows where the neo-capitalistic understanding will lead in 35-40 years if drastic measures are not taken very soon. Fascinated from the money multiplier the 'macro-economists' play the blind cow.

"Expectations therefore have a large effect on economic growth since increased pessimism will lead to less current investment and, subsequently, less future consumption." [207]

→ The author accuses critical experts (about consumption) as 'pessimists'.

→ Less investment will lead to less profit for banks and corporations.

→ People can invest their savings in an own business or in sustainable living.

→ Less future consumption will lead to happy people and peaceful societies.

Investment: Another Method to Multiply Money

"Because capital is a produced factor of production, a society can change the amount of capital it has. If today the economy produces a large quantity of new capital goods, then tomorrow it will have a larger stock of capital and be able to produce more of all types of goods and services. Thus, one way to raise future productivity is to invest more current resources in the production of capital." [208]

→ What is the difference between 'capital' and 'money'? Money we understand as the coins and the bank notes. 'Capital' we understand as an amount of money.

→ 'Capital is a produced factor of production': This a bit unclear. We can say: Production produces capital; which means: Profit is produced capital. And we can say: Capital is a factor used for production. The meaning here is not about 'printing money'.

→ 'The economy produces a large quantity of new capital goods': What or who is meant here with 'the economy'? What is meant with new capital goods? The author writes in a confusing way. We can say: Capital is a good'. We can speak about 'new' capital which means: 'a new amount of capital'. We also can say: The more production, the higher the profit = amount of money (or: capital, or new money, new capital). It's not about

---

[207] McConnell (et al.), p. 120
[208] Mankiw (et al.), p. 534

'printing money'.

→ The author also says: The more (stock of) capital, the more of all kind of products can be produced. To increase production can be achieved by increasing the amount of profit. In other words: Profit can be used for expanding production.

→ The picture can be extended: A firm makes profit and can invest this profit in more production. Or: A corporation makes profit; shareholders get a slice of the cake; and then the shareholders can invest this profit in production firms aiming to make more profit.

→ Investment is discussed here as a tool to permanently increase capital with profit margins. In a system it becomes a wonder machine that produces money. For the owner of capital the machine functions without actively working for such automatic multiplication.

→ This machine should be much more about multiplication of 'bread' for billions of humans.

"The correlation between growth and investment, although not perfect, is strong." [209]

→ In other words: as nothing is perfect, the endless profit-game could also lead to a fatal loss.

"In poor countries, workers lack even the most rudimentary tools and, as a result, have low productivity. Small amounts of capital investment would substantially raise these workers' productivity" [210]

→ This is indeed a strong appeal to the distribution market: Poor countries (or small firms in pool countries) need capital, but they don't have.

→ Poor countries can never, for eternity ever, get out of their misery as they don't have capital and can't create capital.

"An organization that tries to encourage the flow of capital to poor countries is the **World Bank**. This international organization obtains funds from the world's advanced industrialized countries, and uses these resources to make loans to less developed countries so that they can invest in roads, sewage systems, schools and other types of capital." [211]

The mission is excellent, but there are traps: On the one side the interest for loans suffocate their economy. And on the other side the capitalistic market

---

[209] Mankiw (et al.), p. 535
[210] Mankiw (et al.), p. 537
[211] Mankiw (et al.), p. 539

pays as little as possible for their products. As a consequence these countries can never pay back the loan. They must 'sell' their raw resources or rent them for 100 years at a miserable price to the lenders. And here we are in the middle of the capitalistic neocolonialism and exploitation of poor countries. The author doesn't give an insight here. He can't debunk the evil game!

The Mortgage Market

In 2012, Spain has over one million new properties, partly not finished, and an additional one million properties for sale. Some years ago the banks offered 120% mortgage and 40 years for repayment. The prices of the properties have been and still are in the average 65% over-valued. Hundreds of thousands were running to get such a property. Even investors were running for projects of urbanizations; and they also got the best mortgage options. Many banks sold huge amounts of mortgages and got a commission fee. Probably all borrowers had to give a guarantee, for example the home of their parents or land if they had.

A hypothesis could be: there was and is a roadmap from the supreme economic masters. They all knew that many buyers (borrowers) and constructors of urbanizations (owners) will land in a default, called 'bankruptcy'. Now these banks become the masters of the property market; they have the homes and give the mortgage. The day will come, when the banks own 80% of the property market. – This is a way to exploit entire nations and folks; in the end to dominate (dictate) entire governments and folks. Roadmap or not, the reality shows this development in progressive motion.

➔ In both cases, launching a military war or an economic war, the masters always calculate with high damages and victims also on their own side.
➔ More than a hundred million people in America and Europe are today victims of this evil economic war strategically triggered with the 'financial crisis' in 2008.
➔ There are plenty of facts (the results) that show the 'financial crisis' was fabricated in the interest of national continental and global dominance.

The Stock Market

"Stock represents ownership in a firm and is, therefore, a claim to the profits that the firm makes.

A stock is also commonly referred to as a share or as an equity." [212]

→ There are hundreds of millions of small shareholders with an investment of $500 here and $1,000 there, or $5,000 elsewhere. To call this 'ownership' is ridiculous.

→ A claim to the profit a firm makes doesn't guarantee getting a slice of this cake.

→ The value of a share can increase, but also decrease and this down to the bottom.

→ Shares include full risk for capital and profit margin.

→ Today an individual can by with $1,000 an excellent appliance. Let's imagine, the value of a share of $1,000 will be the same in 10 years. But due to inflation, the $1,000 in 10 years will have a purchase value reduced by 30%, not enough to get the same appliance.

The Libor / Euribor Scam

"Libor stands for the London interbank offered rate and is the benchmark for interest rates in the City. Sixteen banks are asked to predict what rate of interest they will be able to borrow at the next day. They send their predictions to Thomson Reuters, which calculates and publishes the benchmarks for the British Bankers Association (BBA).

Euribor is the continental equivalent and has followed a similar pattern.

Thousands of financial products are priced on the Libor (Euribor) rate because it is supposed to represent the real cost of money to the banks.

After Northern Rock went bust and there was a suspicion that Barclays was in trouble, a group of traders deliberately drove down the Libor rate. The lower the rate, the more it appeared that Barclays was healthy and able to survive the credit crunch. At other times, traders colluded with rival bank staff to make profits by driving up the interest rate.

The Financial Services Authority (FSA) says in its 40-page document on the affair that Barclays was involved in manipulating the rate from 2005 and stopped only in 2009. Managers in the division where they worked knew about the practice and compliance officers were informed.

Several banks are under investigation, including Citibank, Deutsche Bank and Royal Bank of Scotland." [213]

---

[212] Mankiw (et al.), p. 552
[213] http://www.guardian.co.uk/business/2012/jun/29/barclays-libor-scandal-faq

➜ It's always the same: "I want to make the best of it … with all means." – Even with a swindle.

"The Libor rate affects about $800 trillion dollars of contracts and all sorts of financial instruments globally, according to experts. Investors of all sizes use the rate as a basis for a variety of financial products; homeowners mortgages, consumers' credit cards and even city governments use derivatives contracts tied to Libor when issuing some bonds." [214]

But nobody really knows how big the derivatives market is with estimates ranging from $600 trillion all the way up to $1.5 quadrillion…

➜ But the actual global GDP in 2011 for example was only around $70 trillion.[215] So what are these hundreds or thousands of trillions of derivates? It's a balloon of hot air, invented by financial institutions and passed around on the markets like a hot potato.

➜ Warren Buffet even goes as far as calling them 'derivatives are financial weapons of mass destruction'.[216]

Financial Intermediaries

"Financial Intermediaries are financial institutions through which savers can indirectly provide funds to borrowers. The term intermediary reflects the role of these institutions in standing between savers and borrowers. Here we consider two of the most important financial intermediaries – banks and investment funds." [217]

➜ The intermediary gets money for this service and this is a cost that especially the small investors, the 'normal' citizens, have to consider.

"Most buyers of stocks and bonds prefer to buy those issued by larger, more familiar companies. The small businessman, therefore, most likely finances his business expansion with a loan from a bank. … A primary function of banks is to take in deposits from people who want to save and use these deposits to make loans to people who want to borrow. Banks pay depositors interest on their deposits and charge borrowers slightly higher interest on their loans. The difference between these rates of interest covers the banks' costs and

---

[214] http://www.forbes.com/sites/halahtouryalai/2012/07/12/libor-lawsuits-are-piling-up-and-could-cost-billions-banks-brace-for-another-big-legal-battle/
[215] http://www.google.com/publicdata/
[216] http://www.fintools.com/docs/Warren%20Buffet%20on%20Derivatives.pdf
[217] Mankiw (et al.), p. 553

returns some profit to the owners of the banks." [218]

→ The important issue here is: Banks demand from borrowers a slightly higher interest on their loans. What is 'slightly' in real figures?
→ If depositors get 3% interest and borrowers (small firms) pay 8% interest or for consumption people pay 18% interest, is this 'slightly higher'?
→ What would happen with the banking business, if consumer loans wouldn't be allowed anymore?
→ Living on consumer loans is anyway not a sustainable economic way of living and it creates a lot of losers and misery.

Investment Funds

"An investment fund is an institution that sells shares to the public and uses the proceeds to buy a selection, of portfolio, of various types of shares, bonds, or both shares and bonds. ... If the value of the portfolio rises, the shareholder benefits; if the value of the portfolio falls, the shareholder suffers the loss. The value of any single stock or bond is tied to the fortunes of one company, holding a single kind of stock or bond is very risky." [219]

→ Portfolio: A private investor can become 'owner' of 5-20 corporations, each with a share value of $200-500.
→ The investor is completely excluded from transparency; the action is thoroughly anonymous or in other words, the investor is an irrelevant 'owner'.
→ The investor can suffer a loss of 50% with part of his shares (some different companies) and 50% gain with the other shares (the other different companies). Who is always the final winner?

"The company operating the investment fund charges shareholders a fee, usually between 0.5 and 2.0 per cent of assets each year." [220]

→ The small investor (or all investors) must calculate this cost added to the loss of profit slices and loss of share value, and the inflation rate.
→ The company receiving the money in exchange with shares or bonds has no liability and never has any risk related to this 'business' with (small) share- or bond- holders.
→ This kind of business is a profound exploitation of shareholders where in most cases only the company is the winner, even if the company goes

---

[218] Mankiw (et al.), p. 553
[219] Mankiw (et al.), p. 555
[220] Mankiw (et al.), p. 555

bankrupt.

→ It is symptomatic that the author does not reveal this picture of risks and exploitation

"The bond market, the stock market, banks and investment funds – have the role of coordinating the economy's saving and investment." [221]

→ This role must be questioned as the liability of companies (corporations) is a criticality, and especially as the traders and financial intermediaries always have a guaranteed income and profit from this kind of 'coordination'.
→ The 'role of coordinating' essentially is making as much profit as possible from such trades.

"To keep things simple, we assume that the economy has only one financial market, called the market for loanable funds. All savers go to this market to deposit their saving, and all borrowers go to this market to get their loans." [222]

→ Making things simple can help to understand the micro-elements or the structural dynamics in the machine, but it also can trivialize and hide all the criticalities of such businesses.

Banks and Bankruptcy

"If a large number of account holders all wanted to withdraw their money as cash the bank is unlikely to have the funds to give to everyone and it would effectively be 'bankrupt'." [223]

→ The most important question is why a large number of account holders would suddenly want to withdraw their money as cash.

"A well-functioning banking system is very important for economic growth because in most countries it's the principal way in which savings are channeled into business investment spending. If a country's citizens trust their banks, they will place their savings in bank deposits, which the banks will then lend to their business customers. But if people don't trust their banks, they will hoard gold or foreign currency, keeping their savings in safe deposit boxes or under the mattress, where it cannot be turned into productive investment spending." [224]

---

[221] Mankiw (et al.), p. 558-559
[222] Mankiw (et al.), p. 561
[223] Mankiw (et al.), p. 630
[224] Krugman, p. 375

→ There is no 'well working banking system' today as everybody can read in the newspapers every day.

→ Savings are channeled into business investment spending: into corporations!

→ Small firms only get a slice of this cake if they can give guarantees: ask small firms in Europe and elsewhere about the guarantees they can give!

→ People do not place a lot of trust in banks, especially in Greece, Italy, Spain (and elsewhere). Billions of Euros have been transferred to other countries due to lack of trust in banks.

→ The compulsive greed is everywhere: 'Spend your money in productive investment.'

Banks and Central Bank

"Banks create money in a system of fractional-reserve banking; the central bank's control of the money supply is indirect." [225]

→ The risk of the system of fractional-reserve banking hits all the people that have deposited their money in the bank.

→ It's the bank that creates here the risk, not the account holders.

→ Central Banks are not infallible and never as independent as they pretend to be.

"If the central bank wants to increase the money supply, it can create currency and use it to buy bonds from the public in the bond market. After the purchase, the extra currency is in the hands of the public." [226]

→ What are the arguments and motives that a central bank wants to increase the money supply?

→ Is there an economic theory or 'law' that makes this supply guaranteed efficient?

→ Is 'in the hands of the public' a true reflection of what happens? Or is it much rather that this 'extra currency' is then in the hands of a few corporations, investors and wealthy individuals who held bonds?

"If, on the other hand, the central bank wants to decrease the money supply, it can sell bonds from its portfolio to the public. After the sale, the currency it

---

[225] Mankiw (et al.), p. 630
[226] Mankiw (et al.), p. 630-631

receives for the bonds is out of the hands of the public." [227]

➔ What are the arguments and motives that a central bank wants to decrease the money supply?
➔ What are the intentioned aims? Does is always work the way they expect?

"The central bank of an economy will set an interest rate at which it is willing to lend to commercial banks on a short-term basis."

➔ Even the Central Banks are money producers.
➔ What are the criteria for setting the interest rate if they are also money multipliers?

"Central bank nowadays more often use a slightly more sophisticated form of open-market operations that involves buying bonds or other assets from banks and at the same time agreeing to sell them back later. When it does this, the central bank has effectively made a loan and taken the bonds or other assets as collateral or security on the loan … The interest rate that the central bank charges on the loan is the refinancing rate." [228]

➔ The statement about 'refinancing rate' does not make the decision making of their interest rate transparent.
➔ The central bank effectively gives loans and takes in guarantees (securities).

"Because deposits and withdrawals at banks can fluctuate randomly, some banks may find that they have an excess of reserves one day (i.e. their reserve ratio is above the level the bank considers prudent or above the minimum reserve ratio, or both), while other banks may find that they are short of reserves and their reserve ratio is too low.

➔ An excess of reserves makes the servant of the king mad as he always wants 'to make more of it' or 'the best it can' for multiplying money.

"Therefore, the commercial banks in an economy will generally lend money to one another on a short-term basis – overnight to a couple of weeks – so that banks with excess reserves can lend them to banks who have inadequate reserves to cover their lending." [229]

---

[227] Mankiw (et al.), p. 630-631
[228] Mankiw (et al.), p. 631
[229] Mankiw (et al.), p. 631

→ Lending money to one another on an 'overnight' basis is really an expression of this compulsive servant: not an hour or day can he leave an amount of money in peace.

→ If a bank needs to borrow money from another bank for a day or for some days, then there is a fire in the house.

→ Here they can extinguish a fire with a high risk to produce somewhere else a new fire.

"If there is a general shortage of liquidity in the money market (because the banks together have done a lot of lending), then the short-term interest rate at which they lend to one another will begin to rise, while it will begin to fall if there is excess liquidity among banks. Suppose, for example, that there is a shortage of liquidity in the market because the banks have been increasing their lending and they need to increase their reserves. A commercial bank may then attempt to obtain liquidity from the central bank by selling assets to the central bank and at the same time agreeing to purchase them back a short time later." [230]

→ How does it come that banks lend too much money? It's greed!

→ There is a law needed that regulates the reserves in a way that eliminates the risks of fire.

"The central bank may also influence the money supply with reserve requirements, which are regulations on the minimum amount of reserves that banks must hold against deposits. Reserve requirements influence how much money the banking system can create with each euro of reserves." [231]

→ The ongoing financial crisis in 2012 shows us that the central banks have not done their job correctly.

"… the less money households deposit, the less reserves banks have, and the less money the banking system can create." [232]

→ The way banks create money is extremely risky.

→ The banking system must completely revise their business concepts.

The Big Picture about the European Bank Sector [233]

---

[230] Mankiw (et al.), p. 631
[231] Mankiw (et al.), p. 632
[232] Mankiw (et al.), p. 633
[233] http://www.ebf-fbe.eu/uploads/Facts%20&%20Figures%202011.pdf

- "By the end of 2010, the number of banks in the EU: 6,825.
- During 2010, banks' assets grew by 3.5%.
- In 2010, European banks registered a high deposit growth of nearly 8%, just over €17 trillion, and loan growth of 4.4%, approaching €17.7 trillion.
- Loan to deposit ratio stood at 103%."

→ During 2010, banks' assets grew by 3.5%: How much is the absolute figure?

→ Deposits: €17 trillion – How much interest do they pay for such an amount of deposits during one year?

→ Loans: €17.7 trillion – How much interest do they get for this amount of loan during one year?

The same source gives us more information: "After an era of high spending and debt, EU citizens and businesses started putting more money into bank deposits; European banks registered a high growth in deposits of almost 8% in 2010, reaching €17.1 trillion. This phenomenon can be partly explained by the fact that the Deposit Guarantee Schemes in the EU now amount to €100,000, a significant increase in most Member States compared with the heterogeneous pre-crisis regime (of at least €22,000)."

The ECB also reports: "…that the total number of non-cash payments in the EU, using all types of instruments, increased by 4.4% to 86.4 billion in 2010 compared with the previous year. Card payments accounted for 39% of all transactions, while credit transfers accounted for 28% and direct debits for 25%. In 2010, the EU-27 average number of transactions per EU Member State was 3.2 billion. In this period, the number of transactions using all types of payment instruments, per million of inhabitants, was registered at the level of 172,836 (it was 163,527 in 2009); an increase of 5.7% per annum."

→ Non-cash payment: 86.4 billion in 2010: How much did they charge in total?

And more insight from this source: "The number of credit transfers within the EU in 2010 increased by 3.8% to 24 billion. The importance of paper-based transactions continued to decrease, with the ratio of paper-based transactions to non-paper-based transactions falling to around one to five. The number of cards with a payment function in the EU remained relatively stable at 726.7 million compared with 725.2 million in 2009. This represented around 1.45 payment cards per EU inhabitant. The number of card transactions rose by 6.7% to 33.9 billion, with a total value of €1.8 trillion, which corresponds to an average value of around €52 per card transaction. In 2010, the average number of card transactions per million EU inhabitants was around 68,051, i.e. 5,000 more than in 2009."

➜ The number of cards with a payment function (EU): 726.7 million: How much do they charge for card issues in total?

Toxic Debt

"Many banks borrow the funds they need from the interbank market. As the sub-prime market collapsed, the exposure to bad debt started to become more obvious and a number of banks reported significant write-downs and losses." [234]

➜ This is an extreme trivialization of the real 'businesses' and 'business methods' during the last years in the banking world.
➜ It also trivializes the immense damages within the banking world and ignores the fact that citizens pay for this evil doing.
➜ The arrogance here is that it hides the hundred million people that suffered losses and extreme damages in their life due to banking practices.
➜ Selling toxic debt (and other practices such as betting, gambling, and 'casino' of all kind) have destroyed entire societies, countries, and the future of a majority of the young generation.

Classical Theory of Inflation

"A rise in the price level means a lower value of money because each unit of money now buys a smaller quantity of goods and services." [235]

➜ Prices go up and down, some more, others less; and some prices remain unchanged.
➜ Price changes also can happen in some regions in a country while in other areas not.
➜ Prices of goods for needs have higher importance and impact in human's life than 'wants'.
➜ From this point of view 'a lower value of money' is very relative.
➜ If prices go up, then for most goods cheaper substitutes are available.
➜ Some goods are produced in better quality or with more additives, therefore have higher price.
➜ Making a lot of noise about general price changes is not the appropriate reaction.

---

[234] Mankiw (et al.), p. 636-637
[235] Mankiw (et al.), p. 643-644

"Demand for money reflects how much wealth people want to hold in liquid form. Many factors influence the quantity of money demands. The amount of currency that people hold in their wallets, for instance, depends on how much they rely on credit cards and on whether an automatic cash dispenser is easy to find." [236]

→ Factors that influence the quantity of money demands are: greed, to have without previous working for it, impatience, obsessions, compensations, etc.
→ Credit cards are another big problem: partly it's a loan problem and partly it has costs: Who profits from each credit card payment of consumers?

"Imagine that the economy is in equilibrium and then, suddenly, the central bank doubles the supply of money by printing large amounts of money." [237]

→ Such an example is absolutely unreal and will not happen except in absolutely disastrous economic situations of a country.

"When an increase in the money supply makes Euros more plentiful, the result is an increase in the price level that makes each euro less valuable. ... the quantity of money available in the economy determines the value of money, and growth in the quantity of money is the primary cause of inflation." [238]

→ The key question is: Is it really the amount of money supply that produces (quasi mechanically) an over-all increase of prices?
→ Probably the problem lies in the world of businesses: Owners of businesses see that people have (more) money and then they simply increase their prices.
→ The primary cause of inflation is not the growth in the quantity of money; it is greed and abuse of consumer's financial potential.

"The greater demand for goods and services causes the prices of goods and services to increase. The increase in the price level, in turn, increases the quantity of money demanded because people are using more Euros for every transaction." [239]

→ The greater demand for goods and services (e.g. America, Europe) is an

---

[236] Mankiw (et al.), p. 644
[237] Mankiw (et al.), p. 645
[238] Mankiw (et al.), p. 646
[239] Mankiw (et al.), p. 647

expression of a sick capitalistic society. The consumer mentality is not healthy and never sustainable.

"When the central bank doubles the money supply, the price level doubles, the euro wage doubles, and all other euro values double." [240]

→ This is again an unreal example, except in cases of disastrous society development.

Hyperinflation

Indeed, "hyperinflation is generally defined as inflation that exceeds 50 per cent per month. This means that the price level increases more than 100-fold over the course of a year." [241]

→ It's time to identify the manipulators that destroy societies through the monetary system.

"The governments of these countries are using money creation as a way to pay for their spending. When the government wants to build roads, pay salaries to police officers, or give transfer payments to the poor or elderly, it first has to raise the necessary funds. Normally, the government does this by levying taxes, such as income and sales taxes, and by borrowing from the public by selling government bonds. Yet the government can also pay for spending by simply printing the money it needs." [242]

→ The causes of hyperinflation also lie in the hands of incompetent politicians, spending their money in many unimaginable mad ways.
→ It's urgent time to identify this 'invisible hand' that indirectly has its fingers in governmental matters.

"When the government prints money, the price level rises, and the Euros in your wallet are less valuable. Thus, the inflation tax is like a tax on everyone who holds money ... Nearly all **hyperinflations** follow the same pattern: the government has high spending, limited ability to borrow, inadequate tax revenue (perhaps because the level of income in the economy is low, or there is widespread tax evasion or a poorly developed tax system or a combination of all these factors), and as a result, it turns to the printing press to pay for its spending. The massive increases in the quantity of money lead to massive

---

[240] Mankiw (et al.), p. 648
[241] Mankiw (et al.), p. 650
[242] Mankiw (et al.), p. 651

inflation." [243]

→ Why does tax evasion happen?
→ Why do governments spend too much money?
→ There is a systemic fault in the tax systems.

"When prices rise, each Euro of income buys fewer goods and services. Thus, it might seem that inflation directly lowers living standards." [244]

→ For the Western world, or parts of it, there is a need to find a lower living standard.

"The primary cause of inflation is simply growth in the quantity of money. When the central bank creates money in large quantities, the value of money falls quickly. To maintain stable prices, the central bank must maintain strict control over the money supply." [245]

→ What and who is behind 'growth in the quantity of money'?
→ Better is to strictly discipline the citizens, firms and corporations.

---

[243] Mankiw (et al.), p. 651
[244] Mankiw (et al.), p. 653
[245] Mankiw (et al.), p. 661

2.5. Public Costs

2.5.1. Government Expenditures

Let's first have an overview taking an example about the United States:

"Government plays two general roles in the economy. It's both a referee (setting the rules that determine relations between business and households) and an actor (collecting money in taxes and spending that money on projects such as defense and education)." [246]

→ Rules that determine relations between business and households are indispensable. But:
→ There are rules that are inefficient or counter-productive.
→ There is a huge lack of adequate rules especially for corporations (banking included).
→ Rules have no effect if reality does not comply due to lack of control.
→ If governments are forced by lobbyism and other 'channels' to create rules or to avoid setting specific rules, then this 'general role' is dictated by the economic masters.

Expenditures of State and Local Governments: [247]

(a) Income

Intergovernmental	21%
Property	16%
Individual and corporate income tax	15%
Sales Tax	19%
Trust revenue	19%
Other	10%

(b) Expenditures

---

[246] Colander (et al.), p. 66
[247] Colander (et al.), p. 67

Education	29%
Public welfare	15%
Health and hospitals	7%
Other	12%
Unemployment compensation and retirement	8%
Environment and housing	7%
Administration and interest	8%
Transportation	6%
Public safety	8%

➔ We can't discuss here the mentioned figures (percentage). Something is anyway wrong here: Education can never be 29%. 'Other' is unspecific. And 'public welfare' can include many things.

➔ The example shows a general problem with such statistics: not compelling, not meaningful.

"… Income taxes make up about 44% of the federal government's revenue, and Social Security taxes make up about 36 percent. That's 80 percent of the federal government's revenues … The federal government's two largest categories of spending are income security and health and education, with expenditures on national defense close behind." [248]

➔ With the increasing financial crisis (2012) and all the new laws and austerity measures (America, Europe) the figures are not significant.

➔ Expenditures for health are too high and can be reduced by 50-65% with the right public education, the adequate personal education, a society living human values, and an environment free of contamination and other high risk factors.

➔ The cost for national defense includes imperialistic wars as we have them again since 1991 from the Balkans to North Africa, Middle East and Far East. An absolute lunacy!

Income and Expenditure of Federal Government

(a) Income

Social Security taxes and contributions	36%
Corporate income taxes	14%
Excise taxes and other	6%

---

[248] Colander, p. 67

Individual income taxes	44%

(b) Expenditures

Health and education	27%
Income security	31%
National defense	20%
Other	11%
Interest	11%

How can we understand all these figures? It doesn't say much:

- Health and education should be separated.
- 'Other': doesn't say anything.
- Why do they mix here 'administration and interest'?
- Unemployment compensation and retirement: should be separated.
- 'Intergovernmental' doesn't allow drawing a distinct content.
- Public welfare: Who knows what and why they spend money here?
- Environment and housing: very vague and should be separated.
- National defense 20%: That's insane and outrageous considering the poverty in US.
- Interest 11%: Immense; sounds insane. Who gets the interest?

→ In fact with such a data overview nobody can understand what all the figures include.
→ This is not a scientific approach; it shows a deviating strategy: say something, but nothing.
→ With such vague parameters politicians can't operate efficiently.
→ Behind such general figures lies deceit and cheat, and manipulations.

Example: Federal Government Spending in Germany:

- General public services
- Health, environment, sport, recreation
- Food, agriculture and forestry water
- Supplies, trade, services
- Economic cooperation and development
- Transport and communications
- Housing, regional planning and local community services
- Commercial enterprises, general real property and capital assets
- Education, training, research and development
- Social security and benefits

- General financial management

Source: German Federal Ministry of Finance. [249]

"The deadweight losses that result when taxes distort the decisions that people make. The administrative burdens that taxpayers bear as they comply with the tax laws … An efficient tax system is one that imposes small deadweight losses and small administrative burdens … Taxes have the effect of changing people's behaviour." [250]

Transformed in simple words we can discuss here:

→ Deadweight loss measures the inefficiency caused from a market distortion.
→ Taxes influence the consumer behavior and with that their way of living.
→ The higher the taxes, the less money people have for personal spending.
→ The efficiency of tax systems must be questioned; it may be completely inefficient.
→ The more taxes come in, the more governments go mad in dealing with money.

"The deadweight loss is the inefficiency that a tax creates as people allocate resources according to the tax incentive rather than the true costs and benefits of the goods and services that they buy and sell." [251]

→ Taxes create inefficiency as people manage their budget according to the tax level.
→ People consider costs and benefits of goods and services within the frame of their taxes.
→ Anti-thesis: People make their budget according to the prices of goods and services, independent from tax level (or tax changes).
→ This statement is vague and lacks proof.

"In any country, tax policy always generates some of the most heated political debates. The heat is rarely fuelled by questions of efficiency. Instead, it usually arises from disagreements over how the tax burden should be distributed." [252]

The intrinsic problems, behind these 'unsolvable' disputes, are:

---

[249] Mankiw (et al.), p. 250
[250] Mankiw (et al.), p. 251
[251] Mankiw (et al.), p. 251
[252] Mankiw (et al.), p. 254

→ It's about distribution of the cake and never about causes of non-productive costs.
→ Governments spend too much money for very questionable projects.
→ Governments spend too much money in a very irresponsible way.
→ Governments spend far too much money in unnecessary defense and war projects.
→ The state administration is not only inefficient, but also extremely costly.
→ Too many politicians have no skills for a reasonable money management.
→ Politicians and ministers deal with money like the masses of stupid people.
→ Governments do not sufficiently inform their citizens about money matters.
→ There is probably everywhere a kind of soft bribery or hard core corruption.
→ People don't trust in politicians and governments; they have serious reason for doing so.

"Vertical equity states that taxpayers with a greater ability to pay taxes should contribute a larger amount. Horizontal equity states that taxpayers with similar abilities to pay should contribute the same amount." [253]

→ There are taxpayers with a greater ability to pay taxes.
→ There are taxpayers with extremely limited ability to pay taxes.
→ The word 'taxpayer' ignores that even poor people pay taxes via VAT (16-25%).

"If taxes are based on ability to pay, then richer taxpayers should pay more than poorer taxpayers. But how much more should the rich pay?" [254]

→ This is a wrong approach to solve the problem of 'how much more should the rich pay'.
→ The problem is that governments spend far too much money for unnecessary projects.
→ Charging the rich with taxes over 25% turns them into enemies of governments and society.
→ The not-satisfiable arrogance and greed of governments creates immense problems.

The design of the tax system: "Indirect tax is a tax that is levied on goods and services bought. Direct tax is a tax that is levied directly on a person's

[253] Mankiw (et al.), p. 255
[254] Mankiw (et al.), p. 255

income." [255]

➔ The real taxes people pay: 'VAT + tax'; or for firms: 'VAT + tax + other fees'; 'other fees' are for example VAT for the rent of premises, fees for licenses and accreditation memberships.
➔ Those who get a comfortable wage are on a tax level of 25-35% + VAT = 43-55%. Sick!

"Almost everyone agrees that equity and efficiency are the two most important goals of the tax system." [256]

➔ Does really 'almost everyone' agree? That's a manipulative statement.
➔ Equity and efficiency in exploitative feudalistic tax systems can never be reached.
➔ Nobody likes to give money to arrogant, ignorant, incompetent, and false institutions.
➔ An arrogant, ignorant, incompetent, neurotic, and false institution can never be efficient.
➔ Even a few minutes in a bar to have a beer or coffee costs a tax! Isn't that insane?
➔ In a decadent society where the truth is lost and hard performance doesn't lead to significant wealth, and high success depends on radical neo-capitalistic principles, there is never a solution for equity and efficiency of the tax system. 'Success depends on each one' is a fairy tale!

Governmental spending: "Budget deficit is an excess of government spending over government receipts. Budget surplus is an excess of government receipts over government spending." [257]

➔ Most governments have a chronic excess of spending.
➔ Governments live self-created debt-bombs of a capacity compared with nukes.
➔ The citizens of most countries would wish to see a governmental budget surplus.
➔ The failure of governmental expenditures is absolutely outrageous.

2.5.2. Pension Payment

"Executive Summary:

---

[255] Mankiw (et al.), p. 243
[256] Mankiw (et al.), p. 260
[257] Mankiw (et al.), p. 245

156

The financial implications of rising longevity, in particular with regard to pensions, pose significant challenges to society. The re-allocation of the financial burden among governments, businesses, and individuals will significantly affect pension systems.

The upward trend in life expectancy and the consequent aging population has led to large unanticipated retirement costs for businesses and governments, particularly in developed countries.

Governments have increased the long-term sustainability of the public finances by reducing the future generosity of state pension entitlements and encouraging greater private sector involvement.

In response to government initiatives, corporate sponsors have closed their defined benefit pension schemes, and moved employees into defined contribution schemes—thus shifting investment and longevity risk onto individuals.

To deal with the legacy of previous commitments, managers have created a range of new solutions for the financial markets, from hedging liabilities to passing all or part of the risk and responsibility to specialist third-party providers.

A huge increase in life expectancy is one of the great achievements of the human race over the past two centuries. Increased longevity has transformed both individuals' lives and their societies, with the most marked changes taking place in the developed world. Actual increases in life expectancy have been far more substantial than previously projected, with the result that governments, businesses, financial markets, and individuals must radically readjust their plans.

Moreover, the current trend shows no sign of leveling off. For example, between 1981 and 2000 the life expectancy for 65-year-old males in the United Kingdom increased by approximately three months for every year, and future life expectancy is widely expected to continue to increase.

Therefore, it is increasingly important that governments, businesses, and individuals consider the economic, societal, and financial implications of an aging society in diverse but important policy areas such as pensions, health care, and long-term care provision. For example, pension liabilities increase by 3% or more for every added year of life expectancy." [258]

- Pension payment is one of the biggest parameters in the governmental expenditures. It affects also the consumers' purchase ability (working people) due to the monthly payments (social security fee).
- The (Western) pension concept is first a matter of modern lifestyle, the collective organization of living together in an organized society; and not a matter of money.
- With the huge increase in life expectancy, the entire population of modern societies is called (challenged) to re-think the value of their living concepts, of human life in general.
- "Working makes free" has an important meaning: works provides satisfaction. Work gives people a feeling to be useful. Work is a self-expression. Working strengthens self-esteem. Working forms a self-identity. Working has a meaning in itself. (Amongst others)
- The modern economy has taken away from the elderly generation these human values; has put them on a storage track, or in a waiting room for the 'exitus'.
- The attitude is: "You are useless, nasty, and a molesting factor in our economic life. We don't want to be reminded that we too, one day will be old. Therefore we pay you in order to get rid of you."

2.5.3. Unemployment Compensation

"Unemployment benefits are payments made by the state or other authorized bodies to unemployed people. Benefits may be based on a compulsory para-governmental insurance system. Depending on the jurisdiction and the status of the person, those sums may be small, covering only basic needs (thus a form of basic welfare), or may compensate the lost time proportionally to the previous earned salary. They often are part of a larger social security scheme.

Unemployment benefits are generally given only to those registering as unemployed, and often on conditions ensuring that they seek work and do not currently have a job." [259]

- Unemployment compensation is one of the biggest parameter in the governmental expenditures. It affects also the consumers' purchase ability (working people) due to the monthly payments (social security fee).
- The (Western) unemployment compensation concept is first a matter of modern lifestyle, the collective organization of living together in an

---

[258]   http://www.qfinance.com/balance-sheets-best-practice/how-to-manage-pension-costs?page=1

[259] http://en.wikipedia.org/wiki/Unemployment_benefits

organized society; and not a matter of money.

➔ One problem lies in the allocation of work in a society. Another problem lies in the highly industrialized production processes.

➔ Establishing the production processes in cheap-wage-countries (e.g. Asia) makes products cheap, but costs of unemployment at home high.

➔ The more the small and medium sized firms are shrinking, the higher the unemployment rate.

➔ The more a country depends on seasonal production and services (e.g. tourism), the higher the risk of instability of working places.

➔ The lack of pioneering vocational education and in general of (low quality) vocational education, the higher the risks of unemployment.

➔ High unemployment rates reflect incompetence, ignorance, arrogance, and carelessness on the side of the governments and the economy as a whole.

➔ High unemployment, especially long term unemployment and unemployment of the youth creates extremely high and dangerous negative externalities at public cost.

➔ The neo-capitalistic economics is not made for equilibrium in society; it's made for those who get richer and richer, especially for the mega-rich people in order to govern governments and to exploit societies.

➔ Without a fundamental change in lifestyle and understanding of human life and society life, the problems of high unemployment rates and negative externalities can never be solved.

Thesis: Unemployment compensation does not solve the problem of unemployment.

"Researchers have also drawn links between higher rates of unemployment and major social problems like higher crime rates and greater political unrest as well as higher rates of depression, heart disease, and other illnesses among unemployed individuals." [260]

➔ Therefore the reasons for such dire problems lie in the ideology of economics and in the management of the economy of a country.

➔ The main actors that create high unemployment should be mentioned: the banks, private banks, the IMF, the central banks, most corporations, big speculation businesses, and incompetent politicians (governments).

➔ The Western warmongers since 1991 together with an immense increase of re-armament that created a global economic imbalance are the culprits, supported by the mega-investors.

---

[260] McConnell (et al.), p. 117

➔ High unemployment is also intentionally produced in order to exploit and even destroy 'unwilling' countries; those who don't follow the orders from the supreme masters on the hidden stage behind the curtains.

2.6. Pro and Anti Growth

McConnell describes the 'antigrowth view': [261]

"Critics of growth say industrialization and growth result in pollution, climate change, ozone depletion, and other environmental problems. These adverse negative externalities occur because inputs in the production process reenter the environment as some form of waste. The more rapid our growth and the higher our standard of living, the more waste the environment must absorb – or attempt to absorb."

→ It's a manipulation to call critical people and experts as 'antigrowth'-people. There is in general no 'anti-growth' attitude, but much more a requirement for a balanced growth or for redirecting production and for giving much more focus on genuine human values.

→ It's a perfidious manipulation and trivialization to speak here about 'some form of waste'; it's about the global disaster of toxic (mortal) contamination and all its dire consequences for humans, species, and nature.

→ To say 'environment must absorb – or attempt to absorb' is making a fool of the very serious problems for the entire humanity and the planet. That's perverse!

→ There are more than 10 mega-parameters of 'negative externalities' that show the facts (see chapter 3)!

"Critics of growth also argue that there is little compelling evidence that economic growth has solved sociological problems such as poverty, homelessness, and discrimination."

→ The author doesn't like 'critics'. But it's not simply about 'critics'. It's about extremely important concerns and dangerous future developments.

→ Poverty, homelessness, and discrimination are the result of many factors, not only a result of lack of economic growth. Again the author fabricates a false picture.

→ Even in the industrialized nations we have 15-25% severe poverty, in

---

[261] McConnell, p. 165 (all following citations)

some countries up to 65%. Millions have lost their home due to this insane 'growth'.

→ In the neo-capitalistic world there exists an immense rejection and even discrimination of pioneering people, critical thinking, and of people highly committed to human values, peace, justice.

→ The author ignores that the governments in America and Europe are full of warmongers, liars, cheaters, psychotic propagandists, megalomaniacs, psychopaths, and very evil people that try to throw billions of people into the abyss.

"Antigrowth sentiment also says that while growth may permit us to 'make a better living', it does not give us 'the good life'. We may be producing more and enjoying it less. Growth means frantic paces on jobs, worker burnout, and alienated employees who have little or no control over decisions affecting their lives."

→ The author hates these critical experts and people: Antigrowth sentiment! The author's arrogance becomes psychotic.

→ The mentioned concerns (from the 'antigrowth sentiment') here are of supreme importance. The author seems to have no idea about the real world, is blinded from his capitalistic ideology.

→ The author makes these critical people to scapegoats. He simply shifts the evil doing of the capitalistic market and on the political stages towards the people favoring 'the good life'.

"The changing technology at the core of growth poses new anxieties and new sources of insecurity for workers. Both high-level and low-level workers face the prospect of having their hard-earned skills and experience rendered obsolete by onrushing technology. High-growth economies are high-stress economies, which may impair our physical and mental health."

→ The 'antigrowth' people have here a clear view. The author is blinded or simply ignores the concerns.

→ Physical and mental health is seriously affected from contamination and the consumer-attitudes. A huge majority of people in the so called capitalistic world is destroyed in mind and soul, and strongly damaged or even destroyed in their physical and mental health.

"Finally, critics of high rates of growth doubt that they are sustainable. The planet Earth has finite amounts of natural resources available, and they are being consumed at alarming rates of economic growth simply speed up the degradation and exhaustion of the earth's resources."

→ There are hundreds of thousands of experts and millions of people that see these serious problems. The author ignores these concerns.
→ There are many very serious experts that say: Humanity can't continue living as usual as there is only one planet, but 3 planets would be needed to get the life standard of the Western world for the entire humanity.

Now, McConnell starts his attack in order to defend 'economic growth': [262]

"The primary defense of growth is that it is the path to the greater material abundance and higher living standards desired by the vast majority of people. Rising output and incomes allow people to buy."

→ 'Greater material abundance and higher living standards desired by the vast majority of people' is the result of brainwashing, dehumanizing, manipulating with the nuclear power of the Western media.
→ The 'material' abundance has become a perverse dimension on the level of the masses of people in industrialized nations. In general this 'material abundance' is concentrated on the level of the very rich people.
→ There is an understanding of growth that does not match with the capitalistic understanding. Growth balanced with genuine human values and authentic culture has another scale.
→ But for sure, most developing countries need to drastically improve their infrastructure, their production and services. They can't. The capitalist history has broken their mental spine and they are chained in debt by Western institutions and corruption copied from America's and Europe's leaders.

"More education, recreation, and travel, more medical care, closer communications, more skilled personal and professional services, and better-designed as well as more numerous products."

→ The author puts everything into one pot. 'More education' is not the same as (more) 'travel' or 'more numerous products'. This is a manipulative statement as part of it is very important and other parts have very critical

---

[262] McConnell, p. 165-167 (all following citations)

aspects.

→ Yes, many developing countries need 'growth' in a general sense, i.e. public education and professional education. Nobody with a clear mind has doubts about these basic needs in a healthy society.

"It also means more art, music, and poetry, theater, and drama. It can even mean more time and resources devoted to spiritual growth and human development."

→ How many people in the capitalistic world enjoy art, music, and poetry, theater, and drama?
→ How many people have the money to enjoy such culture?
→ How many people in the capitalistic world are committed to spiritual growth? Not many!

"Growth also enables society to improve the nation's infrastructure, enhance the care of the sick and elderly, provide greater access for the disabled, and provide more police and fire protection."

→ The 'care of the sick and elderly' and of the 'disabled' has become industrial practices in America as well as in Europe. The 'sick and elderly' are excluded from the dance around the golden calf.
→ Yes, all developing countries need 'growth' in this 'care'. But not at the cost that the Western folks that have to pay with health problems, mental disease, behavior disorder, inner emptiness, etc.
→ The Western world needs police to hit the demonstrating people as they have enough from these economists and politicians permanently cheating and abusing them for their benefits.
→ The 'fire protection': yes, good we have these institutions; but it's a very minor infrastructure compared to all other institutions from society. The author trivializes the concerns.
→ The author plays here a dirty game with hidden manipulations: the 'antigrowth sentiment' does not reject these needs!

"Economic growth may be the only realistic way to reduce poverty, since there is only limited political support for greater redistribution of income. The way to improve the economic position of the poor is to increase household incomes through higher productivity and economic growth."

→ Investments become very fast a trap: They should sell their land, their cultural goods and their raw-resources (including arable land) to get money from the Western investors that then can dictate the governments the right 'democracy'.

→ Investors want guarantees: land, raw resources, cultural goods, etc. They invest money and demand that from this money, part is given as loans to foreign businesses to establish their businesses in these countries in order to exploit these countries.

→ The investors always require 'Western democracy' and the adaptation of neo-capitalistic economics as a condition to investments.

→ The author's ignorance is unlimited! Does he understand anything about history and about how these countries have been destroyed to the core from the Western (neo-) colonialism and imperialism?

"Also, a no-growth policy among industrial nations might severely limit growth in poor nations. Foreign investment and development assistance in those nations would fall, keeping the world's poor in poverty longer."

→ That's not true! It's very arrogant to speak here about a need of 'development assistance'! As no lunch is for free, also this 'assistance' is not for free.

→ These countries must learn to find back their cultural and historic soul.

→ These countries must stand up and fight for their own path.

→ These countries must learn to work hard and to be self-responsible. But this would require throwing the capitalists out of the country.

→ Considering the growth of the world population, poverty will increase and can't be solved with Western capitalistic models.

→ One of the biggest problems to solve global poverty is the horrendous concentration and accumulation of money by a few ultra-rich people.

"Economic growth has not made labor more unpleasant or hazardous, as critics suggest. New machinery is usually less taxing and less dangerous than the machinery it replaces. Air-conditioned workplaces are more pleasant than steamy workshops. Furthermore, why would an end to economic growth reduce materialism or alienation?"

→ New machinery and air-conditions are really not the focus that these 'antigrowth' people have in view. The author deviates from the very serious concerns.

→ Nobody calls for an 'end of economic growth'. The author manipulates again polarizing to the stupid (theoretical) extreme.

→ Economic growth has dehumanized people and extinguished their soul. Most Western people are stupid, conceited, neurotic, egomaniacs, sheep, liars, blabbers, and full of unsolved inner problems that they compensate with consumption.

→ Materialism or alienation does not have its primordial sources in economics. The main sources lie in the archaic public education, in the academic exclusion of human values from scientific aims (and methods), and in a Christianity that is thoroughly a sham.

"The loudest protests against materialism are heard in those nations and groups that now enjoy the highest levels of material abundance! The high standard of living that growth provides has increased our leisure and given us more time for reflection and self-fulfillment."

→ The author hates 'loudest protests' and distorts with such a word the serious concerns these people have. But indeed, these protesters should think about all the benefit our life standard offers to the folks.

→ Sure is, the author does not give any sign that he takes time for reflections and self-fulfillment. He has zero self-reflection, zero spirituality, and there is complete absence of inner fulfillment! He should keep silent and look into his own mirror!

→ How should people be able for the right way of self-reflection and managing self-fulfillment if most of the mind and soul is excluded from official curriculums?

→ How can people focus on self-reflection and self-fulfillment if they are bombarded with thousands of marketing units everywhere and every day?

→ The author's propaganda here for neo-capitalism is not less perfidious than what we know from Goebbels.

→ In most Western countries there is not even 50% of the population that benefit from this 'high standard of living'. 'High standard of living' requires a wage above 8,000 €/$ per month.

→ 'High standard of living' is also a question of comparison: Even the low income population in America and Europe (80% of the population) enjoy a good standard of living compared to the poor people in Asia or Africa.

→ The costs, measured with one parameter, the private car, are very high since 60 years: between 60 and 100 million killed people by car accidents.

Uncountable tons of fine dust that kills millions of people per year.

"Does growth threaten the environment? The connection between growth and environment is tenuous, say growth proponents. Increases in economic growth need not mean increases in pollution. Pollution is not so much a by-product of growth as it is a 'problem of the commons'."

→ The global contamination tells the truth, not the pollution that is here a word that trivializes the criticality; see chapter 3.

→ It's a disgrace how the author declassifies the 'pollution' (including contamination) as a 'problem of the commons'. He fully ignores the moral liability of corporations.

→ Economic growth is the 100% main cause for the horrendous global contamination! Herewith the author is unmasked as an artful perverse manipulator, not less than the propagandists from the Third Reich.

"Much of the environment – streams, lakes, oceans and the air – is treated as common property, with insufficient or no restrictions on its use. The commons have become our dumping grounds; we have overused and debased them. Environmental pollution is a case of negative externalities, and correcting this problem involves regulatory legislation, specific taxes ('effluent charges'), or market-based incentives to remedy misuse of the environment."

→ The commons have become the dumping grounds of the production corporations.

→ The negative externalities are a matter of common property. The author has lost his mind!

→ Again the author only speaks about 'environmental pollution'. But there are some mega-parameters of absolute destructive effects on humanity and the planet.

→ Correcting this problem of regulatory legislation starts with a new micro- and macro-economics and new laws that allows those responsible in the 'free market' and in the science of economics to be held accountable.

"Those who support growth admit there are serious environmental problems. But they say that limiting growth is the wrong solution. Growth has allowed economies to reduce pollution, be more sensitive to environmental considerations, set aside wilderness, create national parks and monuments, and clean up hazardous waste, while still enabling rising household incomes."

→ A new understanding of growth is the right solution.

→ Growth has not allowed for a reduction of pollution. Pollution still increases globally.

→ The authors of the economics are zero sensitive to the mega-parameters of negative externalities.

→ Unbelievable this propaganda: set aside wilderness, create national parks and monuments, and clean up hazardous waste – as if any of the critical mega-parameters would be solved with that.

→ A better solution is: put all these neo-capitalistic experts and all the protagonists of the corporations into prison and let them pay for the global damages and let them also pay directly to the millions of people that have lost their home and existence due to the 'economic crisis' sine 2008.

→ Here the author tries to lure the reader: 'while still enabling rising household incomes'.

"Is growth sustainable? … Yes, say the proponents of growth. If we were depleting natural resources faster than their discovery, we would see the prices of those resources; in fact, the prices of most of them have declined. And if one natural resource becomes too expensive, another resource will be substituted for it. Moreover, say economists, economic growth has to do with the expansion and application of human knowledge and information, not of extractable natural resources. In this view, economic growth is limited only by human imagination."

→ The author is running away from the real problems of negative externalities related to growth (production): Growth, as understood in capitalistic economics, is never sustainable!

→ If the original resources become scarce or too expensive, then simply another resource will be substituted. And this should solve the multiple global problems for the next thousand years?

→ The author is totally ignorant about the immense global problems, including loss of arable land, decrease of water reservoirs, deforestation, drought, heat waves, the damaged eco-systems, etc.

→ The author's rejection gets a new strategy: 'expansion and application of human knowledge and information' that's what 'growth' means. The author distorts words and realities! This strategy of deviation is shameless and devilish!

→ There are then thousands of economic experts and professors that teach all this economic rubbish and perverse lies; and hundreds of thousands of students and more must copy it every year in order to graduate.

→ How is it possible that such 'experts' are allowed to hold the title 'professor' (with top wages) and to teach in academic institutions – Universities – of highest reputation? Speechless!

→ The author is a protagonist of the regicide and deicide! If students like it and follow his path, then they are followers and complicit of the 'crime against humanity and the planet' and abettors of the crimes I call 'regicide' and 'deicide'.

"I can't tell myself a convincing story about where the growth (in yield) is going to come from in the next half century." Vernon Ruttan, 1999 [263]

---

[263] Meadows (et al.), p. 63

3. Parameters of Humanity and the Planet

About the Statistics, Facts and Figures:

- The figures shall draw a general global picture.
- We do not claim to have found the most objective figures.
- Most figures from different sources sometimes vary strongly.
- Figures change every year either to the good or for the worse.
- Even 'serious sources' are only estimates and vary accordingly.
- Statistics are often manipulated or refer to a specific view.
- Everybody can find thousands of facts and figures on the Internet.
- Find the 'right' (objective and all encompassing) figures yourself!
- We cannot verify the real 'more or less' of single figures.
- Experts must calculate exact figures for national or global changes.
- Figures about a field become important in the whole network.
- Figures are important because they express a quantifiable collective human reality.
- We focus on human realities, on 7 billion human lives, on humanity.
- The global picture reaches a new quality with 9-10 billion people.

For creative explorations, thinking and analyzing:

- http://www.worldometers.info/
- http://www.forbes.com/
- http://www.worldbank.org/
- https://www.cia.gov/library/publications/the-world-factbook/
- http://www.globalsecurity.org/military/world/spending.htm
- http://www.thetotalcollapse.com
- http://www.etc-corporate.org/
- http://www.informationclearinghouse.info
- http://www.globalresearch.ca/
- http://www.fao.org/index_es.htm
- http://www.nationmaster.com/index.php
- http://data.worldbank.org/data-catalog/global-statistics
- http://www.gapminder.org/
- http://www.globalissues.org/article/26/poverty-facts-and-stats
- http://www.unhcr.org/pages/49c3646c4d6.html
- http://www.internetworldstats.com/

- http://www.imf.org/external/data.htm
- http://www.greenpeace.org/international/en/
- http://www.who.int/en/
- http://www.poverty.com/
- http://www.theglobaleducationproject.org
- http://www.globalissues.org/article/26/poverty-facts-and-stats

More sources are cited together with the statements.

The biggest of all problems of humanity is global contamination. Once all eco-systems are over-loaded with toxic elements, the entire humanity will be punished in an unimaginable way. For those few millions who will survive it, the consequences will be visible with deformations, mental incapacities, and sadness of guilt for a millennium. There are already irreversible damages of global dimension! You have 6 years left to take drastic measures! If you ignore it, then in 20-35 years the irreversible global damages on all eco-systems will completely and unavoidably change your life!

3.1. Hunger, Food and Water

General short picture: [264]

- Today 4-5 billion people don't have enough healthy food and drinking water.
- 2060: estimated 6-7 billion people will not have enough healthy food and drinking water.

3.1.1. Hunger

- An estimated 2.3 billion people are malnourished, under-fed or starving.
- An estimated 1,000,000,000 people are undernourished.
- 2012: an estimated 3 billion people suffer from hunger, are underfed or malnourished.
- 2050: an estimated 5-6 billion people will suffer from hunger, will be underfed or malnourished.
- Asia and the Pacific have 650 million hungry people.
- Sub-Saharan Africa counts with 265 million hungry people.
- Nearly 30% of all children in developing countries are undernourished.
- "High food prices and lower incomes put poor households at an additional risk of not providing expectant mothers, infants, and children with adequate nutrition." [265]
- Over 9 million people die every year because of hunger and malnutrition. 5 million are children.
- Between 2 and 3.5 billion people have micronutrient deficiency (not enough vitamins and minerals). [266]
- Over 9 million people die every year because of hunger and malnutrition. 5 million are children. [267]

Comparative examples: [268]

---

[264] More figures to find here: http://millionsofmouths.com/info.html
Or: http://www.squidoo.com/world-hunger-facts-1
Or: http://www.worldhunger.org/articles/Learn/world%20hunger%20facts%202002.htm
Or: http://www.fao.org/hunger/en/
[265] State_of_the_World_2011 from: THE WORLDWATCH INSTITUTE
[266] http://www.globalissues.org/article/26/poverty-facts-and-stats
[267] http://www.globalissues.org/article/7/causes-of-hunger-are-related-to-poverty
[268] http://www.globalissues.org/article/7/causes-of-hunger-are-related-to-poverty

- 1.2 billion people suffer from obesity (excess of fats and salt, often accompanied by deficiency of vitamins and minerals).
- In the United Kingdom 30-40% of all foods are never eaten
- In the last 10 years the amount of food British people threw away increased by 15%
- Overall, £20 billion ($38 billion) worth of food is thrown away each year
- In the USA 40-50% of all food ready for harvest never even gets eaten
- Of the food that does eventually reach households, 14% is wasted, resulting in an est. $43 billion wastage
- If food reaching supermarkets, restaurants and cafeterias is added to the household figure, that wastage goes up to 27%.

Macroeconomic conclusions:

→ Food supply is immensely insufficient and more and more in danger.
→ There is a problem of food production and of allocation (distribution).
→ There is a problem of food prices and of lack of money to buy food.
→ Lack of food and money is predominantly in Asia, Africa, and some other areas.
→ In developed countries there is no lack of food, but lack of money to buy food and a lot of food wastage.

3.1.2. Water

- Lack of drinking water or healthy drinking water affects 3.3 billion people. [269] [270]
- 2050: up to 5.5 billion people will suffer from dirty water or lack of drinking water.
- Half of the world's hospital beds are filled with people suffering from water related illnesses.
- People with no access to safe drinking water: 1,400,000,000.
- Up to 250 million people across Africa face water shortages by 2020.
- At least 4.000 children die every day from water-related diseases.
- More people died due to contaminated water than from violence and war.
- Glaciers and snow cover expected to decline, reducing water availability in countries supplied by melting water. These big water reservoirs will be gone in 20 years.
- Billions of people face shortages of water and increased risk of flooding.
- 400,000,000 children have no access to healthy drinking water.

---

[269] http://water.org/water-crisis/water-facts/water/
[270] http://blueplanetnetwork.org/water/facts

- For 3.2 billion people drinking water will be rare in the future.
- 1.3 billion people dispose of dirty and contaminated drinking water.
- 1.8 billion people must walk 2 km or more to get drinking water.
- The United Nations estimates that nearly 900 million people live without clean water.
- Water, the basic ingredient of life, is among the world's most prolific killers.
- People with no access to safe drinking water (August 2009): 1,403,227,749.
- Up to 250 million people across Africa could face water shortages by 2020
- In northern China, the water level is dropping one meter per year due to over-pumping.
- "90% of the developing world's **waste water** is still discharged untreated into local rivers and streams." [271]

Liters of water required to produce one kilogram of food: [272]

- Beef: 15,000 liters
- Lamb: 10,000 liters
- Cereals: 1,500 liters

Some more facts: [273]

- Approximately 70% of all available water is used for irrigation.
- Some 1.8 million children die each year as a result of diarrhea.
- 1.8 billion people who have access to a water source within 1 kilometer.
- Billions of people face food and water shortages and increased risk of flooding
- The highest average water use in the world is in the US, at 600 liters day.
- 1.8 billion people consume around 20 liters per day.
- Almost two in three people lacking access to clean water survive on $1 - $2 a day

Macroeconomic conclusions:

→ Natural water resources are diminishing and increasingly contaminated.
→ Water for agriculture and animal breeding will be scarce in the future.
→ Dirty water is an immense health problem and affects also food production.
→ Illnesses due to dirty or lack of water produces immense public costs.
→ 'Dirty' is extensively related to pollution, contamination, waste, and

[271] http://www.theglobaleducationproject.org
[272] http://www.theglobaleducationproject.org
[273] http://www.globalissues.org/article/26/poverty-facts-and-stats

sewage.

→ Water shortage will lead to a decrease in industrial production (of food).

→ Extensive industrial use of water leads to lack of (healthy) drinking water.

→ Extensive industrial use of water leads to lack of water for small agricultural farms.

→ Extensive industrial use of water causes contamination of the water streams.

→ Over-exploitation of groundwater and decreasing glaciers will have economic effects.

→ There will be strong self-destructive effects for corporations, i.e. profit maximizing.

3.1.3. Death due to Food and Water Scarcity

- 2.2 million children die every year from disease associated with lack of safe drinking water.
- Every year 15 million children die of hunger.
- Between 30.000 and 50.000 babies die in Africa every year.
- People who died of hunger in one day: more than 25,000. [274]
- Over 4 million people die of starvation every year.
- Deaths of children under the age of 5 in the year 2011: 9,000,000. [275]
- Over 3 million deaths due to water related diseases.

Macroeconomic conclusions:

→ More lives have been lost after World War II due to contaminated water than from all forms of violence and war. [276] Macroeconomic mismanagement is responsible!

→ Those in the real world of economics that produce the food and water scarcity and the dirty water are also responsible for the consequences such as suffering, illnesses and death.

→ From a cynical perspective the high rate of death slows down a little bit the population growth. But immense manpower for local business interests is lost; and this is economically inefficient.

→ The phase before death due to hunger and water scarcity or dirty drinking water, there are immense costs due to previous illnesses and suffering. This is an economic waste.

---

[274] http://www.stopthehunger.com/
[275]
http://www.who.int/pmnch/media/press_materials/fs/fs_mdg4_childmortality/en/index.html
[276] http://blueplanetnetwork.org/water/facts

→ Death due to food and water scarcity or dirty water creates enormous sadness and depression to the social environment and reduces the mental capacities of the working people.

3.1.4. Causes of Hunger

- Harmful economic systems are the main cause of poverty and hunger. [277]
- Poverty is the principal cause of hunger.
- Diminution and destruction of agriculture land is a superior cause.
- Destroying 200 million small farmer businesses is a core negative factor.
- Conflicts and (civil) wars are a cause of hunger and poverty.
- The consequences of Climate Change have multiple negative effects.
- Speculation (banks) with food raw material and food products

Macroeconomic conclusions:

→ Those who create (created) the economic systems and those who manage the macroeconomic dimension of real economics are responsible for its consequences such as hunger.
→ Causing poverty and hunger is economically in the long run absolutely inefficient and even counter-productive for corporation's profit interest.
→ Physically and mentally healthy people that can live above the poverty line can manage their sexual activities much better which leads to a significant decrease of the population growth.

3.1.5. Humane Implications

A) To have healthy food and drinking water means:

- Pleasure
- Joy
- Health
- Mental health
- Strength
- Wellness
- Promotes social health
- Gives a feeling for quality
- Makes eating important
- Promotes respect for food

---

[277] http://www.squidoo.com/world-hunger-facts-1

- Eating can (sometimes) become a celebration
- Allows to be occupied with concerns of higher interest / importance
- Makes able to live sex and love with meaningful attitudes

Macroeconomic conclusions:

→ Positive emotional state significantly increases the capacity and efficiency of the working people.
→ Positive emotional state creates constructive contributions to the production processes.

B) Not to have healthy food and drinking water means:

We are talking here about 3-4 billion people!

- No pleasure
- No joy
- No health
- No mental health
- No strength
- No wellness
- Feel ashamed
- Can't be proud
- Can not promote social health
- Can not find a feeling for quality
- Makes drinking for survival important
- Can't find respect for water
- Can't properly wash themselves and their clothes
- High risk for aggressions
- Can't contribute to society with whatever
- Are not efficient manpower
- Completely resigned
- Can not benefit from their education (if they have / had)
- Always occupied and worried to find food and water
- Always occupied with health concerns
- Have a very bad body feeling
- To enjoy and 'celebrate' sex and love is not possible
- Can't develop the force of love (for / with a partner)
- Can't educate their children in a appropriate way
- Are permanently frustrated
- Can't communicate critically about any spiritual/religious truth
- Can't benefit from the inner spiritual source of life

- Contribute enormously to environmental pollution (sewage)
- Have a low esteem of humans (being a human)
- Are running for each cent to get however and from wherever
- Don't trust anybody
- Inner restlessness: nervousness, lack of concentration

Macroeconomic conclusions:

→ Negative emotional state enormously decreases the capacity and efficiency of the working people.
→ Negative emotional state of people produces a lot of failure, including accidents, and with that much unnecessary extra costs.

3.2. Poverty and Misery

3.2.1. Global Poverty

- The UN estimates that 2.6 billion people live without proper sanitation.
- 2050: Easily 4 billion people will live without proper sanitation.
- Today the sewage of 2.5-3.5 billion people goes to the soil, seas and oceans.
- 2050: the sewage of 3.5-4.5 billion people will go to the soil, seas and oceans.
- 4-5 billion people live under poor and extreme poor conditions.
- 50% of all children on the earth (2.2 billion) live in poverty.
- Over 1 billon people have no housing.
- 640,000,000 children have no housing or live in slums.
- 2 billion people don't have access to electricity.
- 2.6 billion people have no access to sanitation.
- 4 billion people have insufficient education.
- 1 billion people are analphabets or can't read or write properly.
- 3 billion poor people who aspire to gaining access to electricity and modern energy services. [278]

Macroeconomic conclusions:

→ Global poverty is not only a dark shadow over the industrialized nations and the billionaires, but it also entails enormous costs for the industrialized nations and the billionaires.
→ If the costs for global poverty are higher than the thin profit sucked out from people living in poverty, then the economic conclusion results in a stupid negative account.
→ If the monstrous public dept is a burden for the following 10 generations, then the burden of the global poverty is globally an even higher economic burden for the coming 25 generations.
→ If there is really such a thing called 'the invisible hand', why then could this 'mysterious being' not stop this dire mess of global poverty, and not even the poverty in Europe and America?

---

[278] http://www.un.org/en/development/desa/policy/wess/wess_current/2011wess.pdf

3.2.2. Economical Conditions

- 1.3 billion people earn less than US$1 per day.
- 1.4 billion people dispose of less that $1.25 per day.
- 3 billion people struggle to survive on US$ 2 per day.
- As many as 2.8 billion people on the planet struggle to survive on less than $2 a day. [279]
- Nearly 50% of the earth population lives from less than $2.50 per day (=$75 per month).
- 40% of Egyptians live on $2 a day or less.
- 80% of the earth's population (5.6 billion) lives from less than $10 per day (= $300 per month).
- 1-1.2 billion people live in comfortable economic conditions.
- 200,000,000 people live in very comfortable or luxurious economic conditions.
- 3.4 billion people disposes of 1% of the world's wealth.
- 2.5 billion people depend on biomass (wood, coal, etc.) for cooking. In the Sub-Sahara, in India or China over 80% depend on traditional biomass for cooking.
- The richest 20% of the world population cover 76.6% of the worldwide private consumption.
- The poorest 35% cover 1.5% of the consumption volume.
- The richest 10% cover 59% of all consumption; and the poorest 10% only 0.5%.

Wealth and Countries

- The world's wealthiest countries (approximately 1 billion people) accounted for $36.6 trillion dollars (76%).
- The world's billionaires — just 497 people (approximately 0.000008% of the world's population) — were worth $3.5 trillion (over 7% of world GDP).
- Low income countries (2.4 billion people) accounted for just $1.6 trillion of GDP (3.3%)
- Middle income countries (3 billion people) made up the rest of GDP at just over $10 trillion (20.7%). [280]

---

[279] http://www.worldwatch.org/node/810
[280] http://www.globalissues.org/article/26/poverty-facts-and-stats#src19#src19

HNWIs: [281]

The world's population of high net worth individuals (HNWIs1) expanded in 2010, as did their wealth.

Globally, HNWIs' financial wealth grew 9.7% in 2010to reach US$42.7 trillion.

The population of HNWIs in Asia-Pacific, at 3.3 million individuals, is now the second-largest in the world behind North America.

Europe's HNWI wealth totaled US$10.2 trillion after growing 7.2% in 2010, while Asia-Pacific HNWI wealth was US$10.8 trillion, up 12.1%.

North American HNWI wealth hit US$11.6 trillion in 2010, up 9.1%.

Latin America saw another modest gain (6.2%) in its HNWI population in 2010 and HNWI wealth rose 9.2%. The Latin America HNWI segment has proved relatively

(2010) the world's HNWIs were still concentrated in the U.S., Japan, and Germany.

Wealth-X World Ultra Wealth Report 2011 [282]

"The fortunes of the world's ultra high net worth (UHNW) individuals have surpassed $25 trillion and is set to increase, spurred by the growth of developing Asia. Wealth-X estimates that the global market of UHNW individuals has reached 185,795. Our intelligence reveals:

▸ North America is home to 62,960 UHNW individuals, and constitutes the largest concentration of UHNW wealth in the world. This region accounts for nearly 33% of the total $25 trillion held by the world's UHNW segment.

▸ Europe has the second largest population of UHNW individuals. The region's 54,325 UHNW individuals have a collective fortune of $6.8 trillion.

▸ Asia-Pacific, with its 42,525 UHNW individuals, represents $6.2 trillion. This region poses the greatest chance of supplanting the old guard of Europe and North America.

---

[281] Capgemini and Merrill Lynch Global Wealth Management are pleased to present the 2011 World Wealth Report
Capgemini and Merrill Lynch Global Wealth Management.capgemini.com
[282] http://www.wealthx.com/articles/2011/wealth-x-world-ultra-wealth-report-2011/

▸ While the Latin American UHNW story has been capturing considerable headlines, its 15,100 UHNW individuals with $2.3 trillion in assets represent roughly a third of the Asian market."

Macroeconomic conclusions:

→ How is life with a wage of $75? It's not even in Asia or Africa a humane life with minimal satisfaction of the indispensable needs. And there is no chance for getting a 'want'.
→ And those who earn more, up to $300, are not much better off. How much profit can a corporation get from this thin cake? And how much taxes will go to the government?
→ Now, masters of the corporations and the tax departments of governments: Calculate the loss of profit and taxes if all these billions of people would be paid $600-1,000. You are the losers!
→ The young generation, especially from the rich and super rich, will lose their legacy and all visions of the elites will be gone like smoke in the air. Is this economically efficient?

3.2.3. Poverty in Industrialized Countries

Selected examples:

- Currently 3.7 million children are living in poverty across Britain overall.
- 22% of the British population live in families with earnings of only 60% of the median (average) income
- Out of the 22% (13 million people), 5.8 million suffer from 'deep poverty' which means they earn less than 40% of the median income.
- In the countries of the European Union, the rate of poverty varies between 10% and 23%.
- At least 80 million people in the EU are 'below the poverty line'.
- Countries with the highest poor population: France, Germany, Italy, Poland, Spain, and the UK.
- 5.8 million Brits suffer from 'deep poverty' which means they earn less than 40% of the median income.
- Across Britain overall there are currently 3.7 million children living in poverty.
- 11.5 million Germans live in poverty (population: 82 million).
- Roughly 100 million people in the EU live below the poverty level or are in danger of doing so. [283]

---

[283] http://www.goethe.de/ges/soz/soz/en6859966.htm

- In 2009 14.6 per cent of the population of Switzerland was in danger of becoming impoverished, which means around 1,140,000 people out of a total population of 7,800,000. 6.7 per cent of the Swiss population is affected by strong material deprivation.
- (In December 2010) 20% of the Spanish population lives in poverty (population: 45 million). 2008: 1.1 million people were considered to be poor. Homeless people: 30.000.
- Spain 2012, February: 22% of households below poverty line, another 30% on the cliff. [284]
- About 9 million people live in poverty in Spain, many without legal support or access to information to enable them to assert their rights.
- Spain: There are nearly 300,000 people who lack Public health coverage.
- Spain: 2 million children are at risk of poverty.
- Spain has one of the highest child poverty levels of the 27 member states of the European Union. [285]
- New report says 25% of Spain's population lives below poverty line. [286]
- The German pension system will lead to mass poverty (says the OECD); most probably this will also happen in other EU-countries.
- In the United States 2012, over 50 million people live below the poverty line; one in five children in the United States live in poverty. (44 million in 2010).
- 3.5 percent of U.S. households experience hunger. Some people in these households frequently skip meals or eat too little, sometimes going without food for a whole day. 9.6 million people, including 3 million children, live in these homes.
- In the U.S., households with incomes below the poverty line: 14.3 percent.
- New official data reveals: "more than eight million Italians, constituting almost 14% of the country's population, live in relative poverty. From among the same number, more than 3 million, over five percent of the whole population, live in 'absolute poverty', unable to procure their most basic needs and services, according to the Italian National Institute of Statistics (ISTAT). Furthermore, every one out of five Italian households lives under the poverty line. In the country's southern regions, every one out of two households lives in the same condition." [287]

Macroeconomic conclusions:

[284]   http://en.mercopress.com/2012/02/24/caritas-spain-22-of-households-below-poverty-line-another-30-on-the-cliff
[285] http://www.typicallyspanish.com/news/publish/article_27905.shtml
[286] http://www.presstv.ir/detail/245070.html
[287] http://www.istat.it/en/

→ Some 3,000 corporations are targeting the 20% of the earth population (1.4 billion) that lives from more than $10 per day. Is the small margin here called 'maximizing profit'?

→ Some 3,000 corporations can target those groups who earn between $10 and $20 per day. Motive: every 50 cents or every dollar can contribute to maximize profit!

→ Can the 3,000 corporations also target those 80% of the earth population (5.6 billion) who earn less than $10 per day? Motive: every five cents can contribute to maximize profit!

→ A radical practice of the principles of economics would require that the corporations only focus on those people as consumers that dispose of at least a $1,000 wage.

→ Poverty in Europe and America is very costly. Poor people reproduce poor people. In the long run, a life of a poor person produces immense public costs.

→ Seen this way: Creating a baby (in Europe and America) easily costs 500 Euros (dollars) per month, increasing with the years up to the age of 18. Then the collateral costs arise and develop during an entire life at the public expense. Economically it's not profitable, neither for corporations nor for the government. Did the state ministers learn anything about economics, benefits, margin profit, and maximizing profit, and so on? We identify here a club of losers!

3.2.4. Human Importance of Having a Home

To have a home requires money that poor people do not have. Having a home concretely means:

- Tenant or owner: "it's my own place to live on earth"
- A safe and protected place / shelter (people, weather)
- A personal, intimate life frame
- A place to relax, recover
- A place to develop life and to grow
- A place for wellbeing
- A place to get / find / create a self-identity
- A place to wash, cook, eat, sleep, spend personal time
- A place for very personal expressions and life style
- A place for love, care, sharing moments with a partner
- A place to prepare for outgoing activities
- A place to give the family members a family-identity
- A place to let arise motivations and personal projects
- A place that promotes social health

- A place to celebrate personal / family events
- A place to develop a personal identity
- A place that allows to live sex and love with meaningful attitudes

Not to have a home concretely means:

- Tenant or owner: "I have no own place to live on earth"
- To live in a unsafe and not protected place / no shelter (people, weather)
- To live without personal, intimate life frame
- To not have a place to relax, recover
- To not have a place to develop life and to grow
- To not have a place for wellbeing
- To not have a place to get / find / create a self-identity
- To not have a place to wash, cook, eat, sleep, spend personal time
- To not have a place for very personal expressions and life style
- To not have a place for love, care, sharing moments with a partner
- To not have a place to prepare for outgoing activities
- To not have a place to give the family members a family-identity
- To not have a place to let motivations and personal projects arise
- To not have a place that promotes social health
- To not have a place to celebrate personal / family events
- To not have a place to develop a personal identity

Not having a home produces:

- Unhappiness
- Distrust
- Strife
- Hopelessness
- Negation of life
- Hate
- Aggression
- Insecurity
- Sadness
- Dissatisfaction
- Inner disruption
- Meaninglessness

Macroeconomic conclusions:

➔ Give to all the people a home and they will work for you; they will invest all potentials and strength, with mind and soul. They will kiss your feet and glorify you. This will create trillions in profits globally! Can you see this mountain of money? It's all for your 'wants', golden bathtub included!

3.2.5. Humane Consequences of Poverty

How do people living in poverty feel? How is their daily life of not so wellbeing? Let's look at this:

- Helpless, powerless, hopeless, desperate, passive, distrusting
- Very low self-esteem, no genuine self-identity, no self-realization
- Fighting for food, drinking water, and some cash every single day
- Fear of violence, disease, illnesses, lack of food and water
- Unable to think analytically about their situation
- Running after every cent just to be able to buy something necessary
- Resigned and consumed with fatalistic attitudes
- Turning towards criminality to get some cash
- Life experiences full of misery, suffering, misfortune, sadness
- Unable to understand and communicate for solutions
- Easily suggestible to radicalism, fatalistic and prone to dogmatic religiosity
- Increasing readiness for aggression, unrest, riots, and revolution

Poverty has immense humane and social consequences with long term effects:

- Poverty makes homeless; homeless people feel lost
- Poverty creates sadness, despair, frustration, aggression, crimes etc.
- Can not develop themselves and grow for a positive self-identity
- Can not find constructive personal expressions and life style
- Can not develop constructive personal motivation for projects
- Can not form any positive life aim
- Have a low esteem of humans (being a human)
- Do not feel wellness, joy, zest for life, no personal pride
- Have high risk of illnesses, infections, disease, etc.
- High risk of aggressions, crimes, addictions, accidents, etc.
- Can not live intimate moments with a partner safely
- Can not relax and recover in a safe way
- Can not experience or promote social health
- Can not give the family members a family-identity
- Can not celebrate personal / family events
- Can not contribute to a social life / to society
- Have a permanent fear of being unprotected
- Can be more easily exploited and abused; don't trust anybody
- No orderly washing, cooking, eating, sleeping, spending personal time

- Personal psychical-spiritual development is impossible
- Responsibility and contributions for society is impossible
- Are unable to constructively master life and to solve their life problems
- Feel ashamed, inferior, weak, vulnerable, depressed
- Can't wash themselves and their clothes properly
- 'Safe sex' is not possible
- To enjoy and 'celebrate' sex as an expression of love is not possible
- Can't develop the force of love (for / with a partner)
- Can't educate their children in an appropriate manner
- Can't contribute to a better local community
- Their aspiration: at least a dirty, stinking hut is better than nothing
- Can't communicate critically about any spiritual/religious truth
- Can't benefit from the inner unconscious source of life
- Contribute enormously to environmental pollution (sewage)

Macroeconomic conclusions:

→ This picture is about 3-4 billion humans and it will increase with another 2-3 billion people within 2-3 decades!
→ Another consequence is expressed in the vulgar saying 'the shit hits the fan' which means here: the shit will slap you in your face. And economically that is not a 'rational choice'.

3.2.6. The Main Causes of Poverty

Extracted from several articles on the internet and interpreted or summarized with a few words: [288]

a) General list: [289]

- Overpopulation
- Global Allocation (Distribution) of Resources
- High Standards of Living and Costs of Living
- Inadequate Education and Employment
- Environmental Degradation
- Individual Responsibility and Welfare Dependency

---

[288] An example: http://www.globalissues.org/issue/2/causes-of-poverty
[289] http://www.fightpoverty.mmbrico.com/poverty/reasons.html

b) Economy:

- Investor speculation businesses, including food speculations
- Global industry and trade: destroyed by / dominated by speculators
- World economy ruled by the Federal Reserve, World Bank, other banks
- Dependent on credits of the western world and therefore 'enslaved'
- Greed for exorbitant profit and speculations, for power and reputation
- Extreme and not justifiable disproportion of wealth and money

c) Industry:

- Industry producing products of very cheap quality for artificial needs
- Corporate groups having destroyed millions of small businesses
- Shopping malls and shopping centers destroying local businesses
- Destruction of agricultural land and exploitation of natural resources
- Miserably paid and humanly exploited by the exploitation industry
- Capitalistic system with extremely unbalanced distributions
- Unlimited capitalism as a rule of thumb in all corporate group institutions

d) Politics:

- Corrupt politicians and CEO's, dominated by investors
- Lobbyists hindering changes of politics and financial systems
- Military, wars and secret services absorbing 30-40% of public money
- Arrogance and ignorance of most leaders around the globe
- Complete unscrupulousness of leaders in all systems of society
- Leaders with a complete lack of reliability in human values
- The most extreme lies and cheat in religious and political positions
- A psychopathic megalomania and religious lunacy (psychosis)

e) Mind and Soul:

- Most people are blinded, brainwashed, manipulated, deceived, lured
- Tremendous lack of integrity and ethics – of the truth – everywhere
- Religions teaching illusions instead of ways to master life and the inner life
- Psychopathic megalomania, religious psychosis, political lunacy
- The pest in the industrialized nations: Narcissism and neuroticism

f) Education:

- An educational system and curriculum that doesn't prepare the youth for life

- Tremendous lack of education for qualitative professional work
- Lack of public education that teaches how to master life and to resolve problems
- Lack of education for personal psychical-spiritual development

Macroeconomic conclusions:

→ We can identify here some important parameters for macroeconomics: Global allocation, living standard, education, environment, responsibility, speculations, greed, wage level, scrupulousness, corruption, lobbyism, balance, mind and soul, integrity and ethics.

3.2.7. The Circle of Poverty

- 1 billion people live in very extreme poverty
- 2 billion people live in extreme poverty
- 1 billion people live in serious poverty
- 2 billion people are at risk to fall close to poverty

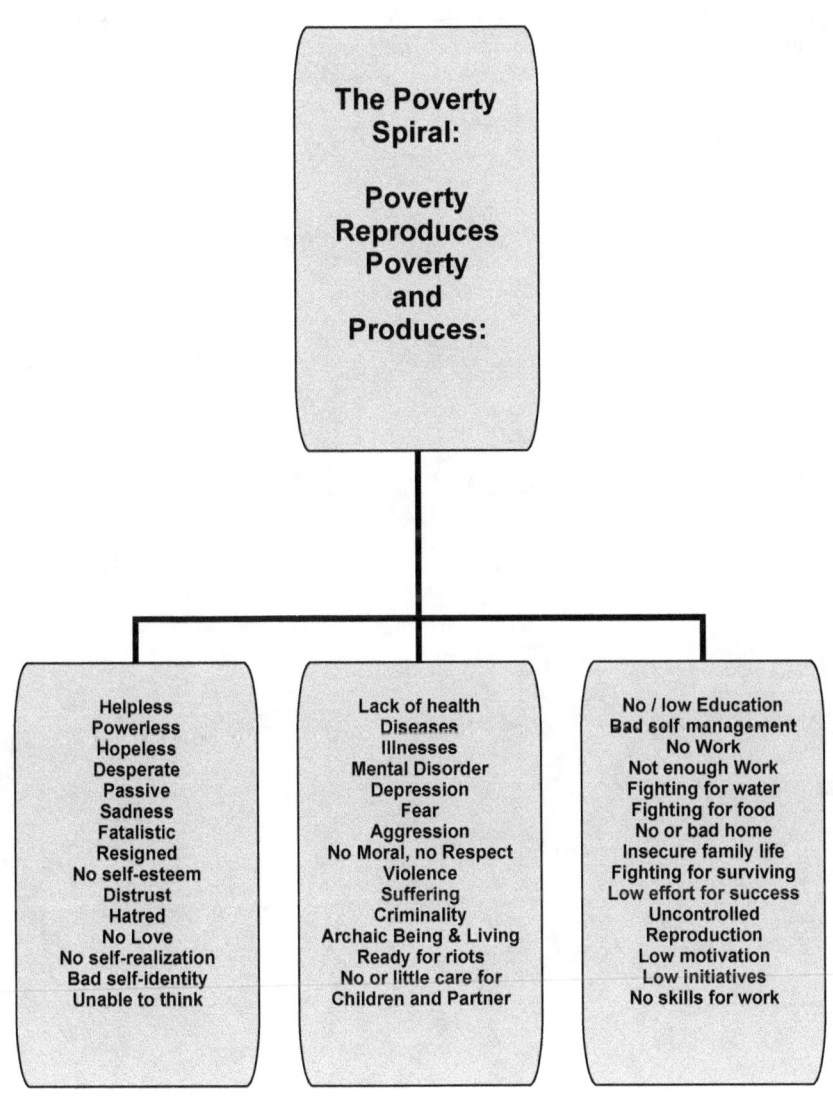

Macroeconomic conclusions:

➔ There is never a way out of poverty without external macroeconomic measures.

➔ The emotional dimension of poverty the long run entails a highly explosive risk.

➔ The future generations will have to pay for the collateral damages of global poverty.

➔ Absolute and significant poverty eliminates dignity and makes people become mad.

➔ General and vocational education together with economic measures is fundamental.

3.3. Agricultural Land, Forest, Oceans

3.3.1. Agriculture

- 500 million small farmers suffer from hunger partly because their right to land (and water) is violated.
- Industrial agriculture has destroyed around 200 million small farmer businesses.
- India: the average landholding fell from 2.6 hectares in 1960 to 1.4 hectares in 2000.
- Crop yields decrease by up to 30% in Central and South Asia.
- Wheat, grain, corn, rice, cocoa, fruit juices, sugar, staples, meat, and coffee are now the new fields for speculators (banks). The consequence: 15-40% price increase.
- Declining crop yield could leave hundreds of millions without the ability to produce sufficient food.
- Crop yields could increase by 20% in East and Southeast Asia, but decrease by up to 30% in Central and South Asia.
- 70 to 90% of the available water is used by the agriculture industry.
- 25-35% of all plant and animal species at increased risk of extinction if temperatures rise between 1.5 and 2.5 C. This will also affect agricultural production.

Macroeconomic conclusions:

→ Agricultural land must be given back to 200 million small farmer businesses.
→ Small farmer businesses must be organized in regional cooperative networks.
→ Top education must be offered to enable all kind of farmer businesses.

3.3.2. Arable Land Loss

- "About 2 billion **hectares of soil**, equivalent to 15% of the Earth's land area (an area larger than the United States and Mexico combined), have been degraded through human activities." [290]

- "It takes approximately 500 years to replace 25 millimeters (1 inch) of topsoil lost to erosion. The minimal soil depth for agricultural production is 150 millimeters. From this perspective, productive fertile soil is a non-renewable, endangered ecosystem." [291]
- By 2010 agriculture fed by rainfall could drop by 50% in some African countries.
- Up to 30 million hectares of (agricultural) land (the size of Italy) is lost each year due to environmental degradation, industrialization and urbanization.
- The average landholding fell from 2.6 hectares in 1960 to 1.4 hectares in 2000.
- Worldwide, soil erosion has caused abandonment of 4.3 million km2 of arable land during the last four decades.
- We are losing 100 billion tons (100 giga tons) of topsoil every year. [292]
- Annually, says the UN's food and agricultural organization, 75 billion tons of soil, the equivalent of nearly 10 million hectares of arable land, is lost. [293]

- Arable land lost in January 2011: 550,000 hectares. [294]
- Climate change is a major factor in damages of agriculture land.
- "Over the past 40 years, approximately 30% of the world's **cropland** has become unproductive." [295]

Macroeconomic conclusions:

→ The loss of arable land will terribly hit the farmer corporations within 2-3 decades.
→ The profit of farmer corporations today will have a high price in the future.
→ Increasing Climate Change will hit corporations and bring them to a fall.

3.3.3. Oceans: Fish and Sea Fruit

- Fishing resources are rapidly decreasing because of excessive exploitation.
- One billion people in the world depend on fish for their principal source of protein.

[290] http://www.theglobaleducationproject.org
[291] http://www.theglobaleducationproject.org
[292] http://www.sustainablesettlement.co.za/issues/landloss.html
[293] http://www.guardian.co.uk/environment/2010/dec/14/soil-erosion-environment-review-vidal
[294] http://www.globalchange.umich.edu/globalchange2/current/lectures/land_deg/land_deg.html
[295] http://www.theglobaleducationproject.org

- Fishing resources are rapidly decreasing because of excessive exploitation.
- The seas and oceans are extremely exploited; fishing resources are destroyed.
- Fishes and sea fruits are 'eating' unimaginable chemical and drug residue cocktails.
- 1 billion people will lose access to fish for their principal source of protein
- Fishing resources are rapidly decreasing

Macroeconomic conclusions:

→ Excessive exploitation of oceans is extremely stupid and in the long run self-destructive.
→ All profit-oriented concepts require a long term view in order to not lose future profit.
→ Why do these corporations kill the cow that gives them milk for decades? Absurd!

3.3.4. Exploitation of Raw Resources

In February 2011, at the World Economic Forum in Davos (Switzerland), the UN Secretary-General Ban Ki-Moon stated that "the world is committing collective global suicide by consuming resources without replenishing them and warned that we are running out of the most important resource of all: Time." [296]

Most corporate groups don't care about environmental destruction or contamination. The 3,000 most important corporate groups produce environmental damages of nearly $2 trillion each year (UN report). [297] The protection of nature and diverse species at risk from the abuse of natural resources, pollution (contamination) of the air and water, and the rapid decrease of the existing number of species is rarely something that the industry or economy cares about.

Facts due to Over-Exploitation

- Most of the bees around the world are sick and billions are dying every year. Bees pollinate over 90 types of vegetables, fruits and grain.
- Most resources are exorbitantly overexploited and within 40 years will be destroyed.

---

[296] http://english.pravda.ru/opinion/columnists/01-02-2011/116741-global_suicide-0/
[297] http://www.guardian.co.uk/environment/2010/feb/18/worlds-top-firms-environmental-damage

- Carbon dioxide (CO2) emissions per year approximately, in tons: 183,000,000,000
- Desertification per year (hectares): more than 12,000,000
- Forest loss per year approximately: 7-10,000,000 (hectares).
- Species that become extinct per year: more than 100,000.
- Days until the end of oil: 15,000 days = 42 years (if consumed at current rates).
- New expectations; the peak of the highest oil production will be: 2014
- At the end of the current century 30% of existing animals and plants will be gone.
- The worldwide destruction of the environment in the interest of profit is unlimited.
- In India Coca-Cola is destroying the food security of countless people by stealing the water and poisoning the water and soil; it is also responsible for ensuring a life of misery for future generations to come.

Facts about exploitation summarized in keywords:

- Resources are exorbitantly overexploited
- Carbon dioxide (CO2) emissions
- Chemical emissions
- Fine dust emissions
- Nuclear waste
- Loss of forests
- Loss of agriculture land
- Desertification
- Deforestation
- Extinction of species
- Days until the end of oil: what next?
- Destruction of nature and environment

Macroeconomic conclusions:

→ Over-exploitation is a madness of the managers of economics and macroeconomics.
→ Over-exploitation with all collateral damages is anti-science and anti-intelligence.
→ All universities and schools teaching such economic madness are as dingy as its practice.

3.3.5. Future Perspectives

The world experienced a catastrophic fall in food production as a result of the financial crisis (low commodity prices and lack of credit) and the adverse weather on a global scale. [298]

- Billions of people face shortages of food
- 1.5 billion people with no access to safe drinking water
- Increasing loss of arable land
- Huge water reservoirs will dramatically decrease
- Billions of people face shortages of food and water

General causes are:

- Agricultural market is increasingly dominated by speculations.
- Exorbitant exploitation is a major factor of lack of resources.
- Exaggerated use of chemicals destroys the soil for hundreds of years.
- Mad greed for exorbitant profit destroyed the agriculture market.
- Climate change is a major factor in damaging agriculture
- Exorbitant exploitation is a major factor of lack of resources

Macroeconomic conclusions:

→ An intelligent management of macroeconomics respects the reasonable use of resources.
→ Responsible leaders in macroeconomics deal with arable land like with the women they love.
→ The children of today's leaders will kill their fathers because they will face a lack of resources.
→ Stupid and blinded macroeconomic masters are already today digging the graves of their children.
→ Arable land, forest, oceans are the source of life and business; once gone, everything is gone.

---

[298] http://agriculture.imva.info/food-prices/agricultural-apocalypse-2010

3.4. Health and Health Care

3.4.1. General Picture

Every year around 240,000 people are diagnosed with skin cancer in Germany – increasing tendency. Every year skin cancer sees an increase of five per cent. Today in April (2011), we already have a greater sun intensity than in August due to the thinner ozone layer.

Breast cancer in Germany: In 2010 59,510 women were diagnosed with breast cancer; 17.286 women died. According to statistics every ninth German woman gets breast cancer. If we calculate this over a period of 10 years we are talking about 600,000 women that get breast cancer: Over a period of 80 years that makes around 5 million women that have breast cancer, are cured or not, or died. How many in Europe as a whole? Estimates would suggest around ten times as many. Incredible suffering, psychically as well as physically and socially! The critical question: Did they all fall ill due to highly toxic contamination of the environment (air, food, products)? It cannot be smoking and the suppressed psyche can also not be the source.

People living in cities are 21 per cent more likely than those living in rural areas to fall victim to anxiety disorders. In the case of depression it rises to 39 per cent... Researchers assume that the cause lies in the fact that so many people live so close together... Already today more than half the world's population lives in cities – tendency increasing.

The widespread misuse of antibiotics is rapidly rendering them powerless against infection.

Each year there are about 440,000 new cases of multi-drug resistant tuberculosis, resulting in at least 150,000 deaths.

An estimated 25,000 patients in the European Union die each year from drug-resistant infections.

"The world is on the brink of losing these miracle cures. In the absence of urgent corrective and protective actions, the world is heading towards a post-antibiotic era, in which many common infections will no longer have a cure and, once again, kill unabated." Most of the blame lies with doctors who overprescribe the drugs. [299]

Another huge problem is the use of antibiotics in food-producing animals. Approximately half of all antibiotic production is used in agriculture. Factory farms routinely give perfectly healthy animals antimicrobials both as a precaution against infection and to promote growth.

Spain: Chronic illnesses from 16 years old: Hypertension (17.2%), Back pains (16.3%), Neck pains (14.2%), chronic allergies (12.0%), Migraines and frequent headaches (8.6%), obesity (16.0%), very overweight (37.7%), under weight at age 18-24 (8.4%), Men with moderate overweight (62.8%) and women with moderate overweight (44.6%).

Short summary:

→ More than one billion (1.5 billion) people are overweight
→ 2.3 billion adults will be overweight by 2015
→ 4 billion people only have access to poor health services
→ In the European Union over 30 million are undernourished
→ More than a billion people suffer from diarrheal diseases
→ Respiratory infections, HIV/AIDS, and tuberculosis
→ Huge illnesses caused by dirty water and malnutrition
→ Diseases caused by bacteria, viruses, fungi and other parasites
→ Hunger causes a variety of illnesses and millions of deaths
→ Alcohol is a major cause of serious illnesses
→ Chemical products and fine dust everywhere influence health
→ Health care expenditure per day: $7,300,000,000
→ 1 billion people have no access to health services

Macroeconomic conclusions:

→ It must be part of macroeconomic thinking that all these health problems have high costs.
→ Unnecessary health costs burden a society with billions of non-productive costs.
→ Clever economists can find out that prevention is much cheaper than these costs.

---

[299] http://www.who.int/mediacentre/news/statements/2011/whd_20110407/en/index.html

3.4.2. Some Single Facts

a) Health care:

- 1 billion have no access to health services and another 4 billion only to poor health services.
- 99 percent of the 536,000 maternal deaths each year occur in the developing world.
- Every year 1.5 million children die due to illnesses caused by dirty water.
- Every year 11 million children under the age of 5 die, half of them due to malnutrition.
- In the European Union more than 30 million people are undernourished, especially people in hospitals and nursing homes, but also 5-15 % of the population in general.
- Germany: Every year around 600,000 hospital patients get infected with dangerous germs. Up to 40,000 patients die every year as a direct result of insufficient hygiene in hospitals.
- Medicare fraud costs Americans US$60 billion each year.
- Approximately 46 million Americans do not currently have any health insurance at all. Approximately 41 percent of working age Americans either have medical bill problems or are currently paying off medical debt. US hospitals overcharge Americans by about 10 billion dollars every single year. Medical bills cause more than 60 percent of the personal bankruptcies in the United States.
- The US health care industry has turned large numbers of doctors, lawyers, health insurance company executives and pharmaceutical company executives into multi-millionaires. America's five biggest for-profit health insurance companies ended 2009 with a combined profit of $12.2 billion. There were more than two dozen pharmaceutical companies that made over a billion dollars in profits in 2008.

b) Diseases:

- Diseases caused by bacteria, viruses, fungi and other parasites are major causes of death, disability, and social and economic disruption for millions of people.
- Over 9.5 million people die each year due to infectious diseases – nearly all live in developing countries.
- Among children under 5 years of age in low-income countries, infectious diseases cause nearly 70 percent of all deaths.
- Infectious diseases, including HIV/AIDS and lower respiratory infections,

cause nearly 40 percent of all deaths in low-income countries and about 18 percent of deaths globally.

- Worldwide, lower respiratory infections, HIV/AIDS, diarrheal diseases, and tuberculosis are among the top 10 causes of death; these diseases along with malaria account for the top 10 causes of death in the developing world.
- An estimated 30-40 million people live with HIV/AIDS with 2.4-3 million deaths every year.
- Over the past 30 years, more than 25 million people have died from AIDS. In 2008, 430,000 children under the age of 15 were infected with HIV and 270,000 died of AIDS. In addition, about 15 million children have lost one or both parents due to the disease.
- 350-400 million Malaria cases are registered per year; with one million deaths.

c) Obesity:

- 50.1 percent of adults across the 27 EU nations are overweight or obese based on the BMI (body mass index) values.
- There are 1,160,000,000 overweight people on earth today.
- Calculations predict that in 2015, 2,300,000,000 adults will be overweight and more than 700,000,000 will be obese (corpulent).
- 2010: more than 72 million adults in the USA suffer from obesity which has turned the condition into a major public health threat.
- Money spent due to obesity in the USA per month: estimated $80,000,000 and per year approximately $1,000,000,000; on weight loss programs: $35,000,000 per month.

d) Chemical products:

- Around 100,000 chemical products are used in Europe. More than 700 carcinogenic elements are present everywhere in the environment of everyday life. They can be found in food, water, soil, air, furniture, electrical devices, computers, carpets, cars, paintings and clothes. Heavy metals in high concentration can also be found in animal bowels, fish and sea food.
- Poisonous substances can be found in food, in the soil, in the air, in the sea, and then in the body of humans.
- About one in three people in the UK will get cancer due to contamination.
- One of four German people in the future will die due to cancer.
- The animals we eat are given large amounts of antibiotics and this not just when they are sick: healthy animals can be fed antibiotics every day because it makes them grow bigger and faster. As a result, people are getting sicker

and sick people are taking longer to get well. The day will come that antibiotics will be over – thanks to chicken farms.

- The sewage that goes into the sea is full of traces of medicines. When eating fish we take in these chemical elements into our bodies. What will be the result for pregnant women and children in the future?
- 11 million Canadians go to hospital every year due to food poisoning (especially from chicken).

e) Results of the Zeitgeist:

- 1,200,000 suicides per year around the globe; that is 1,200,000 human beings!
- Abortions worldwide: more than 40 million per year.
- Over one in 5 Americans has a personality disorder due to alcohol or drug abuse.
- In Europe people spend 11 billion Euros on ice cream, 50 billion Euros on cigarettes, and 105 billion Euros on alcohol.
- Alcohol is a major cause of serious illnesses and early deaths. Exaggerated consumption of alcohol plays a serious role in traffic accidents, crimes, violation, home and working place accidents, arsons, etc.
- Stress, work stress, time pressure and traffic jams result in people constantly being tense. Blood pressure, blood sugar and serum lipid levels increase with stress. Stress promotes cardiovascular diseases such as arteriosclerosis, high blood pressure, heart attacks and strokes.

Macroeconomic conclusions:

→ The sadness is that all intelligent economists and managers of economy are gone.
→ The picture about this collective state of health shows the true face of leaders and economics.

3.4.3. The Anti-Smoking Law

It is said: 6 million people die each year due to the abuse of tobacco around the world. In Germany 140,000 people die every year as a result of smoking. In Spain there are 9.5 million smokers. 56,000 Spaniards die of smoking annually.

In many countries the so-called anti-smoking laws have been implemented. Smoker statistics, which supposedly justify this law, are a complete charade, a monstrous lie and scientifically lacking credibility. This new law serves four

purposes:
1) The citizen has to categorically learn to obey the government, even if the orders from the state and the underlying laws are absurd and economically extremely damaging. This is called: generalized conditioning of behavior, the adoption of standards and laws, and thus it serves to prepare people for much tougher and more absurd laws that are already planned.

2) Nobody shall identify that diseases of the respiratory system are in the most part a result of completely different carcinogenic sources:

- Pollution (fine dust)
- Contamination
- Chemicals everywhere in daily life
- Heating
- Oil refineries
- Chemical factories
- Coal mining industry
- Gold mining industry
- Other mines sourcing for raw material (operating with chemicals)
- Chemical substances in goods
- Chemicals in food and drinks
- Asbestos
- Agriculture industry (chemicals such as pesticides and fertilizers)
- Fine dust emissions from cars (diesel, break pads, tires, tarmac)
- Fine dust and chemical emissions from airplanes
- Fine dust from pavement (car traffic)
- Fine dust from mines and surface mining
- Chemical emissions from the auto industry
- Chemical emissions from the chemical and paint industry
- Pesticides in the agriculture and cotton industry, etc.
- Carcinogenic toxic elements (to promote addiction) added to tobacco

Example: On a bad day, breathing in Mumbai's (or Malaga's) inversion-trapped air is the equivalent of smoking two and a half packs of cigarettes.

Example: After a certain amount of time, the lungs of a person who smokes 40-50 cigarettes a day do not look worse than those of a person that lives in a traffic prone area of a big city.

Has a doctor ever investigated the cause of human deaths in reference to all these much more toxic substances affecting all the everyday environments of people? Are these people not dying from the trillions of tons of carcinogenic emissions and not from smoking?

Aren't many more people dying around the globe every year as a result of the morbid psychical deformations of the leaders in politics, economy and religion, i.e. by delusional wars and exorbitant, perverse and psychopathic material and spiritual exploitation of 5-6 billion people and resources worldwide?

3) The creation of the scapegoat:

- The smoker is at fault.
- The smoker is the bad person.
- The smoker makes others ill.
- The smoker is a danger for society.
- The smoker kills other people ("passive smokers").
- One has to beware of smokers.
- One has to denounce smokers (when they smoke in prohibited places).
- One has to always give severe punishment, if there is a lack of obedience.

Denunciation is a key element of Macroeconomics (Corporations) and politics. On top of this the new law distracts people from the dramatic local, national and global financial crisis and monstrous global contamination.

4) The new anti-smoking law influences social behavior: Smokers talk and like to discuss for hours on end at bars, cafes and restaurants. They criticize politics; talk about the financial crisis, unemployment, social unrest, revolts and demonstrations, and especially about their governments. They share their sorrows and pains, etc. This must be prevented. This new law cuts such discussions in half or completely eliminates them because smokers go less to bars, less to restaurants; or they only stay for a very short time.

The motto: Divide your enemy! The damages go to the hospitality industry and in the end to the entire population, which once again falls into the hands of dictatorship.

Conclusion: Respiratory illnesses and especially cancer are the result of a concentrated combination of many chemical elements and fine dust in the air, in our environment, from the industry, and also as a result of the chemical elements (including pesticides) in cigarettes.

New approaches to the smoking effects:

New research from the Århus University Occupational Medicine Institute shows that Chronic Obstructive Pulmonary Disease (COPD) is not, as generally believed, only a smoker's disease.... According to the survey, some 65,000 Danes have contracted COPD, which in Denmark is also known as Smoker's Lung, without their illness having any connection to tobacco smoke. [300]

Smoking and nicotine have therapeutic effects:

A new study adds to the previously reported evidence that cigarette smoking protects against Parkinson's disease.

An example: "None of the 15,000 people who die from smoking in Australia every year were definitely killed by tobacco!" [301]

The benefit concerns restenosis, that is, the occlusion of coronary arteries. Smokers have much better chances to survive, heal and do well.

Since the benefits of smoking are too numerous and consistent to be attributable to error or random chance, it follows that the established truth asserting that smoking is the cause of (almost) all disease cannot be true – a reality that dramatically clashes with the gigantic corruption of public health, its pharmaceutical and insurance mentors, institutions and media. Therefore, it is constantly suppressed in the interest of public health, but not of the people.

Smokers are actually at lower risk from gum disease.

From the apparent shielding effect against Parkinson's and Alzheimer's diseases to the more intangible benefits associated with well-being and tranquility, smoking tobacco in many ways is definitely good for health: "Smoking Protects against Parkinson's Disease" or "Smoking protects against Alzheimer's Disease", or "Smoking protects against Ulcerative Colitis." [302]

Children of mothers who smoked at least 15 cigarettes a day tended to have lower odds for suffering from allergic rhino-conjunctivitis, allergic asthma, atopic eczema and food allergy, compared to children of mothers who had never smoked.

Carbon monoxide is a by-product of tobacco smoke. A report indicates very low levels of carbon monoxide may help victims of heart attacks and strokes.

---

[300] http://politiken.dk/newsinenglish/ECE1266978/thousands-of-non-smokers-get-copd/
[301] http://www.skepticalscience.com/Smoking-cancer-global-warming.html
[302] http://www.ncbi.nlm.nih.gov/pubmed/15706049

Carbon monoxide inhibits blood clotting, thereby dissolving harmful clots in the arteries.

Smoking may act as a preventative for developing a skin cancer that primarily afflicts elderly men in Mediterranean regions of Southern Italy, Greece and Israel.

Those who smoked cigarettes for more than 4 pack years (i.e., number of packs per day multiplied by the number of years of smoking) were found to have a statistically significant 54 percent decrease in breast cancer incidence when compared with carriers who never smoked.

Nicotine reduces circular muscle activity, predominantly through the release of nitric oxide-this appears to be 'up-regulated' in active ulcerative colitis. These findings may explain some of the therapeutic benefit from nicotine (and smoking) in ulcerative colitis and may account for the colonic motor dysfunction in active disease.

A statistically significant inverse relation between smoking and Alzheimer's disease was observed at all levels of analysis, with a trend towards decreasing risk with increasing consumption.

The benefits of smoking tobacco have been common knowledge for centuries. From sharpening mental acuity to maintaining optimal weight, the relatively small risks of smoking have always been outweighed by the substantial improvement to mental and physical health.

This extremely disproportionate response to a without doubt serious problem is an abuse of power! This perversion of power only exists because those who have the power are effectively perverted; i.e. they are psychically ill. The reaction of state authority also shows they have no wish to apply reasonable measure. They can neither talk nor convince. They have no desire for dialogue. They can only smash with brutal force because their psychical morbidity satisfies itself on the lust of this injury.

Macroeconomic conclusions:

➔ The health concern about smoking is in the core a mental problem of leaders.
➔ Scientists and leaders play the 'blind cow' when talking about smoking.
➔ Destroying bars, cafés and restaurants has become an aim of macroeconomics.

3.4.4. Mental Disorder and Disease

Mental health problems are costing Scotland £10.7 billion a year... The report said almost one in six working people in Scotland have poor mental health, such as depression or anxiety.... They also estimated employers lose £439 million a year through absence caused by mental health issues – 20% more than in 2004-05. The total loss rises to £2bn a year if other factors, such as staff attending work but being less productive because of hidden problems, are included. [303]

Dementia: The total estimated worldwide costs of dementia will exceed 1% of global GDP in 2010, at US$604 billion. About 70% of the costs occur in Western Europe and North America. The report reveals that the number of people with dementia will double by 2030, and more than triple by 2050. [304]

Increasingly psychical disorders are the reason for absences at the work place. Thus, the psychical state of workers produces damages to the economy in the billions.

According to statistics from Germany, in 2006, depression caused damages of 26.7 billion Euros to the economy.

The consumption of antidepressants has tripled in the last 10 years in Spain... The spending on antidepressants represents 47 per cent of the pharmaceutical spending on mental health in Spain.

In the European Union, the most common disorders are anxiety disorders and depression. By 2020 it is expected to be the number one illness in the developed world. "Social anxiety disorder is the most common anxiety disorder and the third most common mental disorder in the U.S., after depression and alcohol dependence." [305]

The WHO has determined that 58,000 people commit suicide every year in the European Union. "In the last 45 years suicide rates have increased by 60% worldwide ... one death every 40 seconds." [306]

People that keep on working with depression instead of seeking treatment cause a damage of 9 billion Euros. A person suffering from depression at the

[303] http://www.heraldscotland.com/news/health/mental-illness-bill-hits-10bn.13258888
[304] http://www.alz.co.uk/media/100921
[305] http://www.webmd.com/anxiety-panic/guide/mental-health-social-anxiety-disorder
[306] http://www.who.int/mental_health/prevention/suicide/suicideprevent/en/

workplace performs half an hour to two hours less than a healthy colleague. 5.2 billion Euros is the sum of the direct costs of treatment. On top of that the cost from the incapacity to work. The total sum for the economy amounts to 15.2 billion up to 22 billion Euros. Every year depression drives around 14,000 people to commit suicide.

One of 100 adolescents between the age of 14 and 18 falls into the grip of anorexia, while 2.4% develop bulimia. Other figures are: Chronic anxiety (6.0%), diabetes (5.9%), depression (5.3%) and asthma (4.3%). All these problems, except for diabetes, have a higher presence in women than in men. [307]

According to data released by the United Nations, three out of every 100 Spaniards is a cocaine addict, making Spain the most addicted country in Europe...19% of all European cocaine addicts are in Spain. [308]

In 2008, with over $14 billion in sales, antipsychotics became the single top-selling therapeutic class of prescription drugs in the United States, surpassing drugs used to treat high cholesterol and acid reflux.

Once upon a time, antipsychotics were reserved for a relatively small number of patients with hard-core psychiatric diagnoses – primarily schizophrenia and bipolar disorder – to treat such symptoms as delusions, hallucinations, or formal thought disorder. Today, it seems, everyone is taking antipsychotics. Parents are told that their unruly kids are in fact bipolar, and in need of anti-psychotics, while old people with dementia are dosed, in large numbers, with drugs once reserved largely for schizophrenics. Americans with symptoms ranging from chronic depression to anxiety to insomnia are now being prescribed anti-psychotics at rates that seem to indicate a national mass psychosis.

Macroeconomic conclusions:

→ If micro- and macroeconomics would be rational, the economy would be very different.

Most people around the globe are highly affected from mental disorder (disease) and from deformed or degenerated psychical functions. A short list of the major mental disorders:

---

[307] http://www.glowm.com/?p=glowm.cml/section_view&articleid=299
[308] http://www.spainreview.net/index.php/2011/03/03/three-out-of-every-100-spaniards-is-a-cocaine-addict/

- Depression
- Social phobia
- Chronic anxiety
- Stuttering
- Sleeping disorder
- Alcoholism
- Headache and migraine
- Speech disorder
- Personality disorder
- Behavior disorder
- Learning difficulties
- Family disruption
- Squalidness (waywardness)
- Aggressive behavior, violence
- Addictions (drugs, medicine, gambling, etc.)
- Morbid (psychopathic) relationships
- Neuroticism
- Narcissism
- Psychopathy
- Psychosis
- Perversion
- Sadism
- Emotional stress
- Megalomania
- Aberration
- Schizophrenia
- Religious psychosis

Macroeconomic conclusions:

→ Production and service sectors would be 50% more efficient without mental disorder.
→ Investors can turn red or blue calculating the higher profit with mentally healthy people.

3.4.5. Psychical Health in Industrial Countries

Let's take Germany as an example of an industrialized country with 82 million citizens. Figures have been collected from the media during the period 2006-2011. The figures obviously vary from year to year or source to source. Today, 2012, some figures may have increased and other figures decreased. The picture as a whole is important:

- 9 million suffer from depression (with 20% having suicidal intentions)
- 10 million suffer from migraine
- 3.2 million stutter
- 8 million have social phobia
- 5 million are dominated by chronic anxiety
- 8 million are at risk to become alcoholic
- 1.6 million are alcoholic and 25,000 die of alcoholism
- Exaggerated alcohol consumption produces economic damages of 20 billion Euros.
- Over 0.65 million suffer from cardiac fibrillation
- Every tenth woman has breast cancer (47,000 new cases 2010)
- One million occasionally have thoughts of committing suicide
- One out of two (three?) people suffer from some sort of sleeping disorder
- 11 million suffer from chronic pains
- 0.8 million have Alzheimer's disease
- 8 million suffer from diabetes B ("prosperity disease")
- 3 million have headaches on a daily basis
- 7 million are plagued by impotence
- 35-45 million are affected by constipation
- 50% of all adults and youth are overweight
- More than 4 million suffer from skin allergies
- Every eighth citizen suffers from respiratory allergies
- Every second child is overweight and suffers from some sort of postural deformity
- 1 million children suffer from asthma
- 14 million young adults have hearing damage (excessive volumes from Mp3 players and nightclubs)
- Every 5th child in the pre-school-age has speech disorder (lack of parental communication)
- Every fifth citizen suffers from stomach burns
- More than 50% suffer from spinal and other back pains
- 90% of all children have a headache either occasionally or very often
- Millions are addicted: drugs, medicine, gambling, consumption, chocolate, eating, etc.
- Over one million people live in poverty
- 70% of all medicaments are consumed by people over the age of 65
- One out of three marriages will end in divorce
- Every tenth child is a victim of violence within its own family
- Every third act of violence happens in a marriage (relationship) and family environment
- In one out of 3 relationships, 50% of women and 50% of men are violent

- Over one million children live on social welfare
- Two in three nursing home residents are badly or not sufficiently nourished.
- 6.3 million people are severely disabled (main cause: accidents)
- Out of 4 million unemployed there are 30% psychically ill from their situation; More than 6 million criminal acts committed per year
- Around 400,000 traffic accidents with over 6,000 victims and 0.5 million seriously injured
- 5-8 million people live in permanent sadness due to losing a beloved person through a car traffic accident
- Millions live in a permanent fear of becoming unemployed, lack of money, catastrophes, terrorism, war, weapons of mass destruction, etc.
- In Germany today there are 360,000 physically or psychologically handicapped children.
- Depressions produce costs (including economic damages) of more than 30 billion Euros per year.
- Nearly 10,000 people commit suicide every year. Three of four are men.
- An estimated 100,000 people try to commit suicide.
- Billions of Euros of damages each year due to psychical stress at the workplace.
- More than one of three Germans will become dement and require special care.
- Nearly one of two women must expect to get Alzheimer's disease.
- 1.2 million Germans have got Alzheimer's disease; with figures increasing yearly.
- New governmental statistics in January 2011: 400,000 Germans have fallen into the trap of compulsive (pathological) gambling – in Germany officially declared as a mental illness.
- Additionally, we have to point out millions of people in the following categories: separated and divorced, partly analphabet, lonely, bedraggled, victims of the economic crisis, victims of accidents, victims of medicine, victims of justice and administration, claimants from environmental catastrophes, homeless, people suffering from stress (noise, pollution, contamination, hunger, cold, etc.).

Macroeconomic conclusions:

→ Is this the society that people want?
→ It is a perverted, thoroughly sick and mad society.
→ Politicians have lost the duties of their ministries.
→ Given that economists have lost their mind, they can't see this economic disaster.

3.5. Contamination, Waste, Sewage

3.5.1. General Picture: Oceans and Water Supply

"According to a new report by the World Bank, urban rubbish generation is set to increase twofold over the next 15 years ... Household waste is set to soar from its current 1.3 billion tons to 2.2 billion by 2025, while the annual cost of managing this mountain of rubbish will rise from $205 billion to $375 billion ... "The challenges are going to be enormous, on a scale, if not greater than, the challenges we are currently facing with climate change. It's a relatively silent problem that is growing daily," Hoornweg told The Guardian ... The rubbish problem not only can be compared to climate change, but is also contributing to it. Greenhouse gas emissions from rubbish disposal, estimated at 5% of total emissions, must also be reduced, the report says. Methane from landfill sites accounts for 12% of total global methane emissions." [309]

We have collected this information from the Internet and from media reports (TV). We want to give importance to the picture as a whole and not to single statements that may be more or less correct.

In the oceans: Sewage and garbage (plastic), poisoning chemical elements, cesium, pesticide, heavy metal and mercury, oil pest, chemicals for agriculture, etc.

Oceans, seas, lakes, rivers, streams and groundwater are contaminated by remains of consumed medicaments: 50-90% go to the sewage, medicaments in urine and feces, also from showering: pain killer, antibiotics, hormones, tranquilizers, cholesterol reducers, medicaments for epilepsy and cancer, birth control pills, and other drugs.

Soaps, shampoos, cosmetics and perfumes contain chemicals that disappear down the drain, and go to the water in the nature: elements from cosmetics, perfumes and hair products. Fishes and sea fruits are eating this chemical soup.

---

[309] http://www.rt.com/news/global-waste-problem-urban-garbage-429/

Farmers give veterinary drugs to their animals, including large amounts of antibiotics. Drug-contaminated sewage sludge is sold as farm fertilizer. Later, these chemicals disappear down the drain and go to the water in the nature. Fishes and sea fruits are eating this chemical soup.

Already today and much more in the future, people around the globe have the chemical cocktail in the fish or sea fruits on their plate.

The artificial female sexual hormones in the anti-baby pill have lasting effects beyond the sewage plant treatment facilities, turning male fish into females.

A teaspoon of fully concentrated Estradiol is enough to cause the male trouts in a river section of ten meters deep, twenty meters wide and ten kilometers long, to turn into females.

Apart from hormones from the pill, fish also absorb painkillers, antibiotics and cell poisons from cancer treatments. Even medicines to treat cholesterol levels are now readily found in pike fish.

Even at low doses, the drug residues in water stop cells from reproducing.

Fish are experiencing reproductive problems as a result of chemical contamination.

Beyond having their sperm damaged, some fish are actually changing sexes due to chemical and medicament elements.

Some water creatures are experiencing organ failure and the inability to grow.

"In the middle of the equatorial **Pacific Ocean** sharks, tuna and other top-of-the-food-bew fish are half the size and their population is 80% smaller in numbers than they were 50 years ago." [310]

More than 100 different pharmaceutical compounds have been detected around the world, affecting fish and wildlife everywhere.

No laws exist to protect the public from pharmaceuticals.

According to a UN study on sanitation, far more people in India have access to a mobile phone than to a toilet. (Statistics 2011: 791 million mobile phone users in India). Immeasurable amounts of sewage go to the nature, the soil,

---

[310] http://www.theglobaleducationproject.org

the water streams, and the oceans.

At least 46 million Americans are drinking water contaminated with trace amounts of pharmaceuticals.

All kinds of drugs are being found in the bodies of fishes near major U.S. cities.

Researchers found drugs for high cholesterol, allergies, high blood pressure, bipolar disorder and depression in the livers and tissue of fishes.

Antidepressants, blood pressure and diabetes medications, anticonvulsants, oral contraceptives, hormone replacement therapy drugs, chemotherapy drugs, antibiotics, heart medications and even codeine are all showing up in the water supplies of American Cities.

Pharmaceutical drug contamination in streams: roughly 80 percent of the streams tested were found to be contaminated.

India's rivers are full of dangerous pharmaceuticals. One Indian River where 90 different pharmaceutical companies dump their waste tested positive for over 21 active drug ingredients. In one river alone, there was enough ciprofloxacin (a strong antibiotic) being dumped every day by drug companies to treat 90,000 people! [311]

It is estimated that 75 percent of India's surface water is now contaminated by human and agricultural waste.

According to a report back in 2009, all kinds of drugs are being found in the bodies of fish near major U.S. cities. Researchers found drugs for high cholesterol, allergies, high blood pressure, bipolar disorder and depression in the livers and tissue of fish.

Sea-life faces extinction, unprecedented in history, because of waste.

Carbon is being absorbed by the ocean at an alarming rate.

"...**Groundwater** pollution is essentially permanent. Water recycles extremely slowly underground, too slowly to flush out or dilute toxic chemicals. Water that enters an aquifer remains there for an average of 1,400 years, compared to only 16 days for rivers." [312]

---

[311] http://www.cbsnews.com/2100-202_162-4752641.html

"90% of the developing world's **waste water** is still discharged untreated into local rivers and streams." [313]

Contaminated water kills 25,000 people every day around the globe, and each year some 20 million children are impaired by malnourishment. [314]

Approximately 150 billion tiny pieces with an average weight of 1.8 milligrams, that is approximately 500 tons of tiny plastic pieces from waste, are currently swimming in the Mediterranean Sea. They serve as food for plankton and therefore for the fish and can easily land on our plates at the dinner table. [315]

Macroeconomic conclusions:

➔ That's why all economists don't drink any water and never eat fishes or sea fruit!
➔ The cocktail of chemicals and pharmaceutics in the human body will globally explode one day.
➔ Bad news: All representatives of economics and all investors will die from contamination.
➔ If economists would realize what they eat and drink every day, they would prefer to starve.

Medicine

Less and less medicine is working to combat illnesses. Antibiotics resistance will become a global problem. The responsibility lies in the massive use of medicines in the industrial livestock farming. There are enough loopholes for producers with high criminal drives.

Around the globe every year millions of tones of antibiotics are being used. Herewith the industrial livestock farming is one of the most important markets for the pharmaceutical industry.

In Germany, nothing related to livestock husbandry is under control. Organized crime dominates. Global corporations don't care what happens to their animals. They seem them as monetary values. It is all about the profit, 15 per cent profit that needs to be retrieved. It doesn't matter how this is

---

[312] http://www.theglobaleducationproject.org
[313] http://www.theglobaleducationproject.org
[314] http://www.waterandhealth.org/drinkingwater/safewater.html
[315] http://phys.org/news/2010-12-billion-plastic-fragments-mediterranean.html

achieved.

Macroeconomic conclusions:

→ Drug residue cocktails actually do cause harm to humans; except to economists.
→ The day the majority of economists read this, the meat market will collapse 80%.

3.5.2. Illustration of the Variety of Contamination

Breath deeply before you read the following paragraph! Prepare a whiskey with ice or a chocolate bar!

- "60% of the most hazardous **liquid waste** in the United States – 34 billion liters of solvents, heavy metals, and radioactive materials – is injected into deep groundwater via thousands of injection wells…" [316]
- 2.6-3 billion people have no access to sanitation; no local sewage treatment!
- Lack of toilets and sanitation facilities costs India nearly $54 billion a year.
- About 200 million tons of human waste is discharged into watercourses yearly.
- More than half of India's 1,170,000,000 people were mobile-phone subscribers, yet only 366,000,000 people had access to proper sanitation in 2008.
- Toxic chemicals released by industries into the air, land, water: 650,000,000 tons of sewage, 60,000 tons of mercury, 36,000 tons of phosphates is dumped into the Mediterranean each year.
- 7,000,000 of tons of plastic debris, industrial chemicals, agricultural waste, petroleum, etc., end up in the oceans every year.
- 250 billion of small plastic pieces are swimming in the oceans; and 500 tons swim in the Mediterranean Sea.
- 46,000 pieces of plastic debris swim on each square kilometer of ocean.
- Medicine residues go through the toilette into the water circles and via fishes back to the food chain.
- Global emission of carbon dioxide will increase until 2030 by 40% up to 40,000,000,000 tons (2006: 29,000,000,000 tons).
- "The increase, a half-billion extra tons of carbon pumped into the air, was almost certainly the largest absolute jump in any year since the Industrial Revolution."[317]

---

[316] http://www.theglobaleducationproject.org
[317] http://www.nytimes.com/2011/12/05/science/earth/record-jump-in-emissions-in-2010-

- Acidification of the oceans is a major threat to marine life and humanity's food supply. It affects marine life and in turn it affects the number of fish.

- The beautiful island in the Maldives that's been reduced to a pile of rubbish: Three-quarters of a million tourists flock to the pristine, white beaches every year. The Maldives dumps upwards of 330 tons of rubbish on the island every day. Each visitor generates 3.5kg of waste per day. Clouds of pungent, toxic smoke rising from open fires, piles of filth made up of plastic bottles, crisp packets and consumer detritus … environmental damage … large amounts of asbestos, lead and other toxic metals have been dumped into the lagoon … sending soot and carbon dioxide billowing into the air … The freighters are now ferrying debris to India instead. [318]

- There is the rubbish that comes from the land, delivered by run-off, storm water drains and the wind-blown rubbish that people leave behind. There is also ocean-based debris; it includes fishing lines and nets, offshore oil and gas rig/platform debris, waste from merchant ships, ferries and cruise liners and garbage from recreational and tourist vessels. Every day, ships jettison 5,500,000 million pieces of rubbish into the sea. [319]

- An estimated 14 billion pounds of trash, much of it plastic is dumped in the world's oceans yearly.

- Today, Americans generate 10,500,000 tons of plastic waste a year but recycle only 1 or 2 % of it.

- Electricity generation in the United States: "The United States 400-plus **coal-fired power plants** emit more toxins into the air than any other single source … Half of all Americans live within 30 miles of a coal-burning power plant, which in addition to mercury, emit more than 361,000 tons of other toxins including vanadium, barium, zinc, lead, chromium, arsenic, nickel, hydrogen fluoride, hydrochloric acid, ammonia and selenium." [320]

- The worldwide fishing industry dumps an estimated 150,000 tons of plastic into the ocean each year, including packaging, plastic nets, lines, and buoys.

- A plastic milk jug takes 1 million years to decompose. A plastic cup can take 50 - 80 years to decompose.

- The traffic emissions: Many tons of oil drops of vehicles go every day into the nature (soil and drinking water): rate of cancer, asthma, depressions, stress, and tickle in one's throat, etc., is increasing.

- Fine dust from cars, industry, oil heating, trains, chemical industry, oil

study-finds.html?_r=2&hp
[318] http://www.dailymail.co.uk/home/moslive/article-2162653/Maldives-island-paradise-Thilafushi-trashed-reduced-pile-rubbish.html
[319] http://articles.cnn.com/2010-04-12/tech/plastiki.kiernan.plastic_1_marine-debris-ocean-based-fishing-nets/2?_s=PM:TECH
[320] http://www.theglobaleducationproject.org

industry, coal and gold mining, etc., produces immense illnesses (respiratory tract) and cancer, millions of times more than smoking.

- The chemical industry, working 24 hours daily, let into the air thousands of tons of poisonous emissions.
- Toxic chemicals released by industries into our air, land, and water in January 2011: 870,000 tons.
- Carbon dioxide (CO2) released in January 2011: 2,000,000,000 tons.
- An estimated 90 tons of gold has been sold in 2010. The dark side: scrupulous exploitation, environmental damages and serious violation of human rights. Gigantic areas of land and exorbitant amounts of water are needed to exploit gold. The extensive contamination is horrifying. Cyanide is used to separate gold from rocks. Cyanide is highly poisonous and deadly. One gram of gold is found in 5 tons of rocks.
- 190,000 tons of asbestos, produced in Canada, are shipped to India, Pakistan, Indonesia, Thailand and Vietnam despite global bans of asbestos. Asbestos is a toxic mineral which causes lung cancer. Asbestos is responsible for 90,000 deaths per year worldwide.
- With over 20 million tones of nitric oxide every year the shipping industry outnumbers the air traffic industry tenfold; with 12 million tons of sulphur dioxide even by one hundred. Carbon dioxide stays in the atmosphere for up to one hundred years. Sulphur dioxide contributes massively to the contamination of the air close to the coasts, especially around areas with harbours.
- Russia has a long list of environmental problems. The total amount of hazardous waste stockpiled in the country is over 30 billion tons. Reversing the environmental damage is a large and complicated topic.
- Pollutants come from cleaning products, furniture, cars, building materials, and the much debated odorless radon gas.
- The accelerated problem of air pollution is determined not only by the increase of the carbon dioxide in the atmosphere but the phenomenon is closely connected with deforestation as well. Trees absorb the carbon dioxide from the atmosphere and in turn release oxygen but with the reduction of the wooded areas like forests and jungles this causes new issues.
- Ships and cruise ships are major water pollutants that are responsible for the deaths of about 65,000 people every year. Calculate for 50 years ahead!
- Power plants that generate the electricity which we rely on everywhere in our society cause about three and half thousand lung cancer cases and over thirty-five thousand heart attacks and this is just in the United States on a yearly basis.
- The chemicals in the water evaporate and fall back on the ground in the form of acid rains.
- There are 74 different kinds of pesticides that have been found in

groundwater, which is used today as potential drinking water.

- Toddlers born to expectant mothers exposed to a common chemical found in insecticides show a slower brain development, a new US study says. Pyrethroid insecticides, including PBO and Permethrin, are commonly used in many homes.

- Space debris: There are now more than 370,000 pieces of junk compared with 1,100 satellites in low-Earth orbit (LEO), between 490 and 620 miles above the planet.

- US estimations calculate $40-100 billion for environmental and economical damages from the oil-spill in the Gulf of Mexico.

- Dioxin is present everywhere in the environment. Dioxin is ultra-poisonous. Improper recycling of electronic scrap produces enormous environmental damages.

- The 3,000 most important enterprises produce environmental damages ('lateral effects') of approximately 2 billion Euros (unknown if per day or month or year).

- Each year, approximately 500 billion to 1 trillion plastic bags are consumed worldwide. That's over one million bags per minute. Billions of them end up as litter each year. The Worldwatch Institute estimates that in the U.S. alone, an estimated 12,000,000 barrels of non-renewable petroleum oil are required to produce the 100 billion bags consumed annually. That's over $500,000,000 the country could be saving to put towards clean, green energy. These plastic bags can take from 400 to 1,000 years to decompose but their chemicals residues remain for years after that.

- Ink found in printers produces fine dust that gets breathed in, which can produce illnesses as well as cancer.

- Billions of batteries in electronic products and cars, which are not correctly disposed of produce contamination that leads to severe health risks and cancer.

- In clothes and shoes there are chemical dyestuff that partly lead to allergies and in some cases even lead to cancer; e.g. colored bras whose dyes get transferred to the skin of the breast.

- If we take a global average life expectancy of 50 years then within 50 years 7 billion people will die. 7 billion corpses that need to be disposed of; staggering figures in the future. Already today, dead bodies contain a high concentration of chemical and medicinal substances. More and more people also have artificial components in their body.

- Biphenyl A: The hormonal effects of biphenyl A is suspected, among other things, to create erection and ejaculation problems, to create infertility, damage the development of the brain and trigger breast cancer. Biphenyl A is found in baby bottles made of polycarbonate, on paper receipts, baby pacifiers, tickets and invoices. Biphenyl A is absorbed through the mouth and skin contact.

- The sperm quality of men in industrialized countries is continually decreasing. Over 500 hormone related substances are responsible for this. These substances are found in a huge variety of products such plastic, insecticide, pesticide, medicines, flame retardants (chemicals), UV-filters in cosmetic products and sun creams.
- Most of the bees around the world are sick and billions are dying every year. Billions of bees have completely died off around the world. The entire human food chain is in danger given that 80% of all edible plants are dependant on bees. Bees pollinate over 90 types of vegetables, fruits and grain. The damage to harvests as a result of dying bees can easily be in the hundreds of billions, if not over a trillion (dollars, Euros).
- The loss of species is increasing at an alarming rate. The reasons are: construction, urbanization, deforestation, overfishing, climate change and invasive species. The diversity of species on our planet provides the basis of the fundamental elements of our ecosystem such as food, drinking water, medicine, wood, etc. Humanity must expect serious consequences in the coming 20-30 years.

Wikipedia: "Smog is also caused by large amounts of coal burning, which creates a mixture of smoke and sulfur dioxide. World coal consumption was about 6,743,786,000 short tons in 2006 and is expected to increase 48% to 9.98 billion short tons by 2030. China produced 2.38 billion tons in 2006. India produced about 447.3 million tons in 2006. 68.7% of China's electricity comes from coal. The USA consumes about 14% of the world total, using 90% of it for generation of electricity."

Macroeconomic conclusions:

→ If this is a consequence of the capitalistic economics, then economics is worse than blabber.
→ The day will come when the children of the investors have totally lost their sperm quality.
→ The corporation business: 'The new sneaking Holocaust oven', or: 'mass murder machine'.

Bioaerosols and Contamination [321]

Bioaerosols are airborne particles that are biological in origin. Bioaerosols are transported by the wind around the globe; with the climate change today – unpredictable "trips".

---

[321] (Info's from the Web (English) and the book: Bioaerosole und ihre Bedeutung für die Gesundheit, Bayerische Akademie der Wissenschaften)

Bioaerosols can be formed from nearly any process that involves biological materials and generates enough energy to separate small particles from the larger substance, such as wind, water, air, or mechanical movement.

Plants, soil, water, and animals (including humans) all serve as sources of bioaerosols, and bioaerosols are subsequently present in most places where any of these sources live.

Bioaerosols have a direct effect on our world on a daily basis, causing many health and welfare effects.

The health hazards associated with bioaerosols can range from more mild reactions such as allergies to much more severe reactions, such as death caused by airborne pathogens.

Welfare effects range from crop and livestock damage to lost tourism dollars and beyond.

While all bioaerosols are biological in origin by definition, an important attribute is whether the bioaerosols are living. Based on this attribute, bioaerosols are categorized into:

Two very important classifications: viable and non-viable. Non-viable bioaerosols are not currently alive and, therefore, cannot multiply; aerosolized pollen, animal dander and saliva, and insect excreta are all forms of non-viable bioaerosols.

In contrast, viable bioaerosols are living organisms that demonstrate microbiological activity and have the potential to multiply. These include airborne bacteria, fungi, and viruses, of which bacteria and fungal spores are the two most prevalent bioaerosols present.

Individual bioaerosols particles can range in size from approximately 0.02 to 100 micrometers in diameter, depending on the type and source. However, they also frequently agglomerate in clusters, thereby forming larger particles.

Important properties characterizing bioaerosols are size, viability, infectivity, allergenicity, toxicity, and pharmacological activity.

For bioaerosols to be infectious or pathogenic (cause disease), it must be viable. However, non-viable bioaerosols can still cause allergies or toxic reactions.

Bioaerosols can produce a wide range of health effects. Recall from earlier that for a bioaerosol to be infectious (pathogenic), it must be viable. However, non-viable bioaersols can still cause allergies or toxic reactions. Allergy sufferers can be affected by airborne biological matter. People with compromised respiratory systems, such as those with asthma and emphysema, can suffer respiratory sensitization attacks caused by bioaerosols as well.

On a daily level, countless people are afflicted with allergies or respiratory sensitization reactions, such as asthma, caused by interactions with fungi, pollen, and dander.

Sources of pathogenic bioaerosols include humans, animal houses, wastewater treatment plants, and biosolids storage units.

Pollen particles not only contain the actual pollen allergens inside, but also carry harmful substances of all kinds (e.g. pollution, fine dust, toxic particles) on their surface.

Indoor air quality: The central air system distributes them to the entire structure, spreading the pathogens incredibly effectively and exposing numerous people as a result. Therefore, the threat of pathogenic bioaerosols is especially potent in indoor scenarios (houses, working places, airplanes).

Phthalates

"Phthalates (…) or phthalate esters, are esters of phthalic acid and are mainly used as plasticizers (substances added to plastics to increase their flexibility, transparency, durability, and longevity). They are used primarily to soften polyvinyl chloride (PVC)…

…Phthalates are being phased out of many products in the United States, Canada, and European Union over health concerns." [322]

→ But production just gets moved to India, China and other Asian countries. The end product such as packaging for food then simply gets re-imported. The corporations are effectively 'forced' to save costs.

Serious health effects related to **Phthalates** are: "Organ system toxicity (non-reproductive), Endocrine system, Reproduction and fertility, Birth or

---

[322] http://en.wikipedia.org/wiki/Phthalate

developmental effects, Persistent and bio-accumulative, Brain and nervous system, Immune system (including sensitization and allergies)." [323]

"**Phthalates** are used in many products, including: automotive components, building materials, vinyl flooring furniture, pool liners and garden hoses cosmetics, perfume and nail polish footwear, outdoor clothing and rain wear inflatable products medical devices such as intravenous and feeding tubing, catheters, blood bags, anaesthetic and dialysis equipment printing inks solvents such as adhesives, lacquers and varnishes sporting goods toys wires and cabling—in many machines and appliances and as insulation for transmission cables and fibre optics." [324]

"Most dangerous are the **Phthalates**. They make the packaging soft and smooth (elastic). But they actuate also like hormones. As a consequence men become infertile. Furthermore these toxics can be found in creams, fruits, milk, oil, sauces, finished products and also in film packaging of meat and fruits." [325]

Summary of effects according to numerous studies:

- There is an association between phthalate exposure and endocrine disruption leading to development of breast cancer.
- High doses have been shown to change hormone levels and cause birth defects.
- Exposure during pregnancy results in decreased anogenital distance among baby boys.
- Boys born to mothers with the highest levels of phthalates were 7 times more likely to have a shortened anogenital distance.
- There may be a link between the obesity epidemic and endocrine disruption and metabolic interference.
- Has showed statistically significant correlations with abnormal obesity and insulin resistance.
- Large amounts of specific phthalates fed to rodents have been shown to damage their liver and testes.
- Initial rodent studies also indicated hepato-carcinogenicity.
- Found a link between allergies in children and the phthalates.
- Found an association between phthalates in the home and asthma, especially in children.
- Found that prenatal phthalate exposure was related to low birth weight in

---

[323] http://www.ewg.org/chemindex/term/480
[324] http://www.productsafety.gov.au/content/index.phtml/itemId/972486
[325] http://www.arte.tv/de/Programm/242,date=3/7/2012.html

infants.
- Low birth weight is the leading cause of death in children under 5 years of age and increases the risk of cardiovascular and metabolic disease in adulthood.
- Statistically significant correlation between urine phthalate concentrations in children and symptoms of ADHD.

3.5.3. Nuclear Waste

The ideology and vision of nuclear power stations is a horrendous lie. Nuclear energy is the most expensive energy that has ever existed. The state even subsidizes the industry with various indirect contributions (tax contributions!). Nuclear energy is the result of the obsession with economic growth. Then you have the tens of thousands of tons of nuclear waste around the globe, which contains a lethal danger and entails billions (of dollars) in maintenance and storage costs. The coming generations will have to pay for today's electricity for thousands of years. Anyone that accepts this is absolutely stupid, evil and devilish! There are no end storage places that are safe; and they will never exist. Possessed by delusion the representatives talk about a "minor risk". Every body already knows this "minor risk", we saw it with Chernobyl and more recently again with Fukushima (Japan). Billions of people can get sick and die in such a nuclear accident. Not to mention the immense contamination of land, seas and oceans. Even entire continents could become poisoned for hundreds of years, including the entire drinking water and agricultural land. Not even the devil could want such a 'minor risk', only those people in the industry that earn billions with this.

- 9 states discharged on 15 locations in the North Atlantic: 115,000t in 223,000 barrels with nuclear waste; now leaking (concentration of plutonium 238).
- Nuclear waste is extremely hazardous for both environment and humans.
- Nuclear waste – many thousands of tons – must be stored for 1,000,000 years.
- Nuclear waste storage must be controlled, protected and administered for 1,000,000 years and will always carry a permanent risk.
- Nobody knows if the nuclear waste storage packaging is safe for 1,000,000 years.
- Repackaging nuclear waste in the future will have to be paid for by future generations. It will be very expensive.
- Nuclear electricity is the most expensive energy humanity has every produced.
- Sweden has stored 9,000 tons of nuclear waste. Hundreds of thousands of

tons are stored around the world.

- Nuclear storage always has a permanent risk.
- Nuclear waste – many hundred thousands of tons – must be stored, controlled, protected and administrated for 1,000,000 years.
- Storage, maintenance, repackaging, and recycling nuclear waste will cost the following generations billions of dollars each year, over and over again.

Macroeconomic conclusions:

→ The economists were drunk when they calculated the nuclear power station business.
→ Doing risky business is fun, exciting, and creates a special mental orgasm.
→ The economic and political attitude: "After me, the deluge! My children can pay for it."
→ Economists, investors, and politicians have lost their mind, intelligence and reason.
→ Not the stupidest person with the tiniest brain would accept such economic calculations.
→ The science of economics preaches profit as a short term ego (or genital) satisfaction.

3.5.4. Special Cases of Contamination

Contamination and Honey Bees

The loss of the honey bee threatens worldwide famine.

All the developed countries of the world are responsible for the collapse of honey bee communities.

In the United States, beekeepers are experiencing unprecedented die-offs of bees, some losing as much as eighty percent of their colonies. Commercial beekeepers in twenty-two states have reported deaths of tens of thousands of honeybee colonies.

A British researcher writes that there are probably many causes for the loss of honey bees, from loss of foraging grounds to viruses, parasites, chemical pollution, and other pathogens that spread quickly from continent to continent. Apart of contamination and pollution, climate chaos and extreme weather seem to be a major factor.

Mass deaths of honeybees affect more than 30 percent of bee colonies in the

US and over 20 percent in some European countries, Reuters reported. [326]

Some 52 of the world's 112 leading crops rely on pollination and honeybee losses can greatly affect the world economy as the value of insect pollination, mainly by bees, is put at about $212 billion.

"Each day 100 living species become extinct, 1,000 acres of peat bogs are excavated and 150,000 acres of tropical rainforest are destroyed. Each day, 2 million tons of toxic waste is dumped in to our rivers and seas, 22 million tons of oil are extracted and 100 million tons of greenhouse gases are released." [327]

Macroeconomic conclusions:

➔ Economics see everywhere a margin for benefit, but never the bees as they are too small.

Oil and Gas

Gas flaring has a global impact on climate change by adding about 400 million tons of CO_2 annually. 90 million tons of heat-trapping emissions are constantly dumped every 24 hours into the earth's atmosphere.

Oil firm Texaco is accused of dumping billions of gallons of toxic waste into unlined pits in Amazon's rainforests and rivers. The poisonous waste has not only contaminated water but also killed wildlife and increased cancer rates in the region. Apart from health issues, the locals say that their homes were destroyed and that their hunting and fishing grounds were polluted, all due to the oil company's actions.

The US state of Louisiana estimates that the damage to the environment and the economy from the oil spill in the Gulf of Mexico could reach 40 to 100 billion dollars.

This oil spill in the Gulf of Mexico was shown around the globe in the media. The oil catastrophe in the Niger delta on the other hand is completely concealed. Since 2006 over 3,000 leaks have been detected there.

Dioxins are organic elements, that can be found everywhere in our environment. They are colorless and odorless, long-lasting and liposoluble

---

[326] http://en.wikipedia.org/wiki/Colony_collapse_disorder
[327] http://www.eradicatingecocide.com/theproblem/

and they are toxic.

The incorrect recycling of electronic waste leads to high Dioxin contamination of the environment.

The United Nations states: Most corporate groups don't care about the massive destruction of the environment. The 3000 mightiest corporation alone cause environmental damages of nearly 2 billion (2000 million) Euros per year.

Macroeconomic conclusions:

→ The economy doesn't even take note of the nature and species around the globe.
→ These 2,000 million Euros for environmental damages (externalities!) must be too small to be considered.
→ Economists calculate only with profit oriented models, never with collateral damages.
→ There is a lust for life and a lust for evil; means: people want to experience both.

Mines and Gold

The constantly increasing price of Gold has increased the destruction of the Amazon rainforests in the Peruvian Madre de Dios six fold.
Between 2003 and 2009 the Gold diggers working with primitive techniques destroyed 7000 hectares of untouched and extremely species-rich rainforest in Guacamayo and Colorado-Puquiri.

44.4 tonnes of Gold were digged out in the second half of 2010. The dark shadow: unscrupulous exploitation, destruction of nature and grave human rights violations.

Gold digging devours massive amounts of land and uses huge amounts of water. The creation of mines violates the human rights of thousands of people who are expelled from their towns and fields.

In Peru rain forests are devoured, in Guatemala Indian folks are expelled and attacked. In the "gold coast" of Africa, in Ghana, the chemicals contaminate rivers and people, and on top of it they lose their homes.

The use of the highly toxic Zyanide is extremely damaging to health and environment. This chemical is used to free the gold from the stone.

To get one gram of golf around five tones of stone need to be exploded. The toxic sludge is massed in huge artificial lakes. When it rains they risk overflowing and causing an environmental catastrophe. Zyanide is absolutely deadly.

Macroeconomic conclusions:

➔ At least we have the gold and can dance around the golden calf; the cost doesn't matter.

Contaminated Fish and Meat

Sewage and garbage (e.g. plastic) polluting oceans, poisoning chemical elements, cesium, pesticide, heavy metals and mercury, oil, chemicals for agriculture, fine dust, etc., in the world's seas are only one side of the ocean's contamination.

The other side: 50-90% of consumed medicines also go into the sewage system. Oceans, seas, lakes, rivers and groundwater are rendered impure by the residue of medicines in urine and feces: pain killers, antibiotics, hormones, tranquilizers, cholesterol reducers, medicines for epilepsy and cancer, birth control pills, high blood pressure tablets, bipolar disorder and depression chemicals, and many more.

Drugs and medicines are not the whole problem: soaps, shampoos, hair products, cosmetics and perfumes contain chemicals that disappear down the drain when washing and showering. They are absorbed by the earth's natural waters.

Fishes and sea fruits ingest this chemical and drug residue cocktail. Researchers also found all kinds of drugs in livers and tissue of fishes. These drug infested fish and sea fruits are then eaten by people around the globe for lunch or dinner.

In the not to distant future this mix of the fish together with meat infested with antibiotics will cause the human body to rebel. Nobody knows the combined reactions of all chemical and drug elements in the future. Nevertheless, enjoy your meal tonight!

The smoking-ban many countries have introduced distracts people not only from the intended "One World Order" and global oligarchy, but also and especially from the extremely serious contamination present in the environment and in the food we eat.

Macroeconomic conclusions:

➜ "Not again! Now, I can't eat anymore fish and meat." Who is the dog in the manger?

Chemicals in Milk

Scientists have revealed that a glass of milk can contain a cocktail of up to 20 painkillers, antibiotics and growth hormones. Using a highly sensitive test, scientists found a host of chemicals used to treat illnesses in animals and people in samples of cow, goat and human breast milk.

Man-made chemicals are now found throughout the food chain. The highest quantities of medicines were found in cow's milk. Milk is contaminated also with the anti-depressant Prozac. The hormones from the contraceptive pill and HRT have been blamed for feminizing fish, leading to male fish producing eggs.

The tests also found niflumic acid in goat's milk, while breast milk contained traces of painkillers ibuprofen and naproxen, along with the antibiotic triclosan and some hormones. If the findings are true for Spanish and Moroccan milk, they could equally be true for milk produced in Britain and northern Europe.

Macroeconomic conclusions:

➜ What's the problem? Children need painkillers, antibiotics, and growth hormones.
➜ Investors and CEOs don't drink milk and they perfectly know why.

Space Debris

More and more garbage is massing in outer space. Around 150 million objects are in orbit. Many are merely a few millimeters in width. 600,000 are bigger than one centimeter. When these pieces collide then they are like a hand grenade.

Macroeconomic conclusions:

➜ Who cares? We don't see these 150 million space debris objects.

The main products of emissions

- Toxic chemicals
- Plastic debris
- Industrial chemicals
- Industrial waste
- Agricultural waste
- Agricultural chemicals
- Petroleum, oil
- Sewage
- Rubbish, garbage
- Household waste
- Nuclear waste
- Emission of carbon dioxide
- Residue of medicines

Oceanic genocide: Between 700,000 and 1,000,000 sea birds are killed each year by marine debris such as discarded fishing lines and plastic bags. An estimated 100,000 marine mammals are killed each year by plastic in the ocean.

Macroeconomic conclusions:

→ It's a waste of time and a loss of money to think about waste and emissions in general.

Drug Residue Cocktails

- Laboratory experiments show: even at low doses, the drug residues in water stop cells from reproducing.
- Fish are experiencing reproductive problems as a result of chemical contamination.
- Beyond having their sperm damaged, some fish are actually changing sexes due to chemical and medicament elements.
- Some water creatures are experiencing organ failure and the inability to grow.
- More than 100 different pharmaceutical compounds have been detected around the world, affecting fish and wildlife everywhere.
- Antidepressants, blood pressure and diabetes medications, anticonvulsants, oral contraceptives, hormone replacement therapy drugs, chemotherapy drugs, antibiotics, heart medications and codeine are all showing up in the water supplies.

- At least 46 million Americans are drinking water contaminated with trace amounts of pharmaceuticals.
- India's rivers are full of dangerous pharmaceuticals. In one Indian river 90 different pharmaceutical elements have been found, from pharmaceutical companies dumping their waste in the river.
- All kinds of drugs are being found in the bodies of fishes near major U.S. cities.

Macroeconomic conclusions:

→ Drug residue cocktails actually do cause harm to humans. How long will it take until such effects start to globally strike down a billion humans?
→ No laws exist to protect the public from such pharmaceuticals.

Other Chemicals in the Water

- Natural oestrogenes
- Synthetic oestrogenes
- Clofibric acid
- Phytooestrogene
- Benz(a)anthracen
- Benzo(a)pyren
- Benz(a)anthracen
- Benzylbutylphthalat
- Bisphenol
- Nonylphenol
- Nonylphenoldiethoxylat
- Endosulfan
- Dieldrin
- Chlordan
- Diethylhexylphthalat
- Dibutylphthalat
- Tributylzinn
- Dichloranilin
- Dichlordiphenyldichlorethylen
- Linuron
- Diuron
- And much more …

Macroeconomic conclusions:

→ As we have here strange foreign words and can't understand the problem we don't care.

→ From which kind of products and production processes do these chemicals come?

Contamination of the Planet

The unstoppable collective suicide of 7 billion, 8 billion, 9 billion, 10 billion.

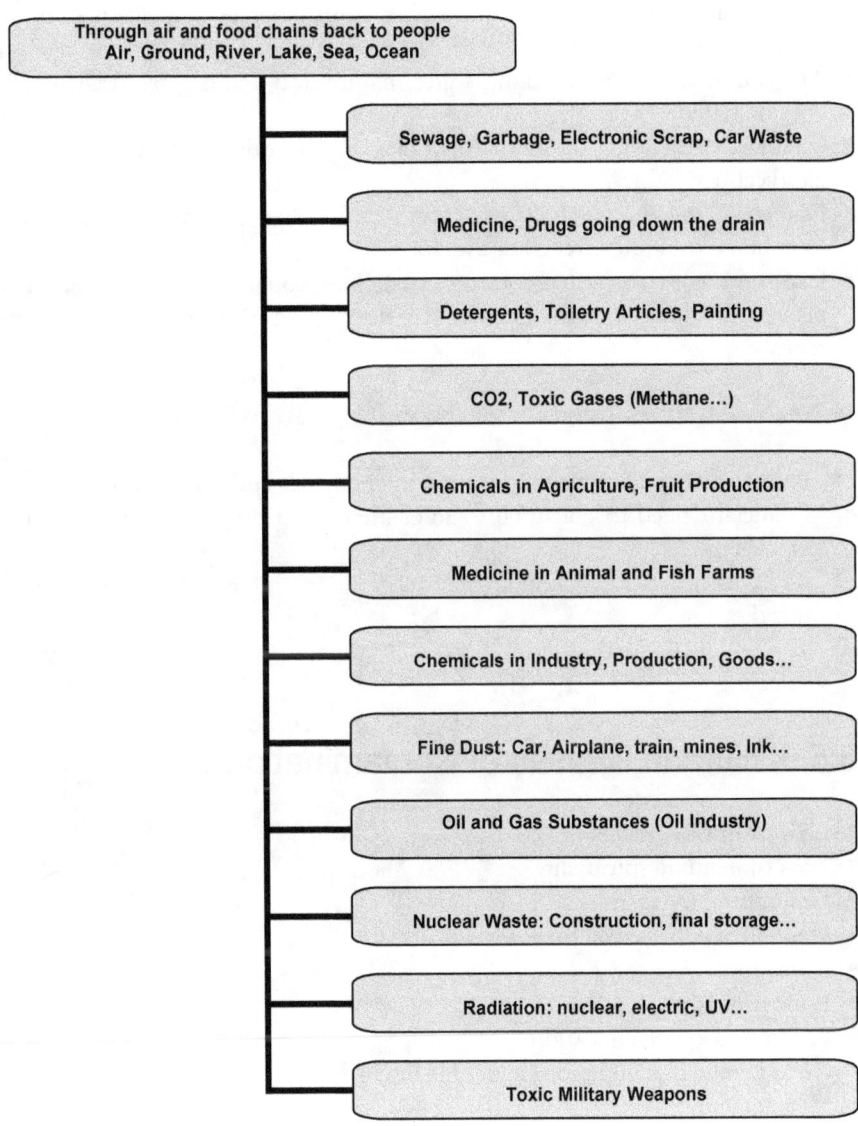

3.5.5. The Result of Contamination

- Millions of people die every year due to fine dust: cars, industry, heating with oil, all kind of mining.
- Hundreds of millions of people die due to chemical emissions from the industry.
- More than 3,000,000,000 people suffer from illnesses and disease due to pollution.
- Air, soil, sea, oceans, drinking water, nature and animals are dramatically contaminated.
- Chemical reactions in human bodies will reduce fertility or create handicapped babies.
- Dying in the future will be very painful due to chemical elements (combined multiple effects) in the body.
- Exposure to two types of common pesticides, rotenone and paraquat, may place individuals at a higher risk of developing Parkinson, a US study reveals.

Macroeconomic conclusions:

→ Politicians need a further education in chemicals and pharmaceutics.
→ Politicians need to consume toxic elements and drugs to understand the problem.
→ Radicalism, terrorism, and archaic religious teachings will increase due to this disaster.
→ The lesson: Industrialized nations will fall into poverty and indescribable suffering.

3.5.6. Human Causes of Contamination

- Loss of human values
- Loss of genuine spirituality
- Unlimited capitalism
- Uncontrolled financial business
- Corruption
- Lobbyism
- Lack of adequate education
- Archaic religions imprisoning people in illusions
- Megalomania
- Narcissism

- Egoism
- Individualism
- Greed
- Loud-moulds
- Religious lunacy disrespecting the human problems
- Unlimited consumption
- Fun oriented society and life style
- Pure hedonism
- Unlimited consumption
- Brainwashed and manipulated (seduced) people
- Life lies
- Religious obsession
- Arrogance
- Ignorance
- Laziness
- Superstition
- Brainless ways of living
- Lack of leadership integrity
- Insensibility and indifference
- Lack of moral education
- Incompetent politicians

Let's summarize the problem:

The pollution and contamination around the globe have brought the planet and all its eco-systems to the brink of collapse; and with that the most probable extinction of humanity in the near future.

Countless poisonous chemical substances can be found in the environment, in the water, in the earth, in rivers and seas and oceans, in animals and fish and in all kinds of food products.

Up to 200 of these chemical elements can already be found in the body of most people. Human-made catastrophes due to contamination are taking on frightening dimensions. Diseases, cancer as well as deformed babies are already today the consequences.

Millions of people are dying every year due to this; and in 10-20 years billions will die as a result.

Billions of people are (and will be) affected in the long-term over hundreds of years due to the consequences, including poverty, misery and terrible suffering.

Macroeconomic conclusions:

→ Incredulous due to such an incredible outrageous contamination disaster and evil doing.
→ Speechless due to the blind economists and politicians with economic responsibility.
→ Dumbstruck due to the stupidity of the educated masses that simply don't bother about it.
→ Unspeakable the absence of moral attitudes and the lack of respect for the creation.
→ The neo-capitalistic micro- and macroeconomics will die like the 30 million died from the pest.
→ Economically all these facts make no sense, a complete loss of profit in the long term.

3.6. Transport Systems

3.6.1. Cars and Public Transport

People like cars. Most people want a car. Here we have a short picture about this 'wonder' vehicle:

- Road Traffic Accidents (RTAs) result in 1.2 million deaths and 50 million injured every year.
- Over the last 50 years more than 60 (100?) million people died and 2.5 billion people were injured due to RTAs. [328]
- WHO: The global annual cost of Road Traffic Accidents is almost 518 billion US dollars. Another source: The global annual cost of RTA is almost 230 billion dollars (2006).
- 10% of all hospital beds are occupied by RTA-victims.
- In 2008, 380,000 people died in Europe as a result of fine dust from road traffic; and millions more around the globe.
- Cars produced in January 2011: 4,500,000; for 2011 as a whole, expectations are 65-70,000,000 (as China enormously increases its car production).
- In 2007 an estimated 73 million cars were produced.

Macroeconomic conclusions:

→ Unbelievable costs for a minimal benefit.
→ The system that will destroy the entire planet.
→ Where are the 2 other planets giving us the resources to produce cars for the next 1000 years?

Car and Lorry Traffic Pollution

1) Exhaust gases, including fine dust (diesel)
2) Fine dust from the abrasion of tires
3) Fine dust from the abrasion of driving surfaces
4) Fine dust from the disk brakes

---

[328] http://www.medindia.net/health_statistics/health_facts/Alarming-facts-about-road-traffic-accidents.htm

5) Traffic noise is also considered as an extremely unhealthy emission

Macroeconomic conclusions:

→ First economic principle: As people don't see the fine dust, it does not exist.

Train Pollution

- Fecal fine dust, fine dust from rail abrasion and iron wheels.

Macroeconomic conclusions:

→ The first economic principle: Speak in a confusing way that is always and everywhere valid or irrelevant, positive or negative at the same time. And never annoy people with verbal fecal fine dust because educated people don't like fecal language as it expresses an anal problem.

Aviation Pollution

- Fine dust, gases and noise (civil, military, sport)

Macroeconomic conclusions:

→ Second economic principle: Any critical approach to economics and its critical externalities is an exaggeration.

Wrecks

- Wrecks of cars and lorries or trucks, all kind of transport vehicles, also trains and airplanes leave behind dangerous metals and chemical elements.

Macroeconomic conclusions:

→ Third principle of economics: Put under the carpet all your concerns, also those about all dangerous metals, chemicals, pharmaceutics, toxic elements in the air, soil, water, environment, food, drinking water, etc.

Oil Tankers

- Oil tankers, pipelines, and oil derricks produce – especially catastrophic accidents – produce an incredible amount of destruction of the world of animals and nature, including sea and oceans. Contamination of soil and drinking water has dramatic long term effects on nature and humans.

Macroeconomic conclusions:

→ Forth principle of economics: Always see and value the benefit for YOUR life standard, satisfaction, and well-being.

Some Examples

- In Germany 55% of the driven car-kilometers are due to holiday and leisure traveling.
- Special holiday pollution: A cruise ship produces the same amount of fine dust as 50,000 cars driving at 130 km/h.
- There is an enormous demand for petrol, diesel, ceresin, and oil; not only from private traffic; probably even more from military use.
- High speed trains consume a lot of electricity and also produce fine dust.
- Traffic noise is also considered an extremely unhealthy emission.
- There are estimated 1.5-2 billion cars and other motor-vehicles (eg. Lorries, vans, etc.) in use worldwide; all producing pollution, contamination, accidents, etc.
- In the air inside certain car models, traces of more than 100 different chemicals can be detected - some of them can cause cancer. Source: Degassing plastics and solvent-based adhesives and coatings. Carcinogenic substances in the interior of a car are not uncommon.
- The concentration of toxins from traffic congestions such as the cancer-causing benzene is about five times as high in the car as in nature. The concentration of toxins in the car also rises sharply when one is stuck in traffic.

Macroeconomic conclusions:

→ Fifth principle of economics: Traveling is the ultimate freedom (benefit, satisfaction) for the ones and creates profit for the others.

3.6.2. Negative Implications of Transport Systems

- Road Traffic Accidents with millions of victims, injured and handicapped people
- Sea traffic accidents (oil tankers) producing mega damages to the environment
- Waste from ships and other vessels thrown directly into the sea (ocean)
- Car and lorry traffic pollution

- Train and airplane pollution
- Cruise ship and in general vessel pollution
- Wrecks of cars, vans and lorries
- Oil tankers
- Noise pollution
- Negative impact into nature, sea life and sea nature
- Enormous global demand of petrol, diesel, kerosene and oil
- Trains, especially high speed trains: high demand of electricity

Macroeconomic conclusions:

→ Sixth principle of economics: Don't be negative. Negative thinking means negative person. And nobody likes negative people.

3.6.3. Cars from Production to Recycling

Raw materials needed: Glass, steel, plastic, copper, lithium, aluminum, iron, plastic steel, wood, cotton, rubber, coconut fiber, chemical elements, detergents, oil, electricity, water, rare elements, paint, leather, and much more.

Exploitation of prime resources produces (mines): destruction of environment, chemical and fine dust contamination (soil, air, and water), very low wages (poverty), exploitation of people, illnesses (cancer), low life expectations of the workers, etc.

Probably more than 1.5 billion people work within this "car production" chain from raw material exploitation to the final buyer of a car including the car maintenance during an average of 15 years (accidents, repair and service, cleaning, traffic lights, car washing, etc.), including insurance providers and damage management (banks for loans, lawyers, insurance companies, police, repair of lateral damages, hospitals, and doctors), and the recycling of the cars.

We must also calculate the millions of machines and tools, including high tech apparatus (robot and conveyor high tech), that are needed to maintain this production chain. Above that during winter there are even more costs: snow removal or salt against ice on the roads, and road damages in general.
Hundreds of thousands of components suppliers are working for the car industry. The effects include: High electricity demand, contamination and environmental destruction (pollution).

Another estimated 100,000,000 people are working in the car repair and service industry, the road building and road repair, including technical equipments and all kind of services (required for road maintenance). Every 2 years or once a year, depending on the location, a car must be checked and get the "technical inspection" stamp for another year.

Not to forget the building constructions for every factory or office building, for the service and administration offices (plus furniture, equipment, stationery) and for the workshops (plus equipment, furniture, stationery).

Global transport of raw material, car components and cars produce: contamination (of air, soil, sea, and oceans), health problems (fine dust), oil, environmental damages, etc. This is a contribution together with the general car traffic to forest decline, to environmental pollution, and illnesses of people.

The car production business is gigantic. These businesses need marketing, an IT-infrastructure, stationery, ink (millions of liters with fine dust emissions), all kind of administration tools, etc. Technical infrastructure requires a maintenance service. Hundreds of millions of emails need to be sent, additionally the costs for internet, telephones, and cell phones.

The best business in the whole lifeline of this "product": from the resource exploitation until the "end" of a car life (recycling), the governments make huge sums of money from taxes, duties and VAT and this every time an element or component "changes hands".

Most of the working people in this chain need a car themselves or need public transport to travel to their workplace: more petrol and more contamination! Effects: contamination and environmental destruction (pollution), including billions of unproductive hours wasted on "traveling" per year.

In the end we should not forget. traffic accidents produce more than one million fatalities and several millions of injured people every single year. There are additional costs and institutions working for: unemployment, handicapped people, loss of manpower, orphans, as well as separation and divorce due to dramatic changes in a family life as a consequence of car traffic accidents, etc.

Identify the lunacy: within the next 20 years an estimated 1.5-2 billion cars will be produced around the globe! Conclusion: fantastic business for the owners of the factories in the production chain, for the CEOs and for some car dealers. But it is lethal for the planet and for the entire humanity!

Macroeconomic conclusions:

→ Seventh principle: Never think in complex dimensions, including the time perspective. It makes life and business too complicated and buggers up profit maximization.

3.6.4. Nuclear Power Stations

Seventy-six operating power stations in Japan, Taiwan, China, South Korea, India, Pakistan and the US are located in areas close to coastlines deemed vulnerable to tsunamis.

Of 442 nuclear power stations globally, more than one in 10 are situated in places deemed to be at high or extreme risk of earthquakes -- in Japan, the US, Taiwan, Armenia and Slovenia.

In every nuclear reactor in Germany there could be a meltdown. All the radioactive elements would be freed, destroying the environment completely in a radius of 400-500 kilometers.

Costs of Nuclear Waste; Example Germany

Nuclear waste is very dangerous for the environment and humankind.

Every reactor has a limited lifespan. At the end, what remains are thousands of tons of contaminated material. Disassembling is done by hand. That is time consuming and very expensive.

The cost of storing nuclear waste is high: 1.8 million tones is the weight of all the nuclear power plants "end material". A third of it, around 600,000 tones, is contaminated radioactively; 10,000 tones so much that they have to go to a nuclear waste repository. This waste has to be stored safely over decades, some even hundreds and thousands (up to one million) of years.

The whole process of dismantling a nuclear power plant costs enormous amounts of money. The bill is footed by the electricity consumer and as is often the case the state or better said the taxpayers.

In Germany the talk is of 3.2 billion Euros until 2013 to dismantle one reactor. End storage several hundreds of millions of Euros more. Add all this together and for the 17 currently operating nuclear reactors we reach a figure of around 55 billion Euros.

Restoration of old nuclear power stations, final storage of nuclear waste, relocation of unsafe nuclear waste storages, and maintenance of provisional and final nuclear storages will cost, for example for Germany, during the next two decades, at least 10 billion with highest probably two or three times more. This means: 20-30 billion Euros (as experts calculated).

Such costs are not in the electricity bills that German citizens get today every month! Who will pay this in the future? The German citizens with their taxes will have to pay such enormous costs.

Macroeconomic conclusions:

→ Eighth principle of economics: Have fun, don't make everything complicated, and copy the principle of public debt. You can relax because others will work and pay for it the next 200 years.

Main Profiteers

- Car and car supplier industry
- Mining industry
- Oil industry
- Governments: tolls, taxes and other fees (yearly)
- Insurance companies
- Hospitals, clinics, doctors
- Lawyers
- Car dealers
- Repair and service industry

Macroeconomic conclusions:

→ Ninth principle of economics: Never mention names or responsible people, institutions, or corporations; always remain vague and very general.

3.7. Climate Change

Don't forget the second and the sixth economic principle!

3.7.1. General Overview

Climate change is without doubt proven by thousands of scientists around the globe: this Climate Change is human made! All the catastrophes due to climate change, in the past, the present and the future will cause unimaginable damages, billions of victims, misery, suffering, poverty, and displacement of entire folks. The greed for money and power of the elite in politics and industry is the main cause. The ignorance of billions of people is the other part of the human cause.

- Probable temperature rise between 1.8C and 4C; or: between 1.1C and 6.4C
- Sea level most likely to rise by 28-43cm; probably up to 1.50 meters.
- Arctic summer sea ice disappears in second half of century
- Increase in heat waves very likely
- Increase in tropical storm intensity likely

20-30% of all plant and animal species at increased risk of extinction if temperatures rise between 1.5-2.5C.

3,000 of the very best scientific experts in the world confirm the human made Climate Change with its frightening consequences.

2005 as the hottest year measured since instruments were first used systematically in the 1880s. Nineteen countries set all-time high temperature records.

The past decade (2000-2010) has been the hottest ever measured.

We are destroying the climate balance and the balance of the eco-systems that are essential to the survival of our civilization, of our children and our following generations.

The 15 nations (of the UN Security Council) warn that global warming can become a threat to global peace. Droughts could lead to food and water wars.

Irreversible destructions of the environment: the Gulf Stream, the glaciers in the Alps and the massive ice caps in Greenland and in Antarctic. Source: the human emitted greenhouse gases, that make the global average temperature rise.

The emission of greenhouse gases speeds up the melting of the ice caps in west Antarctica.

Previously the transformation of an ice age took 5000 years at an increase of 5 degrees. If we continue as today we will reach an increase of 5 degrees in 100 years.

If for example the monsoon rain in India would fail to arrive as a result of climate change, then in one go the food of around 1.2 billion people would be at stake.

Greenhouse gases in the atmosphere now are at 329 parts per million and climbing, with most climate scientists warning that the level must remain below 350 ppm to sustain life as we know it. The Intergovernmental Panel on Climate Change estimates that the measurement could reach 541 to 970 ppm by 2100.

At that point huge parts of the planet, beset with over-population, droughts, soil erosion, freak storms, massive crop failures and rising sea levels, will be unfit for human existence.

As a result of the ice melting: The algal bloom in the Arctic comes earlier. This is a result of climate change, which brings the ice in the North Pole region to melt. This has heavy consequences for the food chain.

In the past 25 years the water temperature of the 160 biggest fresh water basins has risen. Every decade the water temperature has risen by an average of 0.45 degrees Celsius, in many seas up to 1 degree. The biggest increase was registered in Northern Europe, followed by Siberia, Mongolia, Northern-China and South-east Europe around the Black Sea.

Minor temperature changes can already lead to an increase in algae growth. This can destroy the habitat of fish or lead to foreign unknown species reproducing, which in turn changes the natural ecosystem of the Oceans.

More greenhouse gases than ever before: Carbon dioxide, methane and nitrogen oxides are the gases that produce global warming. The more we emit into the atmosphere, the faster climate change develops. The most recent measurements from the global weather organization reveal absolute peak values. Researchers fear, that climate change has already taken on a momentum of its own.

It is clear, that Asia and the Pacific regions are the ones most affected by the changes in climate. The heating of the planet and its consequences could result in masses of migration in the coming decades.

Last year, 89 per cent of the 207 million people that suffered from natural catastrophes lived in Asia. In China floods and landslides in 2010 caused damages of 18 billion dollars, in Pakistan the damages from the floods reached 9.5 billion dollars.

The US space agency NASA has reported the largest collapse of our Earth's upper atmosphere in history, and they don't know why.

Since the Gulf of Mexico oil and methane gas leak our world has experienced its hottest temperatures in recorded history.

Macroeconomic conclusions:

➜ Ministers are enslaved, blackmailed, and controlled by the economic 'invisible hand' (remember the ninth principle of economics: never mention names!).
➜ The alternative hypothesis: Ministers are psychopaths, neurotics, ego-maniacs, cowards; or their wives cook the menu.
➜ In economics the proverb always works: Behind a successful great man is a woman – and behind a deadbeat is also a woman – or in both cases a holy book.

3.7.2. Facts – Examples

a) Ice Melting

- The melting of Arctic and Antarctic ice started in 1990.
- Today each year more ice is melting than the amount of ice that exists in the Alps.
- Glaciers are melting faster than expected and jeopardizing the demand of drinking water.
- The melting of the glaciers in the Himalayas will affect 70% of India's population dependant on agriculture.

- The Arctic summer sea ice will disappear in the second half of the century.
- Glaciers are melting twice as fast as in 1999. Billions of people are affected!
- Melting glaciers will initially increase flood risk and then strongly reduce water supplies.
- According to a new study global warming will result in the defrosting of 30-60 per cent of all permafrost by the year 2200. As a result around 190 billion tones of carbons emissions will go into the atmosphere. As the permafrost begins to thaw they rot and thus set free greenhouse gases especially the damaging carbon dioxide and methane gases.

Macroeconomic conclusions:

→ As a consequence trillions of profit dollars will be lost in the future due to lack of water.
→ The children of the economic and political protagonists must know that they will have no legacy.

b) Rise of Sea Level

- The global average sea level would probably rise by 28-43 cm by the end of the century; but is likely to rise by about 1.4 meters globally by 2100 as polar ice melts.
- Increasing sea level to be expected within 300-400 years: 3-4 meters.
- Many islands and costal towns will be lost already at a global warming of 2°C.
- Methane gas emanating from the bottom of the Arctic Ocean is harmful to the climate.
- The increase in sea level by 100-150 cm by the year 2100 is more than certain.
- UK: Seas could be 1.5 meters higher by the end of the century.

The rise in sea level of the Mediterranean Sea was lower than in the rest of the world due to atmospheric pressure, but since the start of the 21st century the levels of the Mediterranean have regained pace and seem to be accelerating... The sea level in the Mediterranean has risen by between 1 and 1.5 millimeters each year since 1943, but this does not seem set to continue, because it now seems that the speed at which it rises is accelerating"... Since the start of the 21st century the level has already risen by 20 centimeters. During the next 30 years the rise in temperatures and in sea level will continue: estimated 20 cm per 10 year which means, for instance, more than 60 centimeters in 30 years (not only in the Mediterranean Sea). [329]

---

[329] http://phys.org/news/2011-02-sea-mediterranean.html

Macroeconomic conclusions:

→ The tenth principle of economics: Act and grow hidden and very slowly so that people can't see the increase or change.

→ Increase of sea level will destroy within 30-60 years immense amounts of assets and wealth; hundreds of banks, also centuries old private banks will go bankrupt.

→ The young generation today will pay for the faults of the economics' and political protagonists in the future.

c) Facts about Global Warming

- Probable temperature rise between 1.8C and 4C; or: between 1.1C and 6.4C.
- Arctic summer sea ice will disappear in the second half of century.
- The year 2010 is almost certain to rank in the top 3 warmest years since the beginning of instrumental climate records in 1850.
- Warming will have many severe impacts, often mediated through water.
- Increasing global warming triggers an unstoppable chain reaction with unknown effects.
- June 2010 was the warmest month on record worldwide, according to a report from the National Oceanic and Atmospheric Administration. Warmer-than-average conditions were present across nearly all continents, including much of the United States.

Macroeconomic conclusions:

→ Any 'warming' is emotional and therefore irrelevant for economic considerations.

Summary

- The global average sea level will rise by at least 20-30 cm within 20-30 years. During the next 30 years the rise in Mediterranean Sea level will be 2 cm per year.
- Heat waves, drought, fires, rainstorms, floods, tornados, hurricanes, tropical cyclones become more frequent, more widespread and/or more intense.
- 300,000 deaths and 300 million people affected every year by global warming.
- Floods will affect 2 billion by 2050 due to climate change, deforestation, rising sea levels.
- 3.2 billion people will experience water shortages due to climate change.

- Estimated yearly costs of climate change damages (worldwide): over 1 trillion Euros.
- Heat waves with agricultural losses reached $15 billion.
- Climate change could cost the world up to 25% of its entire wealth.

d) Effects of Global Warming

- Areas of the Mediterranean Sea are drying out faster every year. Forest fires will increase.
- Areas around the Mediterranean and other subtropical regions: increase in wildfires and tropical storms.
- Water shortages, heat waves, tropical storms, hunger, and floods will be an ever growing threat.
- 85% of major deltas have seen severe flooding in recent years.
- The area of land vulnerable to flooding will increase by about 50% in the next 40 years.
- Water shortages, hunger, flooding and damage to homes will be a heightened threat.
- Heat waves, rainstorms, drought, tropical cyclones and surges in sea level are among the events expected to become more frequent, more widespread and/or more intense.
- Until 2100 up to 20-40% of the species (plants, animals) are endangered.
- Frequent drought and higher global temperatures could destroy until 2100 up to 70% of the Amazon rain forest. Enormous amounts of CO_2 (carbon dioxide) will increase global warming.
- The US space agency NASA has reported the largest collapse of our Earth's upper atmosphere in history, and they don't know why.
- Since the Gulf of Mexico oil and methane gas leak, our world has experienced its hottest temperatures in recorded history.
- Climate change (global warming) and its consequences will produce an inter-regional movement of population of unknown extent, especially in Asia.
- With earthquakes, heat waves, floods and snowstorms affecting 208 million people, killing nearly 300,000, and costing $110 billion in losses in 2010 alone.

Macroeconomic conclusions:

→ Macroeconomic thinking: As long as we don't see the effects, they do not exist and are neither real nor relevant for cost factor analysis.

e) Thermohaline Circulation

2010: The latest satellite data establishes that the North Atlantic Current (also called the North Atlantic Drift) no longer exists and along with it the Norway Current. These two warm water currents are actually part of the same system that has several names depending on where in the Atlantic Ocean it is. The entire system is a key part of the planet's heat regulatory system; it is what keeps Ireland and the United Kingdom mostly ice free and the Scandinavian countries from being too cold; it is what keeps the entire world from another Ice Age. This Thermohaline Circulation System is now dead in certain places and dying in others. [330]

The Thermohaline Circulatory System, where the warm water current flows through a much cooler, much larger, ocean, effects the upper atmosphere above the current as much as seven miles high. The lack of this normal effect in the eastern North Atlantic has disrupted the normal flow of the atmospheric Jet Stream this summer, causing unheard of high temperatures in Moscow (104F) and drought, and flooding in Central Europe, with high temperatures in much of Asia and massive flooding in China, Pakistan, and elsewhere in Asia.

Macroeconomic conclusions:

➔ It does not affect the models (graphs) of microeconomics and therefore it is also irrelevant for macroeconomics.

f) Floods and Droughts

Gigantic floods displaced 20 million people alone in Pakistan.

In Australia, 28 of the 32 districts have been flooded.

Many places around the world are experiencing larger and more frequent extreme downpours and snowstorms.

Historic drought and fires in Russia killed an estimated 56,000 people.

Wheat and other food crops in Russia, Ukraine and Kazakhstan had to be removed from the global market.

This spring 2011 the majority of the counties in Texas were on fire.

---

[330] http://europebusines.blogspot.com.es/2010/08/special-post-life-on-this-earth-just.html
See   also:
https://groups.google.com/forum/#!msg/globalchange/nIcSyNKrQ3k/y8AKQo_9g7oJ

Before summer 2011, Arizona is fighting the largest fire in its history. Extreme droughts in central China and northern France are currently drying up reservoirs and killing crops.

The acceleration of ice loss in both Greenland and Antarctica has caused another upward revision of global sea-level rise. The numbers of refugees expected from low-lying coastal areas will dramatically increase.

Scientists warn: The record droughts, fires, floods and mudslides continue to increase in severity and frequency. Weather extremes are more frequent and intense due to global warming.

Thousands of scientists have been warning that things will get much worse, if we continue the reckless dumping of more and more heat-trapping pollution into the atmosphere.

Drought is projected to spread across significant, highly populated areas of the globe throughout this century.

20% of the global-warming pollution we spew into the sky each day will still be there in 20,000 years.

Actual consequences of Climate Change are of highest importance for humans: The price of corn has doubled over the last six months. The price of wheat has more than doubled over the past year. The price of soybeans is up about 50% since last June. The price of cotton has more than doubled over the past year. The commodity price of orange juice has doubled since 2009. The price of sugar is the highest it has been in 30 years.

Macroeconomic conclusions:

➔ Shit happens. Humans are not perfect!

g) Superstorms

Superstorms are combined with the cataclysmic destruction of over one-third of Russia's crops due to historic fires and drought, the historic drought in China that is now being warned could cripple their entire winter wheat crop.

Superstorms have pounded Southern Africa leaving their agricultural sector in ruins.

Superstorms have virtually destroyed Sri Lanka's ability to feed itself.

Superstorms killed over 2,000 in Pakistan and destroyed its agriculture sector

Suprstorms produced historic fires and drought in Ukraine and destroyed 20% of their crops, the record cold and snow hitting a European Continent after their worst flooding in decades.

Superstorms hitting Brazil left nearly 700 dead.

Superstorms produced catastrophic drought in Argentina.

To all of this and more, the damage done in the past 12 months to our world's ability to feed its 6.8 billion human beings has been completely destroyed.

- 300,000 deaths and 300 million people are affected every year by global warming.
- Every year an average of over 400 million people are directly exposed to a flood.
- 200 million are to be displaced due to rising sea levels, heavier floods, more intense droughts (other figures go up to 500 million).
- Floods will affect 2 billion by 2050 due to climate change, deforestation, rising sea levels.
- Lack of water threatens one-sixth of the world's population, India, China, and South America.
- 3.2 billion people will experience water shortages due to climate change.
- An additional 600 million people are at risk of famine due to climate change.
- Hundreds of millions will be affected by floods in the future.
- Most of the world's major river deltas are sinking, increasing the flood risk faced by hundreds of millions of people.
- Food speculations increase food prices by 10-40% yet in 2011, unaffordable for billions of people. Hunger will increase dramatically!

Macroeconomic conclusions:

→ People like everything that is 'super', sensational, or exciting.
→ There must be a way to do business and to make profit with such super-parameters!

h) Eco-Systems

As a result of the thawing of permafrost enormous amounts of greenhouse gases are emitted into the atmosphere. Scientists warn insistently of the consequences.

Global warming will lead to the thawing of one to two thirds of the global permafrost by 2200. The atmosphere will have to take on 190 billion tones of carbon dioxide from this.

The permafrost areas in Canada and Russia for example, store large amounts of frozen plants. If they begin to thaw, then these plants rot and release greenhouse gases – especially the very damaging methane (CH_4), but also carbon dioxide (CO_2).

Depending on forecasted scenarios by 2100 only 18 – 45 of today's rainforests would still exist. The tropical forests in South America, South-east Asia and Africa are home to more than half the planet's animal and plant species. The combination of climate change and deforestation forces these species to adapt, migrate or die.

Around 41 per cent of the oceans are badly damaged as a result of direct human intervention; only 3.7 per cent of these waters are still untouched.

Only 15% of Japan's land is suitable for cultivation, meaning they have to import about 50% of their requirements for grain and fodder crops and rely on imports for most of their supply of meat.

Macroeconomic conclusions:

➔ 'Eco' sounds like 'green' and its connotation refers to 'naïve' or 'dreamers'.

Global Warming is Overblown [331]

"Exxon CEO blames the 'illiterate' public for 'overreacting' to global warming. Rex Tillerson, the head of the world's largest oil company, admitted fossil fuels are causing climate change … Tillerson blamed 'lazy journalists' and environmentalists 'manufacturing fear' for 'overblown' concern about the issue.

Rex Tillerson: "Whatever fallout might come from this, he said, humans will be able to adapt' … Tillerson dismissed the dire warnings about

---

[331] http://www.dailymail.co.uk/news/article-2168357/Exxon-CEO-blames-illiterate-public-overreacting-global-warming.html

consequences of possible global warming … We have spent our entire existence adapting ('we'll adapt') … It's an engineering problem and there will be an engineering solution."

Fears about spills, environmental contamination and the disastrous effects of global warming are overblown by environmental groups that 'manufacture fear' and 'lazy' journalists who report their findings without checking that the claims are valid, Tillerson said.

Because of this, he said, the industry's biggest challenge is 'taking an illiterate public and try to help them understand why we can manage these risks.'

→ A better way to see the problem here is: Rex Tillerson needs help from the public to see and to understand the problem.
→ Probability of success of psychotherapy for psychopaths: less than 10%.

Effects of Climate Change

➜ Billions of people are and will be affected by the effects of Climate Change.
➜ Hundreds of millions of people will have to relocate due to damages.
➜ The damages of catastrophes will cost trillions of Dollars per year.

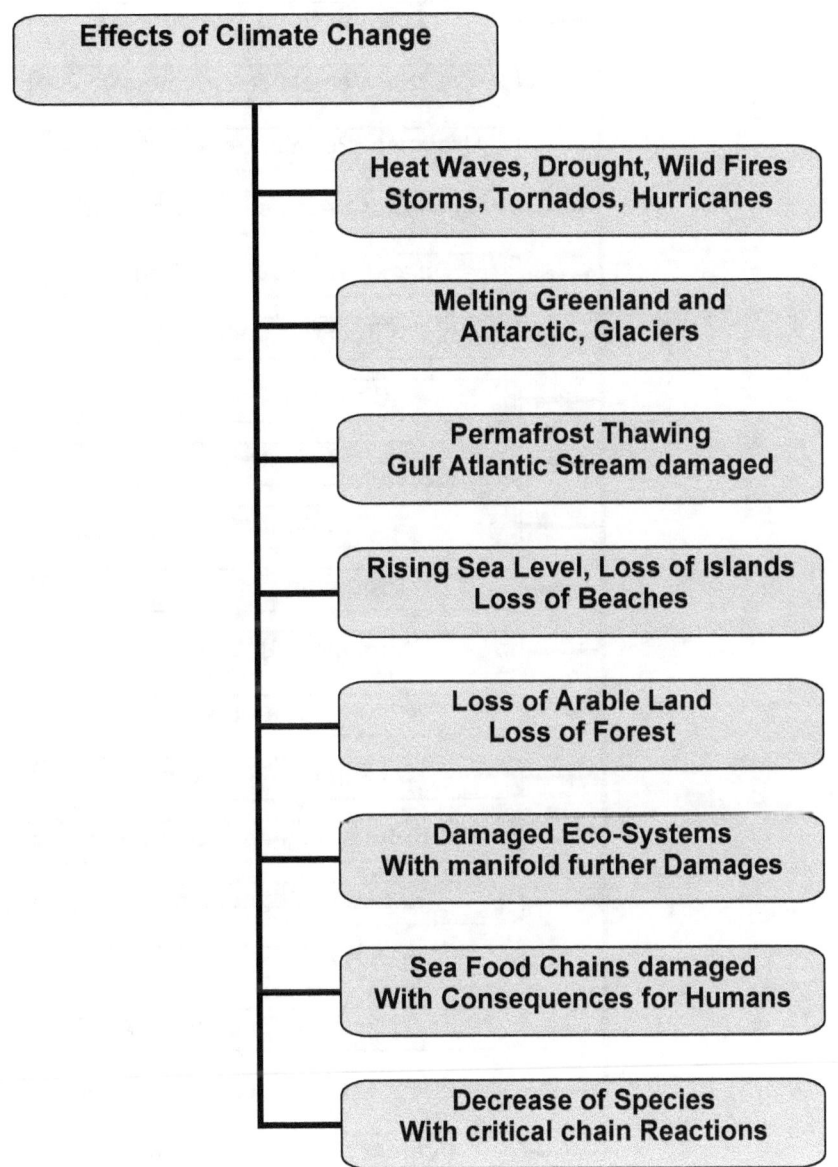

Humans are the Cause of Climate Change

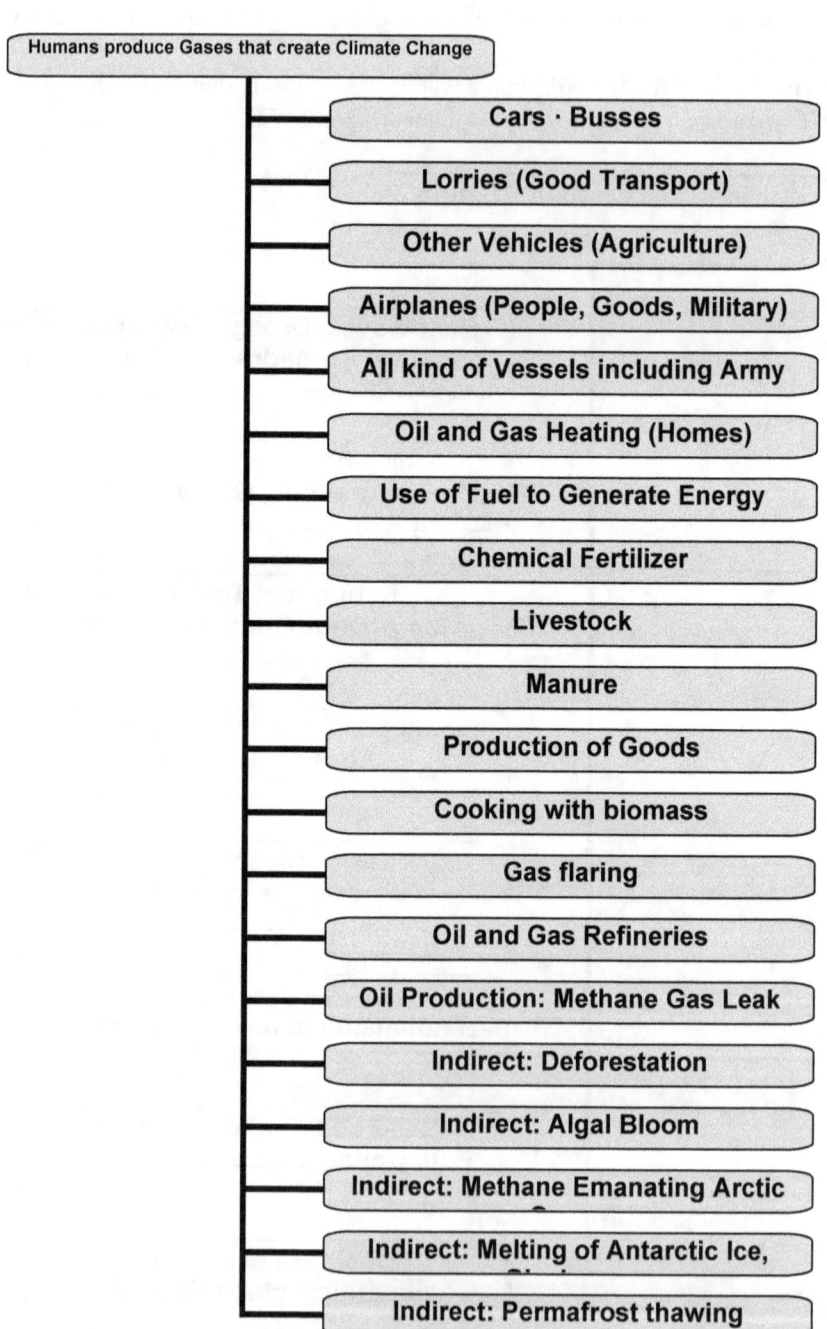

Humans produce Gases that create Climate Change

- Cars · Busses
- Lorries (Good Transport)
- Other Vehicles (Agriculture)
- Airplanes (People, Goods, Military)
- All kind of Vessels including Army
- Oil and Gas Heating (Homes)
- Use of Fuel to Generate Energy
- Chemical Fertilizer
- Livestock
- Manure
- Production of Goods
- Cooking with biomass
- Gas flaring
- Oil and Gas Refineries
- Oil Production: Methane Gas Leak
- Indirect: Deforestation
- Indirect: Algal Bloom
- Indirect: Methane Emanating Arctic
- Indirect: Melting of Antarctic Ice,
- Indirect: Permafrost thawing

3.7.3. Costs of Climate Change

- Costs of extreme weather alone could reach 0.5 to 1 per cent of world GDP in 40 years.
- Impacts of climate change will cost $75-100 billion per year in the developing world.
- The total cost of global warming will be 3.6 percent of GDP, if nothing is done.
- Hurricane damage, real estate losses, energy costs, water costs: US$1.9 trillion per year.
- Floods will produce damages in the trillions of US dollars in the future.
- UN: 500 billion USD in costs for climate damages per year (in developing countries alone).
- Estimated yearly costs of climate change damages: over 1 trillion Euros.
- Costs of 500 billion dollars per year due to climate change only for developing countries.
- The costs of damage from extreme weather (storms, hurricanes, typhoons, floods, droughts, and heat waves) will increase rapidly at higher temperatures.
- A 5 or 10 per cent increase in hurricane wind speed, linked to rising sea temperatures, is predicted to double annual damage costs, in the US.
- Heat waves with agricultural losses reached $15 billion will be commonplace in 30-40 years.
- Climate change could cost the world up to 25% of its entire wealth. Global gross domestic product (GDP) could be reduced by up to 20 per cent due to the damages caused by rising temperatures, droughts, floods, water shortages and extreme weather events.
- In the UK, annual flood losses alone could increase from to 0.2 to 0.4 per cent of GDP once the increase in global temperatures reaches 3°C or 4°C.
- Fighting against climate change could cost the international community up to $20 billion per year.

Macroeconomic conclusions:

➔ Remember the public debt principle: We don't pay for it. The future generations will be forced to pay for it during centuries.

3.7.4. Future Development of Climate Change

Thousands of scientists and thousands of dreams I experienced during the last 30 years draw a frightening picture about our future over the next 20-30 years:

- Rapid climate change will most probably result in a global catastrophe costing millions of lives in chaos, wars and natural disasters.
- A strong and fast increase of climate change could bring the planet to the edge of anarchy. Conflicts and warfare will define human life.
- Widespread flooding as a result of an increase in sea level will create major upheaval for hundreds of millions of people.
- Dramatic shortages of water and energy supply will become increasingly harder to overcome, plunging the world into global war.
- Britain must expect a "Siberian" climate by 2020. Nuclear conflict, mega-droughts, famine and widespread riots will erupt across the world.
- Over the past 50 years around 60 per cent of the global ecosystems have been heavily damaged. Over 40% of the oceans are also significantly damaged due to human behavior. The damages increase exponentially every year. The additional combined damages between interacting ecosystems will produce combined damages of unknown dimensions. In 10-15 years around 95% of the global ecosystems humans depend on will be damaged.

Macroeconomic conclusions:

→ Micro- and macroeconomics has no future in its laws, principles, theories, and statements.
→ It doesn't matter as most people are unable to think ahead in terms of some hours or the next day.

3.8. Criminality and Corruption

3.8.1. Manifoldness of Crimes

- Organized crime threatens peace on earth, development and sovereignty of states.
- Organized crime is one of the biggest economies of the world.
- Organized crime use immense money, weapons, bribes, and corruption.
- Organized crime decomposes politics, blackmail politicians, and abuse military.
- 140,000 people in Europe are abused for human trafficking, especially sexually; profit: $3 billion.
- In Russia 70 tons of hard drugs are consumed; Europe is the supermarket for heroin.
- Corruption: US$5 trillion, approx. 5% of the world's GDP.
- Around the globe 43 percent of companies are affected by economic crime (corruption).
- Up to 80 per cent of international aid to Afghanistan is being lost in international and local corruption schemes.
- The revenue of organized crime worldwide is estimated at 2 trillion US$.
- Damage caused by cybercrime estimated at $100 billion annually; we estimate: $300 billion.
- Over 700,000 people around the globe are trafficked every year for sexual exploitation and forced labor.
- World spending on illegal drugs per year: more than US$300,000,000,000.
- Fossil fuel and nuclear energy industries receive direct / indirect subsidies over $300 billion.
- Bribery and price-fixing influencing public policy costs billions of dollars in lost revenues.
- Malicious computer use such as virus writing and hacking cost businesses globally more than $1 trillion each year.
- The respondents estimated that in 2008 businesses lost data worth a total of $4.6 billion and spent about $600 million cleaning up after breaches.
- The recent recession is only increasing the security risk for corporations, with 42 per cent reporting that displaced workers were the biggest threat to sensitive information on the network.
- 47 per cent of Chinese said they believed the US poses the biggest security threat to their data.
- The average company has $12 million worth of sensitive data residing abroad.

- Companies lost on average $4.6 million worth of intellectual property each year.
- At least one of every three women on earth has been beaten, coerced into sex or abused in some other way, usually by an intimate partner or family member.
- Two million girls between the ages of 5 and 15 are introduced into the commercial sex market each year.
- 6,000 people are executed every year; 95% in the following countries: China, Iran, Pakistan, Saudi Arabia, and USA. In total, 58 countries practice the death penalty.
- Pompously ultraconservative and nationalistic ideals about manliness promote readiness for violence.
- Fundamentalist attitudes (beliefs) promote readiness for violence

Governmental Corruption

Report from 'Transparency International' about Corruption in the European Union; some statements:

"A number of countries in southern Europe – Greece, Italy, Portugal and Spain – are shown to have serious deficits in public sector accountability and deep-rooted problems of inefficiency, malpractice and corruption, which are neither sufficiently controlled nor sanctioned…

Political parties, public administrations and the private sector are evaluated as the weakest players in the fight against corruption across Europe…

Greece, Italy, Portugal and Spain top the list of the Western European countries found to have serious deficits in their integrity systems…

Legal corruption goes beyond bribery and includes influence peddling, for example the excessive and undue influence of lobbyists in the European corridors of power. It skews decision-making to benefit the few at the expense of the many…

In Greece, Ireland, Italy, Romania and Spain, more than 80 per cent of people believe political parties are corrupt or extremely corrupt…

19 of the 25 European countries assessed have yet to implement legislation to control lobbying and those that have often lack enforcement mechanisms and sanctions for non-compliance…

Only 3 national parliaments have appropriate and well-functioning integrity mechanisms for their MPs…

Only 2 out of 25 countries assessed have sufficient protection for whistleblowers in practice." [332]

Macroeconomic conclusions:

→ The way of management of macroeconomics logically leads to the world of crimes.
→ The inhumane capitalistic economics and macroeconomics generates crimes.
→ Crimes have to do with human factors shaped by education, media, and environment.
→ No wonder we have that much crimes as the world of economics is a world of crimes.
→ No wonder we have that much crimes as the world of politics is a world of crimes.
→ No wonder we have that much crimes as the world of religion is a world of crimes.

"Inmates in a Brazilian prison can shave time off their sentences by becoming living sources of green energy. All they need to do is turn the wheel of a bike connected to a power generator.

For every 16 hours of pedaling the inmates have their sentences reduced by one day … The generators the prisoners put in motion charge batteries, which are taken to the city center to power some of the street lights. The two bikes installed in the prison are enough to light six bulbs." [333]

→ I have roughly developed 20 ideas of different machines working with this principle that could be produced on a level of several billion units; and it would change the developing countries within years in an unimaginable way.
→ This is not a Swiss cheese for rats; it's part of the roadmap for a new future of humanity and the planet.
→ 3 billion people could cook their daily meal, make warm water, and would have a little light in their hut or shed.
→ Hundreds of millions of people could make some pocket money with such a 'hobby'. And another two hundred million would have work for the entire life in the future.

---

[332] http://www.transparency.org/
[333] http://www.rt.com/news/brazil-inmates-living-dynamo-167/

3.8.2. The Key Words of Crimes

- Aiding & Abetting
- Arson
- Assault
- Bribery
- Burglary
- Business Crimes
- Child Abduction
- Child Abuse
- Child Pornography
- Conspiracy
- Corruption
- Credit / Debit Card Fraud
- Cyber Crime
- Disorderly Conduct
- Disturbing the Peace
- Domestic Violence
- Drug Cultivation and Manufacturing
- Drug Distribution and Trafficking
- Drug Possession
- Embezzlement
- Extortion
- Forgery
- Fraud
- Harassment
- Hate Crimes
- Homicide
- Indecent Exposure
- Identity Theft
- Insurance Fraud
- Kidnapping
- Manslaughter
- Money Laundering
- Murder
- Perjury
- Probation Violation
- Prostitution
- Public Intoxication
- Pyramid Schemes
- Racketeering

- Rape
- Robbery
- Securities Fraud
- Sexual Assault
- Shoplifting
- Stalking
- Statutory Rape
- Tax Evasion (Fraud)
- Telemarketing Fraud
- Theft / Larceny
- Vandalism
- Wire Fraud

Macroeconomic conclusions:

→ Hunger and extreme poverty are the result of economic and political crimes.
→ Over-exploitation of all resources is a crime against the future generations.
→ Contamination of all kind is a crime against humanity and the creation.
→ The big corporations are a crime against humanity and the creation.
→ The political business destroys democracy and kills millions yearly; therefore is a crime.
→ Climate Change is the result of the economic and political amoral mismanagement.

3.8.3. Global Cost of Crimes

According to a recent study 7.3 million Americans are in prison, on parole or probation, at a cost to the states of $47 billion in 2008. In other figures: one in every 31 adults is in prison, on parole or probation. A survey of 34 states found that these states spent an average of $29,000 a year on prisoners.

Macroeconomic conclusions:

- The financial damages of such crimes are exorbitant: trillions of dollars!
- The administrative costs of such crimes are exorbitant: trillions of dollars!
- The prison costs are exorbitant: trillions of dollars!

3.8.4. Causes of Crimes

- Humans create crime.

- The society creates crimes.
- Life style creates crime.
- Poverty and misery creates crimes.
- Inadequate sexual education creates crimes.
- Neurotic parents create crimes.
- Unlimited greed for money creates crimes.
- Early childhoods with difficult family environments create crimes.
- Lack of love and Spirit, care and understanding, creates crimes.
- Unemployment creates crimes.
- Social injustice creates crimes.
- Amoral politicians are a pattern for crimes copied by countless people.
- Amoral leaders in economy and industry are a pattern copied by others.
- Archaic religions create lies, cheat, deceit, and crimes.
- Lack of psychical-spiritual and ethical education in general.

Macroeconomic conclusions:

→ Many crimes are the result of stupid, neurotic, psychopathic parents and people.
→ All the lies, distortion, perfidious manipulation in the Media produce crimes.
→ The science of economics distorting the truth and the dignity generates crimes.

3.8.5. Punishments and Incarceration

- Nobody is born a criminal.
- No soul is genetically or naturally criminal.
- Society is always co-responsible for serious crimes.
- The current forms of punishment with prisons need to be thoroughly overhauled and changed. The current form is primitive and stupid. The whole system needs to be educational and serve the society as a whole.
- There are over 20,000 people around the globe sitting in prison cells waiting for their execution.
- In 2009 a total of 714 people were executed in 18 U.S. states.
- Capital punishment is the most primitive arrogance of power.
- Capital punishment is an expression of perversion and psychopathy.
- Those in favor of capital punishment are themselves deeply neurotic or psychopathic.
- Those in favor of capital punishment are in their innermost self bound to archaic times.
- Those in favor of capital punishment must be punished.

- War is an exception, yet not a permission for the death penalty. War objectors should not be punished by imprisonment or death penalty. They must serve society in some other form for peace.
- Every form and duration of punishment requires extensive and thorough psychical-spiritual education and formation as well as work for the victims and society as a form of compensation.
- Every type of punishment must be created in such a form, that a relationship with a partner of the opposite sex (and the family if existing) can be lived in a healthy manner, also sexuality.

Macroeconomic conclusions:

→ There are individuals and 'clubs' that try to pull nearly the entire humanity into the Abyss.
→ There are powerful protagonists that act in amoral, criminal and legal ways against humanity.
→ The death penalty does not solve the problem because these people are a 'product' of society.
→ Humanity and the planet must be protected from the economic, political and religious shams.
→ Advocates are perverse, distorted, heavily neurotic, psychopathic and psychotic individuals.

Personal statement:

I have had a thousand dreams about all archetypal processes of the soul that exist, including several dreams about God, the eternal world of all souls, and the global path towards complete fulfillment of the entire humanity. I could not find the slightest argument that God or his Spirit – in other words: 'the source of all life' – would allow the death penalty.

The Federal Prison Corporations: [334]

"Federal Prison Industries, more commonly known as UNICOR, is a wholly owned corporation of the U.S. government that uses penal labor from the Federal Bureau of Prisons to produce various products and services.

→ Corporations use inmates for production and services.

Federal inmates in Oregon and New York are earning between $.23 and $1.15 per hour building solar panels, which are then sold to a range of government

---

[334] http://www.prisonplanet.com/obama-admin-uses-prison-labor-to-advance-%E2%80%9Cgreen%E2%80%9D-agenda.html

agencies."

➜ Corporations outrageously exploit inmates for profit.

The 21st-Century Slaves: More examples how Corporations Exploit Prison Labor: [335]

"In the eyes of the corporation, inmate labor is a brilliant strategy in the eternal quest to maximize profit.

➜ Wherever corporations identify a labor field to make profit, they are there.

There is one group of American workers so disenfranchised that corporations are able to get away with paying them wages that rival those of third-world sweatshops. These laborers have been legally stripped of their political, economic and social rights and ultimately relegated to second-class citizens. They are banned from unionizing, violently silenced from speaking out and forced to work for little to no wages. This marginalization renders them practically invisible, as they are kept hidden from society with no available recourse to improve their circumstances or change their plight.

➜ Inmates, as worker, have no political, economic and social rights; they are second-class citizens.
➜ The corporations can operate with inmates keeping the business hidden from society.

They are the 2.3 million American prisoners locked behind bars where we cannot see or hear them. And they are modern-day slaves of the 21st century.

➜ The modern-day slavery (2.3 million inmates) of the 21st century is unknown.

It's no secret that America imprisons more of its citizens than any other nation in history.

➜ A strange society and there must be a higher reason why America imprisons more of its citizens.

The costs of this incarceration industry are far from evenly distributed, with the impact of excessive incarceration falling predominantly on African-

---

[335] http://www.alternet.org/world/151732/21st-century_slaves%3A_how_corporations_exploit_prison_labor/?page=entire

American communities. Although black people make up just 13 percent of the overall population, they account for 40 percent of US prisoners.

Clearly, the US prison system is riddled with racism and classism, but it gets worse … private companies have a cheap, easy labor market, and it isn't in China, Indonesia, Haiti, or Mexico.

→ There is a significant racism and classism in the United States.
→ The exploitation of prison labor is by no means a new phenomenon.

In 1880, this 8000-acre family plantation was purchased by the state of Louisiana and converted into a prison. Slave quarters became cell units. Now expanded to 18,000 acres, the Angola plantation is tilled by prisoners working the land—a chilling picture of modern day chattel slavery.

→ The collective past is always present until it is collectively reconciled.

Today's corporations can lease factories in prisons, as well as lease prisoners out to their factories. In many cases, private corporations are running prisons-for-profit.

Over the last 30 years, at least 37 states have enacted laws permitting the use of convict labor by private enterprise, with an average pay of $0.93 to $4.73 per day.

→ Lowest wages are an expression of perverse aggression, radical disrespect, and pitilessly breaking the last bit of remaining human dignity.

Some of the largest and most powerful corporations have a stake in the expansion of the prison labor market, including but not limited to IBM, Boeing, Motorola, Microsoft, AT&T, Wireless, Texas Instrument, Dell, Compaq, Honeywell, Hewlett-Packard, Nortel, Lucent Technologies, 3Com, Intel, Northern Telecom, TWA, Nordstrom's, Revlon, Macy's, Pierre Cardin, Target Stores, and many more. Between 1980 and 1994 alone, profits went up from $392 million to $1.31 billion."

→ Here we see the true face of (American) corporations.

Extension of the picture: [336]

"The privatization of prisons in recent years has meant the creation of a small

---

[336] http://www.salon.com/2012/04/19/21st_century_chain_gangs/

army of workers too coerced and right-less to complain … This is a threat to not just established industries; it's a threat to emerging industries.

→ One rule of corporations is: make workers too coerced and right-less to complain.
→ The corporations are psychotically obsessed, also aiming to destroy emerging industries.
→ The author of this report says it clearly: "If China did this – having their prisoners work at subpar wages in prisons – we would be screaming bloody murder."

3.9. Re-armament, Military and Wars

War is on the horizon: "If You Can't Hear the Drums of War You Must Be Deaf" - Henry Kissinger [337]

The last two decades humanity has suffered from many wars: Gulf War I and Gulf War II, Balkan Wars, Iraq War, Afghanistan War, Israel's Wars against Palestinian and Arab people and today the War against Libya.

In not one of these wars was the capitalist coalition, especially not the European Union and the United States, threatened, attacked or in any way in a dimension of collective emergency state of war. All these wars were and are based on lies.

These wars produced millions of victims, injured and handicapped people, of orphans and widows. Hundreds of thousands of soldiers will suffer mentally during their entire life. Millions have been displaced and forced from their homes. Country-wide infrastructure and extensive environments have been totally destroyed. Most released figures are manipulated or distorted.

3.9.1. Perspectives That Form a Picture of War

In numerous countries around the world, US- and NATO soldiers are active since decades. They kill, they murder, they rape, they torture, they torment, they injure, they create handicapped people and psychically ill, they burn babies and women and men, they slaughter, they bomb homes of human beings, they destroy infrastructure, they destroy agricultural land, they destroy the functioning of the administrations and governments, they create hunger and thirst, they produce fear and terror or terrible nightmares, they produce untold agony and calamity, they create strife and sow hate for the coming 100 and more years.

The global military armament business is booming. Germany has a big part of the pie. According to the peace research institute SIPRI the third biggest weapons exporter holds an 11 per cent portion of the global market. Only Russia and the USA export more weapons.

---

[337] http://www.thezimbabwemail.com/opinion/10515-if-you-can-t-hear-the-drums-of-war-you-must-be-deaf-henry-kissin.html

The defense business as a whole has increased by 24 per cent in the past 5 years compared to the period between 2001 and 2005.

The biggest weapons producer between 2006 and 2010 was the USA, laying claim to around 30 per cent of the global weapons industry.

According to a report, other official estimates point to a whopping 2,500,000 Iraqi fatalities as the result of the invasion, in addition to four million children that were left orphaned by the war. The Iraqi Interior Ministry has also released figures pointing to 800,000 individuals that had gone missing in the country by January 2008. Another source reports: Since 2003, over 1,300,000 Iraqi civilians have been killed and an estimated 4.7 million have been displaced as a result of the war. Other statistics speak about 2m - 2.5m Iraqi victims. Most of the infrastructure has been destroyed.

According to UN statistics, Afghanistan produced only 185 tons of opium before the 2001 US-led occupation. Currently, however, the figure stands at 3,400 tons annually.

A Swedish think-tank reports the possession of over 20,500 nuclear weapons by eight nuclear states, including Israel, with 5,000 of them all ready for instant use.

"More than 5,000 nuclear weapons are deployed and ready for use, including nearly 2,000 that are kept in a high state of alert," ...

By the end of November 2010 the number of private military contractors in the United States will surpass for the first time in history the combined number of US Military forces and police officials combined.

US Military: Lies of American Politicians and the Media to start riots, unrest, civil war, war or to intervene with not democratic and not transparent (proxy) activities:

- Vietnam (1964-1975)
- Grenada (1983)
- Panama (1989)
- Iraq (1991)
- Somalia (1993)
- Bosnia (1992-1995)
- Yugoslavia (1999)
- Afghanistan/Pakistan (2001)

- Iraq (2003)
- Venezuela - Ecuador (2008)
- Libya (2011)
- Syria/Yemen (2012)

Macroeconomic conclusions:

→ Nuclear weapons are a permanent threat to folks, nations and humanity. Who cares?
→ A result of war with immense profit is the tons of opium (Afghanistan). Who are the dealers?
→ Victims of wars: babies, children, adolescents, adults, elderly people, animals. Who bothers?
→ Another result of war with immense financial costs is the destruction of infrastructure.
→ The psychological effect of a war is the destruction of the mind and soul of people.
→ Those who give orders for war and those who go to war have a mad aggression in their soul.
→ Lies, cheat, deceit, distortion, perversion, arrogance and amorality characterizes warmongers.
→ Since 1950 the US and NATO are the top warmongers on earth outreaching Hitler.
→ War is always a business for the weapon corporations, all kind of corporations and banks.
→ Riots, civil wars, and wars destroy most or all given national macroeconomic parameters.
→ Macroeconomic interests and money can never be the sole motive of the wars since 1950.

People do not decide about war. Governments decide about war and go to war even if there is no threat for the country. Governments fabricate 'terrorism' and invent all kind of other reasons to go to war. Pre-emptive attack is also an invention. The true motives are on the hidden stage behind the curtains!

3.9.2. Costs of Wars

- June 2010: World military spending increased by 5.9 percent to hit a new record high of $1.53 trillion in 2009.
- Global military expenditure is increasing fast; money spent per year: 36,000,000,000 of US$ with increasing tendency.

- Global military expenditures in January 2011; i.e. during one month: $3,200,000,000.
- The USA has wasted 3,000 billion dollars on wars that have no benefit whatsoever.
- Cost of Iraq War (2001-2010) plus war in Afghanistan: over US$ 1,000,000,000,000.
- Iraq War victims: 1.4 million killed people; 4.7 million displaced; 5 million orphans; 1-2 million widows.
- The Afghan war costs the US taxpayers $300 million per day.
- The war in Afghanistan and in Iraq since 2003 costs the US citizens $3 trillion just for caring for the wounded from both of those two wars over the next thirty years.
- Washington plans to invest $92 billion to expand its nuclear arsenal in the next 10 years.

The US government has admitted selling USD 40 billion worth of private arms worldwide in 2009 with almost USD 7 billion of them going to the Middle East and Northern African countries.... The main recipients of the US arms in 2009 were Japan with USD 4.5 billion, Britain with USD 3.4 billion and Singapore with USD 5.5 billion purchases.

A total of USD 7.3 billion arms were sold to the Middle East and North African nations. Turkey and the United Arab Emirates with USD 1.50 and 1.09 billion purchases respectively, were among the major recipients of the US arms in these regions.

The US military spends USD 20.2 billion annually on air conditioning for the American troops stationed in war-torn Iraq and Afghanistan; including the costs to deliver the fuel to the most isolated places, escorting, command and control, and other support and infrastructure.

The Pentagon's demand for a budget of USD 300 million a day for the Afghan war will put a 'back-breaking burden' on US taxpayers ...

The world's military spending has increased to a record high of $1.6 trillion in 2010.... the top three arms investors are the US, China and Britain ... The Unites States, with extravagant military operations in Afghanistan and Iraq, increased the arms investment by 2.8 percent to $698 billion -- about six times as much as China which is the world's second-biggest spender followed by Britain, France and Russia.

The US Department of Defense (DoD) has wasted almost $50 billion over the past decade, an independent public policy think tank in the United States says. According to a report on the 2012 US defense budget, issued by the Center for Strategic and Budgetary Assessments (CSBA), Pentagon has put some $46 billion since 2001 into developing military systems that were never deployed in the combat fields, Reuters reported Monday. The think tank has suggested in his report that the Pentagon's efforts have produced no meaningful results as far as the modernization of the US military is concerned.

An article in July 2011 reports:

"The latest objective estimate for the wars in Iraq and Afghanistan, made public June 29, is between $3.7 trillion and $4.4 trillion. This doesn't even include the thousands of deaths and injuries among quasi-military contractors … (not included) the "hidden" costs of the war that include enormous medical care expenses over the next 50 years for tens of thousands of badly wounded soldiers, other benefits, equipment replacement, and interest on war debts … (the effective costs) will certainly top $5 trillion in real costs … Defense Department expenses are only half the story. Double the Pentagon's $700 billion for a true estimate of the amount of money the U.S. spent on war-related issues last year. That's $1.4 trillion a year for the United States…. Washington's various other "national security" budgets. That of course includes the costs of Washington's 16 different intelligence services, the percentage of the annual national debt to pay for past war expenses, Homeland Security, nuclear weapons, additional annual spending requests for Iraq and Afghan wars, military retiree pay and healthcare for vets, NASA, FBI (for its war-related military work), etc. When it's all included it comes to $1,398 trillion for fiscal 2010."

Macroeconomic conclusions:

→ Arms factories are booming. They must make immense profit. Who get's the profit?
→ Those who invest in weapon production (and make profit) are those who trigger wars.
→ To increase weapon production, they must trigger unrest, fights, and finance proxy-activities.
→ What do the people that get the profit from weapon production do with all this huge profit?
→ What have been and are the superior (not financial) benefits from all the wars since 1950?
→ Is it possible that the benefits of all wars are higher than all the costs for these wars? (No!)
→ We must include the micro- and macroeconomic costs in those countries

that go to war.

→ Who decides about war as the heads of the states are not those who take the final decision?

→ Who has so much power that they can blackmail governments to go to a baseless war?

3.9.3. US Wars and Aggression

America has intruded in the affairs of at least 50 countries of the world over 130 times during the last 121 years. We give an extract from the source: [338]

While the US troops have intervened in the affairs of Panama eight times (1895, 1901-14, 1908, 1912, 1918-20, 1958, 1964 and 1989), they entered Nicaragua (1894, 1896, 1898, 1899, 1907, 1910, 1912-33), Honduras (1903, 1907, 1911, 1912, 1919, 1924-25, 1983-89) and China (1894-95, 1898-1900, 1911-14, 1922-27, 1927-34, 1948-49, 1958) some seven times each under one pretext or the other during this period under review.

The American forces sailed for Cuba (1898-1902, 1906-1909, 1912, 1917-33, 1961, 1962) six times, they went to Iran five times (1946, 1953, 1980, 1984, 1987-88), and they interfered on four different occasions in Haiti (1891,1914-34, 1987-94, 2004-05) Dominican Republic (1903-04,1914,1916-24,1963-66), Yugoslavia (1919,1946,1992-94,1991-93), Iraq (1958, 1963, 1990-91, 1991-93) and Philippines (1898-1910, 1948-54, 1989, 2002).

The US troops were dispatched thrice to Korea (1894-96, 1904-05, 1945-53), Libya (1981, 1986-89, 2011), Guatemala (1920, 1954, 1966-67), Yemen (2000, 2002, 2004) and Liberia (1990, 1997, 2003).

They were sent on foreign missions twice to nations like Chile (1891, 1964-73), Mexico (1913, 1914-18), Puerto Rico (1898, 1950), El-Salvador (1932, 1981-82), Germany (1948, 1961), Laos (1962, 1971-73), Somalia (1992-94, 2006) and Afghanistan (1998, 2001).

Apart from featuring prominently in World War I and II, the US combat forces have also been active at least once in countries like Argentina, Samoa, Russia, Guam, Turkey, Uruguay, Greece, Vietnam, Indonesia, Cambodia, Oman, Macedonia, Syria, Pakistan, Bolivia, Virgin Islands, Zaire (Congo), Saudi Arabia, Kuwait, Lebanon, Grenada, Angola, Sudan, Albania, Bosnia and Colombia.

---

[338] http://www.thenews.com.pk/TodaysPrintDetail.aspx?ID=43000&Cat=2&dt=4/22/2011

Since the end of World War Two the United States has:

- Endeavored to overthrow more than 50 foreign governments, most of which were democratically elected.
- Grossly interfered in democratic elections in at least 30 countries.
- Waged war/military action, either directly or in conjunction with a proxy army, in some 30 countries.
- Attempted to assassinate more than 50 foreign leaders.
- Dropped bombs on the people of some 30 countries.
- Suppressed dozens of nationalist movements around the world.
- Has spent over 50 trillion dollars on Israel.
- Has masterminded and dictated politics throughout the European Union.

Macroeconomic conclusions:

→ This is a network of small wars and warlike intrusion having the same roadmap.
→ Who is the architect of this roadmap and who gives the orders to realize such lunacy?
→ Do these activities have anything to do with the European or American people?
→ What has been the benefit of all these strife and warlike intrusions? Who benefits from it?
→ Is there any macroeconomic benefit (improvement) that can be seen in financial parameters?
→ If in these interventions there was never a real threat for the US and EU, what was the motive?

3.9.4. US Army and NATO

In 1971, the United States stored 7,300 tactical weapons in Europe. Today they have 200 nuclear warheads in European countries without an all-out accord from Europe. Where are the remaining 7,100 tactical weapons now?

The US Military has more than 1,000 military bases in about 130 countries and another 6,000 bases in the United States and its territories. In total, there are more than 3,000,000 US personnel serving across the planet. Additionally they have an unknown number of so-called secret bases and other bases in the Middle East. There are still 268 bases in Germany, 124 in Japan, and 87 in South Korea. There are also bases in other European Countries.

Global NATO: The U.S. and NATO military alliance has expanded into a globally active 50-nation military network; Germany, Australia, Spain, France, Italy and Japan also on the new war-boat.

The North Atlantic Treaty Organization (NATO) has 24 military bases in Turkey alone.

The annual cost of US intelligence has been made public for the first time and it shows that the overall spending this year (2010) has surpassed $80 billion.

Figures released by the government demonstrate that $27 billion goes to military intelligence and $53.1 billion covers the CIA and some of the other 16 intelligence agencies. Official documents have shown that in 2007 spending was $43.5 billion and as such spending on intelligence has almost doubled since then.

Arms race with new dimensions: 1.5 trillion dollars per year; wars not included.

By the end of November 2010 the number of private military contractors in the United States will surpass the combined number of US Military forces and police officials combined for the first time in history.

The United States could cut its military budget (just the Department of so-called Defense, not counting the hundreds of billions spent through other departments) by 85% and still be the most expensive military on the planet.

President Obama is being given the power to shut down the Internet for any reason he chooses.

In the US, in any case of "state of emergency", the government can take over any goods and wealth, including fruits, vegetables or meat the citizens produce in their own garden; self-evidently without paying or compensating for it.

The US Government now says it has the right to assassinate any American citizen they deem a "terrorist". Under US law only the President can define who a "terrorist" is. Under US law the President's defining of an American as a "terrorist" is not only secret but cannot be reviewed by any court.

Nearly 3,000 of America's top scientists have called for a new investigation of 9/11 because the government's official story was found to be "impossible to have happened in the way it has been officially described".

A study calculated the cost of the Iraq and Afghanistan wars, publicized as the "war against terror" could end up costing the American tax payers $6 trillion.

All the wars of the capitalist coalition since 20 years caused several million fatalities and ten times as many injured and handicapped people, plus untold millions of orphans. There has been an incredible destruction of infrastructures and families along with a burned earth policy of their means of sustenance. Gulf War I and Gulf War II, Balkan Wars, Iraq War, and Afghanistan War with undoubtedly more to come.

A US government audit has found that billions of dollars earmarked for reconstruction projects in Afghanistan cannot be traced. Nearly 18 billion dollars received by thousands of firms to rebuild Afghanistan remain unaccounted for.

The estimated cost to kill each Taliban is as high as $100 million with a conservative estimate being $50 million. Killing 20 Taliban costs $1 billion; killing all the Taliban would cost $1.7 trillion.

1. Taliban field strength: 35,000 troops
2. Taliban killed per year by coalition forces: 2,000 (best available information)
3. Pentagon direct costs for Afghan War for 2010: $100 billion
4. Pentagon indirect costs for Afghan War for 2010: $100 billion
Macroeconomic conclusions:

→ The question is always: Who is the profiteer of such mad politics and legal mendacity?
→ Who profits from such bellicose governmental criminality 'in the Name of the Creator and the Almighty God'?

3.9.5. Alternatives to Military Expenditures

- $1 trillion over a period of 5 years could be spent for a program to repair roads and bridges.
- $1 trillion over a period of 5 years could have hired 15.3 million people out of work for $50,000 a piece. With $1 trillion we could invest in clean energy.
- $1 trillion over a period of 5 years would be enough to provide all people around the globe with healthy drinking water.
- $1 trillion over a period of 5 years would be enough to provide all people

around the globe with sanitation infrastructure.

- $100 trillion over a period of 25 years would be more than enough to provide all megacities, cities and relevant resorts with an efficient public transport system.
- $30 billion over a period of 10 years is enough to provide 1,000,000 school teachers in developing countries at $3,000 per year.

Macroeconomic conclusions:

→ The wars and interventions have created a hate that the victims will not forget for centuries.
→ All these wars have destroyed the substance of the warmonger countries for a century.
→ There is absolutely no financial and social or cultural benefit for the warmonger countries.
→ Without these wars America and Europe could be a paradise like never seen on earth.
→ America and Europe have failed to become a sustainable economic model society for the world.

3.9.6. Motives for Wars

- Need for water, food, and other resources
- Bankrupt financially a country
- Lunacy of a religion; collective religious psychosis
- Dogmatism and fundamentalism of a religion
- Unsolved conflicts between countries from the past
- Sovereignty of stolen lands
- World greed for power
- Geopolitical strategic interests
- Radical ideologies
- Poverty, misery, famine
- Climate change: originator and victims
- Archaic understanding of humans and human life
- Financial interests of the arms industry
- Banking interests financing both sides
- Industrial profit and power interests
- Projection of the evil aspects of humans onto others
- Extreme high rate of unemployment
- Collapse of economy and industry
- Extreme distribution of wealth (financial power)
- Power conservation in unstable political situations

- Political megalomania and psychopathic leaders
- Governmental oppression and exploitation of a folk
- Regional injustice in the most basic services
- Religious claims to have the only true God and belief
- Fundamentalist missions to lead humanity to God
- Brainwashed, manipulated, blinded and exploited folks
- Religious frustration and hate of God
- The planet in danger due to climate change / pollution
- A nation in danger due to overpopulation
- Humanity in danger due to overpopulation and emissions

All motives for a new global war, WWIII are evident today!

The motives of big wars are pathogenic. Narcissism, neurosis and psychopathic, perverse lunacy, obsession and greed, lies and falseness are the source of area-wide murdering, but do not sufficiently explain the roadmap for World War III, which can only be the elimination of humanity, and the destruction of the planet.

The madness of the 'One World Government' of the capitalist coalition, stirred up also by hidden rulers as well as by certain leaders in Christian (Evangelic) circles must have a roadmap in order to succeed. Triggering religious wars against Islam and the Muslim people is only one step of this roadmap (without real religious interests) in order to maximize profit on a level of trillions of dollars.

Macroeconomic conclusions:

→ But now the worst: these entire motives do not explain the history of wars since 1893.
→ When a government (Prime minister, President) decides to go to war, then there are always some ministers, heads of political parties and many politicians that do not agree with such a decision; but they might be forced to agree. The citizens never have a say about going to war or not.
→ It is today and it has always been a religious motive behind wars and colonization.
→ There is only one motive that can sufficiently explain this war history: The deicide!
→ There is a group of people on earth that have inherited a very old legacy aimed at Deicide.
→ This group of individuals is immensely rich and disposes of a global network of financial power.
→ Aiming for Deicide requires first destroying people's mind and soul, and

the lives of citizens.

→ Destroying countries begins with the destruction of the microeconomic and the macroeconomic parameters in a society, then leads to the (financial and democratic) destruction of a country, and finally to the irreversible destruction of the planet.

→ Such an unspeakable destructiveness can only be a religious frustration with and hate for God.

Motives for wars

- Need for water, food, and other resources
- Bankrupt financial situation of a country
- Lunacy of a religion; collective religious psychosis
- Dogmatism and fundamentalism of a religion
- Unsolved conflicts between countries from the past
- Sovereignty of stolen lands
- World power greed
- Geopolitical strategic interests
- Radical ideologies
- Poverty, misery, famine, lack of drinking water
- Climate change: originator and victims
- Archaic understanding of humans and human life
- Financial interests of arms industry
- Industrial profit and economic power interests
- Projection of the evil aspects of humans onto others
- Extreme high rate of unemployment
- Collapse of economy and industry
- Extreme distribution of wealth (financial power)
- Power conservation in unstable political situation
- Originator and victims of emissions
- Political megalomania and psychopathic leaders
- Governmental oppression and exploitation of a folk
- Regional injustice in most basic services
- Religious claim to have the only true God and belief
- Fundamentalist missions to lead humanity to God
- Brainwashed, manipulated, blinded, exploited folks
- Planet in danger due to climate change, pollution
- A nation / continent in danger due to overpopulation
- Humanity in danger due to overpopulation
- Not reconciled history

3.9.7. Trouble Spots

Definition of a 'trouble spot':

A place of recurring turmoil, riots, civil war, religious fights, social and political unrest, especially a country or region where fighting between opposing groups often happens. These places are today 2012:

- Afghanistan
- Albania
- Algeria
- Angola
- Antarctic areas
- Arctic areas
- Armenia
- Bahrain
- Basque (Spain)
- Beirut (Lebanon)
- Bekaa Valley (Lebanon)
- Bosnia
- Burma (Myanmar)
- Cambodia
- Central Iraq
- Chechen (Russia)
- Chiapas (México)
- Colombia (drug war)
- Congo
- Côte d'Ivoire
- Cuba
- Cyprus
- Darfur (Sudan)
- Eastern Congo
- Egypt
- Falkland Islands
- Gaza Strip
- Georgia
- Golan Heights
- Guinea
- Iran
- Israel
- Jammu and Kashmir

- Kosovo
- Kuril Islands
- Lebanon
- Liberia
- Libya
- Macedonia
- Mindanao Island (Philippines)
- Nigeria
- North and South Korea
- Northern Ireland
- Northern Uganda
- Pakistan
- Rwanda
- Serbia
- Sierra Leone
- Somalia
- South Africa
- South Lebanon
- Southern Sudan
- South Vietnam
- Straits of Hormuz
- Syria
- Sudan
- Taiwan
- Tamil (Sri Lanka)
- Tibet
- Tunisia
- West Bank
- Western Sahara
- Yemen
- Zimbabwe
- And more …

Motives for trouble are:

Poverty, hunger, access to water and resources, food price increases, lack of money, financial collapse, high rate of unemployment, high rate of taxes, lack or abuse of human rights, corruption, megalomaniac rulers, exploitation of manpower (slavery) and resources, ignorance towards citizens, lack of democracy, lack of education, dictatorship, mega land ownership, political interests, demands for independence (separation), martial laws suppressing people or minorities, racial apartheid, ethnic conflicts, military coup, extreme ideologies and dominance of religion (fundamentalism), and collective religious psychosis, foreign interference usually by proxy.

Macroeconomic conclusions:

→ Certainly, there have always been troubles due to human matters and dictatorships.
→ But most dictators and many ministers are paid for by sources in America and Europe.
→ Trouble in most countries hinders their development, to live in peace and balance.
→ Therefore there must also be this 'invisible hand' operating with perverse intentions.
→ As nobody sees through these devilish games, it will never end until they fully succeed.
→ The entire microeconomics and macroeconomics is the roadmap for their Deicide!
→ The sole function of a majority of corporations is to provide these mad people with profit.

If you say that all these problems don't really exist, then you are stupid.
If you think that all this is a huge exaggeration, then you are naive.
If this global picture doesn't affect you, then you are a psychopath.
If you feel God will solve these problems, then you are neurotic.
If you feel economics will solve them, then you are brainwashed.
If you feel governments will solve them, then you are a simpleton.
If you feel technology will solve them, then you have lost your soul.
If you reject to contribute to pioneering solutions, then you are a good-for-nothing.

---

4. The Power of Money

4.1. The Masters of the Economy

Everything, but really everything is hijacked by finance: The US, the Dollar, the EU, the Euro, politics, political parties, media, military, IMF, bailouts, labor laws, judicial systems, industry, globally operating corporate groups, shopping malls, etc., is all at the mercy of finance!

Owners, members of the board, CEOs, and managers of the world of finance are not always and not simply citizens of the country where they operate. There are networks of people with 'higher interests' all over countries and continents. As money is but a tool, these people understand their world of finance and direct and know how to use this tool (Weapons of Mass Destruction?).

In other words: Those who command the world of finance do not simply operate in respect of micro or macroeconomic principles, concepts, laws and theories. Taking decisions about billions and trillions of Dollars or Euros means shaping, organizing and controlling entire societies. The borders of nations are not the borders of the world of finance. Therefore the entire world is in the grip of the supreme masters of finance.

If these masters have a religious psychosis, are psychopaths, or operate with false pretenses, then the result for entire societies is catastrophic. There are many banks with economic power that have been built up over the last 150-180 years. All governments depend on banks and therefore also on these masters. The financial crisis that started in 2008 can be interpreted as a result (aim or failure) of the master's economic policy. As all wars require huge financial resources, these masters have been the hidden string pullers of WWI and WWII they certainly have been the hidden puppet masters of wars since 1950s and today the imminent WWIII. Always follow the money (finances) and you will find the motives behind most wars.

Macroeconomic conclusions:

➔ The entire financial system is a tool and not simply 'maintenance' or means of finance for nations.

→ All macroeconomic (financial) aspects of governance are under the control of some masters.
→ The bigger the public debt of a country, the higher is the control of the financial masters.
→ With mortgages, loans, and investments, these masters control people and firms in a society.

4.2. Concentration of Money

Let's summarize some examples of money concentration, follow the money in other words:

US 2011: the rich 'Upper Class' is powerful. In 2009, the richest 5% claimed 63.5% of the nation's wealth. The richest 20% of Americans own 84% of all wealth. The overwhelming majority – the bottom 80% – collectively hold just 12.8%. [339]

→ 80% of people in a country have absolutely no say in all the collective matters of their society.

The leading commodity trader Glencore is valued at $69 billion ... Barclays estimates that Glencore's net income was $3.8 billion last year (2011) and will double to $8.86 billion by 2012. [340]

In Germany experts registered 924,000 cash millionaires last year, an increase of 7.2%... The study shows Germany at third place, after Japan and the United States. The most super rich are found in North America, precisely 3.4 million millionaires. The Asian-Pacific regions follow with 3.3 million millionaires. Expensive status symbols and asset values such as property, luxury cars or art collections are not taken into account. [341]

In 2010 there were around 10.9 million super rich around the globe, an increase of 8.3 per cent compared to 2009. The total sum of liquid assets that the global financial elite dispose of according to the statistics: $42.7 trillion that is around €30 trillion. [342]

Germany has 103 billionaires. The number of millionaires in Germany rose

---

[339] http://www2.ucsc.edu/whorulesamerica/power/wealth.html/
[340] http://www.google.es/#sclient=psy-ab&hl=es&rlz=1W1GGLL_enES324&q=The+leading+commodity+trader+Glencore+is+val ued+at+69+billion+US+Dollars+&oq=The+leading+commodity+trader+Glencore+is+valu ed+at+69+billion+US+Dollars+&aq=f&aqi=&aql=&gs_l=serp.12...4641.4641.0.9141.1.1.0.0. 0.0.218.218.2-
1.1.0...0.0.XdqmfVxe9WU&pbx=1&bav=on.2,or.r_gc.r_pw.,cf.osb&fp=9579e90458fa1ec5&bi w=1280&bih=872
[341] http://zomobo.net/Millionaire-Investor
[342] http://www.ml.com/media/114235.pdf

by 60,100 people in 2009 or an equivalent of 11 per cent up to 779,300. German private investors have amassed a fortune of €5.2 trillion (€5,200 billion). [343]

The rich are becoming richer and there will be more of them: In industrialized nations the number will increase to 55.5 million by 2020. [344]

The wealth amassed by millionaire households is set to increase by more than 100% over the next 9 years. From a total of $92 trillion held by the world's richest in 2011, by 2020 the world's millionaire households will possess $202 trillion, or roughly 4 times current global GDP. Even though much of the move up is attributed to the wealth surge in the developing world … the biggest beneficiary is the United States where the millionaires (those with net wealth of at least $1 million), who currently account for $38.6 trillion of total wealth, will see their assets increased by 225% to $87.1 trillion! [345] [346]

According to one analysis, the total wealth of millionaire households in the 25 economies is forecast to grow from $92 trillion in 2011 to $202 trillion in 2020. The U.S. by 2020 will likely reach $87 trillion, from $39 trillion in 2011. [347]

In 2009, 221,700 Dollar millionaires lived in Switzerland, around 19.7% more than in 2008. Switzerland is amongst the richest nations on earth. 4,000 inhabitants take home a yearly income of over 1 million Swiss francs. 3% of the private taxpayer's possess the same amount of wealth as the remaining 97%. The generation of the over 65 year olds possesses more than half of the private wealth in the whole nation. If we take the real estate assets, pension funds and savings too that brings a sum of over 2,000 billion Swiss francs. Over 120 billionaires live in Switzerland (of around 1,000 billionaires around the globe). [348]

A more extensive analysis is given in Economics II.

Macroeconomic conclusions:

[343] http://www.dailykos.com/story/2011/08/13/1006570/-Power-to-the-Lemmings
[344] http://www.etforecasts.com/products/ES_cinusev2.htm
[345] http://www.zerohedge.com/article/rich-are-about-get-very-very-rich-study-finds-global-millionaire-wealth-set-more-double-2020
[346] http://daviddegraw.org/2011/08/who-rules-america-economic-elite-have-at-least-45-9-trillion-in-wealth-revealing-the-economic-top-0-1/
[347] http://www.ourbroker.com/news/good-to-be-rich-millionaire-wealth-to-double-in-next-decade-051611/
348
http://article.wn.com/view/2010/06/22/le_nombre_de_millionnaires_a_bondi_de_20_lan_pass_en_suisse/

→ The financial elite form the circle around the top-masters and therefore are the sub-masters.

→ The more value a corporation has, the more a corporation can expand or grow financially.

→ The economy is built on the erroneous economic belief that the market dictates human behavior.

→ The science of economics teaches that the global economy can expand without limits.

→ The U.S. and Europe may remain the global centers of wealth up to 2020 – and then what?

4.3. Distribution of Wealth

- 2% of the earth's population (approx. 13 million) own more than 50% of the world's wealth.
- The poorest population, 40% of the earth population, disposes of 5% of the global income.
- The richest population, 20% of the earth population, disposes of 75% of the global income. [349]
- Millionaires hold 38% of the global wealth. [350]
- 11 million people dispose of a wealth of more than $1 million. One in 100 of these millionaires disposes of more than $30 million.
- The world's richest 1% owns 40% of all the wealth, a UN report discovers.
- 10 million millionaires dispose of $41 trillion (2008), home values not included.
- In 2009 the world had 793 billionaires and the net worth of the world's billionaires stood at $2.4 trillion. Now, 2012 the world has around a thousand billionaires. [351]
- The top 20% of Americans has 93% of the nation's financial wealth and the bottom 80% has a mere 7%. [352]
- During the economic crisis the wealth of the 400 richest Americans actually increased by $30 billion. Collectively, those 400 have $1.57 trillion in wealth. [353]
- The HNWI (High Net Worth Individuals) in the U.S., Japan and Germany together accounted for 54% of the world's HNWI population in 2008; wealth of HNWI for 2013 forecast: $48.5 trillion. [354]

Macroeconomic conclusions:

---

[349] http://philanthropy2012.hubpages.com/hub/Things-that-are-wrong-with-the-world-that-could-be-avoided
[350] http://www.unicef.org/socialpolicy/files/Global_Inequality_REVISED_-_5_July.pdf
[351] http://www.forbes.com/lists/2009/10/billionaires-2009-richest-people_The-Worlds-Billionaires_Rank.html
[352]
http://www.alternet.org/economy/145705/the_richest_1%25_have_captured_america's_wealth_--_what's_it_going_to_take_to_get_it_back
[353] http://ampedstatus.com/during-economic-crisis-wealth-of-400-richest-americans-increased-by-30-billion/
[354] http://www.capgemini.com/services-and-solutions/by-industry/financial-services/solutions/wealth/worldwealthreport/worlds_wealth/

→ The money required to renew the world into a paradise with investments of 10 trillion per year exists.
→ From an economic point of view all big problems of humanity can be solved within 25 years.
→ Theories and practices of macroeconomics are a shameless and outrageous failure.
→ The actual distribution of wealth has already destroyed most values of all genuine democracies.

4.4. Rich People are Protagonists

In 2003, Yassir Arafat, in Palestine, had a fortune of around $300 million. With which he belonged to the ten richest rulers of the world. [355]

Other super rich rulers (dead and alive) include the Crown Prince of Saudi Arabia, the Sultan of Brunei, Hans Adam II of Lichtenstein, the Iraqi President Saddam Hussein and the British Queen Elizabeth II. Also on the list you can find the Queen of the Netherlands and Cuba's President Fidel Castro. They all did not make their fortunes with successful ventures. [356]

In more recent lists of high net worth chiefs of state one finds the names of many Arabic oil Sheikhs as well as the King of Thailand, Italy's Silvio Berlusconi, Chiles President and former Prime Minister of Lebanon, Saad Hariri, whose father Rafik Hariri, had amassed millions in Saudi Arabia. [357]

The Pakistani President Asif Ali Zardari, widow of the murdered Benazir Bhutto, was marked as "inexpressibly corrupt". His wealth is estimated at 1.8 to 4 billion US Dollars.

Also in Africa one can find multi-millionaires, such as the King of Swaziland, Mswati III, who is known for his many cars, many palaces and many women.

The wife of the Tunisian President Zinedine Ben Ali is alleged to have taken 1.5 tonnes of Gold.

In 2009, around 10 million people held financial assets worth more than 1 million US Dollars. Nearly every 100th millionaire has financial assets worth more than $30 million, qualifying them as so called super rich. This group held 35.5 per cent of the entire wealth of all millionaires in 2009.

The average millionaire in India will be richer than his counterpart in the US. By 2020, China's rich will hold a fortune of $3.6 trillion ($3,600 billion) Chinese, ranking amongst the top ten richest nations. By 2015 Singapore's millionaires are predicted to hold an average wealth of $4.5 million.

[355] http://www.palestinefacts.org/pf_current_yassir_arafat.php
[356] http://www.cnbcmagazine.com/story/the-worlds-richest-arabs/111/1/
[357] http://www.thenews.com.pk/Todays-News-2-105889-Dr-Baig-leaves-for-Dubai-to-attend-AIM-moot

Egyptian President Hosni Mubarak and his family's net worth are estimated to be around $70 billion (February 2011).

The richest of the rich is no longer an American, but instead a Mexican, the Telecom tycoon Carlos Slim. He leads the list of 1029 billionaires with an estimated wealth of 74 billion US Dollars. Next on the list is Microsoft's Bill Gates, with $56 billion and investor Warren Buffet with $50 billion. Had Bill Gates not donated $28 billion, he would still remain in first place.

The richest European, Bernard Aranult, is in fourth place, with 41 billion US Dollars. The Frenchman owns the luxury goods empire Louis Vuitton-Moët Hennessy (LVMH). More to find here: [358]

It wasn't the Bank managers that skimmed of the most. With a yearly salary of $84.3 million the boss of Viacom (MTV, Paramount, Nickelodeon), Philippe Dauman, led the way. Software producer Oracle's Larry Ellison, came at second place with $68.6 million. Third place was granted to TV mogul Leslie Moonves, from CBS with $53.9 million. [359]

The media bosses came at the top of the ranking. Other big earners included Ford CEO Alan Mulally ($25.8 million), IBM boss Samuel Palmisano ($24.1 million) and oil corporation ExxonMobil's Rex Tillerson with $21.0 million. The best earning German was the former Siemens CEO and today's CEO of the Aluminum producer Alcoa, Klaus Kleinfeld, with $12.2 million. [360] [361]

A list of the wealthiest historical figures is here: [362]

More examples (2010):

- Linde, Wolfgang Reitzle: 2010 Salary €5.45 million; Stock options included: 6.95 million.
- Volkswagen: CEO Martin Winterkorn Salary €9.3 million.
- Daimler-Boss Dieter Zetsche: Salary €8,7 million.
- Josef Ackermann, Deutsche Bank, Salary €8,9 million
- Peter Löscher, Siemens, Salary €8,9 million
- Jürgen Grossmann, RWE, Salary €6,6 million

---

[358] http://www.therichest.org/nation/richest-people-in-europe/
[359] http://www.hispanicbusiness.com/2011/5/9/2010_a_good_year_for_us.htm
[360] http://search.autonews.com/business/finance/CEOs/alan-mulally.htm
[361] http://thinkprogress.org/climate/2012/04/26/471469/exxon-takes-104-million-profits-per-day-so-far-in-2012-while-americans-are-stuck-with-a-higher-gas-bill/?mobile=nc
[362] http://en.wikipedia.org/wiki/List_of_wealthiest_historical_figures

- Michael Diekmann, Allianz, Salary €5,8 million

Israel has 6,000 millionaires and 6 million beggars. Over the last five years, the average income in Israel has increased by 17% and food prices by 25%. Water rates have gone up 40% and gasoline by 23%. The average apartment price has gone up 55% and rent by 27%. [363]

Macroeconomic conclusions:

→ The national and global imbalance of wages and wealth is outrageous and a disgrace.
→ CEOs are protagonists, receivers of orders and not the supreme commanders.
→ Members of boards are controller protagonists and not the supreme commanders.
→ The investors with major participation are the representatives of the commanders.
→ High wealth alone does not mean that these people have a say at the commander level.
→ Universities with the highest reputation in science of economics are not commanders.

---

[363] http://roarmag.org/2011/08/historic-protest-in-israel-over-300000-demand-social-justice/

4.5. Largest Five Personal Landowners on Earth

- Queen Elizabeth II: 6.600 million acres
- King Abdullah of Saudi Arabia: 553 million acres
- King Bhumibol of Thailand: 126 million acres
- King Mohammed IV of Morocco: 113 million acres
- Sultan Quaboos of Oman: 76 million acres

Source: [364] [365] [366]

Queen Elizabeth II, head of state of the United Kingdom and of 31 other states and territories, is the legal owner of about 6.600 million acres of land, <u>one sixth of the earth's non ocean surface</u>.

The Queen's land holding is worth a notional $33,000,000,000,000. She is the only person on earth who owns whole countries, and who owns countries that are not even her own domestic territory. This land ownership is separate from her role as head of state.

Her holding is based on the laws of the countries she owns and her land title is valid in all the countries she owns. Her main holdings are Canada, the 2nd largest country on earth, with 2.467 million acres, Australia, the 7th largest country on earth with 1.900 million acres, the Papua New Guinea with114 million acres, New Zealand with 66 million acres and the UK with 60 million acres. This makes her the richest individual on earth in valuable assets.

Macroeconomic conclusions:

→ Humanity can live with some psychopaths and psychotic rulers, but not an unlimited amount.
→ Such macroeconomic figures show that the world has not changed much since 2000 years.
→ To hold that much land is beyond intelligence, rationality, reasonableness, and Spirit.
→ Economic theories become a mere breeze considering the power and force of these land owners.

---

[364] http://www.whoownstheworld.com/about-the-book/largest-landowner/
[365] http://www.landreport.com/americas-100-largest-landowners/
[366] http://www.businessinsider.com/worlds-biggest-landowners-2011-3?op=1

→ The owner of land decides what can be done on his land, and he gets benefit from the users.

4.6. The Nightmare of Financial Power

Most figures from 2010 and 2011 are irrelevant, like an old newspaper. During the following decades most figures will explode.

- White House's 2012 fiscal budget: $13 trillion in the red, the worst since World War II. [367] [368]
- The global financial crisis has slashed the value of financial assets by $50 trillion (2008). [369]
- The estimated total damage of the financial crisis 2009: $11,900 billion (€7,300 billion). The costs for each human on this earth would be: $1,500. [370]
- The total spent on stimulus should amount to $4 trillion, or about 7% of global GDP, a roughly seven fold increase over current efforts. [371]
- 5,000 CEOs and stockbrokers have destroyed 30% of the world's wealth; and they continue speculating. [372]
- In the next decade the world needs 100 trillion more credit, so they say.
- The profits of the large American companies have reached record levels in the third quarter of this year (2010): Gains of over $1.6 trillion were recorded. [373]

Some more examples about debt and losses (expected increases with every year):

- Bank losses: approximately $1,600 billion
- Loss of real estate values (US and UK): $4,650 billion
- Damage to the world economy: $4,200 billion
- Destruction of asset values: $50 trillion
- Financial Governments spent $10.8 trillion on bailouts

---

[367] http://www.whitehouse.gov/omb/budget
[368] http://www.forbes.com/sites/aroy/2012/02/28/white-house-quietly-increases-budget-for-obamacares-exchange-subsidies-by-111-billion/
[369] http://www.finfacts.ie/irishfinancenews/article_1016145.shtml
[370] The estimated total damage of the financial crisis 2009
[371] http://www.kyklosproductions.com/posts/index.php?p=137
[372] http://theeconomiccollapseblog.com/archives/50-economic-numbers-from-2011-that-are-almost-too-crazy-to-believe/comment-page-1
[373] http://www.dailymarkets.com/economy/2012/04/08/corporate-profits-reached-record-high-in-2011/

- $3.6 trillion was spent on the bailout in the US
- $2.4 trillion on the bailout in the UK
- $3.2 trillion on the bailout in other rich nations
- $1.6 trillion was spent by China and other emerging nations
- The US spent the equivalent of 25.8% of its GDP
- The UK spent the equivalent of 94.4% of its GDP
- The financial burden for each US citizen is $10,000
- In the UK the cost (debt) per person is $50,000 (£31,250)
- The collapse of the Spanish property market resulted in €300 billion in bad debt.
- Over the next five years, the UK government debt is expected to rise from £600 billion to £1.4 trillion, while the US national debt could double to $10 trillion.
- Global debt has reached $75 trillion. [374] [375]
- Germany 2010: Public debt rises to nearly €2 trillion: The debts of the German Federation rose nearly 22% (€230.3 billion) to €1,284 billion. The debt of the German States stood at €595.3 billion at the end of 2010. The debt of the municipalities and local authorities stood at €119.4 billion. [376]

The World Economic Forum says that we need to grow the total amount of debt by another $100 trillion over the next ten years to 'support' the anticipated amount of 'economic growth' around the world that they expect to see ... The entire global financial system is a gigantic Ponzi scheme. It is designed to keep everyone enslaved to perpetual debt. [377]

Macroeconomic conclusions:

→ To these figures one can add a thousand more such figures and then the entire picture clearly shows the immense consequences for nations and the world as a whole.
→ A trivial but very important macroeconomic parameter is: The bigger the amount of money, the bigger is either the benefit or the catastrophe with its costs, depending on its use.
→ The real world of the Economy goes up and down with the movements of billions and trillions of dollars, wealth or debt.
→ Who pays for all the financial damages? The people, the citizens, and every single individual for the next 4-6 generations will have to pay for the amoral attitudes and ineptitude of politicians, CEO's and economists.

---

[374] http://thewe.cc/contents/more/archive/us_debt.html
[375] http://usdebt.kleptocracy.us/
[376] http://alpari-forex.com/es/news/1220558.html
[377] http://www.paulnathan.biz/commentaries/83-the-goal.html

→ Together with the yearly interest payments and the continued increase of future government debt, there is no end in sight for the next 200 years.

→ Some hidden causes lie in the compulsive and psychotic microeconomic theories, graphs, models, theses, and 'anti-scientific' statements, obsessed with greed, profit, and marginal surplus everywhere.

→ Money is a tool and those who command the money flow use this tool for higher interests that do not match with democracy or with the people's satisfaction or wellbeing.

5. Macroeconomics and Political Power

5.1. Macroeconomics and Power of Corporations

In Economics II we have already developed a picture about corporations. We extend the topic with some examples and the advice to first read the picture in the context of microeconomics.

Example: America's corporate tax rate [378]

The tax rate is 35%. But 115 companies pay less than 20% in taxes. That's not even counting 37 companies like Citigroup and AIG that received more in tax credits than they paid.

Example: Tesco and Primark (UK) [379] [380]

Workers producing clothes for Tesco and Primark in the Bangladeshi capital Dhaka earn as little as £0.07 pence an hour for up to 80-hour weeks. British supermarkets are currently exploiting women workers and small scale farmers in poor countries around the globe.

A single mother, 39, with three children earns just £0.38 pence per hour picking fruit that ends up on Tesco's shelves. Some employees receive only the minimum wage, £13.97 a month, far less than the £44.82 needed for nutritious food, clean water, shelter, clothes, education, health care and transport.

Pesticide exposure: "Fruit pickers have no gloves or protective clothing and have to climb wet ladders and pick pears from the trees while they're still wet from pesticides."

Example: Wal-Mart (USA) [381]

The US mega-supermarket Wal-Mart has 2.1 million full-time employees.

---

[378] http://mediamatters.org/research/201205010008
[379] http://uk.oneworld.net/article/view/162703/1/5795
[380] http://www.ekklesia.co.uk/node/9288
[381] The US mega-supermarket Wal-Mart has 2.1 million full-time employees

Wal-Mart is the largest company in the history of the world. Wal-Mart's revenue last year: $405 billion. Wal-Mart would be the 23rd-largest economy in the world (if it was a country).

Every week nearly one-third of the U.S. population visits Wal-Mart's U.S. stores. Wal-Mart is the largest overall employer in the USA, and the biggest employer in 25 states. Wal-Mart operates internationally under 55 different names.

Example: Singapore's rice [382]

Media in Singapore claim that fake rice is being distributed in the Chinese town of Taiyuan, in Shaanxi province. This 'rice' is a mix of potatoes, sweet potatoes, and plastic. It is formed by mixing the potatoes and sweet potatoes into the shape of rice grains, then adding industrial synthetic resins. The low cost of the fake rice is allowing wholesalers to make huge profits.

Example: Corporate group Vale [383]

The Brazilian iron-ore corporate group Vale made a net profit of $17.3 billion in 2010, tripling the figure of the previous year. What isn't accounted for in the mining of resources of all kinds are the damages such as: environmental destruction, contamination, deadly diseases due to fine dust, poverty as a result of miserable pay of the workers and health damages due to dangerous working conditions.

Corporate groups are one of the main causes of global poverty, hunger, unemployment, pollution, contamination, destruction of the environment and the natural eco-systems. Power, greed, arrogance and unscrupulousness are the driving motives. They are carrying out an absolutely diabolical exploitation of all resources and of the workforce without any consideration for health, human life and future generations.

Example: Modern day-slaves in Almeria [384]

The Guardian revealed (February 2011) a report about the exploitation of tens of thousands of migrants (some estimates believe there to be over 100,000) used to grow salad and vegetables for supermarkets.

---

[382] http://veryvietnam.com/2011-01-22/china-makes-fake-rice-from-plastic-vietnam-reacts/
[383] http://en.mercopress.com/2011/05/06/iron-ore-price-doubles-in-a-year-brazil-vale-s-profits-soar-to-6.8bn-in-first
[384] http://www.guardian.co.uk/business/2011/feb/07/spain-salad-growers-slaves-charities

This had been uncovered by investigative journalists enquiring into the €2 billion-a-year (£1.6 billion) hothouse industry of Southern Spain.

- Migrant workers from Africa living in shacks made of old boxes and plastic sheeting, without sanitation or access to drinking water.
- Wages that are routinely less than half the legal minimum wage.
- Workers without papers being told they will be reported to the police if they complain.
- Allegations of segregation enforced by police harassment when African workers stray outside the hothouse areas into tourist areas.

In El Ejido (Almeria) there are more banks per inhabitant than anywhere else in Europe. The Andalusian government turns a blind eye, despite these places being rampant hotbeds of abuse of power and extreme abuse of human rights!

This type of industry exists in many places from Huelva all the way to Valencia: The produce of this industry tastes like paper or at worst is tasteless. The contamination and nurturing quality should also be investigated. But, taste amongst consumers has already degenerated and will continue to degenerate.

The Sumangali System [385] [386]

"...girls sign a contract with mills to work there for 3 years. Afterward, they are not allowed to meet anyone and not even to visit their homes. They stay in the mill hostel where 10-12 girls share one room and there are just 6 toilets for more than 300 girls. They only get a few hours sleep as they work from 8am-8pm and after dinner; they again work till 2am. If they are injured while working or even die, they don't get any compensation. This isn't all though, as they are also harassed by the male staff members. The worst of all is that they cannot even complain about anything during their tenure. They have no rights, no liberties. All this they do because they will get Rs.30,000-50,000 after serving the mill for 3 years, the amount with which they can get married. Sometimes, the mill doesn't even give them the full amount with the excuse of pointing out silly mistakes and the girls and their families are left with just tears."

The benefit of this slavery for German (and other nation's) consumers: very cheap clothes.

---

[385] http://shipra333.blogspot.com.es/2011/09/sumangali-system-in-tamil-nadu.html
[386] http://www.tehelka.com/story_main39.asp?filename=cr050708laterdayslave.asp

Macroeconomic conclusions:

→ Multiply the figures of these corporations by 3,000 and you get the global picture of profitable suffering.

→ Monopolistic corporations dominate the entire market and destroy millions of small businesses.

→ Corporations ignore critical externalities, especially in developing countries.

→ Corporations are very inventive in reducing the quality of raw substances. Less = More Profit.

→ Some corporations are highly privileged in terms of tax rates and freedom in the market.

→ Exploitation of manpower is characteristic for probably all corporations.

→ Corporations are the main cause of global poverty causing unimaginable suffering.

→ No politician, minister or head of state can say something that does not please the owners or the media.

→ If the owners of corporations are not native and cultural citizens, then the country is sold out.

Playing God at any risk is the new game in the economic world: [387]

"Nanotechnology (shortened: 'nanotech') is the study of manipulating matter on an atomic and molecular scale. Generally, nanotechnology deals with developing materials, devices, or other structures with at least one dimension sized from 1 to 100 nanometers.

Nanotechnology is considered a key technology for the future. Consequently, various governments have invested billions of dollars in its future. The United States has invested $3.7 billion through its National Nanotechnology Initiative followed by Japan with $750 million and the European Union $1.2 billion.

...the Davos World Economic Forum in its 2008 annual report indentified nanotechnology as a 'Core Risk' that had the potential to destroy human life on an unimaginable scale.

Health Care Minister Veronika Skvortsova on the mysterious deaths of nearly 200 children in the Indian State of Bihar earlier this month says that our world has suffered its first "nano-disaster" and warns that an 'apocalyptic event' involving nanotechnology is much nearer than anyone will admit.

---

[387] http://www.whatdoesitmean.com/index1590.htm

…in a History Channel broadcast about a futuristic doomsday scenario it stated: In a common practice, billions of nanobots are released to clean up an oil spill off the coast of Louisiana. However, due to a programming error, the nanobots devour all carbon based objects, instead of just the hydrocarbons of the oil. The nanobots destroy everything, all the while, replicating themselves. Within days, the planet is turned to dust."

➔ The hidden motive is without doubt deicide!

"The greatest environmental threat that we are facing is genetic modification: [388]

Behind closed doors, scientists all over the planet are creating some of the most freakish and most bizarre monsters that you could possible imagine, and very few people seem concerned about it.

Scientists claim that they are making our crops stronger, more productive and less vulnerable to insects. Scientists claim that they can alter our animals so that they are more "useful" to us. Scientists claim that genetic modification is only going to "enhance" humanity. But what if something goes seriously wrong?

Rootworms are becoming resistant to the toxins grown inside Bt corn, and this is starting to cause major problems….

Are you sure that the food that you are eating is safe?

Scientists in China have genetically modified 300 cows to produce milk that has many of the same qualities that human breast milk does. So how did they do this? Well, they inserted human genes into the cows.

One U.S. Corporation can now produce a very muscular "monster salmon" which can grow up to three times as fast as normal salmon do.

Now even human babies are being genetically modified. Recently it was reported that scientists have created babies that have three parents.

… 'Human-animal hybrid embryos' that are secretly being created in British labs… Scientists have created more than 150 human-animal hybrid embryos in British laboratories.
The hybrids have been produced secretively over the past three years by

---

[388] http://www.infowars.com/they-are-turning-our-crops-animals-and-even-our-babies-into-freakish-genetic-monsters-what-could-go-wrong/

researchers looking into possible cures for a wide range of diseases ... This kind of mixing of animals and humans is even happening in the heartland of the United States.

In the past two years, scientists have created pigs with human blood, fused rabbit eggs with human DNA and injected human stem cells to make paralyzed mice walk.

By merging humans and technology, those promoting transhumanism believe that humans can become much stronger and much more intelligent. They believe that aging, sickness, disease, disabilities, physical suffering and even death can eventually be totally eliminated.

It is incredibly arrogant to think that we can turn our crops, our animals and even our babies into freakish genetic monsters and that everything will be just fine.

We are ripping nature to shreds and we are rapidly destroying the environment that has been entrusted to us."

➔ The hidden motive is without doubt deicide!

5.2. Macroeconomics and Power of Banks

"Below is a list of the largest banks in the world as of December 31, 2011. The top 10 banks have about $24.7 trillion in combined assets. Two of the Top 5 largest banks are Japanese institutions. Deutsche Bank is currently the largest bank in the world in terms of total assets. The Bank employs over 100,000 people and serves over 20 million customers through a network of about 3,100 branches worldwide. With a market share of 15.6%, Deutsche Bank is also the largest currency trader in the world. Mitsubishi UFJ Financial Group (MUFG) is the second largest bank in the world by assets. The company's main subsidiaries include: Bank of Tokyo-Mitsubishi UFJ, Mitsubishi UFJ Trust and Banking, Mitsubishi UFJ Securities and UnionBanCal Corporation. HSBC Holdings is the third largest global financial institution with about 90 million customers worldwide." [389]

Rank	Bank	Country	Assets ($b)	Date
1	Deutsche Bank	Germany	2,802.71	31/12/2011
2	Mitsubishi UFJ Financial Group	Japan	2,741.52	31/12/2011
3	HSBC Holdings	UK	2,555.58	31/12/2011
4	BNP Paribas	France	2,545.34	31/12/2011
5	Japan Post Bank	Japan	2,542.77	31/12/2011
6	Industrial & Commercial Bank of China	China	2,455.59	31/12/2011
7	Crédit Agricole Group	France	2,434.24	31/12/2011
8	Barclays PLC	UK	2,430.74	31/12/2011
9	Royal Bank of Scotland Group	UK	2,342.66	31/12/2011
10	JPMorgan Chase & Co.	USA	2,265.79	31/12/2011

---

[389] http://www.relbanks.com/worlds-top-banks/assets-2011

11	Bank of America	USA	2,129.05	31/12/2011
12	Mizuho Financial Group	Japan	2,098.18	31/12/2011
13	China Construction Bank	China	1,948.66	31/12/2011
14	Bank of China	China	1,876.98	31/12/2011
15	Citigroup Inc	USA	1,874.91	31/12/2011
16	Agricultural Bank of China	China	1,852.79	31/12/2011
17	Sumitomo Mitsui Financial Group	Japan	1,805.09	31/12/2011
18	ING Group	Netherlands	1,656.74	31/12/2011
19	Santander Group	Spain	1,620.92	31/12/2011
20	Societe Generale	France	1,530.09	31/12/2011
21	UBS	Switzerland	1,510.95	31/12/2011
22	Lloyds Banking Group	UK	1,508.86	31/12/2011
23	Groupe BPCE	France	1,473.88	31/12/2011
24	Wells Fargo	USA	1,313.87	31/12/2011
25	UniCredit S.p.A.	Italy	1,200.31	31/12/2011
26	Credit Suisse Group	Switzerland	1,117.02	31/12/2011
27	China Development Bank	China	992.002	31/12/2011

"The following are the largest and best banks in the world in terms of total assets. The top 10 banks have over $24.4 trillion in combined assets and top 50 banks – about $67 trillion. Three of the Top 7 largest banks are UK institutions. For the third year in a row, BNP Paribas is the largest bank in the world. In 2008, it was the fourth after Royal Bank of Scotland, Barclays and Deutsche Bank. BNP Paribas's four domestic markets are France, Italy, Belgium and Luxembourg. The Bank operates in more than 80 countries and employs over 205,000 people." [390]

Rank	Bank	Country	Total Assets	Date

[390] http://www.relbanks.com/worlds-top-banks/assets-2011

			($b)	
1	BNP Paribas	France	2,792.10	30/06/2011
2	HSBC Holdings	UK	2,690.90	30/06/2011
3	Deutsche Bank	Germany	2,681.30	30/06/2011
4	Mitsubishi UFJ Financial Group	Japan	2,479.50	30/03/2011
5	Barclays PLC	UK	2,395.30	30/06/2011
6	Japan Post Bank	Japan	2,325.77	30/03/2011
7	Royal Bank of Scotland Group	UK	2,319.90	30/06/2011
8	Industrial & Commercial Bank of China	China	2,304.40	30/06/2011
9	Bank of America	US	2,264.40	30/06/2011
10	JPMorgan Chase & Co.	US	2,246.80	30/06/2011
11	Credit Agricole SA	France	2,236.80	30/03/2011
12	Citigroup	US	1,956.60	30/06/2011
13	Mizuho Financial Group	Japan	1,942.60	30/06/2011
14	China Construction Bank	China	1,818.40	30/06/2011
15	ING Group	Netherlands	1,798.60	30/06/2011
16	Banco Santander	Spain	1,785.80	30/06/2011
17	Bank of China	China	1,776.47	30/06/2011
18	Agricultural Bank of China	China	1,773.11	30/06/2011
19	Sumitomo Mitsui Financial Group	Japan	1,652.82	30/06/2011
20	Societe Generale	France	1,590.72	30/06/2011
21	Lloyds Banking Group	UK	1,570.59	30/06/2011
22	Groupe BPCE	France	1,532.53	30/06/2011
23	UBS	Switzerland	1,469.46	30/06/2011
24	UniCredit S.p.A.	Italy	1,331.88	30/06/2011
25	Wells Fargo	US	1,259.73	30/06/2011
26	Credit Suisse Group	Switzerland	1,160.72	30/06/2011

Many websites claim that the most important banks (as well as the central banks of the USA and EU) in the capitalistic world, first of all in the USA, Germany (and in Switzerland), are in the hands of a few Jewish owners or managers in the top positions.

The estimated value of the Rothschild family's wealth is at $500 trillion. [391] Who has more say on earth? They also say that half the world owes these banks billions of dollars. Is this merely a hypothesis? What is fact? What is fiction? What is the plan?

"The Federal Reserve is the central banking system of the United States of America. The Fed sent billions in bailout aid to banks in places like Mexico, Bahrain and Bavaria, billions more to a spate of Japanese car companies, more than $2 trillion in loans each to Citigroup and Morgan Stanley, and billions more to a string of lesser millionaires and billionaires with Cayman Islands addresses." [392]

"Former International Monetary Fund (IMF) Chief Dominique Strauss-Kahn was charged and jailed in the US for sex crimes on May 14th after his discovery that all of the gold held in the United States Bullion Depository located at Fort Knox was 'missing and/or unaccounted' for…. The Central Intelligence Agency (CIA) who provided him 'firm evidence' that all of the gold reported to be held by the US 'was gone' … Gold is regularly exchanged between countries to pay debts and to settle the so-called balance of trade." [393]

Searching with Google 'bank + fraud', 'bank + crimes' we get a picture that allows the hypothesis:

All banking fraud (crimes!) together creates more damages and suffering than all crimes from individuals together around the globe. But, how many bankers are in prison around the globe?

The entire banking system, including speculations, creates more injustice, misery and suffering, including subsequent crimes, around the globe than all big wars created together in the past.

---

[391] http://jubilee2012.50webs.com/the_house_of_rothschild.htm

[392] http://www.cnbc.com/id/43856550/Citi_and_Morgan_Stanley_Borrowed_Over_2_Trillion_From_Fed

[393] http://www.eutimes.net/2011/05/russia-says-imf-chief-jailed-for-discovering-all-us-gold-is-gone/

→ This is not simply an internal fault, or the result of 'imperfect people'. It expresses an essential strategic part of the deicide roadmap.

→ How many economists received a 'Nobel Price'?

→ Isn't it time to clean up this criminal mess with an iron broom?

→ There is never a solution for humanity and the planet without a radical 'clean up'.

Macroeconomic conclusions:

→ The power of the banks over governments is bigger than the power of the governments over banks; or both parties have the other at gunpoint – s stale mate on who blinks first.

→ Who profits from all the debt and the profit (interest)?

→ Where do the massive sums of interest payments and capital flow?

→ Those who try to discuss new monetary systems are at risk of elimination or labeled mad.

→ No politician, minister or head of state can say something that does not please the owners of the media.

5.3. Macroeconomics and Power of Media

It is known that six major conglomerates that make up what is called the mainstream media or MSM control 90% of the shares of large media companies that, in turn, produce 90% of what is read, seen and heard by Americans. From the MSM, the American power elite maintain a systematic and effective control of information, not only within the U.S., but globally.

According to a Canadian magazine published by Global Outlook, six conglomerates control information and entertainment in the United States and in much of the world. They are: [394]

DISNEY, owner of ABC, Touchstone Pictures, Buena Vista, Hollywood Pictures, Caravan Pictures, Miramax Films, the production of documentaries A & F, TV History Channel, Discovery, Disney and others; AOL / Time Warner, which owns CNN, HBO, Warner Brothers, Castle Rock, Time, Sports Illustrated, People, Fortune, Entertainment, Money, Netscape and others;

VIACOM, which includes CBS, Paramount Pictures, Simon & Schuster, Pocket Books, Blockbuster, Showtime, MTV, The Movie Channel & Nickelodeon, BET, Nickelodeon, etc..;

GENERAL ELECTRIC, owner of NBC, CNBC, MSNBC, Bravo, Universal Pictures, and thirteen television stations, and closely linked to the arms and aerospace industries;

RUPERT MURDOCH'S NEWS CORPORATION, owner of Fox TV, DirecTV, TV Guide, New York Post, The Weekly Standard, 20th Century Fox, MySpace and others;

Bertelsmann AG, one of the world's largest media corporations, has the European RTL-TV, Random House, Bantam Dell, Doubleday, Alfred A. Knopf, Vintage Books, and others.

The first five are registered as American and the last one is German. It would make sense to find out who the real owners are of the most important media

---

[394] http://english.pravda.ru/society/stories/21-08-2010/114691-the_global_media_dictatorship-0/

groups around the globe. They represent a religion, an ideology, financial interests of the elite, and an orchestrated media power strategy in order to influence (condition, brainwash, manipulate) humanity.

It is also of highest importance to find out what the media do not say about the state of humanity and the earth, and the hidden actors of politics, religion, economy, industry and media.

Six Jewish led or controlled companies Control 96% of the World's Media [395] [396]

The media use and abuse a great variety of mechanisms for propaganda:

- When people are afraid, they don't think rationally. And when they can't think rationally, they'll believe anything.
- Go after the person's credibility, motives, intelligence, character, or, if necessary, sanity.
- Confuse: Where anti-racists are accused of racism, or in the climate change debate, where those who argue for human causes for the phenomenon are accused of not having science or facts on their side.
- Why lie about the historical facts, even when they can be demonstrated to be false? Well, because dogmatic minds actually find it easier to reject reality than to update their viewpoints.
- If you can find a group to blame for social or economic problems, you can then go on to a) justify violence/dehumanization of them, and b) subvert responsibility for any harm that may befall them as a result.
- Violence becomes synonymous with power, patriotism and piety.
- Bullying and yelling works best on people who come to the conversation with a lack of confidence, either in themselves or their grasp of the subject being discussed.
- The idea is to deliberately confuse the argument, but insist that the logic is airtight and imply that anyone who disagrees is either too dumb or too fanatical to follow along.
- With morality politics, the idea is to declare yourself and your allies as patriots, Christians and 'real Americans'.
- Because the speaker has been blessed by God to speak on behalf of all Americans, any challenge is perceived as immoral.
- Being repetitive, being ubiquitous and being consistent. The message must be repeated over and over, it must be everywhere and it must be shared

---

[395] http://www.freepress.net/ownership/chart
[396]

http://theunjustmedia.com/Media/Six%20Jewish%20Companies%20Control%2096%25%20of%20the%20World%E2%80%99s%20Media.htm across commentators.

- The disdain for education and other evidence of being trained in critical thinking are direct threats to a hive-mind mentality.
- Any attempt to bring the discussion back to the issue at hand will likely be called deflection, an ironic use of the technique of projection/flipping.
- The more someone is losing their temper in a debate and the more intolerant they are of listening to others, the more you can be certain they do not know what they're talking about.
- The fact that a lot of people believe something is not necessarily a sign that it's true.

Source: Theunjustmedia.com

The average Americans watches television 5-6 hours per day. In the average household, at least one television set is turned on more than eight hours a day. Moreover, approximately 75% of those using the Internet frequently watch television at the same time that they are online. [397] Another source says: "The average American watched 34 hours of television each week last year... We'll probably hit an average of 35 hours per week in 2011..." [398]

What the managers and top executives of the state-run British Broadcasting

[397] http://blog.nielsen.com/nielsenwire/online_mobile/americans-watching-more-tv-than-ever/

[398] http://www.tv.com/news/how-much-television-do-you-watch-per-week-24833/

Corporation claim is nothing but sheer lie and falsification ... The BBC is simply a mouthpiece for spreading biased falsehood and untruth ... Throughout the past decades, particularly following the establishment of the Israeli regime in 1948, the BBC has made concerted efforts to function as a mouthpiece for Israel and the Zionism movement... spreads biased falsehood and fabrication simply to please the United States and Israel. [399]

BBC has the second largest budget of any UK broadcaster with an operating expenditure of £4.26 billion in 2009/10 compared to £5.9 billion for British Sky Broadcasting. [400]

They are clearly aware of the fact that this news network is their country's propaganda instrument and once this instrument is derailed and weakened their international influence, and their power to intervene in other countries' internal affairs will diminish dramatically.

The first rule is to view the Middle East through Israeli eyes: Palestinians are terrorists and aggressors; Israelis are victims who retaliate; self-defense is their motive; so is avoiding the truth. [401]

Another rule is to ignore and veil the historical facts and figures regarding the Israeli-Palestinian conflict, "Ignore the historical context", avoid mentioning six decades of dispossession, occupation, and hundreds of preceding years during which Palestine was the Palestinian homeland; also suppress the idea that a Jewish homeland first originated with Zionism's late 19th century's founding and didn't exist prior to that."

Some more statements from such sources:

- Another rule is to suppress or minimize news which is unfavorable and unpleasant to the Israelis: This rule is ironclad and unforgiving; open debate isn't tolerated; facts are suppressed; aggressors are called victims; self-defense is called terrorism; news is carefully "filtered," minds manipulated, and truth conspicuously absent.

- War and militarization are being passed off by mainstream media as "humanitarian intervention".

- Journalists are pressured into accepting media disinformation as routine, as

---

[399] http://www.presstv.ir/detail/182603.html
[400] http://www.oppapers.com/essays/Btec-Business-Level-Three-Unit/992735
[401] http://www.middleeastmonitor.com/articles/middle-east/3581-arab-revolutions-through-israeli-eyes

part of the job.

- Professional journalists committed to truth in media are invariably penalized by their corporate employers. [402] [403]

- This is a system which rewards mediocrity. Those who lie are promised fame, funding and career advancement.

- Those who refuse to abide by the standards of the mainstream media are not only fired, they are blacklisted and their prospects extinguished.

- Journalists who have the courage to say the truth find themselves marginalized and excluded, and therefore often driven into poverty.

Poisonous polluters and right-wing or left-wing ideologues fight against science and reason. Pseudo-scientists are financed from these ideologues (industries, politics) to produce doubt about what is true and what is false. They even buy elected officials with bribes. They spend hundreds of millions of dollars each year on misleading advertisements in the mass media. They hire anti-climate lobbyists to lure politicians. [404]

The extremist ideologues, financed or employed by carbon polluters, undermine the public's respect for Science and Reason by attacking the integrity of the scientists. These extreme ideologues accuse scientists of being greedy extremist ideologues. [405]

To have access to television (for marketing) requires immense amounts of money; we are talking about millions of Euros. Communicating with people is only possible for the super-rich and mega-power people. Who pays the marketing of political programs and political campaigns? The values of democracy are gone!

95% of everything that is really important for the citizens, especially critical circumstances on a local, national or international level and on the earth as a whole are either categorically avoided by the media or presented in extreme simplicity with the intention of depriving the people of the seriousness of the situation.

---

[402] http://www.wix.com/moleman216/the-alternative-voice

[403] http://bbs.chinadaily.com.cn/thread-699052-1-1.html

[404] http://www.rollingstone.com/politics/news/climate-of-denial-20110622

[405] http://www.examiner.com/article/al-gore-s-article-targets-obama-media-and-deniers-for-climate-inaction

Macroeconomic conclusions:

→ Power has replaced the truth and accuses the truth to be false: 100% perversion!

→ The power of the Media is one of the worst cancers on earth, too concentrated and directed by 'invisible' Jewish hands.

→ People's ignorance is always the bliss of politicians, the corporate managers, and the elite.

→ Not even 40,000 experts and representatives of NGOs have a relevant say in the Media.

→ Normal firms, scientific institutes, associations of experts (etc.) have no say in the Media.

→ The Western Media have become one of the most powerful parameters in macroeconomics.

→ No politician, minister or head of state can say something that does not please the owners of the media.

→ If the owners of Media are not native and cultural citizens, then the country is sold out.

5.4. Political Management of the Economy

5.4.1. Lobbyism

Over 13,500 (2009) and estimated 17,000 lobbyists (2012) work in Washington to influence the entire American government. Money spent for lobbyism 2011: more than $3.5 billion [406]

16,500 lobbyists are working to influence the European Union in Brussels. [407]

In the US, corporations spent an average of $200,000 a year on lobbying every politician elected to state legislatures. [408]

The United States, the European Union and many other countries are significantly manipulated, dominated, controlled, abused and exploited by hundreds of thousands of lobbyists, CEO's, institutions, personalities, secret service agents, (co-)owners of banks and corporate groups or educational institutions. Many of them are originally rooted in the interests of other nations.

Nepotism, favoritism, cronyism and informal understandings between businesses, officials and politicians in many places lead to inefficiency and gross waste of resources.

Macroeconomic conclusions:

➔ Lobbyism radically undermines democracy and legal governmental power.
➔ Lobbyism works in the interest of the rich, the superrich, and the corporations.
➔ There is no powerful lobbyism for the citizen's everyday interests and concerns.
➔ There is no powerful lobbyism for the small and medium sized firms'

---

[406]
http://wiki.answers.com/Q/How_many_people_work_as_lobbyists_in_the_nation's_capital_today
[407]   http://www.pacteurope.eu/pact/wp-content/uploads/2012/04/European-Lobbying-EN.pdf
[408] http://en.wikipedia.org/wiki/Lobbying_in_the_United_States

interests and concerns.

→ There is no powerful lobbyism that protects the human values and basic ethics.

→ Lobbyism disfigures and manipulates the importance of macroeconomic parameters.

5.4.2. Politics, Power and Money

General explorations:

With politicians it is first and foremost always about money: money for their own pocket, their privileges and guarantees for a future outside their political career.

Instead of serving the people, politicians first serve themselves, their morbid narcissism and their 'clubs', and the interests of corporations. This makes them fall easy prey to blackmail. They are secretly blackmailed or lured for whatever and whenever. Rarely are they politicians out of vocation or for genuine ideological reasons; Always, but always out of self interest.

Many governments sell or lease agricultural land and provide licenses for others to exploit the resources in their countries. This serves the corporations, the elite, but never the population; especially not as a measure against poverty or unemployment.

Governments misuse and misspend far too much money from taxpayers for their own purposes. For these same purposes they continuously create new laws to limit the rights of the citizens and increase the size of the elite's wealth (economy).

Most government officials have no comprehensive knowledge of the real situations faced by their own people, and of global humanity or the planet's best interests. They are unable to think in complex networks that focus on the past, the present and more importantly the future.

When politicians don't know how to deal with conflicts due to a lack of knowledge, skills and personal character, they react with brutal force. They are not capable of identifying the conflict as a result of their own failures. They are not capable of engaging in meaningful and honest dialogue with the citizens and together work out solutions. Austerity measures are an example of their shortsighted, dogmatic and ignorant reactions.

Most politicians are adept at exaggerating, understating, sweet talking, glossing over, lying, cheating, forging, seducing, manipulating, maneuvering and coming to terms. For these leaders, almost every means is justifiable to achieve their objectives and to use every possible loophole including covert extortion.

Most politicians have an idea of mankind that is from the Middle Ages. Practical politics has not changed for 500 years in its fundamental principles. They 'lead' their people and yet know nothing about human beings or the inner being and genuine needs of humans.

Many politicians misuse God and religion for their own perverse political games.   They violate the   values that earlier pioneers of their own people fought so hard to acquire. Slavery, the conquest and imperialism of the past have merely changed in presentation, form and appearance.

Most politicians do not want truth. The logical conclusion is simple: they are never in the position to solve the big problems in their own country let alone the critical state of humanity and the planet. They always talk about the (essential) growth of the economy, never about quality and balance and never about the 'true human life and value'.

Most women in politics simply copy the patterns of men. In this sense they are nothing but masculine women. The genuine qualities of real (natural) women are not welcome in politics and certainly not, in religion, that has demonized them for centuries. Ultimately as a result of these politics (and religion) their actions will always and must fail.

The state administration, the servant of power is a massive Moloch. Most people that work within the state administration are absolutely incapable of reacting to imbalance and of dealing constructively with the individual situations of citizens. Most of them suffer from feelings of inadequacy in their 'elevated' positions and compensate by working to the letter. Their completely inefficient apparatus sucks up millions if not billions and in spite of supposedly serving the people treats them like human biomass, dealing with them like industrial mass production. Politicians prefer it like this! It's always their mother behind the scene that can be blamed!

Politicians experience maximum lust at the destruction of the Archetypes of the Soul, for example love, truth, marriage and family, the development of an inner life and the power of the inner Spirit. With that they destroy themselves and they destroy the future of their own children, of their population, and of humanity as a whole. This is the way it goes whether in Marbella, Madrid, Zurich, Berlin, Paris, London, in the United States, in Israel, in the whole capitalist coalition as well as in other countries, now completely infected with European capitalism (imperialism), not to talk about contaminated Christianity (for over 800 years). Such development is the result of a roadmap from the masters behind the curtains.

In January 2011 a Swiss politician of highest executive position said (we translate): "I recommend to every woman, that she should get herself a man who is active in the military. Everything else is like at the discount store; you never really know what you are buying." This attitude we already know from the Nazis and from Hitler's loyal followers.

An insider speaks about financial power: 7.7.2011 - Hillary Clinton reviews Spanish government and applauds their servility. She said at the visit of the then President Zapatero and the King Juan Carlos: "There is virtually no important global or military challenge that we are not working on together." Even before that visit, Trinidad Jiménez, Minister of Foreign Affairs cleared all possible doubt by stating that "close cooperation between the U.S. and Spain will be visible in the political, economic and military spheres." Zapatero and the King have sold Spain to foreigners – read: to America; it means: to the owner of the corporation called 'United States'. [409] No Spaniards can see it because no media and no responsible people are talking about it!

Who are these masters destroying societies everywhere with their financial power? What are their true primordial motives? Sexual frustration? Psychopathy? Megalomania? Narcissism? Madness? Religious Psychosis? The roots of all their inner conflicts lie in the failure of their forefathers 2,000 years ago! Through that they have lost their status as 'chosen folk from God'. They have roped in the entire world into their collective unconscious conflict, burdened themselves increasingly with immense guilt and inner pain.

The summer-winter time regulation in Europe is an excellent example to show what politicians do. At the time, when they introduced this change, they had a respectable aim (reducing consumption of electricity). This was a very expensive implementation. Soon later they found out that this aim is not achievable. And today, decades later, we still have these stupid time changes that cost a lot of money twice a year. The world of animals get confused twice per year and hundreds of millions of people as well need to adapt their biorhythm, and are confused for 1-3 weeks. Now today, no politicians wants to put this on the political table aiming for a compromise by continuing with 'back to normal' in the middle of one hour forward and one hour back. It's

---

[409] http://english.pravda.ru/world/europe/07-07-2011/118420-Clinton_reviews_Spanish_government_applauds_servility-0/

about public money wasted for nothing and probably for the coming decades or centuries!

The history of the past 10 years teaches us: The neo-capitalistic coalition, US Army and NATO, chases foreign heads of states and ministers claiming that they have stolen a lot of money from their folks, and built up enormous private wealth. Do you remember Ghaddafi ? Mubarak? There are more in Africa for example. At the same time many banks, corporations, and individuals get richer and richer on a level of billions of dollars and they get increasing power with trillions of dollars and Euros. We must interpret: the governments, the 'kings' in the past, have become the 'servants' of the new 'kings' that were previously the servants of the 'kings'. In all cases the folks pay the price. That's the supra dynamic of macroeconomics. It's not surprising that the classical books about economics do not describe and analyze the real business world, but feed the students of economics and business with 80% junk and 20% facts that are superficial or of low importance.

The common people are blind, brainwashed, misled and deceived, too lazy to think, deformed by the education system, rotten by religion and focused only on their own daily physical and material needs.

Macroeconomic conclusions:

→ Governments generally have far too much money at their disposal. It makes them insane.
→ Governments and politicians are secretly blackmailed or lured for corporate interests.
→ Governments have become the servants of the major corporations and banks.
→ Most government officials have no comprehensive knowledge of the citizens' situations.
→ Governments have no holistic knowledge about the state of humanity and the planet.
→ Ministers are not capable of engaging in dialogue with the citizens and the small firms.
→ Government's practices: understating, lying, distorting, manipulating, and maneuvering.
→ Practical politics has not changed for 500 years in its fundamental principles.
→ Governments misuse God and religion for their own perverse political games.
→ Politicians talk about the growth, but never about quality and balance of life standard.

→ The state administration, servant of power, is a massive Moloch, absorbs too much money.

→ Politicians experience maximum lust at the destruction of the Archetypes of the Soul.

→ The neo-capitalistic coalition, US Army and NATO, chases foreign head of states and ministers claiming that they have stolen a lot of money from their folks for their own sake.

Mediterranean Governance

Governmental spending is of prime importance in macroeconomics: The Spanish government has earned more than a trillion Euros over the past 25 years from tourism as well as from the sale of properties to foreigners (especially in the Mediterranean areas, Balearic Islands, Canary Islands). During the same time the European Union provided further billions to Spain. The Costa del Sol, Costa Blanca, Mallorca raked in billions if not hundreds of billions in taxes, duties and fees.

What did the Spanish government do with these huge amounts of money? They let 2 million homes be built at sales prices with 60% profit that can't be sold now; and they destroyed with this urbanizing madness up to 80% of all natural areas along the ocean.

The attitudes in the world of business and politics are outrageous: corruption and rip off are as high as in an underdeveloped African country. Now, we can imagine where the money is gone. It must compensate another problem: We estimate that around 65% of all members of local governments, including the heads of village or town councils, do not have the necessary knowledge and skills, nor the character and personality qualities to lead their folk and to manage the duties of their job in a permanently changing world with increasing global problems. They live and work with a mind from the previous ages, always adoring their mothers like the Virgin Mary.

A highly relevant macroeconomic question is: Where exactly did this money go? One thing is certain, the money did not go to a nationwide efficient infrastructure (public transport, sewage system, renewable energy, technological research, renewable energy, public education and especially advances in vocational education), nor into a solidly founded and all-sided economy in their underdeveloped Southern regions.

Hard working with excellent professional attitudes is a foreign concept for the majority of Spaniards. They, instead prefer to wait for the masses of tourists that bring every summer fresh cash (paper or coins). Spain's technological pioneering development and innovation is a Fata Morgana. Most claimed innovation is second-hand, copies of other people's ideas. Not many Spaniards want to get their hands dirty, trouble their tiny minds and sweat to learn some complicated technical stuff and invest in a future. Additionally they are too lazy and ignorant to learn about the basics of life and work. Preferring instead to listen to their adoring mummies who encourage these badly educated and pampered individuals by feeding their delusions and telling them: 'Just get a job in the state administration, and you can sit on your arse for the rest of your life, dreaming of the day you will win the National Lottery.'

Bull fighting (killing) is a pleasure for Spaniards. The bull is the symbol for millennia of fertility, male potency, strength, power, and male pride. These Spaniards, symbolically kill their manhood every Sunday, whilst their womenfolk rejoice watching these weak men enjoy killing these strong male attributes, over and over. A sick society with economic consequences: impotent men at home, in the governments, in pioneering science, innovation and production, and in the free market.

That is why today Spain has its self inflicted financial crisis and extremely high unemployment. The same questions have to be asked of Greece, Italy and other Mediterranean regions. All are patriarchal, religion dominated and "macho" cultures. All are seeing a declining birth rate, all register very low sperm count, and all are dependent (the EU and USA masters) and archaic soulless societies. Economic science should investigate and explain with its theories these Southern European contexts! Surely, not even with a trillion Euro, bailout from the IMF and the European Central Bank will the economic problems of Spain, Italy, and Greece, be solved. The macroeconomic consequences will be: Spain, Greece, and half of Italy will fall below the status of 'developing countries'.

Macroeconomic conclusions:

→ The way governments spend public money is of prime importance in macroeconomics.
→ Many governments have no long-term perspective in spending public money.
→ The attitudes for human values in the world of business and politics are outrageous.
→ Working hard with excellent professional attitudes is a prime condition for the economy.
→ Education is relegated to spreading dogma, lies and religious mythology.

The 9/11 Attacks and Costs of War

The 9/11 attacks on the World Trade Center in New York is probably still vivid in most people's memory. It was an act of terror, ordered by Osama Bin Laden, or so they say.

Yet 3,000 scientists (!) in the USA question this: they say the events never occurred as they have been portrayed in the media and presented by politicians. They say the buildings could never have collapsed by just the airliners' impact. The buildings were 'prepared' with special explosives on all floors in order to create the collapse. The whole scenery of those events was orchestrated by the secret service of the USA (CIA) and Israel (Mossad). It is not a matter of economic science to find out the truth here, just let the evidence guide you.

The aim they say was to create a reason for war, to invade and occupy Afghanistan and Iraq. This however is said to also be but a small element of the global plan for the 'One World Order' of the capitalist coalition, including the occupation and possession of oil fields around the globe and the weakening of Russia, China and the whole Islamic world.

Of high economic interest is the financial aspect of terrorism:

How many people died through terrorist attacks, orchestrated by Bin Laden, Al-Qaeda and other similar groups around the world? There were some 3,000 from the World Trade Center. To these can be added perhaps 1,000 deaths from individual terrorist attacks around the world. This does not include terrorist outrages in Iraq, given that these are understood as part of the war. We are perhaps talking about 4,000 deaths to date since 9/11 caused by 'terrorists'. This adds up to approximately 400 victims per year or 33 per month. This is indeed a terrible tragedy, a miserable suffering for those left behind and obviously not justifiable.

But let us compare these figures with some other figures:

➜ Over 42,000 deaths from Road Traffic Accidents in Europe alone (every year).
➜ 380,000 deaths from fine dust (cars), in Europe alone (every year).
➜ Over 46,000 deaths from Road Traffic Accidents in America alone (every year).
➜ 400,000 deaths from fine dust (cars), in America alone (every year).
➜ Millions of deaths around the world due to contamination, also every year.
➜ 3-4 billion people living in poverty, so that 1,000 people can earn billions.

Do you understand? Something is fundamentally wrong here with the economic theories: The proportions are not comprehensible: Wars to fight terrorism with around 4,000 victims spread over 10 years, or 33 victims per month. At the same time trillions of dollars are spent on weapons and all the wars since 9/11. And when we relate the figures with the victims from road traffic accidents per year. Such disproportions indicate extreme lies!

Macroeconomic conclusions:

→ Governments do not want the truth and measure realities on different scales.
→ Governments distort values of high human importance in order to justify evil doing.
→ Governments ignore the economic and human factors of road traffic accidents.
→ Governments have two-faced, immoral and perverse attitudes, in matters of wars.

The Holocaust Law as a Principle of Economics

We do not want to explore here the historical event of WWII and the Holocaust, nor the figures and circumstances of the real genocide. It's sad anyway. Our interest is: In many states there are laws that prohibit anyone from critically investigating or even critically expressing oneself about the Holocaust. In actual fact most of the critical investigations do not deny the Holocaust; the murder of Jews during WWII. The critical statements and observations are usually related to the alleged number of '6 million Jews' and about the subject matter of what can be defined as murder and what can be defined as victims of war. Here it's about a fact of figures and the interpretation of a word.

Critics claim that it was never 6 million Jews who were murdered, that such a figure is impossible. One thing can be said as a matter of fact: It is not important if it was 6 or 3 or 'only' half a million victims. It is and will remain a terrible genocide. The economic and psychological consequences however are extremely different: Compensation payments and collective (German) guilt as a means for endless political manipulation (blackmail and extortion) come to a new light. Israel and generally affected Jews have received billions of DM, USD and EUR to date. Here it's about benefit and profit; either way it's about money.

As a follow up, one must also integrate the judgment of other collective murders in the 19th, 20th and 21st century. From what figure can one talk about 'genocide'? To this topic there are far worse hypotheses (evil allegations?): Jews (Zionists) proposed their plan to Hitler of murdering millions of Jews, in order to subsequently lay claim the right to Palestine and as blackmail for massive financial payments in the future. We can compare the figures and interpretations with the figures of victims of private car traffic accidents for the last 50 years: higher than the victims of WWII. For the sake of industrial profit and governmental taxes! Here and elsewhere with human topics (e.g. absolute poverty, hunger, dirty water, etc.) it's about externalities and collateral damages. There are always enormous collateral damages with wars (e.g. Vietnam, Afghanistan, and Iraq).

There are at least 100 historical and scientific questions that would need to be clarified on this Holocaust matter. However the Holocaust laws prohibit this. These circumstances (figures, interpretations, comparisons) make the whole Holocaust affair extremely suspicious: indeed something very explosive is being covered up, something that nobody is allowed to uncover or discuss.

Digging in the marsh is strenuous and in the end nobody wants to know the truth. Revealing the truth is collectively punished: in a relationship, in family life, in our social life, in the industry (production), in the world of religion, politics and the science of economics or the real economy.

On the other side digging and fully showing the truth is a fundamental human need, principle of science, also of social sciences, but thoroughly ignored in the neo-capitalistic science of economics!

Macroeconomic conclusions:

➔ Politicians hide or manipulate macroeconomic parameters or they simply lie about them.
➔ Macroeconomic facts are 'elaborated' to make people and corporations feel comfortable.
➔ The collective pays for the failure of authorities, institutions, corporations, and government.
➔ The way governments operate with facts, figures, interpretations and comparisons is distorted.

5.4.3. Maturity of Politicians

The Defense Minister in Germany (May 2011) was a 39 year old attorney. The Foreign Minister is a homosexual, married to a man. From a psychoanalytical view we must say: Could a 39 year old have the maturity, moral integrity, life experience and wisdom necessary for such a position? Age alone surely does not provide wisdom and moral integrity. The life experiences alone neither. Homosexuality is a very complicated neurosis, marked by a disturbance in the balance of the male and female pole; also related in a deep libido disorder to the mother and father. On top of that the use of the 'Marriage'-Archetype for a same-sex relationship is a desecration of the eternal 'Marriage'-Archetype. This is nothing but a political cabaret, distorting reality!

In Spain there was (2011) a government minister who was born in 1971 and another in 1976; both are women. Can a 35 or 40 year old person have the maturity, moral integrity, life experience, human knowledge, personal psychical-spiritual foundation, knowledge and skills to manage a government department with global perspectives, and the corresponding wisdom necessary for such a position? That's also a political cabaret! Give to such a government €100, €300 or €500 billion bailout, and then, after a few years you will need 50 years to find out where the money has gone. That's a macroeconomic issue, nothing new for many developing countries, e.g. in Africa!

The people should start to think about what relevant skills and psychical-spiritual preconditions (free from neurosis, psychosis and psychopathy) a person should have in order to be in a position of the highest political responsibility in order to carry out and manage in the interests of the people. This question should be asked around the world, regardless of culture or form of government. It is especially valid for church office holders (e.g. minister, priest, monk, bishop, cardinal, Pope) and for religious teachers of all kinds. In the future, those who violate the Archetypes of the Soul should never be allowed to fill top leadership positions in a society if humanity wants to have a good future!

It has been clear for a long time now that the people in Europe and America feel that governments have long lost touch with the healthy and genuine needs of the people. The citizens say: 'governments and political leaders cheat, lie, twist and distort'. They only act in their own interest. They are doing nothing against poverty in their own country. They are doing nothing for the long-term benefit of their citizens. So, herewith we are back to macroeconomics!

Macroeconomic conclusions:

➔ A majority of politicians lack maturity, moral integrity, life experience and wisdom.
➔ Neurotic, psychotic and psychopathic politicians can't properly manage

the concerns of a society.

→ Governments have long lost touch with the concerns and genuine needs of the people.

→ The arrogance and ignorance of politicians towards their own folk is beyond imagination.

5.4.4. The Perversion of Power

We present here a longer part of an article admitting that we can't prove the truth; but it shows a picture widely known around the globe:

"I was involved in the payment, in the direct payment in cash to a person who killed the president of a foreign country. I was in the meeting where it was decided to give this cash money to the killer... I know that certain people who are Bilderbergers were involved in such orders.... We had to pay on the instructions of foreign powers for the killing of persons who did not follow the orders of Bilderberg or the IMF or the World Bank for example.... the biggest banks in Switzerland are involved in unethical activities.... its trillions, completely unaudited, illegal and besides the tax... most of the directors of Swiss banks are not locals anymore, they are foreigners, mostly Anglo-Saxon, either American or British... they destroy our society and destroy the people world wide just for greed.

... They seek power and destroy whole countries, like Greece, Spain, Portugal or Ireland and Switzerland will be one of the last in line. And they use China as working slaves. And a person like Josef Ackermann, who is a Swiss citizen, is the top man at a German bank and he uses his power for greed and does not respect the common people. He has quite a few legal cases in Germany and also now in the States. He is a Bilderberger and does not care about Switzerland or any other country... They have huge amounts of money available and use it to destroy whole countries.... The real aim is to destroy Europe.... the big Swiss banks, because they are not Swiss anymore, most of them are led by Americans.... a kind of exclusive elite club that has all the power and everybody else is impoverished and down.... The EU is under the iron grip of Bilderberg....

...The big banks are training their staff with Anglo-Saxon values. They are training them to be greedy and ruthless. And greed is destroying Switzerland and everybody else... We are confronted with really ruthless criminals, also big war criminals. It's worse than genocide. They are ready and able to kill millions of people just to stay in power and in control.... Question: In the structure of Bilderberg, is there an inner circle that knows the plans and then there is the majority who just follow orders? Answer: Yes.... Bilderberg was founded by Prince Bernard, a former member of the SS and Nazi party and he also worked for IG Farben, who's subsidiary produced Cyclone B." [410]

The main issue here is not the people in this event or the content itself. It is about 'democracy' that has been a hollow word for a long time. The oligarchy of the capitalistic financial markets has the power. The population merely serves for exploitation for their 'One World Government' aims. Rarely somebody gets into the government without a lot of money or without being promoted by 'important' personalities and institutions.

Politics serves those that have and want to have more. More recently politics serves the political and religious psychosis: For the new World Governance. This also means: against Islam. With this the people will once again have the never-ending religious war at their doorstep like every few centuries. Remember the 'Crusades' from the 12th to the 14th century? This is exciting for the Pope! It has been like this for 2,000 years. Religion abuses politics and politics abuses religion. Both in turn misuse the people. Who is the actual culprit here? What has this got to do with macroeconomics? A hypothesis could be: it was and still is only about stealing money or making profit.

'Justice' today is in many democratic (and other) countries nothing but a lie. Laws protect political crimes, political corruption, political mendacity and hypocrisy. The judicial system is a macroeconomic pillar that allows big businesses to operate and to manage their life and wealth.

When you look at the outcome, then you know what is wanted or approved. This is what the governments, and the politicians want and approve:

- The people are helpless.
- The people are ensnared.
- The people are lied to.
- The people are brainwashed.
- The people need to be blind.
- The people should shut up.
- The people should not think.
- The people are chained to credit.
- The people are allowed to buy a car.
- The people should suffer from emissions.
- The people must suffer in general.
- The people are allowed to have a cell phone.
- The people should lose themselves in the Internet.

---

[410] http://www.henrymakow.com/revelations_from_a_swiss_banki.html

- The people are allowed to have fun.
- The people can speculate.
- The people should consume.
- The people should use credit cards.
- The people should be (relatively) poor.
- The people can have a swimming pool.
- The people can have a walkway.
- The people should feel lust when shopping.
- The people should go to the doctor.
- The people should go to the pharmacy.
- The people can go on holiday.
- The people cannot have a soul.
- The people should not ask questions.
- The people should see lies as the truth.
- The people should see neurosis as something healthy.
- The people should see lunacy as a mission.
- The people should experience narcissism as wellbeing.
- The people should get meaningless things cheap.
- The people must adapt.
- The people who are critical need to go into psychotherapy.
- The people who do not follow the lunacy must be punished.

There are too many politicians that are imprisoned in pathogenic narcissism, neurosis and psychopathy, perverse lunacy, obsession and greed, lies and falseness, intrigues and maneuvers. They only serve themselves, the elite and their power. Many ministers and heads of states in Europe and elsewhere do not govern; they do execute the orders from the supreme masters. They barely serve the people. They all disregard and abuse the Archetypes of the Soul. They are far too uneducated for the issues they manage, especially in their understanding of the psychical-spiritual being.

There are many laws that merely serve politicians themselves, their power, the wars, the elite, the exploitation and misuse and in many cases infringe the basic rights of every human being. The Holocaust laws hinder the truth and the exact (objective, neutral) establishment of the truth; it serves the lies and hidden benefits.

On the other hand new laws must be established to prohibit the brainwashing of people. New laws are also necessary for the protection of the environment, the planet and every human being. Too many laws and forms of punishment are only there to oppress the people, create mistrust and hatred and to ultimately sow fear and suffering. All those who created these laws must be held accountable, absolutely all of them.

Macroeconomic conclusions:

→ Too many laws and forms of punishment are only there to oppress the people.
→ 'Justice' today is in many democratic (and other) countries nothing but a lie.
→ Politics serves the political and religious psychosis: For a new World Governance.
→ Religion abuses politics and politics abuses religion. Both in turn misuse the people.

5.4.5. Destruction of Democracy through Money

"The power elite consist of those with tremendous amounts of both wealth and power in our world. Like any group, the power elite has both individuals and factions which are inclined to promote their own self-serving interests, and those who are more interested in serving the greater good. Many scholars who have spent considerable time studying this group have found that there are factions within this elite group which at times fight against each other, while at other times they work together for common goals." [411]

The elites do what all elites do. They launch more wars, build grander monuments to themselves, plunge their nations deeper into debt, and as it all unravels they take it out on the backs of workers and the poor. [412]

The collapse of the global economy, which wiped out a staggering $40 trillion in wealth, was caused when our elites, after destroying our manufacturing base, sold massive quantities of fraudulent mortgage-backed securities to pension funds, small investors, banks, universities, state and foreign governments and shareholders. [413]

The elites, to cover the losses, then looted the public treasury to begin the speculation over again. They also, in the name of austerity, began dismantling basic social services, set out to break the last vestiges of unions, slashed jobs, froze wages, threw millions of people out of their homes, and stood by idly as

---

[411] http://www.hidden-knowledge.net/lessons/05a_power_elite
[412]
http://www.truthdig.com/report/item/this_time_were_taking_the_whole_planet_with_us_20110307/
[413] http://www.rense.com/general93/next.htm

we created a permanent underclass of unemployed and underemployed. [414]

As Sigmund Freud grasped in 'Beyond the Pleasure Principle' and 'Civilization and its Discontents' human societies are as intoxicated and blinded by their own headlong rush toward death and destruction as they are by the search for erotic fulfillment. [415]

And the elite are all at the mercy of finance. Who owns the significant financial institutions and who has the say in the world of finance?

The elites destroy the core of societies in Europe and America; also in this way for example:

British society is witnessing a swift end to traditional family life with 46% of children now born to unmarried mothers… nearly half of all children will go through the trauma of seeing their parents divorce before they are 16… A child in a single-parent family is 75% more likely to struggle at school, 70% more likely to become addicted to drugs, 50% more likely to develop a drinking problem and 35% more likely to be unemployed in adulthood. [416]

In Germany a third of singles are against marriage. Many unmarried Germans want to remain unmarried. Only 43% of them can imagine getting married sometime in the future.

On the Internet and in the media one can find many critical observations with respect to politics. The facts of yesterday are forgotten or covered up with new facts. A lot is interpreted and assessed subjectively. Depending on the side of the political questioning or the analysis one will find completely different pictures of a concern. By using a few examples we intend to motivate questions and hypotheses, which could lead to further questions and meticulous investigations. One or the other critical observations may be seen as a conspiracy or allegation.

We understand the political topics and facts here as a starting point for economic hypotheses, which the science of history and economics, free from ideology and specific interests should explore.

Macroeconomic conclusions:

---

[414] http://www.bibliotecapleyades.net/sociopolitica/sociopol_globalelite62.htm

[415] http://www.studioeight.tv/phpbb/viewtopic.php?f=12&t=22492

[416] http://www.presstv.ir/detail/175459.html

→ All mentioned critical aspects of political acting lead to immense misuse of public money.

→ Lack of political integrity, knowledge and skills produces immense loss of public money.

→ Political mismanagement causes poverty, amorality, immense collateral damages, and costs.

→ The weak success of democracy has been destroyed and sold to the financial elite.

→ Politicians are humans and as a human they have destroyed hundreds of millions of lives.

→ Governments in America and Europe are responsible for 4 billion lives in extreme misery.

→ Coward ministers and head of states are fully responsible for war and its consequences.

→ The best possible pioneering and advanced concept, theory and practice of micro and macroeconomics can't have success with ignorant, amoral, coward, hypocritical, neurotic, psychotic, and psychopathic politicians.

→ New pioneering and vanguard academic programs, free of the insane neo-capitalism, must be offered in order to build up a new generation of leaders that will save humanity and the planet.

6. Systemic Macro-Key-Faults

6.1. Systemic Faults in Macroeconomics

- The definition of 'economy' and 'macro-economics' is not clearly elaborated.
- It is not elaborated which other systems are in an economically relevant relation.
- The interrelations with other relevant systems of society are vague and incomplete.
- The topics of 'macro-economics' and 'economy' are not structurally organized.
- All essential macro-parameters of economics are based on ideology, not on science.
- Most terms are confusing, misleading, and open many doors for interpretation.
- The preponderantly technological approach ignores the laws of nature and mind.
- Many theses and statements are not even a good journalistic elaboration.
- Ignoring 95% of the mega-parameters is an outrageous deceit and manipulation.
- All human related terms are superficial and express a highly reduced understanding.
- Many interrelations between parameters exclude other factors of immense influence.
- The entire banking system is presented in a much reduced, naïve and unreal picture.
- There is in general no holistic approach, but everywhere are labyrinths without exit.
- Many statements are clearly misleading, manipulative and rigidly constructed.
- There is no pioneering thinking or a critical creative and an intuitive thinking.
- Economics did not learn anything from the century's failure in the real world.
- There is everywhere an immense lack of care for the details in the real world.

- The entire micro- and macro-economics is anti-evolutionary, evil, and monstrous.
- There are many provocative, cantankerous, and intrinsic motives for wars.
- The extrapolation of all parameters of economics in the end leads to deicide.
- Ignored is that there has been and is a titanic fight between government and economics.
- Economics ignores the costs of all mega-parameters, understanding them as 'externalities'.
- An inadequate understanding of humans can never make any economic 'model' work.
- The criminal energy on the side of the economic top-leaders is simply not discussed.

6.2. Systemic Faults in Bailouts

What they say it is: "The European sovereign debt crisis is an ongoing financial crisis that has made it difficult or impossible for some countries in the euro area to re-finance their government debt without the assistance of third parties." [417]

A government like any individual or business has income (mainly through taxes) and expenditures (building roads, police force, maintenance, etc.). Like many individuals and businesses, the government doesn't always have the income at the time of the expenditure. Some bills come early, some have been postponed and end up accumulating and somewhere along the line, government leaders decide that the advice from economists (Just go get some money from the market) is the easy way out. In any case, the neighboring countries are doing the same, so why not.

But then one day comes the problem: On the one hand repayment gets postponed and borrowing becomes like a free for all, grab what you can frenzy. On the other hand the lenders (other countries, institutional investors such as the IMF, etc.) start to put pressure on interest rates and repayment schedules. The whole house of cards threatens to collapse.

The situation gets declared as a 'sovereign debt crisis' and the whole financial mess becomes like a giant arena where gladiator fights gladiator. Germany pulls its strings to make it harder (and more expensive) for Spain to borrow money. France demands payment from Greece for money lent. And so forth. The vicious circle is in full gear.

The small players begin to crumble. Greece finds itself in the position where it can no longer get money on the market without accepting huge increases in interest rates. So while Germany can still borrow money at 5%, Greece now must pay 25%. The best comes when the big boys come to the rescue.

The IMF shareholders sit together and 'offer' Greece a 'bailout'. In effect: A sum of money with many strings attached. Greece, which can no longer finance its day to day operations (pension payments, building roads, paying civil servants, etc.) given that it cannot raise funds on the market, is forced to accept the bailout (with all the strings attached). The true story is: The bailout

---

[417] http://en.wikipedia.org/wiki/European_sovereign-debt_crisis.

is not a 'rescue' or a 'saving from bankruptcy'. It's the opposite!

Here's an analogy: You are on a boat that is sinking. Your friend fell over board but is clinging on, so he doesn't drown. You and the other people on the boat have a "meeting" and decide that the friend should be 'saved'. You throw him the life vest but the condition is that he must let go of the boat (as it risks drowning the boat with all other passengers). Your friend who is struggling to hold on, decides (due to coercion) that it is better to take the life vest and let go than to risk not being able to hold on, or worse, that the others take drastic action to 'remove' him from holding on. This is the bailout. It's the time bomb disguised as a first aid kit!

Watching from the seats around the arena, we have the public – the masses. The majority doesn't understand anything about the 'technicalities', but everyone thinks they know better than the other. So they are easily influenced and quickly divided. With a little help from the experts, the division is quickly provided with order, those for, those against and those panicking.

In practice it happens like this: The leaders tell the people: If we don't accept this bailout we risk going back to the Stone Age. Those who don't understand immediately believe. The ones who have some intelligence, see the trick but cannot communicate to the ones who don't understand, another set, is so oblivious to everything that they simply decide to rebel (and end up getting together on a main square and 'occupying' it).

The underlying truth however isn't so complicated: The small player is crushed and the big boys are left standing. What should happen is that the country defaults and declares bankruptcy and starts off with a clean slate. From there on, the country needs to simply manage its finances in a way that avoids taking on debt. Income distributed and planned according to expenditure. In practice it happens like this: Some expenses you cut (you can live without), others you invest to increase future income. You find a balance to survive.

Banking Crisis and Bailouts

The banking crisis bailouts are similar but even less complex. These are private institutions that in some cases have gambled away the money of their customers, in other cases simply mismanaged their financial planning. In any case, the situation is that they have 'holes'.

The day to day operations are under threat of existence. The banks are made up of four key elements: clients, employees, managers and investors. The clients deposited their money and were happy to get a free set of wine glasses. The employees were simply robots or soldiers that executed orders. The managers at the steering wheels of the operations were seduced with great pay packages and bonuses and the investors raked in the yearly profits while salivating from their mouths.

When the problem of the 'holes' came to light, the clients begin to flee with their money, the employees close their eyes in fear of losing their jobs and the managers hand in their resignation and jump ship or go into early retirement (with a big fat bonus of course). The investors who all along raked in all the profits from the mismanagement are far away in hiding, counting their money.

The government sees the problem and steps in to 'rescue' the banks with a bailout. The media hypes up the whole controversy and the spectators watching the gladiator battle are again unable to decipher the whole situation. One expert says one thing, another something else. In the end a few 'heads roll' (some top CEOs have to sit on a chair and listen to a bunch of pretentious arbitrators and judges and then accept a verbal smack on their wrist) and the bank as a corporation receives a fine (maybe 10-20 million USD, maybe 100 million USD) that goes into the pocket of the government. But the investors who were the ones, who gained all the profits, are safe in their golden palaces.

Fact is fact: Just like energy, money does not simply disappear. It does not simply get destroyed or vanish. What happens is it goes from one place to another. So if a bank mismanaged their funds (or worse: strategically cheated clients and robbed their money), then this money has to be traced, found, confiscated and redistributed to the victims.

But that's too complicated for the general public and too time consuming for the government (who has its own problems). So one or two bankers (traders for example) get painted as the black sheep (oh, they were rogue traders who blew billions on bad investments), the CEO gets a public interrogation (and then lives happily ever after) and the investors who horded all the money that was mismanaged (stolen, cheated, defrauded) are gathering around a bonfire in a forest somewhere far away chanting in a circle 'LMFAO'.

LIBOR Interest Rates Scandal

This recently 'uncovered scandal' is another charade. Barclays was 'caught cheating'. The result: The CEO resigns but announces a counter attack (claiming it was the Bank of England that instructed them to do so) and thus guaranteeing that the legal case takes years to resolve. The government comes in as the charming knight on the white horse and slaps a 400 million plus pound fine on Barclays and pockets the money. But all the millions of victims of this crime (the homeowners who paid higher than necessary mortgage rates, the small business owners who paid higher than necessary interest rates on their bank loans, the consumer that paid higher than necessary interest rates on their credit card bills, etc.) are left out standing in the rain. And again, we have the investors who cashed out their winnings who are free from wrongdoing, free from legal obligation or consequence and not even in the public eye of the whole scandal.

Real Estate Crash

What they say happened: Millions of individuals, couples and families were given mortgages even though it was unrealistic that they would be able to pay them back. The homeowners were greedy and couldn't wait to get their hands on a property without having to work for it. The banks were in a trance like there was no tomorrow. Somewhere along the line, someone pulled the plug and the house of cards came crumbling down.

What really happened: Some investors made a lot of money (those that cashed out early), others were left standing when the music turned off (and couldn't find a place to sit), the homeowners lost their homes (if they couldn't continue paying) and the banks suddenly had hundreds of thousands of properties in their asset box. Some small mortgage brokers were handcuffed and painted as the black sheep. Some banks received huge sums of money from the government to cover the 'holes'. And the public woke up with a hangover.

Buying Stolen Goods

In most countries it is illegal to buy stolen goods and even if the purchaser was unaware of the fact that a good was stolen, they are still liable. Why then are none of the investors who were all too happy to cash in on the profits from dodgy, illegal, criminal, fraudulent, abusive operations not brought to justice? Effectively what we have is the crime bosses walking free (albeit richer than before) and everyone else in the chain suffering the consequences.

Debt is like a Drug

Sooner or later you become an addict (you can no longer live, operate, function without it). Sooner or later the vicious circle kicks in (you need more debt to keep living, operating and functioning). At some point you hit the curb (some collapse, some die, others face consequences for the rest of their lives). When the situation gets out of control, the government steps in, jails a few dealers and victims and confiscates what it can. The only ones left standing are the winners who cashed out their profits!

So if as citizens or governments, we want solutions let's call a spade a spade and a thief a thief. But let's keep our sanity and our intelligence. There is effectively no need to even throw anyone in jail. All that is needed is a tracing of the illicit profits and the redistribution to the victims. Then to ensure it doesn't happen again, everyone is educated in a simple and transparent form about what happened.

6.3. Systemic Faults in Politics

- Those who want to make political career have to go up a very challenging ladder.
- First of all they have to decide about an ideology and with that the right political party.
- As a member of a political party it's a must to be active and all-over friendly to get attention.
- The candidate must expand his connections and stay in contact with promoters.
- A candidate has many competitors and all claim to have the right leadership power.
- A candidate is always confronted with other members that proclaim their solutions.
- At the basic level of a political career a candidate must regularly contact many citizens.
- Once the candidate sits in a local or provincial parliament, he has stronger competitors.
- On this higher level the candidate must knock at many doors to present himself.
- Even if at this political low level, the candidate will be lured from all kind of lobbyists.
- Now, the candidate wants a seat in the provincial government. He must travel a lot.
- To become known by the party members and the citizens is indispensable: time consuming.
- The day arrives; the candidate sits in the provincial parliament. Strong fights start.
- The candidate is lost as many cooks want to prepare the same menu; to have a say.
- Practical constraints dissolve ideological ideals and force to distorted compromises.
- After a first year, the provincial minister finally understands how it works between the doors.
- There is a lot that he didn't know and he feels that he does not have the appropriate knowledge.
- Politicians do not have much time for further education or for collecting information.
- The information the provincial minister gets on the table are selected

information.
- From now on his plans and decisions are based on selected information and compromises.
- After 2 years the candidate realizes that he is simply a manager of the ongoing machine.
- Starting the third year the minister must already carefully think about the next elections.
- He can bring forward some projects, bring in new stimuli; but everything is micro-level.
- With the fourth year he must begin to spend up to 40% of his time for the next election.
- The provincial minister finally has become a member of the national committee party.
- Now he is fully engaged in the next elections and in meetings all over the country.
- He learnt to speak in a way that he gets majority supporters to get a national minister seat.
- Such activities are very time consuming (at public cost) and require promising a lot of 'benefits'.
- The candidate for the upper echelon has little time for his family; has already lost his soul.
- He learnt to twist, distort, trivialize, lie, deviate, deceive, and operate in a clandestine way.
- Finally he gets the national ministerial seat and the games continue on a perfidious level.
- Most of the resort is completely new for the beginner; he talks a lot and plays down the tasks.
- Every day some lobbyists knock at his door, or send him information with demands.
- He spends 40% of his time with telephone calls, talking, reading documents, meetings or travelling.
- He is the defense minister now, but he has no idea about the devilish geopolitical games.
- Although he is used now to practice Machiavelli's principles, he is naïve towards others.
- After two years he finally realizes that he is imprisoned in a dark labyrinth without exit.
- He needs much of his time to protect his seat for the future with the soft soap principle.
- With the end of the third year he learnt not to touch the hot potatoes and to hide the truth.
- His ideology, ideals, and political values are gone; remain as a verbal relict

in his speeches.

- At the next election he loses the seat and gets an interesting job from a corporation.
- The following ministers, a majority new, restart at zero, and change the previous decisions.

Most probably a majority of politicians and members of governments do not even have 5-10% of the knowledge and skills of critical network-thinking in our Economics I, II, and III.

In contrast to that, the masters of economics know very well how they operate with their study books and in the world of corporations and banking. The supreme masters manage their project during their entire life. And then one of their children becomes the successor. These people have their institutional power legacy through generations. They do not need the voice of the stupid citizens. They are the genius master minders and laugh about the naïve (democratic) politicians they have in their iron fist through public debt, media control, and other tools.

➔ The key fault is: such a democratic system never allows for a long-term management of national projects and there are too many competitors that always claim to have a better solution.

➔ From some governments one can get the impression that the innermost drive the politicians have lies in their biography since early childhood: always the father, the mother, the teacher, the professor, the priest and finally their partner (husband, wife) had the last word and these politicians had no say at all in their private life. But now, as politicians they blindly compensate with far too much incompetence and immaturity, but with the same stubbornness they experienced and the defiance they had when they were in the age of the terrible twos.

➔ From this view it's not surprising that the masters of economics go for their throat and dance on their nose.

6.4. Systemic Faults in Education

Most of the state universities are far too big, operating like the mass industry and completely neglecting the (inner) being as part of teaching in all areas of study. The social sciences (philosophy, psychology, education, sociology, business, tourism, politics, journalism, etc.) 'sell' a predominantly inefficient and inappropriate bulk product (knowledge) with very heavy ideological and elitist molding.

Since hundreds of years they teach about the 'old human being' but not about the 'evolutionary psychical-spiritual human being'. It is unacceptable that politics, which generally has an image of human beings from the Middle Ages, gets to have a say in the content of such study programs.

Social sciences must also be allowed to be taught at private academic institutions. The state shouldn't meddle in the content. The state must officially recognize private academic institutions and their academic titles.

Most people are too lazy to learn, especially too lazy for self-realization and psychical-spiritual development. They avoid every serious human challenge for the truth and for love. They are hypocrites, blind sheep, big mouths, and they mostly talk a lot of rubbish and nonsense. They only make fun of true love, about human values and the inner Spirit. They piss on the Archetypes of the Soul. These people are good-for-nothing and only pollute the world with their ways of living and their stupid and perverted gossip. This must now come to an end!

→ The key fault is that public education is still founded on an archaic understanding of humans and human life.

6.5. Systemic Faults in Religion

More than 6.5 billion people are brainwashed and deformed in their soul. They are trapped in dark psychical and spiritual labyrinths, in religious psychosis, in stupidity, in arrogance and ignorance. Religions have failed! Even their officials are trapped within.

There are approximately 2.4 billion Christian, who believe, that Jesus Christ will descend from heaven physically with 10,000 angels (armed with swords), to come and free the people. This Jesus Christ is even expected to come and clean up the mess, which people around the planet created. They further believe that Jesus from Nazareth, an exceptional miracle maker, died on the cross for the sins of mankind. On top of all this they are obsessed with the idea that God is 'forgiving' (like Mom or Dad) and will simply just take everybody into Paradise.

That is stupid, naïve, primitive, blinded, neurotic, perverse and all around completely psychically ill. This belief shows the extreme laziness and hypocrisy of Christians. This whole thing is nothing more than a ridiculous trap: Once you are in it you are poisoned and won't be able to get out anymore. The powerful and super rich are laughing their heads off, because this stupidity and blindness conveniently serves them and their interests.

Billions of believers and millions of priests as well as hundreds of self-declared Messiahs have misused the name of the true prophets for power and war, for genocide, for stealing land and commodities, for narcissistic satisfaction, out of stupidity or dishonesty and out of a spiritual aberration or religious psychosis. Nearly everything that remains is nothing but lies and deceit. All this has got nothing to do with the true and eternal Archetypes of the Soul.

Fact is: Christians need to find the truth themselves and they need to develop their psychical-spiritual salvation and reconciliation on their own for the actions ('sins') they committed against the Archetypes of the Soul, against themselves, against humanity and against the planet.

→ The key fault is the exclusion of the inner archetypal psychical-spiritual processes as the foundation of religion.

6.6. Key Faults of Barbarity

Everywhere around the world there are far too many lies and liars, far too much falseness, fakeness, stubbornness, sadism and a complete lack of respect as well as lunacy, unscrupulousness, arrogance and ignorance.

There are far too many people that poison everything with their amorality, perversion, greed, megalomania, dogmatism, fundamentalism and their religious psychosis.

Everywhere you go people are brainwashed and manipulated, exploited like slaves and defrauded with spiritual labyrinths. They are all treated like a soulless human bio-mass. Most of the time this makes the select more powerful and wealthier as the bulk of the people gets poorer and more disenfranchised.

Far too many people live with facades and masks, twisting and distorting reality. They are mere copies of the Zeitgeist. They make empty promises and assurances. They do everything in their power to undermine justice and the truth.

Many even think that they can actually solve the problems of the local population with money. Political and military power must enable solutions. Often it is religious psychosis that gives them the drive.

The truth was lost a long time ago! Nobody wants it anymore. The truth no longer has any 'power'. This is the triumph of pathogenic narcissism, political and religious psychosis, lies and perversion, and last but not least also of the stupidity of the people! Nobody can find their way out of this maze. This is also the key fault of society and human life.

Truth and a good personality do not exist without the psychical-spiritual formation and respect for the Archetypes of the Soul.

Many places on this earth have become soulless:

→ No love
→ No hope
→ No trust

→ No faith
→ No truth
→ No honesty
→ No fairness
→ No business morals
→ No service quality
→ No balanced prices
→ No disposition to learn and change
→ No environmental protection
→ No hygiene control
→ No efficient and professional skills
→ No interest to learn for love and business
→ No interest for personal psychical-spiritual formation
→ No respect for the genuine inner needs
→ No leisure offers for the soul and for creativity
→ No respect for the Archetypes of the Soul
→ No love with the inner Spirit

Certainly there are exceptions, in individuals and business.

→ The truth has lost; Lies have taken its place.
→ The real good has lost; it can never win by itself.
→ Love has lost; People are rotten to their innermost core.
→ The inner Spirit of humans barely stands a chance anymore.
→ All Archetypes of the Soul have been abused and destroyed.

The key fault is that in all societies, in all households, in all businesses, and in all relationships the truth has lost and lies have taken its place.

6.7. The Lost Humanity

Clarification of 'Conspiracy'

The word 'conspiracy' is thoroughly abused and misinterpreted. Those who dig for example in the fog of political or economic realities are not the agents of a conspiring act. They do not come together to make an agreement and plan to commit a crime, fraud or political wrongdoing. These people do not act subversively. They are not evil, lying, or treacherous people. They are not preparing anything in secret. They have no mad purpose. They all investigate facts, analyze facts, and try to interpret and understand what is behind visible scenery. Their result can be referred to as 'hypotheses' or 'proven theory'. It is quite typical for the representatives of economics and politics, also from the media, to convert the meaning of this word into the opposite in order to defame the people that reveal facts and search for the truth; they call these investigating people 'conspirators' and their result a 'conspiracy'. That's a dirty strategy to protect wrong and criminal doing and their master minders.

Many writers speak about the powerful 'invisible hand'; we give some examples to stimulate digging and all-sided critical thinking: [418]

Most of the major events of world significance are masterfully planned and orchestrated by an elite coterie of enormously powerful people who are not of one nation, one ethnic grouping, or one overridingly important business group. They are a power unto themselves for whom those others work. Neither are these power elite of recent origin. Its roots go deep into the past.

The control of the US, and of global politics, by the wealthiest families of the planet is exercised in a powerful, profound and clandestine manner. This control began in Europe and has a continuity that can be traced back to the time when the bankers discovered it was more profitable to give loans to governments than to needy individuals. [419]

These banking families and their subservient beneficiaries have come to own most major businesses over the two centuries during which they have secretly and increasingly organized themselves as controllers of governments worldwide and as arbiters of war and peace.

---

[418] http://www.newdawnmagazine.com/articles/the-elite-the-great-game-world-war-iii
[419] http://www.newdawnmagazine.com/articles/the-elite-the-great-game-world-war-iii

The US is controlled through the privately owned Federal Reserve, which in turn is controlled by the handful of banking families that established it by deception in the first place. [420]

Here is a 'High Cabal' that has made US what it is … This 'High Cabal' is the 'One World Cabal' of today, also called the elite by various writers. [421]

The elites own the media, banks, defense and oil industry. They own the US military, NATO, the Secret Service, the CIA (and other secret services), the Supreme Court, and many of the lower courts. They appear to control, either directly or indirectly, most of the state, country, and local law enforcement agencies.

It was 1774 when Amschel Mayer Rothschild stated at a gathering of the twelve richest men of Prussia in Frankfurt: 'Wars should be directed so that the nations on both sides should be further in our debt.'

The elites own numerous 'think tanks' that work for expanding, consolidating and perpetuating its hold on the globe. The Royal Institute of International Affairs (RIIA), the Council on Foreign Relations (CFR), the Bilderberg Group, the Trilateral Commission, and many other similar organizations are all funded by the elite and work for it. [422]

The Tavistock Institute on Human Relations, Shaping the Moral, Spiritual, Cultural, Political and Economic Decline of the United States of America, was established in 1913 at Wellington House, London for manipulation of public opinion. [423]

The Tavistock Institute has a $6 billion fund and 400 subsidiary organizations are under its control along with 3,000 think tanks, mostly in the USA.

The modern science of mass manipulation was born at Wellington House London.

Bernays was a nephew of Sigmund Freud, a fact never mentioned, and developed the technique of engineering consent. [424]

---

[420] http://www.globalresearch.ca/index.php?context=va&aid=8518
[421] http://www.bilderberg.org/st/SecretTeamChapter01.htm
[422] http://imperialtwilight.wordpress.com/category/the-globalist-web-of-subversion/
[423] http://educate-yourself.org/cn/tavistockarticlesindex04jun04.shtml
[424] http://www.scribd.com/doc/6921657/Goebbels-todays-mass-mind-control-Part-1

Bernays "pioneered the use of psychology and other social sciences to shape and form public opinion so that the public thought such manufactured opinions were their own".

Their supreme principle: Absolute behavior control is imminent...

80% of US electronic and print media are owned by only six large corporations. The distortions, lies and fabrications, incessantly are pouring out of this media, a propaganda and brainwashing organ of the elite.

Who rules East Europe commands the Heartland: Who rules the Heartland commands the World-Island: Who commands the World-Island commands the world. [425]

For America the chief geopolitical prize is Eurasia... About 75 percent of the world's people live in Eurasia ... Eurasia accounts for about 60 percent of the world's GNP and about three fourths of the world's known energy resources.

For decades Israel has violated well established precepts of international law and defied numerous United Nations resolutions in its occupation of conquered lands, in extra-judicial killings, and in its repeated acts of military aggression. [426]

For decades the US has provided Israel with crucial military, diplomatic and financial backing, including more than $3 billion each year in aid. [427]

Although this group makes up only about 3% of the US population, they wield immense power and influence - vastly more than any other ethnic or religious group.

Since the 1960s, this group has come to wield considerable influence in American economic, cultural, intellectual and political life. [428]

This group played a central role in American finance during the 1980s, and they were among the chief beneficiaries of that decade's corporate mergers and reorganizations.

Though barely 2% of the (US) nation's population is from this population group, close to half its billionaires are from this (population group). [429]

---

[425] http://en.wikipedia.org/wiki/Halford_Mackinder
[426] http://www.freearbvoice.org/readerscorner/jewishLobby.htm
[427] http://www.rense.com/general27/jlobby.htm
[428] http://www.ihr.org/leaflets/jewishlobby.shtml/

The chief executive officers of the three major television networks and the four largest film studios are members of this group, as are the owners of the nation's largest newspaper chain and the most influential single newspaper, the New York Times.

The group's economic influence and power are disproportionately concentrated in Hollywood, television, and in the news industry. [430]

This group alone had contributed 50 percent of the funds for [President Bill] Clinton's 1996 re-election campaign.

In a few key sectors of the media, notably among Hollywood studio executives, members of this group are so numerically dominant that calling these businesses ('foreigner')-controlled is little more than a statistical observation.

They (Jews) are a major source of money for Democratic candidates.

Hollywood is run by members of this group. It's owned by these ('foreigners').

The three most important groups pressing America into war (WWII) were the British, these 'foreigners', and the Roosevelt administration.

Their greatest danger to this country lies in their large ownership and influence in our motion pictures, our press, our radio, and our government.

The group's connection thoroughly pervades affluent financial, commercial, social, entertainment, and art circles.

Hardly a month goes by without a new TV production, a new film, a new drama, new books, prose or poetry, dealing with the subject, and the flood is increasing rather than abating.

The Jews' suffering (from the Holocaust) simply does not merit comparable attention. Overshadowed in the focus on the group's victimization are, for example, the tens of millions of victims of America's World War II ally, Stalinist Russia, along with the tens of millions of victims of China's Maoist regime, as well as the 12 to 14 million Germans, victims of the flight and

---

[429] http://www.lovearth.net/ThePowerfulJewishLobby.htm
[430] http://www.henrymakow.com/jewish_leader_laments_decline.html

expulsion of 1944-1949, of whom some two million lost their lives. [431]
The well-financed Jewish media and 'educational' campaign is crucially important to the interests of Israel. [432]

Organized Jewish groups have exploited the Nazi Holocaust to deflect criticism of their country and its own morally indefensible policies ... [433]

The Holocaust may yet turn out to be the 'greatest robbery in the history of mankind'.

I've never seen a President standing up to (these groups). They always get what they want.

If the American people understood what a grip those people have got on our government, they would rise up in arms. Our citizens certainly don't have any idea what goes on.

Israel and the Jewish organizations, in collaboration with this country's pro-(Jewish) Christian fundamentalist 'amen corner', are prodding the United States - the world's foremost military and economic power - into new wars against (the Foreigner's) enemies.

(Foreigners) wield immense power and influence in the United States. The (foreigners) dominates the U.S. political system. The ('foreigner') lobby is a decisive factor in US support for (their foreign country).

Through complex analysis we become more and more aware of a horrendous picture. A massive global octopus, full of falseness, lies, misrepresentation, distortion, deadly poison, political and religious psychosis, perverse lust to kill of an indescribable and never before existing dimension and power, has got nearly the whole humanity in its iron grip. In the hidden reality of politics, economy, media and religion there is a diabolical titanic battle that has been ongoing since 150-200 years.

There are no solutions for a new macroeconomics in the interest of humanity without the complete disclosure of the truth about this global octopus! Humanity needs to be enlightened up to the minute details. This also means: the entire history since the Middle Ages up until today must be entirely re-written.

---

[431] http://www.rense.com/general27/jlobby.htm
[432] http://www.codoh.com/node/866
[433] http://desip.igc.org/AkramFinkelsteinHolocaust.html

Mainly the drive of this group's clandestine activities has nothing to do with religion, nothing with Christian or Jewish belief. Criticizing Israel's government or this clandestine group has nothing to do with religion or with race, but much more (even only) with economics and politics.

Most people are cowards. The Pope and his Cardinals are cowards. Mot Christians are cowards. The governments and the politicians are cowards. That's why we have such a nightmare of history and the current economic and bellicose disasters.

→ The key fault is that a small selected group can have such immense financial power to indirectly and clandestinely govern much of the world; simply due to public cowardice.

6.8. Economics of Christianity

An estimated 2.2.-2.4. billion people have grown up and live in Christian countries, countries that are culturally and educationally shaped from the history and presence of Christian religion. Even those who do not believe in most of their dogmatic teaching, including the so called 'atheists', are shaped in their mind and soul from Christian 'mental good'.

Economics understand 'Education' as a positive externality. We understand Christianity also as a so called 'positive externality', enormously influencing in many ways the entire economy and society. The picture we draw here will make clear that Christianity is preponderantly a very critical externality. Its effects on humans are absolutely not positive, but desired from and of indirect benefit for politics and economics.

Christianity is also a mega-institution consisting in a million and more churches ('households'), countless properties, own banks, millions of 'working people' (for the church), and operating own businesses. There are also many Christian institutions and authorities that have a say in politics and the economy. Churches are producers and consumers.

→ Religion is a mega-parameter of society and economy.

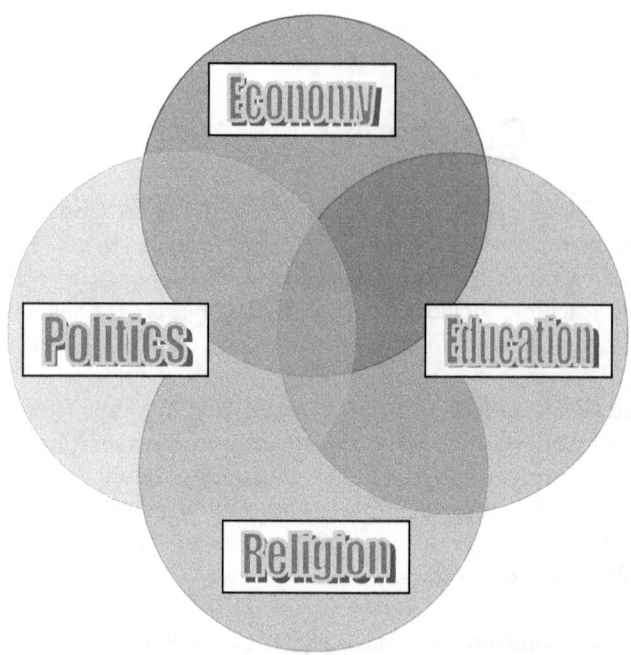

We could also say: Politics, Education, and Religion are 'Positive Externalities' from the Economy (Economics). Seen that way, we must re-write the entire History.

Recall: There is never a Solution for Humanity without the Truth! If you believe that the sum of your knowledge covers at least 1% of the truth, then you are mistaken, also and especially in matters of religious or political believes. If certain authorities in politics and religions said in the past and say today, and even if millions of authorities said in the past and say today *'That is the truth'*, then this is not proof and does not mean that it is really the truth. It is not the tiniest bit of proof.

Assets of the Vatican

"The Church has 20-22% of all the real estate, a quarter of Rome and the Vatican." [434]

"The Vatican's real estate is worth about 700 million euro ($1.21 billion), not including its priceless art treasures, (according to) Ivan Ruggiero, the Holy See's chief accountant." [435]

---

[434] Dagospia.com
[435] http://www.catholicarrogance.org/Catholic/Vaticanpalace.html

"...the Catholic Church (is) into the ranks of the top billionaire corporations of the twentieth century." [436]

"World's Biggest Stock Broker: The Catholic Church, therefore, once all her assets have been put together, is the most formidable stockbroker in the world. The 'Wall Street Journal' said that the Vatican's financial deals in the U.S. alone were so big that very often it sold or bought gold in lots of a million or more dollars at one time.

Therefore, the Vatican was, and still is, the most redoubtable wealth accumulator and property owner in existence.

The Vatican has large investments with the Rothschilds of Britain, France and America, with the Hambros Bank, with the Credit Suisse in London and Zurich. In the United States it has large investments with the Morgan Bank, the Chase-Manhattan Bank, the First National Bank of New York, the Bankers Trust Company, and others. The Vatican has billions of shares in the most powerful international corporations such as Gulf Oil, Shell, General Motors, Bethlehem Steel, General Electric, International Business Machines, T.W.A., etc. At a conservative estimate, these amount to more than 500 million dollars in the U.S.A. alone." [437]

"The Catholic church is the biggest financial power, wealth accumulator and property owner in existence. She is a greater possessor of material riches than any other single institution, corporation, bank, giant trust, government or state of the whole globe." [438]

The Roman Catholic Church is practically everywhere around the globe. There is no secret service from any country that has such an intimate access to people's soul and real life; and to the people's secret pocket money. There must be a reason why American Presidents a few months after election do the Pope the honor of visiting him with private audience. Others, especially European heads of state, go to Israel when they are elected, also with strange unknown motives. What other than economic interests can explain such special honor? The relationship structure is obvious: the servant visits the 'king' and never the other way round!

Vatican Bank: Assets worth 6 billion Euro, 25 thousand clients. [439]

---

[436] http://www.cai.org/bible-studies/vatican-billions
[437] http://www.chick.com/reading/books/153/153_10.asp
[438] http://www.chick.com/reading/books/153/153_10.asp
[439] http://vaticaninsider.lastampa.it/en/homepage/the-vatican/detail/articolo/ior-16389/

Properties of the Vatican: 4 institutes of nuns, 300 parishes, 250 catholic schools, 200 non-parish churches, 200 houses generalities, 90 religious institutions, 65 nursing home, 50 missions, 43 colleges, 30 monasteries, 20 nursing homes, 10 hospitals, 16 monasteries, tourism: 200,000 beds (estimated turnover 4,5bn), etc. [440]

Let's roughly estimate that 500,000,000 million Christians from the total of 2.2.-2.4.bn Christians are working; and they pay the Biblical taxes of 10% to their local Church for their services 'in God'. If we theoretically calculate a $100 per year and worker, all the Churches get together a sum of $50,000,000,000 per year. That's a fine business! But we assume the amount is much higher. Furthermore many old people leave their assets to the Church. Also, many Churches have additional businesses and income (profit). So we could estimate a total sum of $250,000,000,000 per year minimum. But who knows, if the right experts would dig here and calculate with one billion 'tax- and donation'-providers, they would probably find two trillion dollars of income and 'assets-gifts' per year. However, Christian Churches as an economic system are a mega-parameter in the economy.

Christian Churches are free of taxes.

Christianity; World Council of Churches: A worldwide fellowship of 349 churches seeking unity, a common witness and Christian service. [441]

→ Questions for a global perspective: Assets? Turnover? Revenue? Profit? Undeclared income?
→ Christian population: 2.2-2.4bn people. Market value of such a consumer population?
→ As no lunch is for free, what is the hidden deal behind these tax free churches?

The Unholy Bible

60 Gospels existed in the first centuries. At the end, the ecclesiastic authorities chose 4 editions, written between the years 70 and 120. Not one has been written by an eyewitness! And not one original Gospel exists, not even first transcripts. The authors of the original texts are unknown. No apostle has ever written such texts! Nobody has written down what Jesus said. The first 100 years after his death no historian even took notice of him.

---

[440] ICI and Vatican TEMIS, Ma8 18, 2007.
[441] http://www.oikoumene.org/

Countless copyists redacted and copied over and over again the texts of the Holy Bible, added, changed or deleted pieces. Over 2,000 diverse text variations and 250,000 variations of reading exist today. And these texts are translated today with many errors into 1,100 languages and dialects!

These texts in a rarely accountable manifoldness are simply mission letters, mythological tales, religious edifications, legends, with a lot of anecdotes and fictional stories, with each copywriting new additions and eliminations, smaller and bigger changes. All texts are made by unexampled lies, falsifications, and displacements. The contradictions are countless. The constitution of the Holy Bible does not allow for an understanding of these texts as 'holy' or 'inspired from God'.

In the Gospels you will find innumerable statements that are quoted billions of times by churchgoers: And Jesus said: "…"; or: "I am …". Fact is: Nobody knows what Jesus said! Such words are even presented as authentic words of God! This is called 'brainwashing' and 'manipulating with lies'.

Critical Bible research says: All stories in the Old Testament and New Testament are legends, myths, sagas, fictions, anecdotes, full of manipulation and deceit. The Bible is a chaotic and corrupted collection of texts. There is practically no real historical substance. The four Gospels are never a biography of J.C.!

Today it is proven that the Christian dogmas already existed in the Middle East and Far East, at Jesus' time as well as thousands of years before his epoch: the spiritual procreation, the physical resurrection, the mother of God, the son of God, the savior, the messiah, the prophet, the angels, the devil, God, the eternal life, the paradise, hell, the miracles, the dogma of the trinity, the crucifixion as a sin offering, the story about Adam and Eve, the natural death as a punishment, the creation as the beginning of the salvific history, and all the sacraments such as baptism, the remission, the last supper, etc. Nothing is new and authentically Christian in that sense!

Considering the development of these texts it is an absurdity to allege that God has written or dictated these texts, or that these texts have been written by inspiration through God. There, where lies don't lead further, there is the need for an untouchable 'belief'. It's absolutely perverse to teach and claim: our belief lives from the relationship to the Holy Bible, inspired by the Holy Spirit. But indeed: the belief can't be better than these texts.

All the Christian dogmas, teachings and practices have got absolutely nothing to do with any part of the psychical-spiritual life (the inner life, the psychical-spiritual organism) of a person, of psychical-spiritual development, and of a constructive self-forming for living and growing with love and the inner Spirit. Christian dogmas, teachings and practices completely ignore what makes a person to a genuine human being.

Sources of the Bible

The Book: Chaotically plugged together anthology of unrelated texts, that hundreds of anonymous authors, publishers and copywriters created, reworked, translated, falsified and 'improved'. It is proven, that the texts from the Bible (Old and New Testament) were always continuously changed. Political power interests always played a role in the creation of the Bible texts. It is proven, that much did not and could not have happened as stated in the Old Testament. There are many oral and written sources of unknown origins and stories. Some texts date back to the time 250-100 BC, others from the time around 539 BC. The 5 books of Moses were not written by Moses; they are also not 3200 years old. Historical facts were inflated, distorted, mixed up and placed into a different time. There are many unknown authors and thousand fold editing of the texts over many centuries. Many essential untruths have been determined in the Old Testament. The texts of the Bible that relate to previous times were only written down much later.

The essential texts of the Bible (Old Testament) originate from the late 7th century BC. There are countless contradictions in the Bible. In the Bible there are Commandments that without doubt originate from the Old Babylonia, from the Hammurabi Codex. In many old civilizations there were myths about floods, also in India, China and America. Much already originated from the Epic of Gilgamesh from the Mesopotamian region.

There are many parallels between the Bible (Old Testament) and the Epic of Gilgamesh. Most of the religious customs and values have their roots in the Asia Minor and Egyptian region. The archaeological analysts come to the conclusion, that the Old Testament is fully the work of subsequent editors. All the analysts see the Pentateuch as a 'mosaic from different sources'. The Bible itself turns out to be an artifact with many erratic statements from different societies.

Content of the Bible (BC)

- The Old Testament is based on testimonies and talks of the creation of the earth, the prehistory of mankind, the election, the history of salvation. The contents are put together out of a variety of texts: Tales, stories, law collections, testimonies, pieces of wisdom, chronicles, liturgical and poetical texts, lamentations, love songs, family sagas, legends…

- The aim of the one-God-movement was and is, to create a world epic as collection of historical scrolls, memories, sagas, popular tales, anecdotes, Kingly propaganda, prophecies and ancient composition, partly original, partly copied from previous editions.
- The creation of the world according to old Sumerian beliefs is similar to the stated one in the Bible.
- The birth of Moses, his childhood and youth are consistent with legends from the time in the Mesopotamian region.
- The exodus from Egypt with Moses never happened.
- The Ten Commandments can already be found – in somewhat different form – already in the Egyptian Books of the Dead.
- Nearly everything is legend and never historiography.
- Most of the texts are adapted to the political interests of the given times.
- The savage story, that Abraham sacrificed his son at the will of God, is legend.
- The mass exodus of the Jews from Lower Egypt, from the Delta region, never happened.
- Monotheism was not an invention of the Israelites.
- Jericho never had a wall and did not even exist at the time that Joshua was said to have conquered it.
- A federal state of Israel and Judaea never existed.
- Countless conceptions and tales in the Bible originate from other civilizations and religions.
- Essential parts of the story of Israel played out very differently from the way the Bible portrays.
- A settlement of Israel through Abraham never happened.
- Different archaeologists place the time of Abraham in different epochs, that differ by up to 1000 years.
- The contradictions in the story of Abraham are indications that Abraham hardly could have even existed.
- Biblical and archaeological information indicates a concoction of cults.
- There are historical facts that make it impossible that Isaac ever existed.
- The whole story about Jacob is false.
- All the portrayed facts and findings are clues, that the legends about Joseph were a complete invention.
- The incidents of the 12 sons of Jacob in Egypt are to be seriously put in question.
- The ascertained data from excavations in Egypt are not compatible with Moses data from the invented Pentateuch.
- A mass exodus from Egypt under Ramses appears to be completely

implausible.

- There are no indications of any mass exodus under a Moses.
- The exodus of 600,000 people from Egypt is invented.
- The invented Moses could not have been hindered by Edom.
- Myths are subsequently condensed into historical fact.
- Moses' laws: It is incomprehensible, why God would promise a land that first needs to be conquered with war and religious-racist mass murder.
- The exodus from Egypt is a conglomeration of legends from different epochs.
- The book of Joshua is a collection of sagas, heroic tales and local myths.
- An over 100 year invasion under Joshua could hardly have occurred.
- The factual life of Israelites is hardly described in the Old Testament.
- A 'golden age' of Israel under David and Salomon is simulated.
- There are no archaeological findings of the structures of a kingdom of David.
- Large kingdom or a central administration, as portrayed in the Old Testament with a temple city Jerusalem, did not exist in the times of Judah.
- The people in Israel-Palestine were up until the end of the 8th century B.C. illiterate.
- The Genesis (1st book of Moses) is a concoction of various nomadic tales.
- The archaeological findings, or rather the non-findings clearly indicate that the invasion under the King Josia did not take place.
- With false stories about the King Omri, Ahab and Isebel the true story of Israel is camouflaged according to plan and Jerusalem placed at the center.

The Vulgate

- In the year 367 A.D. the first binding 'Holy Scriptures' (a collection of scrolls) commissioned by the Pope was created by Jerome: the 'Vulgate'.
- Vulgate: Latin translation, originally Greek (New Testament) and Hebrew (Old Testament).
- Previously numerous Latin translations existed, each one considerably differing from the other.
- The roman-catholic church declared the Vulgate as 'error-free'.
- But later errors were found, already in 1590 the new 'error-free' edition was released ('Editio Sixtina').
- Already in 1592 this was then replaced by the new 'error-free' Editio Clementina.
- In the year 1598 another corrected and 'error-free' declared version of the Bible was released.
- This 1598 corrected Vulgate, the 'Editio Clementina', remained in use until the year 1907.

- Pope Pius X, then replaced the Vulgate, with the Nuova Vulgata – the fifth 'error-free' edition.
- Herewith the new Vulgate was again declared 'error free', from God as 'creator' and dictated by the holy Spirit.
- In 1870 the Pope Pius IX declared the edition at the time as 'miraculous revelation', from the Apostles out of the mouth of Jesus Christ received dictated from the Holy Spirit. Yet the 'error-free' doctrine lasted until 1907.
- In 1870 the council declared the infallibility of the Pope.
- At the time the pre-existence of the soul before the birth of the being and reincarnation was also taught.
- One must be aware of the fact that at the time of Jerome any deviation from the catholic state religion meant the death penalty. Jerome wanted to become Pope. He obviously had to adapt to the interests of the Pope and the authority! Shortly before that Christianity was declared as the sole religion of the state in the entire Roman Empire.
- Already in the year 326 the Emperor Constantine began with the persecution of dissidents. Jerome had to execute a duty in a totalitarian state. In such a situation one must work to the interest of the state religion!
- The oldest conserved Greek texts from the New Testament originate from the 4th and 5th century.
- The ancient Christians that rejected the virgin birth of Jesus were considered a sect.
- The Gospel of St. Matthew did not know a virgin birth of Jesus, instead a natural procreation through Joseph and Mary. The idea of a virgin birth originates from ancient idolatrous cults.
- The new church office followed ancient pagan idolatry and influence from the stat the contents of the texts (Vulgate).
- The new (Christian) state religion in the year 380 systematically burned all the old Christian scriptures. Source texts and several other Gospels were eliminated by the newly established Church. There are pressing suspicions that the biggest library in ancient times, in Alexandria were burned down on purpose in the interest of the new state Church. There were already then so called sect hunters.
- There are Early Christian sources that the Early Catholic and later the Roman-Catholic Church destroyed.
- There are numerous essential contradictions in the Bible that reveal, that the many authors with differing knowledge and consciousness worked on this 'Holy Book'.

Creation of the Bible

- The authors of the four Gospels are unknown; the names are made up.
- The four Gospels were written around 70-100; the authors are unknown.

- The Pauline epistles came about around the year 50. But Paul did not know Jesus, knew nothing about him.
- J.C. died around the year 30; and there is not a single witness from the time.
- Numerous religious texts are not integrated; the Apocrypha.
- There is no biographical knowledge about most of the protagonists in the Old Testament and the New Testament.
- Nobody knows, what Jesus Christ taught (said). There is practically nothing concrete that one knows about this person. And yet, in the Bible it constantly says: "And Jesus said…"
- Selected texts indicate little about truth and falsifications within a text.
- Many texts do not have any declared authors and no authenticity as 'source text'.
- There are many Early Christian texts and fragments that were not integrated into the Bible.
- There are ways of reading and interpreting that can never lead to a single truth.
- There are almost as many text forms as there are copies.
- Translators are not always precise; sometimes also not concentrate, careless or incompetent.
- Changes and compositions always had to conform to the views and interest of the papacy.
- The Bible is a conglomerate of copies of copies and translations of translations.
- Texts can be forged, texts can be wrongly translated, new texts can be added, the meaning changed through sentence construction, something of one's own can be integrated, something can be 'put right' (in order to falsify), texts can be excluded, etc. and the originals can be burnt.
- Critical books always ended up on the list of forbidden books since the beginning of the Christian state religion.
- The Bible was written by completely different, mostly unknown people with differing ideas and views and at different times.
- The Bible is the book of the Christian churches that has been thousand fold changed always according to private, ecclesiastic and political interests.
- The Bible today is created to a complete works, of all the previous reigning interests of the past 3000 years.
- The Bible can never be the pure 'word of God' and the 'dictation of the Spirit'. There are no comprehensible reports, apart from a few archetypal dreams, that also need to be put into question.
- Nothing, absolute nothing is 'authentically' documented about the prophets, Abraham or Moses, Christ, the Apostles, the Gospels or from God and Spirit.

- Nothing in the Bible or in the Church is 'error-free', 'unflawed', 'untouchable', or 'infallible', especially not the Pope or the Magisterium.
- If everything is declared as the 'word of God', then one obtains a grotesque, chaotic, neurotic and schizophrenic image of God; it appears that everything has gone astray on a fatal religious Psychosis.
- The environment of the origination of the 'Holy Scriptures' is not 'divine', rather: Power, wars, hate, power struggle, political interests, intrigues, murder, papal crimes, perversions, powerful and influential people, forgers, religious evildoers, etc.
- The many gruesome events of mass murder that according to the Bible were arranged, advocated, supported or even accomplished by a vengeful God himself are absolutely insane.
- The Roman-catholic Church is since a long time a rigid, even fossilized, psychopathic power apparatus, rooted in thinking from the Middle Ages, still as devilish as the inquisition of the times.
- The world view of the Bible, including the ideas about the creation of the world and the human being correspond to the spiritual horizon and knowledge of human beings from around 2000-3500 years ago.
- 2000 years of Christian and Christian Church history have prevented timings and contexts to be seen scientifically and historically in true form.

→ In its history Christianity has probably killed, murdered, and let starve and die over one billion people. The economic benefits were the cake for governments, the masters of the economy, and the consumers in the 'free market'.

Motives to Believe

- Humans are lazy, lazy to think, sluggish, superficial and don't want to learn anything.
- Humans want easy, fast, simple and direct solutions for their salvation.
- Humans are submissive to authority, easily deceivable and easily enslaved.
- Humans are like blind sheep, driven herd animals and followers.
- Human are cowardly and fearfully paralyzed by social pressure.
- Humans believe in 'holy lies' because they themselves lie, live in lies.
- Humans believe in archaic nonsense, because they themselves are archaic.
- Humans want to belong, otherwise they are alone and excluded.
- Humans do not want to take responsibility for the truth.
- Humans need the belief, in order to live their quarrelsomeness.
- Humans cannot give up their belief, because they are stubborn.
- Humans live their sick cantankerousness with their belief.
- Humans are scared of the shock that the truth can release.

- Humans have such a small ego, that they refurbish it with belief.
- Humans think they are better with their belief, than non believers.
- Humans are scared of life and therefore cling to their belief.
- Humans themselves play a false, deceitful, deceiving game in life.
- Humans are psychically on the stage of development of a small child.
- Humans can live their own, open or concealed arrogance with their belief.
- Humans choose illusions over the strong facts of life and humane being.
- Humans hope for the redemption of their unconscious complexes with belief.
- Humans compensate their human weaknesses with their belief.
- Humans have enormous concealed guilt, partly real and partly self suggested.
- Humans increase their extremely low and bad self value with their belief.
- Humans expect help from God and J.C. instead of helping themselves.
- Humans compensate their weak, instable self-confidence with their belief.
- Humans flee from themselves and their own inferiority with their belief.
- Humans think that with belief they can tame their 'unworthy' compulsiveness and lust.
- Humans see their life as unworthy and low; create balance with belief.
- Humans cannot live themselves and need the 'mother church'.
- Humans have not been loved and hope to receive the love of God with their belief.
- Humans have experienced suffering and in their belief experience comfort and relief.
- Humans strengthen their own imperiousness and their tyrannical personality.
- Humans don't have a genuine self-identity and find it in their community of believers.
- Humans conceal with their extremely low psychical-spiritual development with their belief.
- Humans do not have any substantial self enlightenment and do not want any.
- Humans do not want to see, how their own parents are completely archaic.
- Humans suppress their hate of their father, mother and life with their belief.
- Humans are sickened by themselves, their own body and flee into belief.
- Humans have an increased feeling of triumph, being in the "true" belief.
- Humans are submissive and masochistically bonded in their drive to religion.
- Humans are orally unsaved and nurture themselves through fixation on belief.
- Humans do not have any substantial knowledge, to question themselves or

others.

- Humans are scared, to look at themselves in the inner mirror.
- Humans are scared, to recognize the devilish lies of the church.
- Humans fear to recognize themselves, how they are deceived by the religion.
- Humans loose their ground, when they recognize 'infallible' truth as a lie.

→ These are the best consumer conditions for 'free operations' from the side of the corporations as well as from the politicians, especially the governments.

Corrupted Religion

Politicians of the Christian-oriented party need their naive, blind followers. Politicians in general want this type of human being, so that they can do what they want. The military needs this type of human being, as a soldier, as submissive cannon fodder. The military can declare their military action as act of God, and 'in the name of God'. The industry needs this type of human being, to make maximum profit.

If the Pope and the Bible lie, Christians believe the lies, so also politicians can lie. The big media have it easy with their games of deceit and distortion. Brainwashing, manipulation and propaganda only functions with this type of human being. Most of the billionaires base their wealth and their power on this type of human being.

If the people are focused on the suffering Jesus Christ, then they bear a lot of suffering. If the people are fixed on the after life and the relieving Paradise, then they accept poverty. If the people believe in the authorities of the Church, then they protest very little against state powers.

If the people are psychically and spiritually weak and submissive, then the politicians are strong. If religion can deceive people without being detected, then those in power can as well. If people have their soul at the mercy of the Church, then they give their life at the mercy of those in power. If people let themselves be exploited by the Church, they let themselves be exploited by the state.

Those in power around the world, the leaders in politics and the economy as well as the elite think they are the winners in this power game. But history teaches us: The last winner standing is always the papacy und with that the institution that leads the entire Christianity (the churches of the world church council included).

Those that rule heaven (the souls of all people including those in power in the economy and government) rule (with the illusionary world of Dogma), the people (humanity) and with that the world: this was and is the politics of the Roman-Catholic Church and of the Christian religion since the creation of the first Vulgate.

Herewith the papacy determines war and peace on earth; even if the religious power loses, it will ultimately always be the winner, during war and after war. Politics use and misuse religion and religion uses and misuses politics.

This is how it has been 1000, 2000, 3000 and 5000 years ago; and this is how it will go in, until the new, genuine, truthful and evolutionary religion reaches its breakthrough – or until both eliminate each other together with humanity as a whole.

→ There is never a solution for humanity without a complete catharsis and a new understanding of religion, politics and economics.

Christian Dogmas

All the Christian dogmas, teachings and practices have got absolutely nothing to do with any part of the psychical-spiritual life (the inner life) of a person, of psychical-spiritual development, and of a constructive self-forming for living and growing with love and the inner Spirit. Christian dogmas, teachings and practices completely ignore what makes a person to a genuine human being.

→ Form a life and business-oriented view, the Christian education does not promote any useful and constructive knowledge and skills for living and the world of work and business.

What kind of love and relationship do the people live with their partner if they mutually ignore all these aspects of inner life we all have? And what is the result? It is the same kind of result as the one expressed and produced by the Christian dogmas, teachings, and practices! Lies and games and sadistic suppression everywhere, over and over again, with the result of a complete neurotic being and living, not rarely psychopathic! This produces an immense hidden suffering and failure worldwide!

→ Christian dogmas, teachings and practices do not express any ability to understand people's real inner psychical-spiritual life. That's why we have contamination, climate change with is consequences, the destruction of the world of nature and animals, an incredible amount of victims of traffic accidents, wars and terrorism, misery, poverty, and countless amoral and criminal people around the globe.

Christian Churches also teach: not being Christian is a lost being and life, and therefore all non-Christians are evil and bad people, never people of God. Logically they can't get to heaven.

➔ That's why most of the Christian Churches want the total collapse, the last big war, the destruction of the earth, and the elimination of humanity: to show to the rest of the world's souls that they are the only religion that has the truth and therefore that they are the sole folk going to heaven.
➔ Very neurotic! Very perverse! Totally psychopathic! The most evil psychosis! A frightening danger for humanity and the earth! It must be a horrifying nightmare for the super-rich and the UHNW and their heirs around the globe.

Defeat of the Truth

All wisdom, all human values (love, hope, truth, peace, justice, spirit, the Archetypes of the Soul, etc.) and all the wise men together never stand a chance against politics, the financial power, the media, the industry, the official religion and the huge masses (billions) of brainwashed, blind, neurotic, malformed and driven people.

Add to that the fact that the state of humanity and the earth is so catastrophic and heading towards the complete annihilation, and that people will be squashed and hardly have room for their psychical and spiritual freedom.

The search for the truth in the Christian religion leads people to incomprehensible facts. Nothing in the entire universe can be so brutally devilish as the lies and the falseness of the Christian religion, its deeds and its consequences. They totally infected the world of politics and economics.

On the other hand the search for the truth leads to the truth about religion. With that the total breakthrough is given for politics and economics. But the people don't want the truth behind all the lies, distortions and falsifications. Even those that uncover the lies of the religion, politics, economy, industry and business world don't want the real truth.

➔ Today there is not one word related to the spiritual and religious concern that has not been misused, disfigured, falsified, emptied, or perverted.
➔ With only a few million exceptions, seven billion people are brainwashed and totally disfigured in their truthful being and becoming.
➔ In Economics, Politics, and Religion we find everywhere the same

systemic faults.

The Sick or Uneducated Human

- An inferior, unreasonable human of minor value
- An unidentified animal without instinct
- A blind, brainwashed human biomass
- A conceited bigmouth without truthfulness
- A being full of lies, self-lies and life-lies
- A deformed, distorted, disfigured human being
- A crushed, chained and suppressed being
- An artificial, superficial vivid object
- A very weak, adulterated copied product
- A greedy, ravenous, insatiable monster
- An uninformed, ignorant, dull, primitive creature
- A naive, gullible and easy seducible sloth
- An archaic, perverse, psychopathic driven creature
- An inner weak beast, strengthened only by external things
- An inflated narcissist with a completely disfigured ego
- A follower, copycat, stereotype of the collective
- An animalistic being with a completely rotten inner core
- A hypocritical, pitiable, embarrassing figure of fun
- A cushy, lazy, indolent, fastidious human biomass
- A very low-thinking, even unable to think pre-hominid
- A boring, bossy person too lazy to learn
- An ego-driven, blind 'I do what I want'-machine

The Evil Man

- A vivid, chaotic, emotional, energetic biomass
- A highly bred, self-alienated, mad being
- A bragger, impostor, bluffer, gambler
- A lying, false and brutal creature unable to love
- A destroyer, breaker, spoiler, embitterer, hater
- An inutile, only taking and stealing being
- A suppressing, displacing, falsifier, decomposing, distorting person
- An obsessed, religious-psychotic driven person
- A slave, exploited, abused, misused, violated, raped person
- An exploiting, enslaving, desecrating, oppressing thief

- A babbler and talker poisoning the environment
- A devil, a beast, a thoroughly evil being
- A bellicose, a warlike, predacious, killing beast
- A lunacy obsessed figure, a global mass killer
- A destroyer of nature, the species, the climate and the planet
- A liar, dispraiser and destroyer of psychical-spiritual values
- An unreasonable, scrupulous, violent, relentless creature
- An indifferent, irresponsible, dull inferior human
- An insane, tricky, inhumane being
- A human poisoning trust, hope, love, Spirit, the truth
- A deicide, a killer of the truth, a destroyer of the Spirit, a hater of love
- A frightening nightmare in the name of Jesus Christ
- An absolute sad and hopeless case for God and the Spirit

The Guilt of People

- People want lies, falseness, perversion, illusion, a mentally ill religion and psychopaths.
- People are hypocrites, cowards, narcissists, neurotics, materialists and mentally ill people.
- People are self-opinionated, greedy, stubborn, egoistic, ignorant, arrogant, false and too lazy to learn.
- People are too coward to question the authority of the politics, religion, media, economy and education.
- People have unscrupulously exploited, enslaved, and killed billions of people and used lies to lead wars.
- People have driven the planet and humanity to the abyss with your greed and arrogance.
- People yourself have chosen and elected the mentally ill and megalomaniac leaders in politics and religion.
- People have not learnt anything from history; in return you now have the concealed dictatorship, the police state.
- People blindly believed your politicians out of laziness; now you are victim and offender in your own folk.
- People don't want the truth or the inner values, nor the inner Spirit, and neither true love.
- People disdained the Archetypes of the Soul and with that ultimately also yourselves and humanity as a whole.
- People can all talk without thinking, but self realization and psychical-spiritual development you all reject.
- People all want a good life, but you all accept, that for that billions of

people are exploited.
- People provoked the financial crisis yourselves, because you all wanted without first working hard for it.
- You have sold all human values and natural resources for the soul to monsters.

The Christian Pest

- The Christian, who believes in lies and forgeries, is himself the victim and a liar and forger.
- The Christian, who believes in the distortions and falsifications, will himself be distorted and even falsified.
- The Christian, who believes in absurdities, becomes absurd himself and lives in an absurd manner.
- The Christian, who believes in a corrupt work and corrupt leadership, becomes corrupt himself.
- The Christian, who believes in dogma, is stubborn, inflexible, rigid and compulsive.
- The Christian, who believes in the self-righteous teachings of the church, becomes self-righteous himself.
- The Christian, who believes in the oppressive rules and commandments, becomes the oppressor himself.
- The Christian, who believes in the miracles of Jesus, then hopes for a miracle and loses his life.
- The Christian, who believes in the dehumanization of Jesus and Mary, dehumanizes himself.
- The Christian, who believes in the intervention of God on earth, is kidding himself.
- The Christian, who believes in help by means of worshipping the cross or a wall, ends up in madness.
- The Christian, who believes in the vile spiritual fraud, he will even cheat and dupe.
- The Christian, who believes in absurd magic rituals, he himself lives with stupid magical attitudes.
- The Christian, who believes in the cross of death and suffering, lives in constant fear of death and suffering.
- The Christian, who believes in the content of religious songs and sings along, ends up in psychosis.
- The Christian, who believes in the salvation of the church, is lazy, naïve, gullible, stupid and ignorant.
- The Christian, who believes in the doctrine of Adam and Eve, is a mentally poor, lost instinct creature.

- The Christian, who believes in the perverse sexual teachings of church leaders, becomes somewhat perverse.
- The Christian, who believes in celibacy and the religious ideal of the woman, is never able to love.
- The Christian, who believes in the high dignitaries of the Vatican, can never distinguish God from the devil.
- The Christian, who believes in the magic of redemption and salvation, is lazy and becomes more and more rotten.
- The Christian, who believes in the power of the 'Urbi et Orbi' blessing, is a hypocrite and a coward.
- The Christian, who believes in neurotic, psychopathic and psychotic teachings, becomes so himself.
- The Christian, who believes in the teachings of the diseased labyrinth, will find no escape and only war.
- The Christian, who believes in God's help on the battlefield, is himself guilty of being at war.
- The Christian, who believes in the transformation of the St. Mass, becomes a danger to humanity.
- The Christian, who believes in dogmas without the psychical-spiritual organism, will never find himself.

The Guilt of the Church

- Throughout its history, Christianity has killed, murdered, liquidated, driven to death more than a billion people and led to starve billions of people, all in the name of Jesus Christ.
- Throughout its history, Christianity has tortured, raped, violated, abused, oppressed and exploited billions of people in the most perverse ways, all in the name of Jesus Christ.
- Throughout its history, Christianity has lied to, misled, deceived, brainwashed, manipulated, deluded, stupefied and led billions of people astray in the name of Jesus Christ.
- Throughout its history, Christianity has stolen to a frightful extent, looted, robbed, expropriated, destroyed and driven to brutal poverty billions of people in the name of Jesus Christ.
- Throughout its history, Christianity has enslaved and chained over a billion people, taken away their freedom and dignity and paid for their work with abysmal contempt in the name of Jesus Christ.
- Throughout its history, Christianity has provoked more riots and rebellions, more wars than any other religion, as well as led the biggest and worst wars directly and indirectly in the name of Jesus Christ.
- Throughout its history, Christianity has enriched itself immensely, created sinecures, betrayed, cheated and in diabolical way exercised power over

people and their souls in the name of Jesus Christ.

- Throughout its history, Christianity has mentally infected billions of people with ignorance, arrogance, ruthlessness, megalomania and psychosis, and with lies and falsehood in the name of Jesus Christ.
- Christianity is the main cause of the contamination, pollution, climate change, destruction of ecosystems, the destruction of resources and the destruction of the planet in the name of Jesus Christ.
- Throughout its history, Christianity has made the lie to the truth and deformed love to sadism, perverted the true inner Spirit into a fool and mocked peace and justice in the name of Jesus Christ.
- Throughout its history, Christianity has created an incredible amount of narcissism, neurosis, obsession, insanity, psychosis, megalomania, perversion and crime in the name of Jesus Christ.
- Throughout its history, Christianity has sown cowardice, hypocrisy, duplicity, hatred, fear, guilt, depression, distrust, hopelessness, and psychological and physical violence throughout the world in the name of Jesus Christ.
- Christianity was and is seduced, driven and energized by the lust of death, suffering, the torturing, the guilt, the blood and the destruction of humanity in the name of Jesus Christ.
- Throughout its history, Christianity has polluted the politicians, poisoned, demoralized, and made them mentally ill, incompetent in terms of managing people and blinded by the lies of religion in the name of Jesus Christ.
- Throughout its history, Christianity has distorted and deformed people with fairy tales, fantasies, superstitions, myths, legends, anecdotes, illusions, and heresies in the name of Jesus Christ.
- Christianity makes people infantile, blind, obedient, subservient, inept to think, adaptive, naive, trusting and neurotic sheep in the name of Jesus Christ.

It is high time for a complete catharsis and a totally new beginning! Christians either want the renewal, or Christianity will perish! No one except me can perform this enormously divine work!

Guilt Calls for Learning

On the one side:

- People have made terrible mistakes; but they can profoundly learn from it.
- People have missed chances to take the right decisions for a prosper development.

👎 People have ignored and neglected the most important human values.

👎 People have forgotten the immeasurable values of their cultural and social history.

👎 People have lost themselves in running for superficial and egoistic purposes.

👎 People have lost themselves in a dark labyrinth of political and religious fights.

👎 People have missed chances to do politics and business with the inner Spirit for humans.

👎 People have played with lies, cheat, deceit, distortion, delusion, empty promises.

👎 People have forgotten that they only have one earth and that they must care for it.

👎 People have ignored that all humans on earth are a divine creation to be formed.

👎 People have not seen that they destroy their society with centralized rigid regulations.

On the other side:

👍 People must change their view, their thinking, their ways of living and their attitudes.

👍 People must find new faith in themselves, in their inner Spirit, in their inner potentials.

👍 People must become creative, innovative and pioneering for new solutions.

👍 People must decisively give an effort much stronger than ever before in the history.

👍 People must aspire to new goals with strength, endurance and perseverance.

👍 People must cooperate, talk, discuss without taboos and take decisions together.

👍 People must listen to each other with respect, trust, openness and understanding.

👍 People must work together for a new holistic and a sustainable development of societies.

👍 People must go through a catharsis and complete renewal for the future generations.

👍 People must solve the immense global problems with their soul and not with wars.

→ People must unify humanity for a cooperative, balanced, peaceful and equitable path.

Wise Men Required

Without a doubt we can assume, that today around the globe there are people that are very wise, that seek and live a genuine inner spirituality. They have learnt a lot about life and about people, learnt a lot about the deepest meaning of life, about hope, the truth, justice, peace, and the innermost meaning of life. They experience the spiritual power inside through meditation, contemplation and many also through their dreams.

→ They all belong to the most valuable people that exist on earth.

These wise people have experienced and know, how much most people ignore their inner being and how these people are and live totally self-alienated. They have experience and know about the inner suffering of billions of people.

They also know about how the lies, the life lies, the cheating and deceiving, the falseness and evilness, the distortion and twisting create endless suffering, despair and hopelessness.

All these wise people have deep in their heart, the desire, that people around the globe find their fortune and their fulfillment, that freedom and justice reigns over the earth, and that all people find within themselves the inner transcendental source. Many of the wise people, women as well as men, have a certain smaller or bigger access (inner experience) of the existence of the transcendental world that means they found the spiritual world.

Many of these wise people, partly also members of an official religion, are actively anxious, to help other people find their way to psychical-spiritual fulfillment. Many may have their own, somewhat bizarre ideas about spirituality. Certain organizations however are extremely astray and even teach absurd ideas and practices; we won't touch on this subject here.

We can certainly assume, that such wise people existed over and over again over the past centuries amongst many civilizations around the globe and that they always existed. They also existed 1000, 2000, 3000 and more years ago in all civilizations around the globe. They told people about their experiences, shared their knowledge and organized themselves in communities. Already in the second subsequent generation this word of mouth knowledge become alienated from its substance, manipulated, distorted and misused for different interests. Subsequently people created legends out of this substance and these – later biographically unknown people – were given names and a story.

There are wise men as protagonists in the Bible. There are also prophets, men of God, saviors, messiahs, priests, teachers of wisdom, enlightened personalities and those sent by God – however one wants to define those terms. Most probably most of these very wise men failed out of known reasons: power of the established religious institutions, political and local cultural circumstances. The masses could neither read nor write; most of these people were overwhelmingly poor, stupid, submissive to authority, and had a magical experience of their existence.

One had to sell the people supernatural illusions, already based on the reason of (word of mouth) marketing. The failure of such a mission is practically preconditioned. Only fragments of their being, actions and teaching stood the test of time; partially mixed creatively or with strategy with other ideas and knowledge from other cultures and with distorted (untruthful) historical facts. With that given individual or institutional interests, most of the genuine, authentic knowledge was extremely or even totally distorted.

7. Macroeconomics for a Sustainable Roadmap

→ There is no solution for humanity and the planet without the 'inner truth'.
→ There is no solution for humanity and the planet without wise men and women.
→ There is no solution for humanity and the planet without holistic education.
→ There is no solution for humanity and the planet without catharsis and reconciliation.
→ There is no solution for humanity and the planet without the inner source of life.
→ There is no solution for humanity and the planet without the vivid collective unconscious.
→ There is no solution for humanity and the planet without a complete re-construction.
→ There is no solution for humanity and the planet without living the Archetypes of the Soul.
→ Wise men and women must unify at a new 'round table' in order to guide humanity.

7.1. Mega-Parameters of Economics

Each of these parameters implies hundreds of billions if not $1-2 trillion costs per year:

(The list is not complete!)

- Population growth
- Poverty and economic imbalance
- Lack of primary needs and infrastructures
- Lack of healthy food
- Lack of healthy water and water for agriculture
- Decrease of underground water resources
- Glaciers melting (water reservoirs)

- Decreasing agriculture land and soil degradation
- Deforestation, desertification, decomposition
- Over-exploitation of seas and oceans
- Over-exploitation of raw resources
- Irreversibly damaged eco-systems
- Species reduction and elimination
- Contamination: chemicals, pharmaceutics
- Contamination: fine dust, waste, nuclear waste, sewage
- Collateral effects of the transport systems
- Nuclear waste and its maintenance
- Climate change with consequences for production
- Drought, flood, fire, tornados, storms, hurricanes
- Disease and all kind of illnesses, accidents
- Mental and behavior disorder of all kind
- Crimes and corruption
- Rearmament, military and wars
- Unrest, trouble spots and radicalism
- Mega-cities and its social-mental effects
- Reparation of damages and measures for protection
- Decrease of human values, dehumanization
- Destruction of democratic values, principles
- Increasing money demand globally for living

Effects of Mega-Parameters

A first short approach requires a differentiation between causes and effects.

Parameters (cause):

- Contamination
- Pollution
- Destruction
- Damages
- Diminishment

Parameters (effect):

- Affects human body
- Affects mind and soul
- Affects social life
- Affects species
- Affects ecosystems
- Destroys human values
- Destroys environment
- Destroys resources
- Puts the planet in danger
- Puts humanity in danger
- Creates risks of unrest and wars

Parameters (agents):

- Human's characteristics
- Institutional characteristics
- Society's characteristics
- Political characteristics
- Religion's characteristics
- Media's characteristics
- Educational characteristics
- Economic characteristics
- Ethical characteristics

Parameters (non-productive costs): damages, destruction, elimination, prevention

- Short term costs
- Long term costs
- Who pays for the costs?
- The cost's long term effects

→ There are direct costs that are burdened on the global economy.
→ There are indirect costs due to destroyed systemic resources.
→ There are the costs for repair, protection, and prevention.
→ There are the not definable costs from the loss of human values.
→ The total costs of these parameters exceed $20trillion per year.
→ These parameters are 'mega-parameters' that dominate the economy.

7.2. No Hope due to the 'Clubs'

Professor Vicenç Navarro (Universidad Pompeu Fabra) hits the nail on the head; we summarize the essence: Today, with economics, it's like with the dogma in the middle Age: the earth is the center of the universe. Today we see a similar situation in economics: replacing the religious attitude, supported by the establishment, by economists and by the financial systems (and financed by the Church) makes politics, finances and the economy of a country. The dogma is the neo-liberal dogma. A short view about the 'economic crisis' shows how erroneous they are. The (economics') clergy today and the new (economics') Church have created this enormous crisis in order to implement their politics of austerity at favor of themselves. This dogma, despite of its enormous failure, continues to be broadcasted by the media. [442]

To really understand the neo-capitalistic 'macroeconomics' it is indispensable to search with Google and to dig into all directions. We do not assert that all the information that can be found in the Internet is true. But there is a lot of information one can comprehend and explore scientifically: from assumed facts to hypothesis and from there to thesis or proven facts. The world today can't be adequately understood without getting a bigger historical picture of the financial institutions and their masters since centuries.

A quick glance at the membership of the Club of Rome (the organization that commissioned the report 'Limits to Growth') and one finds high ranking members from banking, economics and even nuclear physicists.[443]

On the one hand, one would assume with such high profile members that something came of the initial report first published 40 years ago; on the other hand it is clearly evident that the membership is infiltrated with members from vested interest groups.

Here's another good one: A 30 second Google search on Dr. Ricardo Díez-Hochleitner, the 'Honorary President of the Club of Rome' and where else does he belong?

http://www.fundacionbertelsmann.org/cps/rde/xchg/SID-65304396-

---

[442] http://www.elplural.com/2012/07/01/el-dogma-economico-neoliberal-y-las-politicas-y-estafas-que-promueve/
[443] http://www.clubofrome.org/?p=2419

ECCE24FD/fundacion/hs.xsl/6509.htm

http://www.idea.int/about/board/diez-hochleitner.cfm (the ones that are now)

Oh, that name rings a bell … Are they not the ones implementing electronic voting? Perfecting the 'voting fraud'? Yes they are!

http://www.conspiracyplanet.com/channel.cfm?channelid=31&contentid=947

What else is this IDEA? See here:

http://www.quotaproject.org/

Another path to destruction! From the country that now has kindergartens where it is forbidden to call boys 'boys' or girls 'girls':

http://www.heraldsun.com.au/news/the-other-side/pc-preschool-bans-words-him-and-her/story-e6frfhk6-1226082516997

Puh, and isn't Sweden the one 'wanting' Julian Assange on a pure fabricated claim of consensual sex without a condom. It's like a bank claiming it was robbed after a customer used the ATM machine with his own credit card!

But back to Dr. Ricardo: Where else is he?

http://www.futurefoundation.org/

Uff … Sounds like heaven … Future & Foundation. But a short extract from their latest work:

"The Next Thousand Years television series, an outgrowth of the Humanity 3000 Program, is an ambitious step in the Foundation's efforts to live its mission. The four-program series is based on the most current scientific information and the thinking of the best minds on the planet, to give the audience some comprehension of the potentials for the evolution of human culture during the next thousand years. Viewers will gain a richer understanding of the past and present, then look through windows opened by scientific discoveries and technological advances to consider the question: Where does humanity go from here?"

'Scientific discoveries' and 'technological advances' for the new 'The 1000

Year Reich'.

The key to further darkness! The highway to collapse ... More science, more technology, less human ... Ouch! Evolution gone ... Roadmap to hell!

No, but maybe they have good intentions, no? Well here's some more about them:

http://www.futurefoundation.org/resources/index.htm

Wow, welcome to science fiction!

http://www.arlingtoninstitute.org/

http://www.arlingtoninstitute.org/wbp What is this 5 year old analysis?

http://www.foresight.org/ Oh, this one is straight from heaven, ready to play God on earth!

And it's not alone: http://www.extropy.org/

"Extropy Institute continues to support critical research and development of sciences and technologies of human enhancement." Sounds like 'penis enlargement'.

Science + technology + human enhancement = Another replacement for God!

And more:

http://www.crnano.org/

http://longnow.org/

http://www.altfutures.com/

http://www.thevenusproject.com/

http://www.thevenusproject.com/downloads/ebooks/Jacque%20Fresco%20-%20Designing%20the%20Future.pdf

But surely it cannot all be true?

A picture says more than 1,000 words:

http://www.abc.es/Media/201110/14/13817221--644x362.jpg

And now, don't tell anybody that you found even more links for critical thinking:

http://www.whale.to/b/sp/blood.html
http://www.israelect.com/reference/WillieMartin/Rothchild%20[D].htm
http://www.lovethetruth.com/books/13_bloodlines/rothschild_02.htm

→ 'The Thousand Year Reich' is in motion. The supreme masters have immense power. There is no chance for politicians, the UN, the religion, or all the organizations and institutes, or individuals of good will. The key-power of such insane aim is concentration of money and the essential condition for success is private and public debt up to the utmost extreme.

→ Even if only half of these reports would be true, questions arise about the true wirepuller of World War One and World War Two, all the wars since Vietnam with motives based on fabrications, and the imminent final mega-war already gradually in motion.

→ There are a lot of psychoanalytical considerations that make much of the official presentations about the actors of WWI and WWII as something 'impossible'; it's simply not comprehensible from this view and even more questionable in the economic context and in the context of all wars since the Vietnam War.

→ The energetic psychological potential of psychopathy and psychosis can have the potential to kill 10,000 or even 100,000 people, but never to make war with 20 million, 60 million or 100 million victims.

→ To have a clear view in matters of economics, religion and big wars, one must think and create hypotheses about the absolute impossible beyond imagination, even if the entire world would say about such hypotheses: 'such madness is never possible'.

→ Microeconomics and macroeconomics are built up with ideologies, lies, cheat, deceit, manipulations, dehumanization, trivialization, belittlement, exaggerations, camouflage, fabrications and sham. This is evil and partly diabolic. The dynamic of most economic parameters is undoubtedly regicide and deicide; and this satanic at the utmost extreme.

7.3. Living Planet Report RIO + 20

(Living Planet Report 2012 special edition RIO + 20 – WWF.org)

WWF's mission is to stop the degradation of the planet's natural environment and to build a future in which humans live in harmony with nature, by conserving the world's biological diversity, ensuring that the use of renewable natural resources is sustainable, and promoting the reduction of pollution and wasteful consumption.

→ To stop the degradation of the planet's natural environment would require a reduction of the big corporations up to 75%. They will never agree.
→ How can humans live in harmony with nature if they can't live in harmony with themselves and with others?
→ Sustainable renewable natural resources are of primordial importance, but not at cost of arable land or wood.
→ Reduction of pollution and wasteful consumption requires a complete new life style, including a new understanding of the core meaning of life. The folks will bluster in pure rage if they must give something up.

We have the ability to save our home, to protect our planet. Not only for our own benefit but, above all, for generations to come. We have the solutions. Everyone can make a contribution by making better choices in how we govern, produce and consume. Taking better care of the planet is in our hands. André Kuipers Astronaut, European Space Agency

→ The ability to save our home and to protect our planet is given, but nobody wants to change their way of living and their 'wants' to save the planet (our home).
→ You may have technical solutions. But with technology nothing can succeed. The approach for solutions is here fundamentally wrong and inefficient, an empty hope.
→ How can politicians and governments make better choices in the way they operate? They simply can't. They are imprisoned, blackmailed, threatened, and do not understand the global picture and its momentum.
→ Taking better care of the planet is not in our hands. Those who govern the world have no interest in losing profit and economic power.

We are living as if we have an extra planet at our disposal. We are using 50 per cent more resources than the Earth can provide, and unless we change course that number will grow very fast – by 2030, even two planets will not be enough. But we do have a choice. We can create a prosperous future that provides food, water and energy for the 9 or perhaps 10 billion people who will be sharing the planet in 2050.

→ Therefore we need two planets; or: the Western folks need to reduce consumption by 50%. Go and tell this to the Americans, the Europeans and other folks of Western culture! They will get in an unimaginable rage.
→ Changing the 'course' must rapidly start as the result would only come in effect in 10-15 years. You can't change the macroeconomic structures just like that.
→ We can create a prosperous future, but this would imply a completely new understanding of human values, human internal life, and strong spiritual attitudes.
→ Who can guarantee that with 10 billion people on earth the population growth will definitely stop? Already 8 billion, and even more 9 billion or 10 billion people will cause globally enormous stress.

We can ensure there is enough water for our needs and also conserve the healthy rivers, lakes and wetlands from which it comes.

→ No, there will not be enough healthy drinking water in 30-40 years. Already most of all water resources are irreversibly damaged. It will take 100 years for part-reparation.

This can and must be the moment for governments to set a new course toward sustainability. Jim Leape Director General WWF International said.

→ To set a new course toward sustainability is a trivialization of the complexity of all the global problems.

Living Planet Report 2012, Full Report, Chapter 4)

There are solutions for living within the means of one planet. The report recommends 16 'better choices' from a global One Planet perspective. We list the 'parameters' that require changes:

1) Significantly expand the global protected areas network

→ This will affect the speculation business

2) Halt loss of priority habitats

→ The contamination is in motion and unstoppable due to 3,000 corporations

3) Restore damaged ecosystems and ecosystem services

→ Corporations produce damages of $5 trillion per year. Who pays for restoring?

4) Significantly reduce inputs and waste in production systems

→ Reducing use of raw material leads to a decrease of production. Reducing waste is costly.

5) Manage resources sustainably

→ Destructive exploitation is cheap. Sustainable resources have higher costs.

6) Scale-up renewable energy production

→ The owners of nuclear power plant will not accept it; coal mining is very contaminating.

7) Change energy consumption patterns

→ Not possible without declaration of 'emergency state'; people and businesses will not agree.

8) Promote healthy consumption patterns

→ Food is already contaminated; cheap food is of low quality; and good food is unaffordable.

9) Achieve low-footprint lifestyles

→ How will Americans, Europeans, and the city people in China change their lifestyle?

10) Value nature

→ People do not value the truth nor human values; how can they value nature?

11) Account for environmental and social costs

→ Capitalistic economics want to maximize profit. They laugh if you tell them about such costs.

12) Support and reward conservation, sustainable resource management and innovation

→ Economics wants free markets and has here the say and they hate governmental interventions.

13) Share available resources

→ No lunch is for free! How can you share with those who earn less than $300 per month?

14) Make fair and ecologically informed choices

→ 'Fairness' does not exist in the free market and neither in the banking systems.

15) Measure success 'beyond GDP'

→ Yes, for sure. But how can we implement this while politicians need growth for their debt?

16) Sustainable population

→ Go and make 5.5 billion people (that earn less than $300) clear that they should use contraceptives!

7.4. The Disaster of Collective Failure

The accumulation of the destructive mega-parameters every decade

- Population growth
- Poverty and economic imbalance
- Lack of primary needs and infrastructures
- Lack of healthy food
- Lack of healthy water and water for agriculture
- Decrease of underground water resources
- Glaciers melting (water reservoirs)
- Decreasing agriculture land and soil degradation
- Deforestation, desertification, decomposition
- Over-exploitation of seas and oceans
- Over-exploitation of raw resources
- Irreversibly damaged eco-systems
- Species reduction and elimination
- Contaminating chemicals, pharmaceutics
- Contamination: fine dust, waste, sewage
- Nuclear waste and its maintenance
- Climate change with damages for production
- Drought, flood, fire, tornados, storms, hurricanes
- Disease and all kind of illnesses, accidents
- Mental and behavior disorder of all kind
- Crimes and corruption
- Rearmament, military and wars
- Unrest, trouble spots and radicalism
- Mega-cities and its social mental effects
- Reparation of damages & measures for protection
- Decrease of human values, dehumanization
- Destruction of democratic values, principles

→ The collective unconscious contains the collective history of mankind!
→ Humanity is in permanent interaction with the collective unconscious!
→ The explosive content of the collective unconscious is the superior threat!

								2040-2050
							2030-2040	2030-2040
						2020-2030	2020-2030	2020-2030
					2010-2020	2010-2020	2010-2020	2010-2020
				2000-2010	2000-2010	2000-2010	2000-2010	2000-2010
			1990-2000	1990-2000	1990-2000	1990-2000	1990-2000	1990-2000
		1980-1990	1980-1990	1980-1990	1980-1990	1980-1990	1980-1990	1980-1990
	1970-1980	1970-1980	1970-1980	1970-1980	1970-1980	1970-1980	1970-1980	1970-1980
1960-1970	1960-1970	1960-1970	1960-1970	1960-1970	1960-1970	1960-1970	1960-1970	1960-1970

Unstoppable Increase of Mega-Parameters

Population growth

Poverty and economic imbalance

Lack of primary needs and infrastructures

Lack of healthy food and drinking water

Lack of healthy water and water for agriculture

Chemicals, pharmaceutics, fine dust, waste, sewage

Drought, flood, fire, tornados, storms, hurricanes

Deforestation, desertification, decomposition

Over-exploitation of seas, oceans, raw resources

Decreasing agriculture land and soil degradation

Decrease underground water resources, Glacier

Damaged eco-systems and species elimination

Decreasing agriculture land and soil degradation

Illnesses, mental and behavior disorder of all kind

Trouble spots, rearmament, military and wars

The Interrelations of the Vivid Mega-Parameters

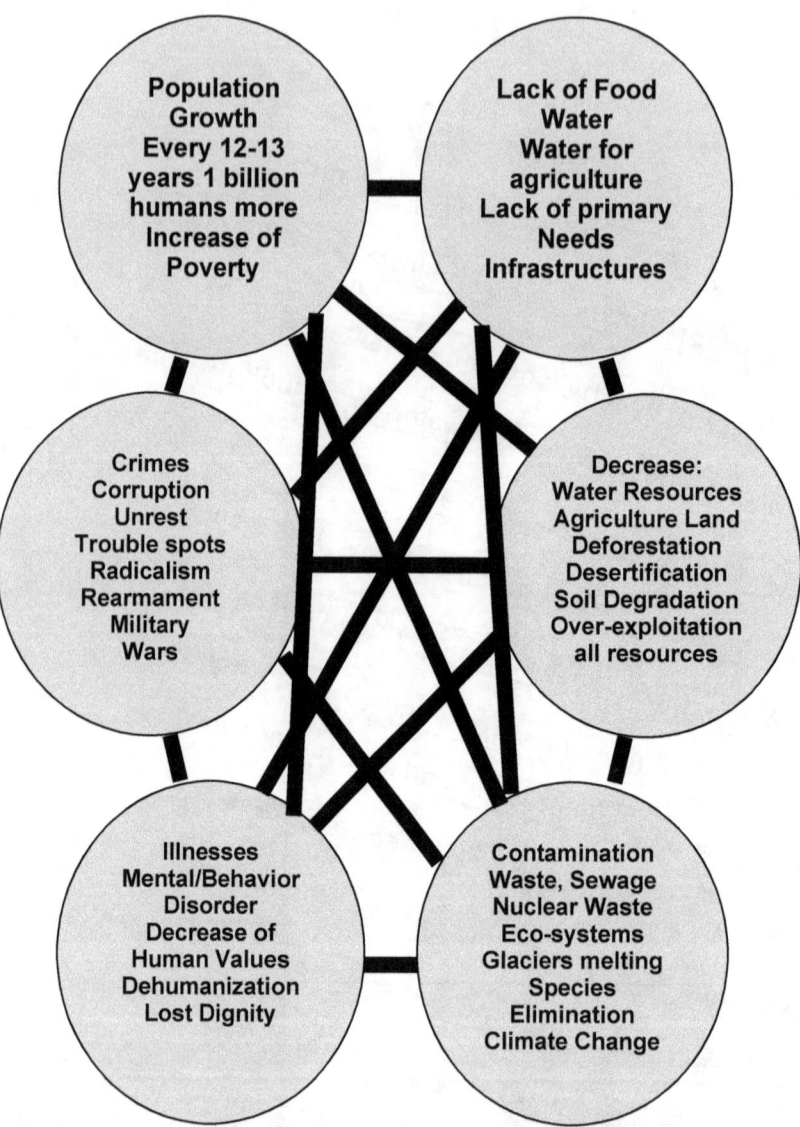

The Failure

- 2.2-2.4 billion Christians failed.
- 1.5-1.8 billion Muslims failed.
- Other religions also failed.
- All kind of spiritual teaching failed.
- Over one billion atheists failed.
- Millions of politicians failed.
- Millions of economists failed.
- Millions of public schools failed.
- Most academic education failed.
- Millions of media outlets failed.
- Millions of CEOs and managers failed.
- More than a billion parents failed.

→ All systems are affected from the insane deicide-virus!

The United Nations has completely failed. It is rotten to the core. It is misused and abused by a select few self-serving super powers and never really respected. Humanity needs an alternative to the UN: The **"Free Nations"**. The preliminary outline is lying on my table. The ethical and spiritual authority is me, clearly given by the above reasons.

→ The Mission of Buddha and other Asian masters of wisdom could not provide a breakthrough. The people have failed!
→ The chosen Jewish folk could not provide a breakthrough. They already failed 2,000 years-ago and lost their 'chosen status'!
→ The Mission of Jesus Christ and the Prophet Mohammed could not provide a breakthrough. The people have failed!
→ An estimated one hundred thousand wise masters since 3,000 years could not provide a breakthrough. The people have failed!
→ More than 6.5 billion people are brainwashed and deformed in their soul. They are trapped in dark psychical and spiritual labyrinths, in pathogenic narcissism, in neurosis and psychopathy, in obsession and greed, in lies and falseness, in political and religious psychosis, in stupidity, in arrogance and ignorance. Like this they will never find a real solution for humanity and the planet! They fail and will continue failing!

The great majority of humanity suffers psychically: depression, anxiety, aggression, compulsion, guilt, psychosis, schizophrenia, sleeplessness, nervousness, obesity, despair, inferiority, lack of self-confidence, lack of love, hate, stubbornness, inner void, senselessness, hopelessness, alienation, mobbing, mistrust, addictions of all kind, neglect, behavioral problems, relationship problems, inability to love and to communicate, etc.

The majority of humanity suffers physically as a result of human-made factors: diseases and cancer due to contamination and pollution, victims of traffic accidents and fine dust, victims of catastrophes and climate change, victims of the ozone hole (skin cancer), suffering from work and environment stress, suffering from poverty, suicide and suicide attempts, constipation, anorexia and obesity, etc.

The majority of humanity suffers financially: exploitation of the workforce, distribution of wealth and income, poverty, unemployment, speculation of the banks and the taxes of the government, an estimated 65% of all taxes are lost due to misspending, political inefficiency, costs associated with catastrophes (climate change) and contamination (and pollution), costs due to the destruction of eco-systems, costs from the exorbitant armament and militarization, participation in wars, storage of nuclear waste (as well as the dismantling and storage of nuclear power stations in the future), costs due to hotspots, interest payments and repayments of public debt, that are not even feasible over 200 years in many nations, etc.

The majority of humanity suffers spiritually-religiously: an archaic religion, that is characterized through neurosis, psychopathy, manipulation, fairy tales, myths, superstition, falsifications, lies, perversions, distortions, deceit, fantasies, legends, religious psychosis and an absolute inefficiency in terms of psychical-spiritual formation, love, Spirit and management of the inner and outer life.

The majority of humanity is psychically and spiritually completely deformed, mentally manipulated, self-alienated, enslaved and exploited. Whole nations are systematically lied to and seduced. Lies have replaced the truth. Lunacy and psychosis are the admired values in many societies. The adults destroy the future of their children! The earth is sliding towards the abyss. Politics, the economy, industry, media, education and religion have completely failed! Most leaders in many countries are hypocritical, cowardly, false and mendacious and act on the moral level of child molesters. The octopus celebrates its triumph.

We agree with the urgency of finding global solutions. There are good ideas and visions for a global renewal. But there are serious psychological and social factors that hinder solutions:

- Fame, power and fortune have corrupted most innocent souls.
- Perversion has become main stream.

- Lunacy attracts admiration.
- Hope is abused.
- Courage is raped.
- Individuality is slaughtered.
- Money is the lure spirit.
- Religious psychosis has replaced the genuine spiritual inner path.
- The truth has lost; Lies have taken its place.
- The true good has lost; it can never win by itself.
- Love has lost; People are rotten to their innermost core.
- The Spirit of God, who speaks through dreams, barely stands a chance anymore.
- All Archetypes of the Soul have been raped, abused, and completely destroyed.

Characteristics of Economics, Politics and Religion (Christianity)

The 'Trilogy of Economics' uncovers the neo-capitalistic concept. We thoroughly identified the following essential characteristics in economics, politics, and religion (Christianity):

Confusing, misleading terms	Immense negative externalities
Ideological principles and 'laws'	Destructive functions ignored
Abuse of valuable terms	Destructive dynamic of functions
Unproven generalizations	Destroying mother Earth
Manipulation of words and realities	Extremely hostile
Abuse of scientific authority	Anti-human dynamic
Ideological (dogmatic) concept	Psychotic dynamic
Fundamentalist rigid thinking	Total lack of relevant moral
Lack of pioneer and creative spirit	Authoritarian false consciousness
Static and rigid parameters	Stolen the vivid Archetypes
Technocratic or illusionary thinking	Immature agents in the system
Absurd constructions	Soulless archaic leadership
Not science, not even good journalism	Exploitation of humans
Most statements fabricated	Enslaving physically, mentally
Expresses imbalance	Brainwashing and

	dehumanizing
✎ Produces injustice, imbalance	✎ Abuse of humans
✎ Archaic concept of humans	✎ Extreme exploitative, destroying planet
✎ Ignoring spiritual intelligence	✎ Rejecting the truth
✎ Simplified, reduced humane image	✎ Befogging, putting facts into the fog
✎ Excluding inner human values	✎ Trivializing, embellishing, hiding
✎ Rigid humane patterns ('types')	✎ Distorting, trickery, deceiving
✎ Ignored human differences	✎ Fooling, cheating, misleading
✎ No holistic (systemic) approaches	✎ Bigotry and cowardice everywhere
✎ No respect for humans and the planet	✎ Extreme stubbornness and arrogance
✎ Vague interdependences/interrelations	✎ Theatre, falseness and lies everywhere
✎ Ignored complexity, manifoldness	✎ Neurotic, narcissistic, egomaniac
✎ Household diverseness ignored	✎ Hidden unlimited megalomania
✎ Ignored learning potential	✎ Excessive compulsion and greed
✎ Performance potential neglected	✎ Inflated and psychotic ego and theories
✎ One-sided linear views of aims	✎ Madness and lunacy beyond imagination
✎ Infectious Fata Morgana theories	✎ Psychopathy (absence of humanity)
✎ Exaggerated rational function	✎ Sadism, perversion, lust for suffering
✎ No holistic equilibrium parameter	✎ Control freak, domineering
✎ Systemic oriented efficiency	✎ Paralyzed from mother's awl
✎ No match with human reality	✎ Pursuit from totalitarian father
✎ Immense collateral damages	✎ Main source of all mental disorder
✎ Preponderantly inefficient in the real world	✎ Exhaustless source of quarrels
✎ Ego-driven glorifications, worship	✎ Extremely obsessive and

	possessive
✿ Immense lack of care for realities	✿ Provocative cantankerousness
✿ Nutrient for ego-trips and strives	✿ Intrinsic motives for wars
✿ Anti-evolutionary, evil, monstrous	✿ Complex dynamic leads to deicide

→ Calling this 'science' is outrageous. The consequences are devastating. Doom is programmed!

7.5. The Psychological-Spiritual Approach

The Process of Dehumanization

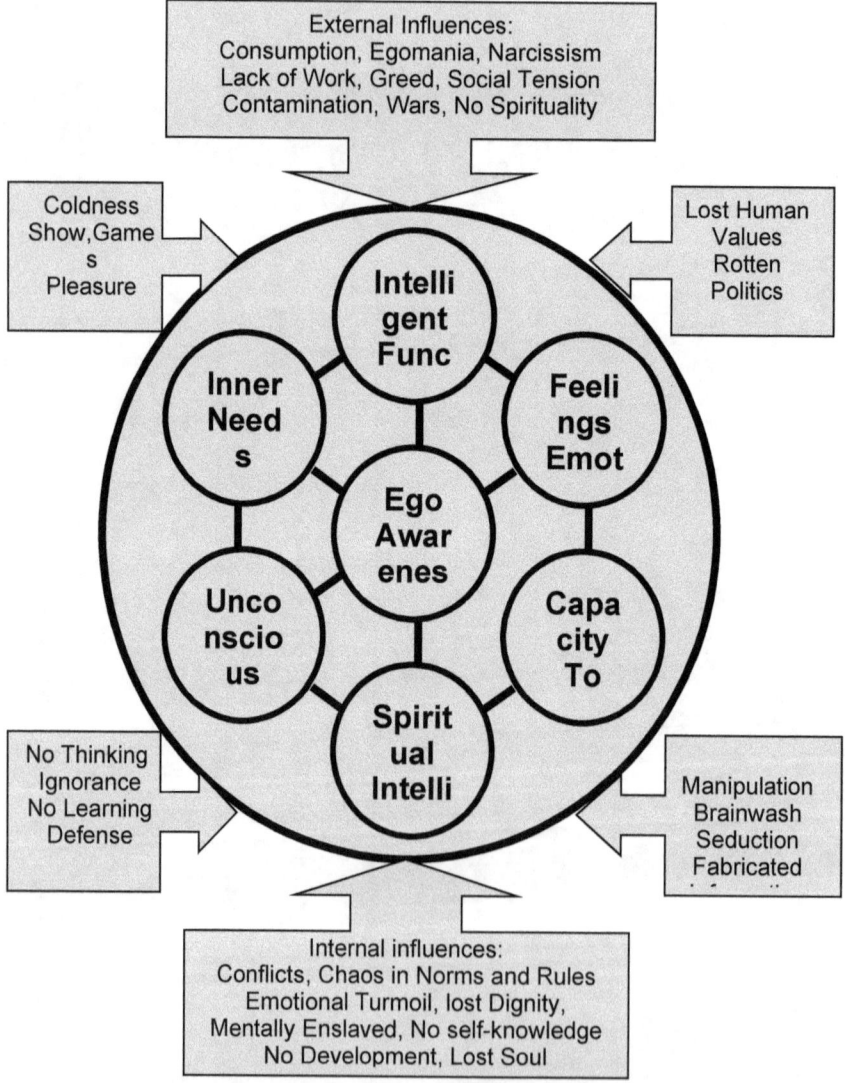

→ A huge majority of people are absolutely overwhelmed from all the influences and challenges.

→ They are unable to deal with all the burdens and forced to reject, suppress, or ignore them.

→ The spiral of destructive development of all the psychical functions has become unstoppable.

→ To escape from oneself and from life remains to be the only solution to survive however.

If we assume that there is a God unifying all positive values and potentials, then there is also the opposite – at least on Earth. The failure of all archaic religions makes it impossible for people to identify this 'evil opposite being'. God can't be destructive ('evil' in a human understanding). As we have identified everywhere in theories of economics and the real market (production) world an enormous unlimited destructive dynamic, we now know where we have to search for finding this 'evil opposite being' in the absolute extreme.

Another approach is given through the archetypal human values:

- A life with love, truth, honesty, happiness and truthfulness.
- Authentic satisfaction and fulfillment of the genuine inner needs.
- Understanding oneself, one's behavior and life, and other people.
- Efficiency with knowledge and skills to deal with life.
- Being free of biographical burdens and unconscious complexes.
- Authentic, integral, self-realized and strong personalities.
- Ideals, norms, values, and rules that are constructive towards life.
- Capability to understand and constructively manage feelings.
- Living sexual needs and longing for affection with love.
- Solving difficulties, crises, problems and conflicts for peace.
- Outstanding self-management that provides a strong self-confidence.
- Correctly interpreting dreams and meditating provides the best development.
- Preparing a happy relationship and family life with education.
- Elaborating quality of life with thorough and networked thinking.
- Living the meaning of the Archetype "Marriage", leads to complete fulfillment.
- Meaning of life, anchored within, centered in the inner Spirit.
- Environment and business world for the soul of people.

- An all-encompassing positive life philosophy for living and growing.

These positive human values are founded on the Archetypes:

- The complete acceptance of the inner life and the dedication towards it.
- The discovery and formation of psychical forces and functions.
- The formation and living of the genuine inner self through conscious formation.
- The integration of the inner Spirit as a guiding power (dreams, meditation).
- Carrying out the process of 'dying and rebirth' (inner renewal).
- The development of the unification with the inner opposite gender pole.
- Integrating the spiritual principles in ethics, behavior and meaning of life.
- Bringing the inner and outer world into a balance, anchored within.
- Achieving the fulfillment of wholeness and completeness (Individuation).

Higher levels of psychical-spiritual developments are for special spiritual vocations and are the 'archetypal' authority that stands above all religions, political institutions, and economics.

The Archetypal experiences express themselves in dreams and are the result of spiritual, psychical, theoretical, meditative and practical processes, including a lot of experience and learning about life, human beings, societies, cultures, humanity and the state of the earth.

→ The key question is whether humans and the entire humanity want to stand for these archetypal human values or to accept the opposite – the 'evil opposite being'.
→ Everywhere in human's life are economic and political factors fundamentally determining human's life either for benefit or for misery.
→ Economics, corporations, politics and governments can't reject or ignore taking a decision of pro or contra the Archetypes of the Soul. Not taking a decision is always a decision for the 'evil opposite being'.

Before we explore the options for a new roadmap, we want to have a closer view on what the 'market' offers us as solutions. Our short comment can be understood as questions or critical statements:

7.6. The Immense Practical Problems

One problem that hinders to even begin discussing solutions is the completely pompous and stubborn state administration. The supreme authorities, politicians and especially government members are all rigid in defensiveness and focused on ego, power and greed. There are many local, regional and national members of government that enormously enrich themselves on the goods and possessions of the people. They misspend and misallocate huge tax incomes. But they do nothing, really absolutely nothing that in consideration of the global disaster would actually be needed. They have no interest to live or promote the Archetypes of the Soul.

Many governments have racked up horrendous debt and misspent finances: for the 'Big War' and the 'One World Government' of the capitalistic coalition. They are also responsible for wars, unrest, poverty, financial crises, high unemployment, climate change, contamination and the man-made catastrophes of all kinds over the past 20 years. The following generations will have to pay for this even with their blood. Indeed it is odd that the people around the world actually put up with this.

Most people cannot identify and recognize the infantile ties they have to their mother and father, or the bond to the church and the Bible. They don't want to learn anything about themselves or about life. They approvingly swallow the monstrous lies and illusions because they themselves want to live lies and illusions. Political responsibility isn't something they are interested in. They actually don't want any responsibility whatsoever, not even for themselves or for their own life.

The modern Titanic of today already has horrifying leaks and is driving towards the abyss at unstoppable speed. The millions of well-off, rich and super rich, the millionaires and billionaires around the world cannot be so incredibly stupid to believe they will survive in their suite on the Titanic? Or can they?

With regards to the tragedy of the 'unsinkable' Titanic one thing must be made clear: Only the captain was responsible for the sinking of the Titanic! Consequence: The captains around the world are the biggest problem: They do not recognize the danger of such a downfall. Or they simply don't want to take any efficient measures against it because it could damage their career. Then there are those who with perverted lust are wishing for this danger and ultimately even provoking this downfall. They are abusing their power for their lunacy obsessed 'One World Government" (the 'Fourth 1000 Year Reich') or out of personal frustration (love, happiness, sex, and fulfillment).

One has to take away all the power from these doomed captains without long discussions. With all legal means, one has to defy their orders, which are based on their pathogenic narcissism, their power obsession, their megalomania, their religious psychosis and their messianic psychosis.

The word 'legal' in this context however also poses delicate questions; for example: What should be done, when the people are not able to get rid of their tyrants, their incompetent, amoral, greedy, perverse leaders and politicians? The problem goes both for the people as well as for the police, the secret service and the military. Without a global collective solidarity for the Archetypes of the Soul there will be no breakthrough towards a new paradisiacal era with love, peace, and the inner Spirit. Intelligent and rational thinking are essential, but are never enough for solutions! The truth remains above the law!

Despite the massive defensive bulwarks set up against solutions there is hope: The creative potential in the soul of many people, especially when utilized with the inner Spirit and the collective promotion of the Archetypes of the Soul, will make solutions for humanity and the earth possible; solutions, that today nobody can even begin to imagine. For that we first need collective conscious education about the truth.

→ There are no solutions without fundamental changes in the entire banking and corporation systems.

→ There are no solutions without fundamental changes of the public education; a complete new understanding of humans and human life is indispensable.

→ There are no solutions without the truth!

→ There are no solutions with old-fashioned ways of thinking, with dogmas and ideologies, with power and violence, with ignorance and arrogance, with megalomania and religious psychosis.

→ There are no solutions without regard for the genuine inner and world needs of the people – and this around the globe.

→ There are no solutions without networking in a global and future-oriented perspective.

→ There are no solutions without a new education and without a new understanding about human beings.

→ Ultimately there are no solutions without the Archetypes of the Soul, whether for superlative holiday resorts nor for humanity as a whole!

The big majority of humanity needs to declare: "I confirm the willingness, to live and work within the truth and the Archetypes of the Soul, and to respect these in full extent." This is: Living in the truth!

Additionally it must be said that there is never practical success without education, skills, understanding, communication, co-operation, pioneering thinking, vanguard thinking, spiritual intelligence, clarification, creative development of ideas, and adaptation to local (cultural) singularities, will power and assertiveness. The solutions are without a doubt extremely challenging.

Seen like this: It is about 'all or nothing' and about 'archetypal evolution or downfall' for the supreme masters, the powerful, the rich, the normal earners and for the poor. Who would not want the breakthrough to hope and bring solutions for humanity without political and religious lies?

Do the people really not want to live with the truth? Do the people really not want to protect the truth to save humanity and the earth? Do the people perhaps want to "crush", "destroy" and "eliminate" or even "kill" the Archetypes of the Soul and the inner Spirit?

→ Humanity is on the breakthrough for a new Age: Armageddon or Catharsis and Renewal!

7.7. The Start of the Solutions

A series of solutions are on offer:

- The Natural Laws of the Chaos Theory?
- Millionaires and Billionaires together with Financial Power?
- Corporate Groups with Industrial and Economic Developments?
- Western Democracy with its Politics, Politicians and Values?
- Chinese Politics with its Philosophy and Values?
- Indian Politics with its Philosophy (Buddhism) and Values?
- Arab Politics with its Social Philosophy and Values?
- Russian Politics and Power with the Perestroika Ideology?
- Western Dictatorship and Military Power with Martial Laws?
- One World Order implemented by the US/NATO (ruled by who)?
- Christianity with the Bible and its Religious Institutions?
- Islam with the Koran and its Religious Institutions?
- A Savior with 10,000 angels descending from Heaven?
- World War III, eliminating 50-75% of the Earth's Population?
- Natural Catastrophes eliminating 50% of the Earth's Population?
- The Archetypes of the Soul lived and practiced by billions of people?
- A new understanding of economics and the economy?

You want a new world, a good future for yourself, for your loved ones, for the young generation today and for the coming generations, for humanity and the planet as a whole. Therefore, forget your 'bunker' (ego-) mentality and get rid of your stubbornness.

The state of most people around the globe, the societies around the world, is very bad: brainwashed, manipulated, narcissistic, arrogant, ignorant, superficial, neurotic, psychopathic, perverted, obsessed, infantile, stupid, stupefied, cowardly, hypocritical, gossipy, mendacious, stubborn, blinded, sightless, greedy, too lazy to learn, without discipline, lacking character, unable to think, self-opinionated and driven by consumption. Self-evidently there are exceptions.

The elite in most countries, especially in the capitalist coalition (in essence the Jewish-American-Israeli Elite) has created a disfigured and deformed human biomass out of humanity, in order to use it for their lunatic and psychotic means. The Soul of humanity is seriously ill to the core.

A massive global octopus, full of falseness, lies, misrepresentation, distortion, deadly poison, political and religious psychosis, perverse lust to kill of an indescribable and never before existing dimension and power, has got nearly the whole humanity in its iron grip. The global history since over 100 years is essentially very different from that what is portrayed in history books or taught in schools and universities.

Most nations have an incredible psychical-spiritual potential, to pave ways for solutions in their own countries and solutions for the huge global problems of humanity and the planet. Many nations have the moral and intellectual potential to build a new evolutionary and psychical-spiritual humaneness, rooted in the innermost of the soul and free from ideology and dogmatism. In order for the whole world to renew itself!

→ People need to find their healthy pride, their inner values, and their self-confidence.
→ People must use the potential of the intelligence, love, the soul and the Spirit within.
→ People must first find themselves, their genuine inner human being and their life.
→ People must form, develop, balance, center themselves and become a unity.
→ People must find the truth, the real facts and the genuine inner spiritual force.
→ People must permanently educate themselves with relevant information (internet and books).
→ People must convince others of the severity of the critical state and the dangers.
→ People must improve their lifestyle in the interest of the inner values.
→ People must develop local solutions together with others and do the best possible.
→ People must take responsibility so that the potentials can breakthrough.
→ People must unite with others in solidarity in clubs, networks and associations.
→ People must accept that all this doesn't work without effort, time and costs.

The hopeful future begins with catharsis and renewal. A new humane life is needed. New forms of society and new ways of living are needed. A renewal of nations is needed. A new world is needed. A new political system is needed. A new, genuine form of democracy is needed! A new religion is needed: a humane religion or simply an efficient spirituality, free from dogmatism and fundamentalism, founded within and built up from within with love and Spirit, with the highest values of the soul, the inner humaneness. And with that the Octopus can and must be completely eliminated.

This is the absolutely new, comprehensive catharsis and renewal in content, importance and dimension that has never before existed in humanity!

With over 3,000 dreams about all Archetypes of the Soul, about God, about the spiritual world, about the true source of religion, and about the sick psychical-spiritual life of the people I am 100% certain that I have the appropriate possible solution. These dreams have formed the biggest mission of all times. Without the slightest doubt this is the mission for humanity. In a dream I spoke to humanity and told them: "I did not come here to this earth from millions of light years away to play here the idiot!"

The 'invisible hand' is something like an economic parameter. This 'hand' has been since centuries and is today and will be operating tomorrow everywhere in human's life and in most systems of societies. It's still an unanswered question what Adam Smith really had in his mind about this strange magic and nearly mystic omnipresent and omnipotent being. It must be something he couldn't speak out about without getting his life in danger. But it's so easy to reveal this mystery: simply find the right replacement for the word 'hand' and you understand the history since 2,000 years and the problems of humanity and the planet today.

The last 20 years this neo-capitalistic macro-economics has systematically and globally lured with chocolate or a plush toy most of the young generation, starting with early childhood, has penetrated in the core of these innocent humans, has destroyed their mind and soul, has dehumanized them with irreparable life long consequences.

Where will this lead humanity when this 'invisible hand' has already systematically destroyed all human values, all components of the soul, the innermost of the mind, the creative and pioneering spirit of people, the inner Spirit, and all Archetypes of the Soul including all supreme Archetypes such as 'spiritual King' or ' Messiah' or 'God'? The 'invisible hand' smashed all of them and most people simply copy such evil doing without knowing that they do. Here we are again with the roadmap of regicide and deicide!

There are hundreds of thousands if not millions that want a global renewal. There are many experts and institutions that work with commitment on finding the right solutions. But they can't address billions of people around the globe. They don't have the financial power to build up a global network of institutions to prepare the educational foundation. There are the 3,000 corporations and the supreme masters of the monetary world. The Chinese and Indian governments have lost their mind. Some African governments are out of mental control. Obama couldn't believe what is fact when he started as President and accepted to become a marionette of the supreme masters. Other governmental people have been drowning into a marsh of psychotic madness. The religions are trapped in a dark labyrinth with false and coward top leaders, and holy texts full of sham. There are the governments and politicians that struggle in their daily matters and their power strife. There is the most powerful economic world that can't be changed just like that. There are the hundred thousand people driven by ego-trip with their solutions for humanity and the planet. And there is objective inherent constraint in many complex networks and interconnections.

And all relevant macro-parameters are incessantly growing for the next 10, 20, and 30 years. The most critical aspect of this growing process is the inertia of the critical macroeconomic parameters.

→ The best strategies for renewal can't work considering this immense rock-solid wall of mental and structural resistance.

Just to mention one example to show where the difficulties of solutions lie: I calculated with experts some projects for Spain: Spain could be free of public debt within a 10-year-project. Spain could become an economic leader in the world; also within this decade. The problem is, the Spanish character, the country's systemic corruption, and a wide spread mental deficit that hinders pioneering solutions do not allow such success.

7.8. Principles of Constructing the Roadmap

Psychological Effects of Economic Factors

Economic Factors form Personality

- Determine mobility
- Influence self-esteem
- Can make dependent or free
- Form self-image (self-identity)
- Stimulate mood and emotional state
- Establish self-confidence
- Determine personal living quality
- Promote or block inner potentials
- Set the chances for (further) education
- Can produce social tensions or balance
- Money creates money and potentials
- Poverty creates poverty
- Determine ways of mastering life
- Exclude understanding of human being
- Can provoke mental disease
- Can disrupt relationship and family
- Promote or hinder vocational education
- Boost power or powerlessness
- Does not strengthen spirituality
- Can promote fulfillment or produce emptiness

Effects of Western Lifestyle

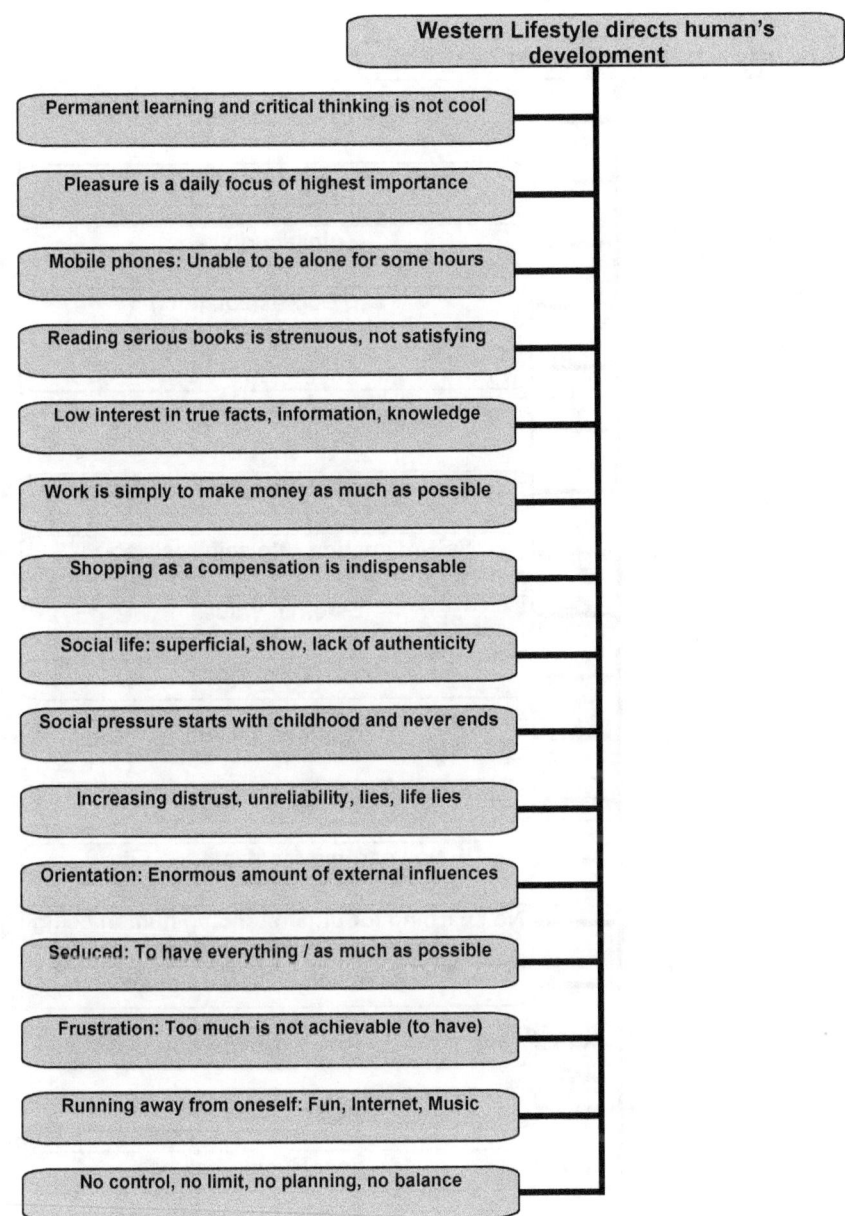

Western Lifestyle directs human's development

- Permanent learning and critical thinking is not cool
- Pleasure is a daily focus of highest importance
- Mobile phones: Unable to be alone for some hours
- Reading serious books is strenuous, not satisfying
- Low interest in true facts, information, knowledge
- Work is simply to make money as much as possible
- Shopping as a compensation is indispensable
- Social life: superficial, show, lack of authenticity
- Social pressure starts with childhood and never ends
- Increasing distrust, unreliability, lies, life lies
- Orientation: Enormous amount of external influences
- Seduced: To have everything / as much as possible
- Frustration: Too much is not achievable (to have)
- Running away from oneself: Fun, Internet, Music
- No control, no limit, no planning, no balance

Society Transmits Wants, Rules and Values

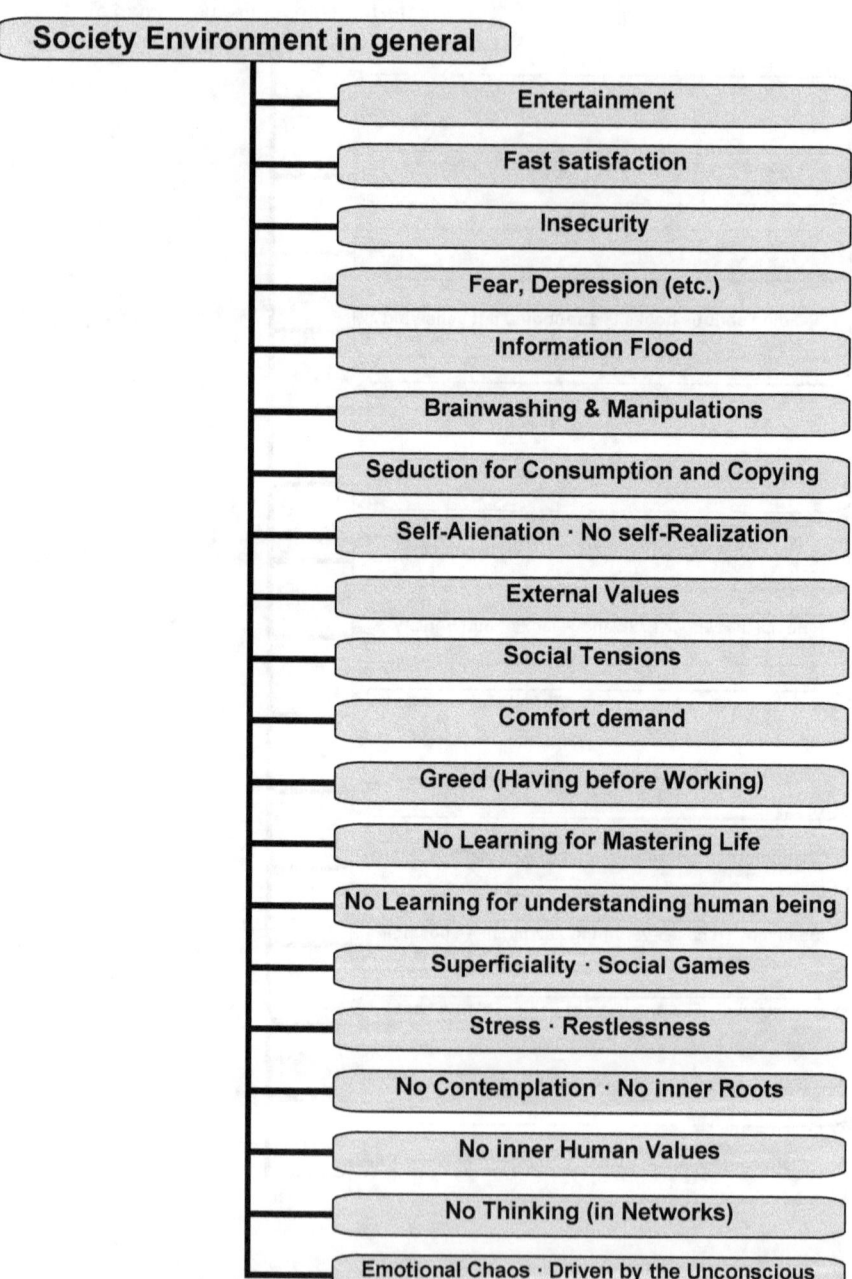

Society Environment in general

- Entertainment
- Fast satisfaction
- Insecurity
- Fear, Depression (etc.)
- Information Flood
- Brainwashing & Manipulations
- Seduction for Consumption and Copying
- Self-Alienation · No self-Realization
- External Values
- Social Tensions
- Comfort demand
- Greed (Having before Working)
- No Learning for Mastering Life
- No Learning for understanding human being
- Superficiality · Social Games
- Stress · Restlessness
- No Contemplation · No inner Roots
- No inner Human Values
- No Thinking (in Networks)
- Emotional Chaos · Driven by the Unconscious

<u>For the leaders:</u> Either you understand humans as 'rats', and then use pharmaceutics, electro shocks, and whips, or you educate them as human beings in an adequate holistic way!

<u>For alls human beings:</u> Either you want to be 'rats' and then you know what you have to expect; or you want to form your entire psychical-spiritual being with the Archetypes of the Soul.

Mental Inefficiency of People

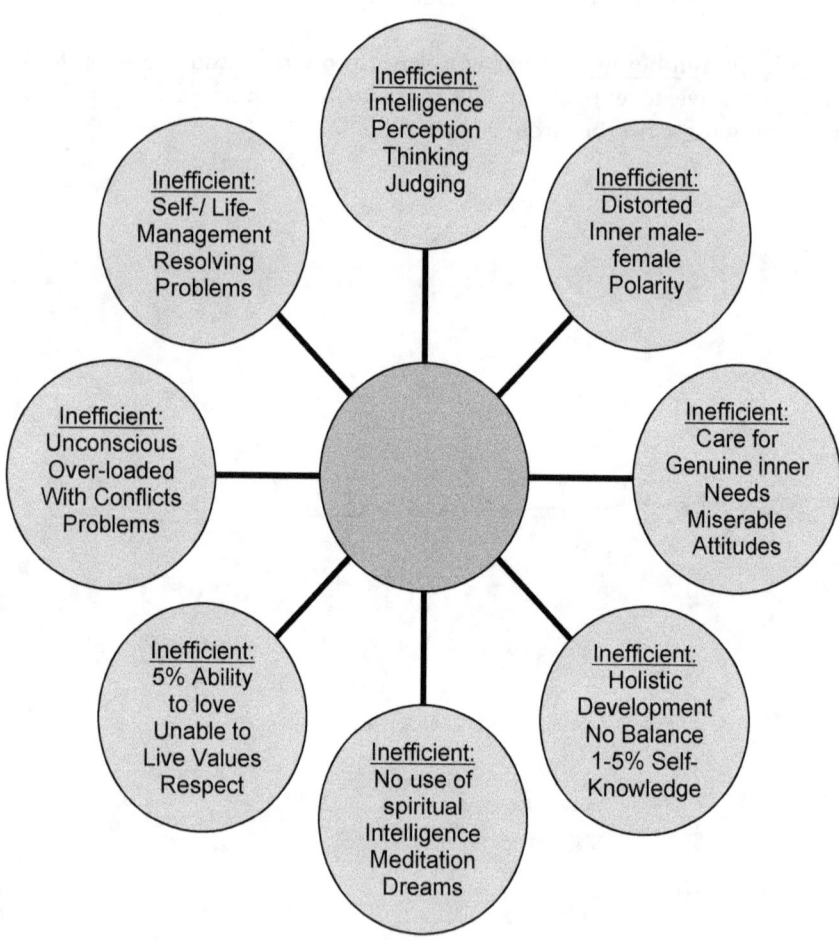

Structure of Analysis for Critical Topics

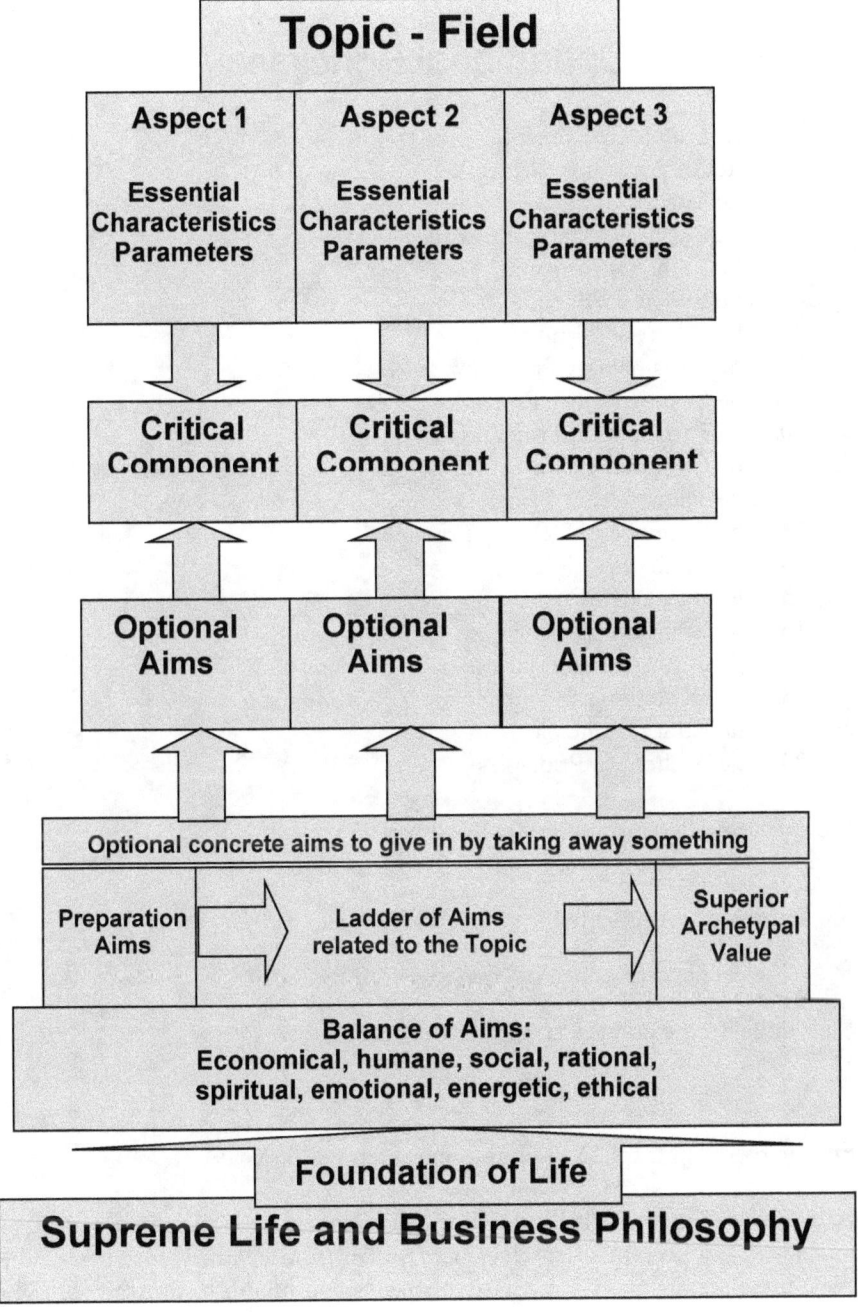

7.9. The 20 Operational Principles

1. The Humanity Principle
2. The Responsibility Principle
3. The Growth Principle
4. The Quality-Quantity Principle
5. The Catharsis Principle
6. The Renewal Principle
7. The Pioneering Principle
8. The Sustainability Principle
9. The Compensatory Principle
10. The Participation Principle
11. The Communication Principle
12. The Transparency Principle
13. The Priority and Urgency Principle
14. The Inertia Principle
15. The Balance of Cost Principle
16. The Educational Principle
17. The Performance Principle
18. The Evolutionary Principle
19. The Ethical Principles
20. The Archetypal Principles

Indispensable Parameters of the 'Roadmap 25':

- Immense investments for pioneering projects

- Globally new structures of economics for balance

- Globally new political structures for peace

- Globally implementing the Archetypes of the Soul

➔ The roadmap takes 25 years and must start within 6 years!

As a thousand individuals like to wear a divine robe, to be on the top stage of humanity, and present themselves with stolen (non-vivid) Archetypes of the Soul, there are herewith some nasty obstacles that hinder to manage the right roadmap.

The last hope arises when all the superior masters on the stage behind the curtains realize that they will lose everything; or their children reject to continue working with the master plan that they inherit from their fathers and forefathers.

→ Humanity first needs a lesson!
→ Until that day it is impossible to implement any constructive roadmap.

7.10. Strategy for the 'Roadmap 25'

No arguments against the 'Roadmap 25'

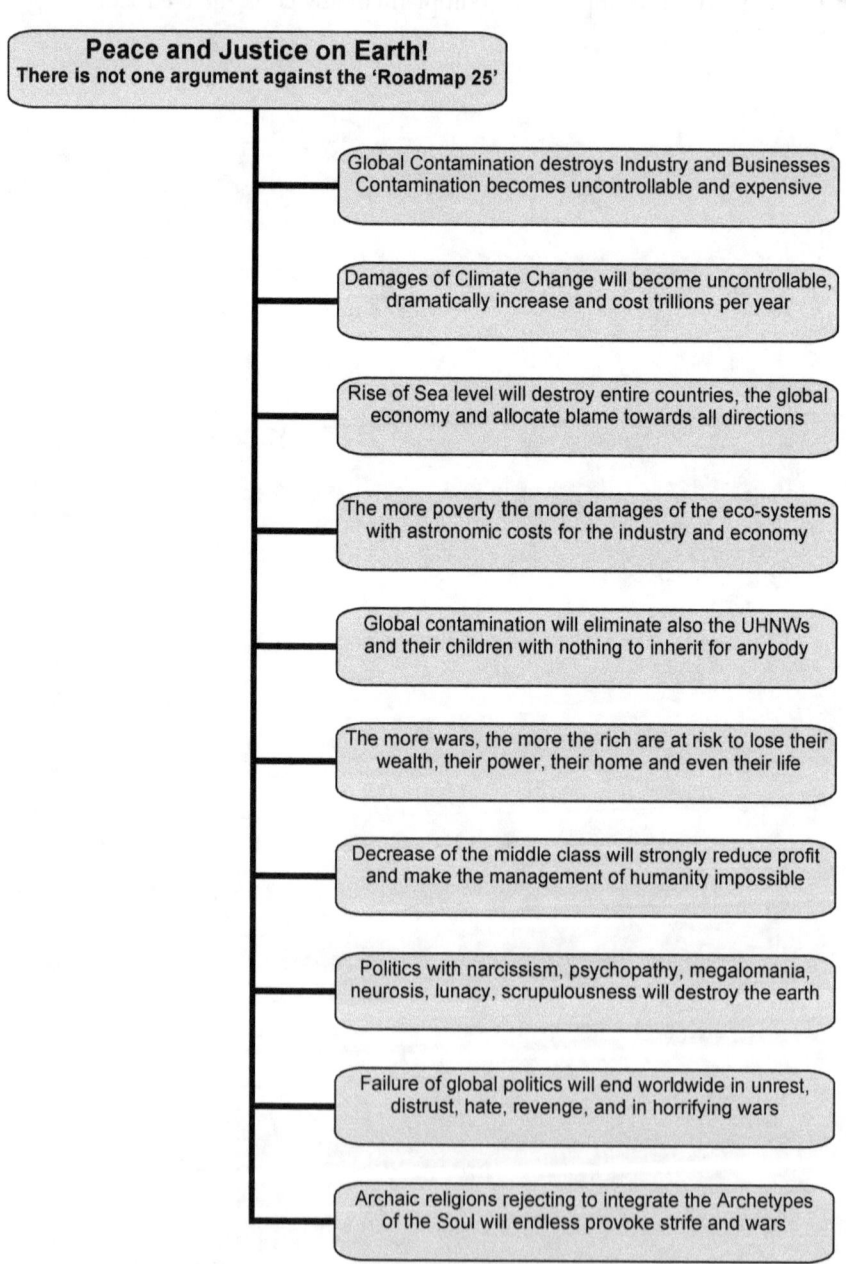

Peace and Justice on Earth!
There is not one argument against the 'Roadmap 25'

Global Contamination destroys Industry and Businesses Contamination becomes uncontrollable and expensive

Damages of Climate Change will become uncontrollable, dramatically increase and cost trillions per year

Rise of Sea level will destroy entire countries, the global economy and allocate blame towards all directions

The more poverty the more damages of the eco-systems with astronomic costs for the industry and economy

Global contamination will eliminate also the UHNWs and their children with nothing to inherit for anybody

The more wars, the more the rich are at risk to lose their wealth, their power, their home and even their life

Decrease of the middle class will strongly reduce profit and make the management of humanity impossible

Politics with narcissism, psychopathy, megalomania, neurosis, lunacy, scrupulousness will destroy the earth

Failure of global politics will end worldwide in unrest, distrust, hate, revenge, and in horrifying wars

Archaic religions rejecting to integrate the Archetypes of the Soul will endless provoke strife and wars

Strategic Principals of the 'Roadmap 25'

A) Facing the Defense Mechanisms

People have and use a lot of defense mechanisms, always when they should make changes:

Ignoring	Simplifying	Overvaluing	Fabricating
Selecting	Minimizing	Giving opposite value	Ideologizing
Lying	Exaggerating	Making noise	Indoctrinating
Hiding	Deviating	Embellishing	Trivializing
Suppressing	Detracting	Looking away	Ridiculizing
Projecting	Intriguing	Perverting	Radicalizing
Distorting	Denying	Instrumentalizing	Reshaping
Deceiving	Replacing	Demonizing	Polarizing
Cheating	Compensating	Magic interpretation	Annulling
Disfiguration	Provoking	Discrediting	Playing indignation
Displacing	Devaluating	Dogmatizing	Putting down
Turning into the opposite	Falsifying, mixing facts with lies	Putting rumors in the air	Putting curtains of fume

→ People must become aware of their defense mechanisms and become responsible!

B) Strategic, Tactic, and Organizational Principles

- There is no solution valid for everybody and everywhere
- Each topic, area, culture, folk need its specific approach
- Each country has its own variety of criticalities
- One must start even if all others still reject solidarity
- Any intervention in a topic has effects within its network
- Changes of a mega parameter influences other mega parameters
- Intervention is not successful if collateral effects are ignored
- People must be educated for changes and renewal
- People must be informed before decisions and actions
- People must feel the innovation as their wish and idea
- People must see the advantage and benefit of a change
- Libido-ties must be redirected to the new implementation

- Obstacles must be taken away before an implementation
- Democratic proceeding is not possible with uneducated people
- People are lazy, greedy, stubborn, neurotic, egoistic, obsessed
- Immense effort is necessary to educate people for renewal
- Nobody gives away personal benefits and advantages freely
- Urgency because of increasing damage comes before importance
- Taking away something requires replacing it with something new
- Essential: eliminating and completely replacing it or part renewal
- The bigger the matter of change, the longer the preparations take
- Complex changes must be divided into small changes step by step
- Small changes sometimes can be done within a short period
- 80% preparation and planning; and 20% renewal or complete change
- Changing a society needs a minimum of 25 years for sustainability
- Planning changes requires to strongly focus on the young generation
- Changes must focus on age groups: 6-12, 13-17, 18-29, 30-49, 50-67, 68+
- Changes must also focus on urban criteria (village, town, big town, city)
- Citizen's networks of max 5,000 people must be created for contributions
- Networks of specific population groups must be created for contributions

Constitution of the 'Roadmap 25'

1. GOD IS EVERYTHING
God is the fountainhead of all life; and God is also the Spirit. Each human soul is created from this fountainhead and lives in eternal development. Value, promote and form the human being and the all-sided balanced human life; live and grow from your inner being with the inner Spirit and with love.

2. ONLY GOD IS GOD
You shall not abuse God or the Spirit for egoistic and compensatory purposes, or greed for power, self-enhancement, exploitation of humans and the earth. Nobody is entitled to ban or condemn humans in the name of God. Jurisdiction in the spiritual world is solely and exclusively reserved for a true Messiah and the spiritual kings in the world of the souls.

3. YOUR LIFE AND AIM
Regularly take enough time to contemplate about you, your life, your fellow human beings, humanity and the earth. The highest aim in your life is to aspire and to live your all-sided balanced completeness in the evolutionary development. A human is a human through his psychical-spiritual organism. Herein lies begin and aim of the human evolution.

4. MARRIAGE AND FAMILY
The marriage between man and woman is untouchable and shall not be abused. Dignify being father and being mother as a high value of being and living. To educate a child is a demanding responsibility that requires formation, and has to be embedded in the polarity of man and woman as a couple, or in individual cases as a kinsman like or friendship like community.

5. VIOLENCE AND PUNISHMENT
You shall not be violent against humans or kill humans. A state has never got the right to kill a human as punishment or to violate humans physically or psychically; not even in the frame of a persecution or investigation. You also shall not provoke other humans in such a way or put them in a desperate situation so that they become violent.

6. LOVE AND SEXUALITY
Live your genuine physical and psychical needs in a balanced and healthy way. Do not act against love or the inner Spirit. You shall not devalue the natural sexual needs, nor suppress them, nor live them in a perverted way. Live your sexuality with your opposite partner in a human way and with love. Do not create a baby if you are not prepared and not mature for the consequences, educationally and financially.

7. PROPERTY RIGHT AND POWER

Do not exploit humans and institutions. You shall not take away from other people or from institutions what is their right to possess. Humans, economy and states do not have the right to exhaustively exploit resources. No human, no institution and no state shall have enough power to create a national or global imbalance. Jurisdiction requires fairness, transparency, balance, justice, free from feudalistic spirit.

8. AUTHENTICITY AND RESPONSIBILITY

Acknowledge yourself and love yourself. From this state love the human being. You shall not make a wrong image of yourself. You shall not ignore, suppress or displace the realities with the purpose of gaining advantage or damaging humans or institutions. You shall not cheat others. You shall never abuse political, economic, and religious or media power.

9. SOCIAL STRUCTURE

Society, state and humanity shall be created and developed in the attitudes of love and rooted in the inner Spirit, in a way that each human can realize his potentials and grow in a protected life frame. It is an absolute imperative from God that society and humanity shall not be militarized.

10. EARTH AND ITS NATURE

Protect with your way of living the nature, the richness of the earth and its resources in the interest of the community of humans and the genuine human needs – also for the future generations. In the interest of the conservation of the earth and of humanity, all folks shall live with highest regard for the psychical-spiritual values and the vivid Archetypes of the Soul.

Literature – Economics I, II, III

Antonioni Peter, Flynn Sean Masaki: Economics for Dummies. Wiley 2011. Chichester, West Sussex, England.

Arum Richard, Roksa Josipa: Academically adrift. Limited Learning on College Campuses. University of Chicaco Press 2011. Chicago. London.

Brandon Craig: The Five-Year-Party. Benbella Books 2010. Dallas.

Chinn Menzie D., Frieden Jeffry A.: Lost decades. Debt Crisis and the long recovery. W.W. Norton & Company 2011. London.

Colander, D.C.: Microeconomics. 8th edition. McGraw-Hill 2010. New York.

Dasgupta Partha: Economics. Oxford University Press. 2007. New York.

Hacker Andrew, Dreifus Claudia: Higher Education. Times Books Henry Hold 2010. New York.

Haralambos Mike, Holborn Martin: Sociology. 7th edition. Collins 2008. London

Kamenetz Anya: DIY U Edupunks, Edupreneurs, and the Coming transformation of Higher Education. Chelsea Green Publishing 2010. White River Junction VT.

Krugman Paul, Wells Robin, Graddy Kathryn: Essentials of Economics. Worth Publishers 2011. New York.

McConnell Campbell R., Brue Stanley L., Flynn Sean M.: Macroeconomics, Principles, Problems, and Policies. 19th edition 2012. McGraw-Hill. New York.

McDowell Moore, Thom Rodney, Frank Robert, Bernanke Ben: Principles of Economics. 2nd European Edition. McGraw-Hill Higher Education 2009. Berkshire.

Mankiw N. Gregory, Taylor Mark P.: Economics. 2nd edition. South-Western Cengage Learning. 2011. Hampshire. United Kingdom.

Meadows, Donella, Randers Jorgen, Meadows Dennis: Chelsea Green Publishing. 2004. Vermont.

Palmer Parker J., Zajonc Arthur: The Heart of higher Education. Jossey-Bass 2010. San Francisco.

Smith Adam: The Wealth of Nations. First copy 1776. Edition 2010. Simon and Brown. www.simonandbrown.com

Other Publications (English, German) from Dr. Edward Schellhammer: www.edwardschellhammer.com

www.ingramcontent.com/pod-product-compliance
Lightning Source LLC
Chambersburg PA
CBHW051437170526
45166CB00001B/26